Law, Meaning, and Violence

The scope of Law, Meaning, and Violence is defined by the wide-ranging scholarly debates signaled by each of the words in the title. Those debates have taken place among and between lawyers, anthropologists, political theorists, sociologists, and historians, as well as literary and cultural critics. This series is intended to recognize the importance of such ongoing conversations about law, meaning, and violence as well as to encourage and further them.

Series Editors:

Martha Minow, Harvard Law School
Michael Ryan, Northeastern University
Austin Sarat, Amherst College

Narrative, Violence, and the Law: The Essays of Robert Cover, edited by Martha Minow, Michael Ryan, and Austin Sarat

Narrative, Authority, and Law, by Robin West

The Possibility of Popular Justice: A Case Study of Community Mediation in the United States, edited by Sally Engle Merry and Neal Milner

Legal Modernism, by David Luban

Surveillance, Privacy, and the Law: Employee Drug Testing and the Politics of Social Control, by John Gilliom

Lives of Lawyers: Journeys in the Organizations of Practice, by Michael J. Kelly

Unleashing Rights: Law, Meaning, and the Animal Rights Movement, by Helena Silverstein

Law Stories, edited by Gary Bellow and Martha Minow

The Powers That Punish: Prison and Politics in the Era of the "Big House," 1920–1955, by Charles Bright

The Powers That Punish

Prison and Politics in the Era of the "Big House," 1920–1955

Charles Bright

Ann Arbor
THE UNIVERSITY OF MICHIGAN PRESS

HV
9475
M52
m533
1996

1999 1998 1997 1996   4 3 2 1

A CIP catalog record for this book is available from the British Library.

Library of Congress Cataloging-in-Publication Data

Bright, Charles, 1943–
    The powers that punish : prison and politics in the era of the
 "Big house," 1920–1955 / Charles Bright.
        p.   cm. — (Law, meaning, and violence)
    Includes index.
    ISBN 0-472-10732-1 (cloth : acid-free paper)
    1. Michigan State Prison—History. 2. Prisons—Michigan—Jackson—
History. 3. Corrections—Political aspects—Michigan—History.
4. Michigan—Politics and government. I. Title. II. Series.
HV9475.M52M533   1996
365'.9774—dc20
                                                            96-9954
                                                            CIP

Contents

Acknowledgments

This book grew out of the unique teaching environment of the Residential College at the University of Michigan. It was in pursuing collective research projects with undergraduates that I first became interested in Michigan history and discovered the rich and largely untapped resources of the state's several archival collections. The need to do "research within reach" drew me back to these topics every other or third year, and echoes of the students' energy and enthusiasm spurred me to continue the work whenever time allowed. My thanks in particular to John Knox, Adrienne Eaton, Roy Doppelt, Jody George, Ellen Leopold, Chris Culliton, Nick Griffin, Jake London, Erica Freedman, and David Waldstein.

Over the years a number of people who witnessed events described in this book consented to interviews; several have since died. My appreciation goes especially to George Kropp, William Kime, Robert Northrup, Albert Fingel, Murray Van Wagoner, G. Mennen Williams, Niel Staebler, and Thomas T. Thatcher for their kind cooperation. I also owe a large debt of gratitude to the folks at the Michigan Historical Collection in Ann Arbor (especially Nancy Bartlett) and the State Archives in Lansing (especially Leroy Barnett).

Many colleagues and friends have read portions of this text or otherwise given me encouragement and support. Special thanks to Jonathan Simon and Raymond Grew as well as to Roger Rouse, Fred Cooper, Susan Harding, Michael Geyer, Francis Blouin, Kim Scheppele, and Jeff Evans, none of whom, of course, bear the slightest responsibility for the flaws and failings that may now appear. My thinking, especially on issues of power and resistance, has been greatly influenced by discussions I have listen to or joined in at the regular faculty colloquia on Comparative Studies in Social Transformations at the University of Michigan. My thanks to these colleagues collectively.

I would like to dedicate this book to Michael Bright, who came along during its long development and, while caring little for its content, made it all worthwhile, and to Susan Crowell, who has made this (and everything else) possible: so small a return for so very much.

Chapter 1

Introduction: The Prison and Its Political Contexts

This book is about a maximum-security penitentiary in its historical and political context. It is an attempt to study the prison as a site of power in modern society. The central argument, developed in a narrative history, is that there exists a deep interconnection between the constitution of the political realm and the construction of carceral regimes. This is not only to say that prisons are derived from politics or that prison officials and politicians interact in the public sphere (though this clearly happens). It is also an attempt to see a dual and simultaneous construction: the constitution of the political sphere is also the constitution of the disciplinary order inside the prison. This formulation tries to get beyond a plain Marxist claim—that prisons are instruments of power, expressing ruling-class ideologies and policing priorities and imposing upon the poor and the powerless the disciplines of the powerful (though, again, this is clearly the case)— and to move toward Foucault's understanding of power as a field of relational practices that invests those upon whom it is exercised and is transmitted by and through those whom it constitutes.[1]

In this conception power is not a possession of some but a strat-

---

1. A convenient collection of essays in a Marxist tradition may be found in David F. Greenberg, *Crime and Capitalism: Readings in Marxist Criminology* (Philadelphia: Temple University Press, 1993); a perusal of the early years of the journal *Crime and Social Justice* will yield more. A systematic treatment of the origin of the penitentiary in a Marxist vein is Dario Melossi and Massimo Pavarini, *The Prison and the Factory: Origins of the Penitentiary System*, trans. (London: Macmillan, 1981). This study appeared in Italian in the same year as Michel Foucault's now classic treatment of the same issues appeared in English as *Discipline and Punish: The Birth of the Prison* (French ed., Paris: Gallimard, 1975; trans. London: Penguin, 1977). Students of U.S. prisons have largely resisted Foucault's influence, though Thomas L. Dumm sought to apply his categories in *Democracy and Punishment: Disciplinary Origins of the United States* (Madison: University of Wisconsin Press, 1987).

egy of all, whose effects may be measured as domination but whose practices are found in the micro-moves, maneuvers, tactics, and techniques deployed within a field of power relations. The prison is constituted in and by these relations, and it retails them upon others. It is one position of power formed up in a field of combinations, rivalries, and alliances that make some more powerful than others and frame the terms of dominant discourse. Thus the process of constituting a public sphere, of defining the terrain of ideology and practice for political activity, of "calling things to order"[2] in a formal framework that disciplines discourse, contains the possibilities and congeals alliances for governing, is also, simultaneously, the process of forging normative standards, deploying disciplinary forces, and bringing things to order behind the walls in an articulation of control strategies and correctional goals that offers a coherent account of what prisons are doing to whom and with what results.

This view of the prison entails a somewhat different reading of politics and its impact upon the prison than is common in available studies of punishment.[3] When scholars have focused on the history of a prison or state prison system, they have tended, perhaps inevitably, to view politics as a set of external inputs and legislative interventions that affect conditions or operations in the prison but are also evaded or co-opted by its managers. This perspective, in turn, sustains the reigning interpretive paradigm of prison historiography that

---

2. I first heard this illuminating phrase used by Geoff Eley in a comment made at a conference on "Power" sponsored by Comparative Studies in Social Transformations at the University of Michigan (UM) in January 1992. For discussion of the public sphere, see the collection edited by Craig Calhoun, *Habermas and the Public Sphere* (Cambridge, Mass.: MIT Press, 1992).

3. There is a small handful of recent histories of state prisons or prisons systems: Shelley Bookspan, *A Germ of Goodness: The California State Prison System 1851–1944* (Lincoln: University of Nebraska Press, 1991); Mark Carleton, *Politics and Punishment: The History of the Louisiana State Penal System* (Baton Rouge: Louisiana State University Press, 1971); Paul W. Keve, *A History of Corrections in Virginia* (Charlottesville: University of Virginia Press, 1986); and Donald Walker, *Penology for Profit: A History of the Texas Prison System, 1897–1912* (Austin: Texas A&M, 1988). On the Federal Bureau of Prison, see Paul W. Keve, *The McNeil Century: The Life and Times of an Island Prison* (Chicago: Nelson-Hall, 1984); and *Prisons and the American Conscience: A History of U.S. Federal Corrections* (Carbondale: Southern Illinois University Press, 1991). For older studies, see the works cited in n. 21. More polemical but informative accounts include Min Yee, *The Melancholy History of Soledad* (New York: Harper's Magazine Press, 1973); and the essays collected by Erik Olin Wright in *The Politics of Punishment: A Critical Analysis of Prisons in America* (New York: Harper, 1973).

sets reform "impulses" from outside against the inert forces of tradition and control inside, in a recurrent struggle between "conscience and convenience."[4] Obviously, a move to treat prison and punishment regimes as part of political order, not derivative of it, invites a more interactive view—one that considers, in specific contexts, how the prison intervenes in politics, contributes to the formation of political combinations, and underwrites the credibility of political discourse.

The relationship of prison and politics, and in particular the parallel and simultaneous constitution of these realms, poses questions that cannot, in my view, be addressed abstractly or normatively; they require a close reading of historical dynamics in a particular time and place. For this reason, I have radically narrowed the focus of study to the state of Michigan in the period between 1920 and 1955. In doing this, I am not abandoning the more general inquiry, but pursuing it in more intimate detail and with greater historical specificity. The site chosen for study is not entirely arbitrary. In the first half of the twentieth century Michigan was on the leading edge of economic, social, and political development in this country. Its automobile industry was at the center of—and gave a name to—what scholars often call the "Fordist" regime of production, accumulation, and labor relations. With the boom, bust, and recovery of industry between 1920 and 1950, moreover, state politics in Michigan underwent a dramatic reconfiguration in both content and practice, as the politics of exclusion and patronage, characteristic of post–Civil War Republican power in the North gave way before the mass mobilizations and reform politics of the New Deal. This was also the era of the "big house" penitentiary in American penology, when a specific combination of industrial corrections and reform ideology shaped carceral regimes. Michigan was not perhaps the leading innovator in this approach to penal discipline, but at the height of the "big house" era, the state built a huge new penitentiary at Jackson, the largest walled institution in the world and a model facility that exemplified the key principles of industrial penology and also, almost instantly, its many limits and contradictions. It is in the simultaneous and interactive transformations

---

4. The title of the second volume of David Rothman's standard study of disciplinary institutions in the United States, *Conscience and Convenience* (Boston: Little, Brown, 1980).

of politics and penology in Michigan during this period that I found the key elements of the argument presented in this book.

In moving to a narrower, if richer, historical terrain, my intention was to get closer to the dynamics of power, public order, and punishment that I wanted to study. It was not to develop a "case study" of something else, prefigured elsewhere and implicitly more important, but to study something for what it was. Thus, in developing the institutional history of Jackson prison, I have tried to avoid treating it as a sample of some general theme in U.S. corrections or as a specific example of some larger, generic process of prison reform and its frustrations. By the same token, I have tried not to generalize from the experiences of this particular prison to statements about incarceration or carceral practices in general, and I have been wary of the temptation to turn the lives of inmates or prison managers at Jackson into concentrated expressions of some essence of the prison experience as a whole. My intention has been to capture the specificity of this prison in its historical epoch and to understand how Jackson prison occupied space in the political geography of the state of Michigan over time.

In developing the political end of the story, I have had to range rather far afield because the narrative of Michigan history is so poorly developed. Aside from a thirty-five-year-old political treatise[5] and the biographies of two Michigan governors in the period,[6] the historical field covered in this study is practically barren; this has necessitated more elaborate excursions into Michigan political history than might be expected or may be to the taste of some readers. But a necessity born of circumstances has also reinforced my inclination to reposition the history of the prison itself. As the story of Michigan politics took shape, I became less concerned with Jackson prison as an expression of some theme in American penology and more interested in Jackson's position within a field of political power. In the process I moved beyond simply marking the moments

---

5. Stephen and Vera Sarasohn, *Political Party Patterns in Michigan* (Detroit: Wayne State University Press, 1957). This book was a compilation of material on electoral reform that Stephen Sarasohn, then an assistant professor at Wayne, had in hand when he died, at age thirty, in 1955.

6. Sidney Fine, *Frank Murphy: The New Deal Years* (Chicago: University of Chicago Press, 1979); and Frank Woodford, *Alex J. Groesbeck: Portrait of a Public Man* (Detroit: Wayne State University Press, 1962).

of significant political intervention in the life of the prison—the laws passed, the investigations launched, and the reforms initiated—toward a fuller examination of the terrain of power itself and the role of the prison in reproducing it.

This attempt to develop a situationally specific account of how politicians, institutional administrators, and prisoners constructed, dialectically, prison routines and practices over time and within a particular, albeit changing, political context could be used to extrapolate broader generalizations, about the changing norms and values of free society, on the one hand, or about the changing patterns and character of criminal behavior, on the other. But these are not within the purview of this study. I am very uncertain about what can or should be inferred about the life of crime (or "deviant subcultures") from a study of inmates in prison. Not only does the everyday operation of the prison have little to do, except rhetorically, with the control of crime, but categories such as "the crime problem" or "criminal underworlds" are not preexisting things to be found; they are constituted in the activities, records, and lore—the effects—of the criminal justice system. By the same token, I am wary of the implicit functionalism of prison scholarship that treats punishment regimes as an expression of changing norms and values in free society or sees in carceral practices a mere extension of what people on the street think of crime and criminals. These assumptions are not, in my view, self-evident, and they feed the powerful preoccupation of prison studies with questions of "what works" (which tell us why wrongdoers misbehave and how they might be corrected) instead of with questions of "how it works" (which tell us about the operations of power in society, among and upon everyone). I have tried to keep the focus here squarely on the institutional mediations of politics and prisons—less on what is mediated than on how the process of mediation created its own realities. In this way I hope to encourage a move away from the standard themes in the American historiography of prisons, in which humanitarian aspirations for reform beat against reactionary institutions, and toward a greater appreciation of the prison as a site of power, in which the seemingly monolithic mass of the "big house" can be seen as a highly unstable terrain of contestation, improvisation, improbable ideologies, and impermanent coalitions of power.

Locating the Argument in the Literature

The analytic inspiration for this study is eclectic, drawing on many traditions without standing in any. But there is an immense wealth of material to work with—in the many sociologies of prison that have studied inmate social structure and the internal dynamics of the penitentiary, in the histories that have charted the course of prison reform and meditated upon the recurrent failure of the penitentiary to rehabilitate its charges, and in the theoretical treatments that have studied penal institutions in their interrelationships with, among other things, the moral order and social solidarities (Durkheim), the capitalist mode of production (Rusche and Kirchheimer), or the archipelago of disciplinary techniques (Foucault).[7] It was here that I found the analytic challenges and insights that came to inform this study. While avoiding a full review of this literature and eschewing any attempt to assess competing theories of punishment (a project that has in any case been recently and superbly done),[8] I can try briefly to anchor this study of Jackson prison in the relevant fields of debate and perhaps, thereby, further clarify the notion of a dual and simultaneous construction of prison and public spheres.

American sociology has long been interested in the prison as a composite model, albeit bizarre and dysfunctional, of a community in action. Donald Clemmer's seminal study of the Menard (Illinois) "big house" set the standard of academic debate for forty years.[9] Strongly influenced by the "culture-subculture" dichotomies of the Chicago School, Clemmer studied how prisoners became identified with "primary groups," developed distinct rituals, argots, and solidarities, over against authorities, and thus defined a specific inmate culture that inured them in criminal habits and deviant associations and blocked all efforts at reformation. He was not especially interested in

---

7. Durkheim's thinking on punishment can be found in *The Division of Labor in Society;* and his essay "Two Laws of Penal Evolution" published in the *Année Sociologique* in 1901. Georg Rusche and Otto Kirchheimer's classic is *Punishment and Social Structure* (New York: Columbia University Press, 1939), which was largely penned by Rusche; Foucault's principal meditation on prisons and punishment is, of course, in *Discipline and Punish.*

8. See David Garland, *Punishment and Modern Society: A Study in Social Theory* (Oxford: Clarendon, 1990).

9. Donald Clemmer, *The Prison Community* (Boston: The Christopher Publishing House, 1940).

the "informal" economy of the prison, although he was deeply skeptical about the utility of industrial work,[10] and, while he sketched a picture of "unregulated leisure" (gambling, drinking, sex), he did not explore the internal networks that organized these illicit activities, nor did he connect these to the official administration of the prison. His prison was made up of isolated individuals, falling out and forming up among themselves, and finding in these precarious solidarities a defense of deviant behavior that "deepen[ed] criminality and antisociality" and annealed them into lifelong criminals.

In the postwar era, sociologists, in an effort to establish a "value-free" social science, deepened and extended Clemmer's thesis while backing away from his moral engagement. Strongly influenced by Talcott Parsons and the paradigm of the "social system," this new generation of academic investigators—Sykes, McCleery, Korn, McCorkle, and, somewhat later, Cressey, Messinger, and Ohlin[11]—developed a picture of the prison as a functionally integrated system, relatively self-contained and internally coherent. To do this they introduced prison administration as a player behind the walls and set it against the solidarities Clemmer had sketched, developing in this move an analysis of the tenuous relationships of accommodation and standoff that characterized the interactions between keeper and kept and made prison society cohere. This exposed for study the embattled hierarchies among inmates and the links between and among inmate "leaders," and it brought into focus the possibilities of corrupt collusion among certain prisoners and elements of prison administration in the interest of keeping the institution quiet and satisfying elementary needs. Without gainsaying the meanness and formlessness of Clemmer's prison, the new sociology sought to clarify the lines of order and organization that gave functional coherence to

---

10. Ibid., 275 ff.

11. Donald Cressey, "Prison Organization," in *Handbook of Organizations*, ed. James March (New York: Rand McNally, 1965); the essays in Donald Cressey, *The Prison: Studies in Institutional Organization and Change* (New York: Holt, Rinehardt and Winston, 1961), esp. Richard McCleery, "The Governmental Process and Informal Social Control"; the work of the Group on Correctional Organization, sponsored in the late 1950s by the Social Science Research Council, collected in Richard Cloward et al., *Theoretical Studies in Social Organization of the Prison* (New York: Social Science Research Council, 1960); Lawrence Hazelrigg, ed., *Prison within Society: A Reader in Penology* (New York: Doubleday, 1968); and Gresham Sykes, *Society of Captives* (Princeton: Princeton University Press, 1958).

prison society and made available a series of "roles" that inmates and managers alike took up and played. Embedded in these lines of mutuality and accommodation were, of course, the seeds of riot, and, as we shall see in chapter 4, the postwar prison sociologies were able to develop a powerful explanatory model for prison upheavals by examining what happened when collaboration was withdrawn and functionally settled roles were rearranged.

By the late 1960s, a third generation of prison sociology had arisen to challenge these functionalist paradigms.[12] Responding to the failure of individual treatment programs and to a demographic shift in prison populations toward younger, darker inmates, these sociologists sought to break down the conceptual walls that separated prisons from a larger social universe. Their claim was that the functionalist effort to define and bound a "relatively self-contained social system"[13] had produced an artificial distance between prisons and the free world, making prisons too separate, inwardly oriented, and self-cauterizing and thus neglecting the continuous traffic of people and cultural influences moving between prisons and the streets.[14] Although in part a response to the proliferation of gangs inside, this shift of focus was primarily an attempt to come to grips with the persistent failure of the "big house" prison to reform or rehabilitate its inmates. At the center of debate was the problem of how to locate the prison: Was it to be seen as a separate society, formed on the margins and full of marginals, which then socialized its inmates to a distinct and impervious criminal culture that insured the failure of rehabilitational interventions? Or was the prison part of society, its interior culture suffused with mores and practices from the street that, once imported into the prison, remained so strong and were so continuously replenished as to insure that the prison would have no effect on

---

12. The best studies in this new vein were John Irwin, *The Felon* (New York: Prentice-Hall, 1970); *Prisons in Turmoil* (Boston: Little, Brown, 1980); and (with Donald Cressey), "Thieves, Convicts and the Inmate Culture," *Social Problems* 10 (1962): 142–55; and the work of James Jacobs, esp. his study *Stateville: The Penitentiary in Mass Society* (Chicago: University of Chicago Press, 1977); and the collection of his essays in *New Perspectives on Prisons and Imprisonment* (Ithaca: Cornell University Press, 1983). The essays collected by Albert Cohen et al., *Prison Violence* (Lexington, Mass.: D. C. Heath, 1977), are also useful.

13. The phrase is McCleery's, in Cressey, *Prison*, 158–60.

14. A strong statement of this is by John Irwin, "The Big House: The Great American Prison," in *Contemporary Corrections: Social Control and Conflict*, ed. C. R. Huff (Beverly Hills, Calif.: Sage, 1977), 37–38.

its charges, one way or the other? Did prison make criminals or merely house them? As the newer sociology inclined toward the latter position, it also cleared the ground for studying the more technically professional, managerial regimes that were emerging during the 1970s and were disposed neither to corrupt collusion with nor rehabilitational interventions upon the incarcerated. While this turn produced some highly sophisticated studies of bureaucratic rationalization and administrative renewal, as in the work of James Jacobs,[15] it also fueled a more conservative, policy-relevant tangent that "found it difficult to swallow the notion that the 'society of captives' is somehow beyond better government"[16] and, in devising administrative means to bring these deviants to heel, effaced the prisoner altogether, either as an object of correction or a subject of informal collusion.

In many ways this long debate over prisonization has run up a dead end. Positions have been overstated: in cracking open the functionalist prison, critics misrepresented Clemmer, who always insisted that "today's penitentiary is not a closed culture" and that prisoners "brought into the prison the ways of society;"[17] and they may also have understated the disorienting effects of incarceration. Clearly, prisoners do come to prison from social worlds that impart values and attitudes not easily erased; just as clearly, the prison is an irreducible physical space that shapes the lives of its charges. What gets called "prison culture" is some sort of an amalgam, born of a reworking and reconstitution of elements, contingent in its directions and specific to time and place. As a vessel of containment, the prison succeeds only partially and temporarily; its disciplinary effects are thus bound to be fragmentary and diverse. This would suggest that the key nexus is not between prison culture and street culture but, rather, between the fragmented yet hugely powerful disciplinary presence of the institution working upon unwilling incarcerants, both intimidated and resistant, who bring to this encounter resources, practices, and values drawn from the street and from the inner world of the prison. Such an

---

15. See esp. "Prison Violence and Formal Organization," in Cohen et al., *Prison Violence*.

16. Here the work of John DiIulio is representative: *Governing Prisons: A Comparative Study of Correctional Management* (New York: Free Press, 1987); and *No Escape: The Future of American Corrections* (New York: Basic Books, 1991).

17. Clemmer, *Prison Community,* ix–x.

engagement cannot be considered wholly functional, nor are its determinants easily confined to the prison.

Yet the impasse in sociology runs deeper, for, in order to build a
sociology of prisons, it was necessary to dehistorize the subject. Specific studies (of Menard-Joliet, Trenton Penitentiary, Walla Walla, the
Hawaii State Prison), for all their particular differences, became the
foundations of general statements that deliberately effaced the "little"
distinctions and abstracted back toward the abiding laws of penal
motion. In the process a presumption of fixity, of timelessness, crept
in. The prison is forever the same (Clemmer), or it moves in cycles
(Sykes) from collaboration to standoff, or it swings like a pendulum
(Irwin) between an "inherent tendency towards harshness" and the
meliorating influences (from outside) of reform. Yet all its key elements remain the same, hence generalizable. Each new study adds to
and elaborates the emerging picture of "the" prison, and debate
among sociologists becomes a movement toward a more perfect understanding. There is an implicit historicism here, of course—not so
much a history of specifics as a theory of history. The cycles and
pendulum swings do have directionality: "The overall movement,
though slow, was towards less and less overt brutality and punishment."[18] And sociologists have always seen themselves as part of the
progress in scientific knowledge and hence of the reform movement
in penology; typically, Clemmer put it best:

> As humanitarianism increases and as the sciences which deal
> with human nature improve their techniques of treating the mal-
> adjusted, and as other better methods . . . are found to deal with
> violators of the law . . . the criminality of the offender, which is
> currently increased by the methods used, may well be decreased
> in that brave new world somewhere ahead.

But this belief in the perfectibility of knowledge not only reinforces
the impression that the thing being studied is somehow "fixed" and
immobile, waiting to be revealed and examined; it also highlights the
extent to which the sociology of prisons has always been centrally
concerned with the question of what works—or more exactly, with
what currently does not work and might be made to work. As accu-

---

18. Irwin, *Prisons in Turmoil*, 27.

mulating doubts about the rehabilitational goal have combined with a loss of faith in the workability of the project, the whole sociological enterprise was becalmed.

There is, of course, a world of difference between a debate over the reformational effects of prison and a discussion of how prisons are organized and operate. In focusing on the specific history of Jackson prison, I put aside concern for what worked and focused instead on how the prison was run. In this move the sociologies proved enormously helpful. Indeed, the history of the sociology of prison is itself a history of the penitentiary. Clemmer's study is a penetrating examination of the specific moment in a twentieth-century prison when the industrial "big house" collided with the world depression; Sykes's study of corrupt collusion between inmates and administration certainly captured one possible path of development in the industrial "big house" during the 1940s, even if he did not begin to imagine the criminal scope of management-by-accommodation that was achieved in Michigan; and the attempt of functionalist sociology to understand the sources of prison riots, while probably not applicable to all riots at all times,[19] had specific relevance for the study of the crisis of the industrial model and the contradictory elaboration of a therapeutic alternative at Jackson prison. While avoiding universalist discussions and eschewing an essentialist picture of prison life, I was able to draw upon the detailed observations of sociologists to make better sense of a specific history. In doing so, however, I have had to grapple instead with the time-bound interpretive schemes of historians studying the prison.

The central vision of U.S. prison history, which crystallized in the Progressive Era and soldiers on to this day, is a decidedly whiggish one of embattled but persistent progress against the forces of brutality and vengeance.[20] Again and again, historians have studied the course

---

19. Bert Useem and Peter Kimball (*States of Siege: U.S. Prison Riots, 1971–1986* [Oxford: Oxford University Press, 1991]) have made much of this point in their attempt to debunk Sykes explanation and install their own (in my view, equally dubious) explanatory model.

20. The classic treatments are Harry E. Barnes, *A History of the Penal, Reformatory and Correctional Institutions of the State of New Jersey* (Trenton, N.J.: MacCrellish and Quigley, 1918); and *The Evolution of Penology in Pennsylvania* (Indianapolis: Bobbs-Merrill, 1927); Orlando Lewis, *The Development of American Prisons and Prison Customs* (New York: The Prison Association of New York, 1922); and Blake McKelvey, *American Prisons: A Study in American Social History* (Chicago: University of Chicago, 1936). But

of reform, developed in enlightened, often religious, circles, usually in the context of moving critiques of prevailing practice, inaugurated after a sustained public campaign, only to be blunted and dissipated by the combined forces of habit, tradition, custody, and cruelty. In every case, however, the thwarted reforms have left permanent traces upon the prison, and over time a steady, if unspectacular, progress has been made: prison conditions have gotten better, enlightened practices have become more pervasive, and the promise of effective rehabilitation has drawn ever closer to realization. Like the sociologists, most historians in the time they wrote saw themselves as part of an unfinished saga; indeed the histories were often written, at least in part, to assess the gains made and to affirm good intentions.

As with the sociological tradition in the United States, the historiography of prisons has seemed determined to abstract a general history of American corrections from what can be known about particular prisons. Most national surveys of prison history rely on examples drawn from various state prison systems to establish general trends or developments; often "American" penology becomes the amalgamated history of a few state systems, such as those in New York, Pennsylvania, and California, which have a reputation for innovation and progressive practices but whose development says little about most states (whose prison history is not written) or about the southern states (whose prison systems were markedly different). This pick-and-choose technique has produced a history of general trends and movements that often proves resistant to specific applications and tends also to overrepresent the progressive forces at work in corrections. Alternatively, historians of state prison systems have too often sought to amplify the significance of provincial findings or to contextualize their conclusions by linking quite particular histories to the national trends already elaborated by others. This not only has the effect of naturalizing the account of one place, at one time, into an aspect or example of something else, but it also reinforces the preoccupation of the historiography as a whole with reform and progress.

---

the themes are carried on in later studies of state prison systems: W. David Lewis, *From Newgate to Dannemora: The Rise of the Penitentiary in New York, 1796–1848* (Ithaca: Cornell University Press, 1965); Negley Teeters, *The Cradle of the Penitentiary: The Walnut Street Jail at Philadelphia, 1773–1835* (Philadelphia, 1955); and more recent texts cited in n. 3. See also Estelle Freedman, *Their Sisters' Keeper: Women's Prison Reform in America, 1830–1930* (Ann Arbor: University of Michigan Press, 1981), which is built around the same interpretive paradigms.

The most sophisticated and convincing treatment in this tradition displays both problems. David Rothman's two studies of the American penitentiary drew upon a disparate wealth of specific cases to build a general narrative and, while highly critical of the faith in uplift that informed the standard histories, retained the teleology without the whiggish verve.[21] Frequently giving an ironic twist to the march of progress (the original penitentiaries were, in his argument, devised as a way to go back rather than forward), Rothman nevertheless preserved the basic directionality of change, toward better, improved, or at least less brutal prisons, and, while he sought to locate the springs of change in social and ideological developments, rather than in the minds of well-intentioned reformers, the formulation he devised ends up running in the familiar direction: from general social changes to new ideas about crime and criticisms of prevailing punishment practices to the crystallization of a new reform agenda, formulated by a cadre of leading lights in a handful of the usual states and aimed at prisons from the outside. Thus a basic "from-to" narrative receives a more complex historical treatment while preserving the stark opposition between the advocates of reform and prison administration and effectively reinstalling the standard narrative sequence: well-intentioned prison reforms batter against institutional walls, behind which even the most modest gains are quickly co-opted to the priorities of institutional order and custodial control; good conscience is thus transformed into quotidian convenience, as backsliding and disappointment follow with an inevitability that only predicts a renewed round of high-minded efforts to promote long-needed reform.

If nothing else, however, the imagery of change must become more nuanced and inchoate when brought to ground in a specific context. As will become plain in chapter 3, the rhetoric of reform was always part of custodial talk in the Michigan "big house" at Jackson; indeed reform was embedded in the disciplinary strategies of the prison right through the first half of the twentieth century. Reform ideas did not enter the prison as alien, external currents; they were an aspect of bringing things to order on the inside. And the carriers of

---

21. David J. Rothman, *The Discovery of the Asylum: Social Order and Disorder in the New Republic* (Boston: Little, Brown, 1971); and *Conscience and Convenience: The Asylum and Its Alternatives in the Progressive Era*. An excellent critique of Rothman's first volume is by Adam Hirsch, *The Rise of the Penitentiary: Prisons and Punishment in Early America* (New Haven: Yale University Press, 1992).

reform were rarely newcomers to the prison but, typically, people already working in the system who appropriated and developed reform ideas in the context of other routine activities or as weapons in bureaucratic turf fights.

In all, then, the study in hand suggests a somewhat different sequence: general social changes generated not so much new ideas in whole cloth as rubs and tensions between and among prevailing institutions and practices; people who inhabited positions therein, or traveled the interstices between them, responded—whether creatively or defensively—to specific conditions, pressures, and crises and found or developed appropriate languages to explain, illuminate, and rationalize what they did. Whether action guided words or words action, it is clear that reform ideologies and quotidian management were coeval and combined forces, always at work in the state prison. Reform currents took shape and moved among a multitude of sites, through a myriad of openings that were discovered in the context of everyday practices and treated as either apertures or ruptures by those occupying these sites. In this sense the opposition between movement and stasis—change and the status quo—is even less tenable than that between reform and custody or conscience and convenience. Everybody was moving, fast or slow and in multiple directions, combining progressive rhetoric with everyday imperatives. Reform had no "head," only multiple voices and nuances that occasionally clustered or galvanized into coalitions for action as opportunity arose but, more typically, filtered into and through other activities, as postures, positions, and ways of seeing issues that arose in specific contexts.

For practical purposes, then, I have come to understand prison reform as a process of formulating plausible accounts of carceral control in changing circumstances. This helps to remind us that the function of punishment cannot be taken for granted just because the institutions are established and the buildings set in concrete. Prison administration is continuously trying to construct meaningful accounts of itself, of what is being done in prison, how, and with what effect. In constantly, even opportunistically, adapting their rhetoric and tailoring their ends to conform to new constraints and discursive turns, however, prison administrators cannot, in a twinkling, overturn institutional practices or renovate their buildings. The means of punishment have a specificity of their own. While the aims and objectives of punishment may change rapidly, often "re-explaining" the means in new circumstances, the means of punishment are rooted in a genealogy of practices and structures that have their own history and, very often, consequences that were quite unintended. Means thus remain distinct from ends and cannot be subordinated to them; indeed they often outlive and reinvent the ends. At the same time, however, it is the technologies of punishment, not its aims and intentions, that actually seize upon incarcerated bodies and dig their marks into real people. The history of these engines of punishment, while distinct, is not necessarily antithetical to the rhetoric of aims and needs to be studied in its articulation with reform currents in the prison, not as its antithesis. For the process of bringing things to order in the "big house" always meant aligning practices and rhetoric in ways that naturalized new problems to existing institutions and reconciled means and ends within a coherent account of punishment that carried conviction both inside, as a regime of carceral discipline, and outside, as a contribution to social order.[22]

We may expect to find a surer grasp of this dual construction of public order and prison discipline if we turn from the histories to more theoretical treatments of punishment. The work of Rusche and Kirchheimer, and indeed all Marxist analyses of punishment,[23] has sought to avoid the minds of reformers and the ideal sequences of good intentions by studying punishment as a function of class relations. For Rusche and Kirchheimer this led to a somewhat mechanical equation between the conditions of punishment and the requirements of the labor market in capitalist production. Simply put, their argument was that, when the labor supply was abundant, punishment became more destructive, reflecting a cheapening of the social

---

22. This paragraph owes much to discussions with Jonathan Simon, whose book *Poor Discipline: Parole and the Social Control of the Underclass, 1890–1990* (University of Chicago Press, 1993) applies many of these themes to the history of parole practices in California.

23. Rusche and Kirchheimer, *Punishment and Social Structure*. Further essays by Rusche did not appear in translation until the 1970s. See "Labor Market and Penal Sanction: Thoughts on the Sociology of Criminal Justice," *Crime and Social Justice* 10 (1978); and "Prison Revolts or Social Policy: Lessons from America," ibid. 13 (1980). See also the texts cited in n. 1; and the essays in Douglas Hay, ed., *Albion's Fatal Tree: Crime and Society in Eighteenth Century England* (New York: Pantheon, 1975), including, in particular, Hay's piece "Property, Authority and the Criminal Law"; and Edward Thompson's parallel study of *Whigs and Hunters: The Origins of the Black Act* (London: Allen Lane, 1975).

value of human life; when labor was in short supply, punishment became more humane, turning toward the rehabilitation and re-inclusion of felons or at least a more productive use of their labor power. The conditions of punishment were thus firmly tied to Rusche and Kirchheimer's famous principle of "less eligibility": the treatment of convicts would always, but only, be relatively less pleasant than the conditions faced by the lowliest elements of the free labor force.

The key insight at the core of this analysis was not, in fact, about the labor market as such but about the liberal or bourgeois social vision that arose with the capitalist mode of production: the agitation of eighteenth-century reformers against brutality and atrocity in punishment, Rusche and Kirchheimer argued, embodied a basic presumption that there existed a bond between the protection of the material foundations of bourgeois society and an *apparent* equality and humaneness in the administration of justice. Humane treatment was thus linked to class interests, and, for Rusche and Kirchheimer, this set in motion the contradictory historical conditions that led to the invention of the penitentiary in the early nineteenth century: a burgeoning surplus of labor that brutalized punishment (less eligibility), on the one hand, and a liberal interest in preserving the class foundations of bourgeois society through more humane treatment (penal reform), on the other, combined and grated to produce innovation—a shift in punishment modes toward new institutional methods that aimed at doing not only something worse but something different. The penitentiary embodied a double objective, attempting through isolation, work, and discipline to improve prisoners as an aspect of punishing them. Reform was thus part of discipline from the outset and grounded always in class concerns.

Rusche and Kirchheimer's historical account has long been criticized for reductionism and factual inaccuracy; nor can it be said that they developed an adequate analysis of the American case, where the isolation, silence, and segmented disciplines of the European prison (chronicled by Foucault) gave way, early on, to congregate systems of gang labor and crude sociability.[24] In the United States a scarcity of

---

24. Georg Rusche, who wrote most of the original draft of this text, apparently developed an account of the divergence between U.S. prisons (tending to congregate labor) and European practices (which clung to isolation and make-work disciplines). But this material was excised from the published version on the advice (to the publishers) of American criminologists, who did not like it. See Dario Melossi's review article, in *Crime and Social Justice* 9 (1978).

labor and relatively high wages not only made the disciplinary promise of the penitentiary highly attractive but also quickly drove prison managers toward experiments in the use of their charges as productive (and remunerative) labor. The logical extension of a system of punishment-as-work in a society in which work was plentiful and labor scarce would probably be the Southern chain gang, not the modern penitentiary, but we will find in the operation of the Michigan "big house" during the 1920s a measure of the possibilities opened up to prison administrators by an industrial boom and a relative shortage of labor. There was room for prisoners to be made productive, and productivity was achieved through a relatively lax system of internal discipline and the proliferation of informal incentives for collaboration. Why Michigan pursued this entirely unique trajectory will take more careful explanation (chap. 2), and what prisoners did with the opportunities provided by an industrial model prison is a distinct issue that we shall address directly; but we may note here that, until the Depression rang down the curtain, an industrial model penitentiary not only put prisoners to work and ordered an internal regime built on jobs and the remunerations available from jobs, but also established a plausible account of how this regime might promote the reformation of felons and their eventual reintegration as productive workers into industrial society. Moreover, because the state of Michigan built a new penitentiary at this moment, it proved possible to adapt the means of punishment to this new articulation of ends. The demise of this industrial avenue of carceral development and the eventual adaptation of the internal control regime to the general loss of employment will require closer study (chap. 3), but the loosening of links between prison work and the labor market clearly undercut the coherence of the carceral narrative and turned the new prison at Jackson into an orphaned means without clear rationale. We will return to Rusche and Kirchheimer's thesis after this complicated story is told.

Although Foucault expressed his debt to Rusche and Kirchheimer,[25] his approach to punishment was altogether more subversive and original. Far from seeing the prison as a derivative expression of social conditions under capitalism, Foucault found *in* the prison the synaptic pivot for a whole new economy of power. The modern mode of punishment originated, not in "the superimposition

---

25. In *Discipline and Punish* he singles them out for praise (24–25).

of the human sciences upon criminal justice," but in the disciplinary
techniques deployed inside the prison. Because, in Foucault's conception, power operated upon the body and materialized as an effect of
its practice, the critical point of analysis were the apparatuses and
practices themselves, not grand theory or reform agendas. In this
sense Foucault turned back into the prisons and reconnected with the
sociologies that tried to understand the mundane operations of the
penitentiary.[26] But in fact, Foucault did not study the actual operation
of prisons so much as their principles of operation—in particular, the
way disciplinary techniques drawn from the military, the monastery,
and the workhouse colonized the prison and transformed its operations. For Foucault the consolidation of disciplinary procedures for
enclosing and partitioning space, enforcing drill, sequence, and regular routine, and producing knowledge by the continuous monitoring
and observation of the object under surveillance were the nexus of a
new kind of power. For it was this "political economy of detail" that
constituted the individual who also, then, became the object of discipline and, more broadly, that became, by sorting and distributing its
objects, the power to constitute the social domains that were then the
targets of rationalized disciplinary interventions.

The core of this carceral order, and its central metaphor, was
Bentham's panopticon, through whose constant, noiseless operation
the "tactics of individualizing disciplines" were imposed on convicts.
The panopticon appealed to Foucault because, in his reading, it created permanent effects even though the act of surveillance itself was
not continuous; precisely because the system operated upon the
mind, grounded in an expectation of being watched all the time, any
time, the panopticon so internalized the normative codes that surveillance, imagined more than real, intervened before the offense. The
inmate-criminal learned to check himself. In this way power could be
intensified, while coercion was lightened, its actual exercise even rendered unnecessary, and a much deeper mastery of the soul could
proceed with less painful infliction on the body. The effects of a
power that "invests human bodies and subjugates them by turning
them into objects of knowledge" could thus become less negative

---

26. Garland makes this a central contention in his treatment of Foucault, claiming
that his study, like that of Clemmer, Sykes and, others, is entirely about the detailed
workings of the prison (*Punishment and Modern Society*, 150–51).

(exclusionary, repressive, and censorious) and more able to release new forces (constitutive, productive, and inclusionary).

Foucault located the prison on a cusp, facing two ways. On the one hand, its mechanisms of observation and correction bore down upon the incarcerated felon: "The prison with all the corrective technology at its disposal is to be resituated at the point where the codified power to punish turns into the disciplinary power to observe; . . . at the point where the redefinition of the juridical subject [the offender convicted] by the penalty *becomes* a useful training of the criminal [the inmate incarcerated]."[27] At this point the prison took a "certain excess" beyond the sentence. This added claim upon the penalty, exacted after judgment, exclusion, and deprivation of liberty, aimed at transforming the penalty required by law into a socially useful modification of the criminal. All the surveillance operations of carceral routine—the biographies, descriptions, topologies, classifications, and case comparisons—bore not upon the crime, but upon the life, and worked to establish a "criminal being" before the crime, "even outside it." The constitution of the offender as the object of knowledge thus produced a new, "delinquent" being, "the little soul of the criminal, which the very apparatus of punishment fabricated at a point of application of the power to punish and as the object of what is still called today penitentiary science." Punishment was not about controlling crime but about constituting the "known criminal."

On the other hand, in Foucault's view this panoptic arrangement proved infinitely generalizable and easily transferrable; the disciplinary technologies spread out from "specialized institutions (prisons) to functional institutions with specialized roles (schools, hospitals) to productive sites (factories) through preexisting institutions under renewal (the military, the family) to new apparatuses of the state for surveillance (the police)"—in a great "swarming" across society. In this sweeping imagery the prison acted as an anchor in an archipelago of disciplinary procedures. Discipline, having colonized the prison, now, through the prison, colonized the penalty, eliminating all other possible forms of punishment, precisely because it so effectively concentrated the disciplinary techniques of surveillance. Now, spreading outward in a capillary proliferation, it "enters into every grain of individuals, touches their bodies, and inserts itself into their actions

---

27. Foucault, *Discipline and Punish*, 224.

and attitudes, their discourses, learning processes and everyday lives."[28]

The prison remains the anchor and central metaphor of this process, and to this disciplined society the prison offers the soul of the delinquent created in punishment. This delinquent is, on the one hand, the promise of useful correction, the criminal transformed into the object of disciplinary interventions. The delinquent "child of carceral practice" embodied both the exclusion of the criminal and the re-inclusion of the penitent, combining in one unified object both punishment and correction, discipline and reform. On the other hand, the appearance of this delinquent, as the constituted object upon whom discipline can be brought to bear, radically narrowed and resolved the focus onto a visible crime problem: "From the vague, swarming mass of a population practicing occasional illegality . . . [the] vagabonds . . . unemployed, beggars, and 'bad characters' of all kinds . . . is substituted a relatively small and enclosed group of individuals on whom a constant surveillance may be kept." The delinquent that punishment creates thus becomes, for Foucault, "the vengeance of the prison on justice," in that the categories, descriptions, and knowledge that went into his constitution colonize the criminal justice system and inform the police about their criminal objects. Thus the operation of carceral discipline serves to highlight "the form of illegality that seems to sum up symbolically all the others": the foreign-born bootlegger of the 1920s, the desperado gangster of the 1930s, the dysfunctional psychopath of the 1950s, and the black drug dealer of the 1980s. It is this utility of the prison in the production of "usable illegalities" that, in Foucault's view, enabled it to survive and flourish in the face of continual evidence that it failed to correct criminals or control crime.

Foucault did not write history, although he marshaled historical material to great effect. His aim was to construct, not a narrative sequence of cause and effect, but a genealogy of difference that highlighted two moments in the history of punishment and clarified insights about modern methodologies by juxtaposing these with an other, stranger practice that went before. This methodological move had the effect of telescoping or collapsing the history of actually exist-

---

28. Foucault, "Prison Talk," in *Power/Knowledge*, ed. G. Gordon (New York: Pantheon, 1980), 39; quoted in Garland, *Punishment and Modern Society*, 138.

ing prisons and penal practices into an almost ideal type representation of the new carceral modes, in order that these might be set against the exquisite tortures and casual targeting of the ancien régime and the genealogy of difference elaborated. As numerous scholars have shown,[29] the development and deployment of the new disciplinary technologies proved, in practice, far more fragmented, halting, and uneven than Foucault allowed. And, as the study of Jackson prison will plainly show, stubborn difficulties attend any attempt to lay Foucault's artfully effervescent yet doggedly relevant analysis beside the historical particularities of a single institution.

Nor could Foucault admit agency. A deeply passive, retrospective voice dominated his writing. The metaphor of a "swarming" singled out no one by name. The meticulously domineering, relentlessly oppressive, irresistible movement of discipline was, inescapably, the objectification of human beings. In the exercise of power there were no agents doing the work of disciplining, for to have agents was to raise questions—"by whom? in the name of what/whom?"—that Foucault did not admit. Indeed, his entire theory of history amounted to a massive refusal of intentionality and movement. Any hint of teleology, whether liberal or Marxist, any intrusion of progress, from-to, any directionality that might affirm what is in terms of what had been, was muted in favor of a genealogy of practices that admitted no internal contradictions or dialectical necessity. Foucault's unwillingness to allow the present to be legitimated by appeals to evolutionary movements in history—or to be delegitimated by appeals to some other, utopian or idealized future—meant that it was impossible to admit the possibility that the modern system of domination was open to challenge or could even collapse.

Without agency, moreover, there could be no opposition. Foucault routinely conflated objectives and practices in the construction of genealogies, eliding the project or intent of punishment with its actual effects, as if statements of intention in the past were no more than descriptive material for the historian. Foucault clearly understood that the correspondences were not unproblematic—that new disciplinary mechanisms constituted a program never fully realized or

---

29. Michael Ignatieff, *A Just Measure of Pain* (London: Macmillan, 1978); David Garland, *Punishment and Welfare: A History of Penal Strategies* (London: Gower, 1985); and Patricia O'Brien, *The Promise of Punishment: Prisons in Nineteenth Century France* (Princeton: Princeton University Press, 1982).

perfected. There was a necessary slippage between the social world that is constituted, classified, and normalized by knowledge as a potentially rational (and rationalizable) object of power and the lived (but unknowable) worlds that discipline tries to know, which are always less ordered and rational than they are made to appear. Indeed there is probably no more poignant moment in *Discipline and Punish* than the encounter between the vagabond and the judge:

> The judge: One must sleep at home. - [the vagabond]: Have I got a home? - You live in perpetual vagabondage. - I work to earn my living - What is your station in life? - My station . . . I have my day station and my night station. In the day, for instance, I hand out leaflets free of charge to all the passers-by; I run after the stage-coaches when they arrive and carry luggage for the passengers; I turn cart-wheels on the avenue de Neuilly; at night there are the shows; I open coach doors, I sell pass-out tickets; I've plenty to do. - It would be better for you to be put into a good house as an apprentice and learn a trade - Oh, a good house, an apprenticeship, it's too much trouble. And anyway the bourgeois . . . always grumbling, no freedom. - Does not your father wish to reclaim you? - haven't got no father. - and Your mother? - No mother neither, no parents, no friends, free and independent.[30]

Yet in Foucault's hands this gap, or slippage, between disciplinary visions and disorderly actualities did not suggest the existence of, nor did it open space for, oppositional possibilities. The movement of disciplinary techniques against the "tolerated illegalities" of the old regime was, for Foucault, persistent, relentless, and implacable. The world that discipline made was always constituted independently of the worlds, discourses, or opinions of the putative subjects of discipline. Without actors and objectives there could be no one to resist. There could be gaps—unfilled, unregulated, insubordinated spaces— but there was no contention, certainly no contention that might deflect the swarming of disciplinary practices or reshape the nexus of knowledge and power that rested upon these disciplines.

Many have lamented Foucault's indifference to resistance.[31] A

---

30. Foucault, *Discipline and Punish*, 290–91.
31. See Garland, *Punishment and Modern Society*, chap. 7; Barry Smart, "Foucault, Sociology and the Problem of Human Agency," *Theory and Society* 2, no. 2 (1982); and

power that constitutes identity and creates its own subjects is apparently without limits—unidirectional, always spreading, deepening, reaching further, and irresistibly rendering speechless all subjectivities, passions, and opinions. The effort of some historians, most notably Patricia O'Brien, to show that resistance and oppositional culture flourished in the panoptic prisons of nineteenth-century France, would seem to be beside Foucault's point; for the things that O'Brien studied—homosexuality, tattooing, subcultural argot, and other oppositional practices—would presumably become grist for panoptic surveillance and thus be transformed into the official argot and classifications of criminality and attached to the codified knowledge arising from surveillance that constitutes the "known" targets of disciplinary action. Yet it is precisely at this point of appropriation that the history of an actually existing prison can help us resist Foucault's implacably self-contained logic. We may embrace his central insight, that the prison is inseparably linked to the constitution of power in society, its disciplinary order the anchor of disciplines swarming across other social institutions. We may accept his argument that the act of constituting both power and discipline is not merely a process of the intellect, expressed in ideologies and intentions, but also of practices, embedded in everyday activities. But we must also insist that Foucault was quite wrong about the unidirectional spread of discipline and, in failing to study the history, as opposed to the essence, of everyday practices, was unable to see how much prisoners participated in the process of bringing things to order behind the walls.

The Possibilities of Resistance

In turning to the problem of resistance, we move against a powerful current that runs through most of the sociology, history, and theory of punishment: the impulse to silence the prisoners. The majority of the population in any prison are studied as the objects of discipline, the obstacles to effective rehabilitation, the problems to be managed, even the beneficiaries of reform efforts—but always as entities to be acted upon, not as agents themselves. This no doubt reflects their

Foucault, Marxism and Critique (London: Routledge, 1983); and Mark Poster, Critical Theory and Poststructuralism: In Search of a Context (Ithaca: Cornell University Press, 1989).

disenfranchised status and captures the invisibility that has always been imposed on those "sent away" for their crimes. It also reflects the proclivity we have observed in academic studies to generalize from the particular to some larger theme or premise, to abstract from concrete histories of particular prisons, in particular times, to generic statements about something else. The first effacement in this operation is the prisoner. But above all, the silence of the convict is an extension of the basic assumption that informs the carceral regime of the penitentiary as well as most theories and students of it—namely, that prisons are supposed to do something to the inmates, change them, render them anew, make them into compliant, obedient, adjusted, even good, people. Because prisoners are the objects of the system's work, they cannot be empowered as participants.

It is, to be sure, no easy matter to recapture prisoners for history. It's hard enough to know what is going on behind the walls and barbed wire fences today, let alone in the past. The prisoners at Jackson in the period of this study are cocooned in the administrative records, transcripts of investigations, and news reports of scandals that tell us that they existed; their words come to us as they were recorded, reorganized, and re-presented by others, as part of a bureaucratic paper trail that is almost entirely independent of, and in most respects antagonistic toward, the worlds and worldviews of the prisoners they encode. And, while we may safely assume that most prisoners imported into the "big house" something of their lives, their values, and their culture from the outside, the historian must, as we have noted, be very cautious in running inferences back from the institutional beings created by the official record to the "criminal underworld" or the "problem of crime," and we must emphatically resist the keeper's perspective that sees inmates as only criminals. In all these ways Foucault's work interrupts and challenges efforts to know "the other" in another time.

Yet at the same time, for all the possibilities of turning it into something else, resistance is obviously pervasive inside prison. Where stiff discipline is applied, rather crudely, to unwilling, often unruly, incarcerants, various kinds of hostility, defiance, opposition, and resistance are bound to arise. It is a common and widely shared stance among prisoners to be hostile to authority, although this rarely amounts to collective action. Indeed, attempts at inmate solidarity in the face of the carceral regime are always riven with crosscutting

hatreds and intramural feuds based on ethnicity, race, status, sen-
iority, and plain criminal "badness." Thus, while resistance in prison
is often a full-throated defiance, ringing with verbal aggression and
violent hostility, it almost never topples and rarely directly challenges
authority. Rather, it tends to be capped, contained, and turned in-
ward, finding interior channels of expression and becoming com-
pressed in the narrow and unyielding spaces behind the walls.
Prisons ooze anger and resentment. And it is here, in the corners and
interstices, that patterns of resistance, defiance, or oppositional posturing take on more polymorphous forms of grumbling, backtalking,
conniving, pilfering, evasion, and sabotage. These are the weapons
of the weak in any circumstance, and in prison they produce the
complex Brechtian maneuvers of space taking and self-activity that
Alf Lüdtke, in another context, has called *Eigensinn*.[32] I have found
this notion extremely helpful. For the practice of cooperating while
holding out, getting along without going over, playing the game without buying into it—seeking a space in which to be, not in resistance or
in complicity—captures, in prison, precisely that ambivalence of
compliance that Lüdtke saw as fundamental to the patchwork of appropriation and response, acceptance and distance, that defined
"workers' spaces" as their own: being by oneself or with one's mates
but, in all events, "'winning distance' from the commands or norms
from above and from the 'outside.'" Not only is *Eigensinn* (the reap-
propriated spaces of self-activity, in Lüdtke's usage) an implicit space
in prison life—one actually promoted by authorities when they encourage prisoners to "get with the program" and "do their own
time"—but its existence at the intersection of defiance and compliance, where a nonacquiescent resignation, a noncompliant consent,
proliferates, amounts to a major foreshortening of Foucault's omnipresent and totalizing discipline.

Resistance in prison, treated as indirect, glancing "shadowbox-
ing" with an authority that cannot be overturned, is of course easily
transformed by prison officials into something else—into the aimless,

---

32. A useful definition is in Alf Lüdtke, ed., *The History of Everyday Life: Historical
Experiences and Ways of Life* (Princeton: Princeton University Press, 1995), 313–14: *willful-
ness*, in the sense of "self-will" or "one's own meaning," but linked semantically with
aneignen (to appropriate or reclaim). See also his article "Organizational Order or Eigensinn: Workers' Privacy and Workers' Politics in Germany," in *Rites of Power: Symbolism,
Ritual, Politics*, ed. Sean Wilentz (Philadelphia: University of Pennsylvania Press, 1985).

inchoate roiling of all those asocial and dysfunctional behaviors that brought "them" to prison in the first place; it becomes "their problem," having nothing to do with "us." But, taking it for no more than what it is, we may take up Lila Abu-Lughod's point about the diagnostic possibilities of resistance. Studying the patterns and practices of resistance from *within* systems of domination, she argues, "teaches us about the complex interworkings of historically changing structures of power,"[33] exposing how domination works by making it work against those who resist it. This may serve to remind us that the disciplinary practices that, in Foucault's imagery, swarm over society and diffuse into the microcircuits of social relations, are also, simultaneously, concentrated behind prison walls. The small irritations and anxieties that you and I may feel about omnipresent surveillance and implied (or panoptic) disciplines become congealed into powerful hatreds and paranoias inside the prison.

Yet at the same time, where the panoptic effects are intensified, so too are the gaps and limits of discipline most plain. Where little is held in reserve and the options of free choice are the most constrained, human ingenuity becomes, as it were, concentrated as well and more sharply focused on the forces bearing down. Thus, if prisons are on a cusp, they are not only at the cutting edge of disciplinary techniques, anchoring an archipelago of practices extending out into society; they also display, inside, the raw edges of the deep struggle—chaotic, confused, perhaps aimless, usually disorganized, often mute and muddled—between discipline and its objects. While we may study systems of domination themselves (their logic and operations) or how domination bears down on people (documenting oppression), it is only when we pay close attention to how domination is contested that we actually "see" it working. And here we may push Abu-Lughod's point, for it is not just "we" (as scholars or observers) who see through resistance how domination works; prisoners do as well. For seeing is like surveillance; it produces usable knowledge, and what prisoners come to "know" about how the carceral regime operates becomes, for them, in practice a kind of oppositional surveillance that constitutes counter-identities and amplifies their power to contest and survive.

---

33. Lila Abu-Lughod "Honor and the Sentiments of Loss in a Bedouin Society," *American Ethnologist* 12 (May 1985): 245–46.

This is the clearing from which to see the prison as a contested terrain. The keepers watch the kept and are watched back. Both "see," "know," and "constitute" the other, in Foucault's terms. It is thus impossible to understand how a prison works without taking account of how prisoners try to gum up the works. Historically, most of the rules and regulated routines of the "big house" were forged in a cat-and-mouse dialectic between custodial imperatives and inmate inventiveness. To be sure, prison authorities often saw resistance where there was none; seeking a comprehensive supervision, they readily assumed that malingering, wandering, gossiping, space taking, and other signs of inmate self-activity betokened insubordination. Conversely, prisoners who defied a rule or challenged a guard or became involved in the oppositional subcultures that flourished in the prison could find their self-expression duly noted and filed, their acts of resistance transformed into the topologies of "childishness," "criminal disposition," "perversion," or "madness" and incorporated into the knowledge that arises from surveillance. Cat-and-mouse stratagems thus turned into labeling games.

In the abstract, however, such labels and classifications are neither fixed nor absolute; they express knowledge that "arises" from the surveilled. The official regime—the way it distributes prisoners, segments the day, orders carceral spaces, and calibrates routine—registers a quest for knowledge, for information and comprehension, and thus incorporates the calculations and inventiveness of those who are incarcerated. In this sense discipline not only constitutes its subjects but is constituted by them. And within the official regime thus devised, prisoners then inhabit the spaces, invest the order with human smells and passions, live across the categories, challenging and reshuffling the distributions, and appropriate the classifications as claims, statuses, and openings that transform disciplinary domains into terrains of limited but real possibility. Patterns of resistance, oppositional posturing, self-activity, and space taking (*Eigensinn*)—as well as the prison cultures these self-expressive efforts create and sustain—reflect, but also inflect, the regimes of domination they contest.

My interest in inmate resistance at Jackson is not an armchair invitation to romanticize prisoners—there are few nice guys and no heroes in this story—but, rather, to see prisoners as participants shaping the carceral regime at Jackson, even as this regime played its part in the political practices of the state of Michigan. This helps locate the prison more precisely in a larger conceptual terrain and allows us, briefly, to reconnect with our earlier discussion of politics and the prison. For the recent sociological interest in the traffic between prisons and the streets has been largely concerned with a critique of Clemmer's "prisonization" argument and with efforts to understand why prisons do not, after all, reform inmates. Yet a full picture of the linkages between prisons and the outside would involve the transportation of practices and values along two conduits, at the "bottom" among criminals sentenced and sent to prison from social worlds that are heavily policed and at the "top" among administrators and officials, appointed and deployed to run the prison, often as extensions of the very police agencies that produced their incarcerated charges.

In this sense oppositional structures in the prison congeal and clarify oppositional relations in society at large. And the conduits of connection continually convey changes, both in the patterns and composition of criminalized populations and in the political preoccupations and allegiances of policing authority, that register larger movements shaping American society. Carceral society thus brings crime and political power together in the production of everyday prison life. Derived dialectically from the antagonistic yet symbiotic relationship of keeper and kept, prison society is forged of what prisoners, with their scanty resources, can make of what authorities render available and make possible. Power, though always unequal in its deployment and often brutally applied to compel compliance, is rarely one-sided or total; indeed, everyday compliance is ordinarily won by the kind of deals and accommodations that corrupt power. And it is the negotiable nature of the production of prison life that produces a complex and deep interplay, even an interpenetration of oppression and corruption, an admixing of criminal practices with the power deployed to suppress it.

In the pages that follow I will report many crooked deals and shady goings-on and will have occasion to note the tendency for boundaries to blur and the worlds of keeper and kept to elide. My fascination with the corrupt practices that pervaded prison management in the 1920s, 1930s, and 1940s and in the lurid scandals that attended the overthrow of these practices in the 1940s and 1950s is not especially salacious, although the stories do make good retelling. Nor am I interested in pushing the assertion that all politicians are crooks (though common usage in the public sphere is suggestive) or that all convicts are politicians (though the ordinary slang of prisons is also suggestive). But one finds in the history of Jackson prison a deep symbolic and symbiotic association between politics and crime *inside* that replicates the more complex interaction of the two *outside*. What made Jackson prison distinct was not its separation or distance from free society but its rendition in another space of fundamental and abiding dynamics in free society, in which power shaped the criminal universe by patrolling it, but tended also to be criminalized in this operation. The prison—at least in the period studied here—revealed in more concentrated and focused surroundings what went on outside, namely a continuous interaction between the constitution of power and the delineation of crime, between building ruling coalitions for governing and defining, sorting, classifying, arranging, and policing criminal practices.[34]

The Shape of the Argument

Three themes held my attention and form the core of the historical chapters that follow. In exploring the parallel constitution of political order and carceral regimes, it seemed necessary, first, to focus on practices. This meant getting beyond the events of politics or the intentions of politicians to an examination of *how* politics was practiced, how power relations were organized and ordered, and how these practices, forged in the everyday conduct of politics, shaped the environment and conditioned the terms of survival for all political practitioners. In telling the story of how the new prison facility at Jackson was built in the 1920s (chap. 2), my focus is on the interactions between patronage politics and industrial penology. I was interested in how political practices (party organization, electoral combat, and patron-client relationships) and prison management practices (control regimes, work routines, and reward structures) were articulated, aligned, and reproduced over time. In pursuing this study of practices a broader theme is established: prison managers, operating within, not outside, the political terrain of the state, shaped their regimes of control inside in accordance with the conditions of their

---

34. Inspiration for this comes from reading Peter Linebaugh's suggestive study of *The London Hanged: Crime and Civil Society in the Eighteenth Century* (Cambridge: Cambridge University Press, 1992).

political survival outside; this in turn conditioned power relations and determined the everyday opportunities of prisoners living in Jackson. The prison thus became a window into state politics, even as the practice of politics in the state illuminated the internal ordering of the prison.

As becomes apparent in the discussion of industrial corrections, it was necessary to recognize, secondly, that practices, even when habitual and automatic, are not unreflexive. Historical actors think, explain, and rationalize their actions continuously; the managers at Jackson and their political overseers in state administration were not passive role players but had agendas of their own and ways of talking about these agendas that were sensitive to the political winds and calibrated to be politically relevant. In studying the upheavals that occurred in the practices of patronage politics and, simultaneously, in the central tenets of industrial penology during the 1930s and early 1940s (chap. 3), I was interested in how politicians and prison officials moved to reinvent their practices and the principles governing these practices, experimentally, in the context of what was possible or seemed likely within a rapidly changing terrain of power. As prison managers fought among themselves in the great bureaucratic turf wars of the 1940s, and politicians explored the possibilities of scandal in the construction of reform platforms, both were groping for a formulation of practices and public speech, of means and ends, that would be coherent and salient in the circumstances of the moment. In this they were producers of ideology. By placing the discourse of corrections at the synaptic pivot of an analysis of prison and public spheres, I came to appreciate the critical importance of rehabilitation and reform rhetoric as a rationalizing language that gave meaning to prison work, a public policy point to corrections, and a practical orientation to inmates seeking to make their lives more tolerable and their eventual release more likely. Aligning the elements of correction discursively and allying these with the prevailing themes of politics made the system cohere and gave guidance to historical actors within it.

Thirdly, just because practices were aligned in ways that offered a coherent account of the carceral project and linked it to available political positions did not mean that the resulting power regime of the prison functioned unopposed. A major aim of this study has been to give agency to prisoners, as participants in the constitution of the carceral regime and, by extension, in the political realm that shaped the internal order. In studying the great riot that occurred at Jackson in 1952 (chap. 4), I am attempting to engage the question of resistance in prison and to understand, through a specific history, how subalterns, the objects of power, were able to talk and act back in ways that shaped the regimes of power that subordinated them. By setting the conflicting contemporary explanations of the riot against a historical account of its antecedents, moreover, I have tried to make plain the role of ideological formulations not only in giving coherence to power regimes but in grounding those regimes in subject populations and securing, however tacitly and reluctantly, the assent of those it seeks to rule. In the process of doing this, the inmates at Jackson ceased, in my mind, to be objects of incarceration—examples of criminals, let alone of criminal types, to be managed and, if possible, changed—and assumed the status of fellow travelers in this history, coresidents of the institution, with names and distinct personalities, whose activities had a determinant impact upon how the prison was run. This line of analysis in turn lays the ground for concluding reflections on the historical specificity of the "big house" penitentiary and, by extension, on the limits of Foucault's conception of modern discipline.

These three themes—the practices of power, the elaboration of coherent accounts of power, and the countervalence of resistance—are not separable. They form continuous and interactive threads throughout the historical narrative. The chapters are arranged chronologically, but each is organized around a moment or event, which is then explored on several levels—through the worlds of state politicians, prison administrators, and prisoners at the institution. This procedure seemed most appropriate to the task of mapping power relationally, in fields of continual interaction, in which causality gives way to conjuncture and explanations emerge not from on high, but from the thick of description and from the contingent interplay of practices and ideas embedded in the everyday world of historical actors.

Chapter 2

Prohibition, Patronage, and Profit: Building the New Prison at Jackson

In the summer of 1924 the state of Michigan commenced building a new penitentiary at Jackson. When it was finished ten years later, this modern, state-of-the-art facility enclosed fifty-seven acres within its thirty-foot-high walls and contained cell space for about 5,500 inmates.[1] The State Prison of Southern Michigan generated its own electricity and heat, operated its own water and sewage treatment facility, and maintained a host of basic services for its captive population: a post office, newspaper, and radio station (with headphone receivers in every cell); a hospital with physicians, nurses, and dentists; a library, theater, bank, telephone system, bakery, garage, laundry, dairy, barber shop (with fourteen barbers), tailors, printers, carpenters, variety stores, schools, and churches (with three chaplains). The prison also farmed nearly five thousand acres of state and leased land, raising most of its own vegetables and meat (310 head of cattle, 6,000 chickens, 600 pigs), and it maintained one hundred acres of orchard.[2] It was, as no one tired of saying, the largest walled institution in the world.

It was also, as most wardens would later insist, far too big and

---

1. The precise capacity of the new prison was always unclear; while under construction, it kept getting bigger, and, after completion, its capacity limits were variously put at between fifty-three hundred and fifty-eight hundred. Its actual population ranged over six thousand in the early 1950s. The variations reflect general housekeeping procedures, especially the use made of tiers in particular cell blocks; how disciplinary, hospital, and secure spaces were organized; and, most particularly, how many prisoners could be housed in the farms surrounding the main prison.

2. Figures taken from the report of the warden of SPSM (Joel Moore), Michigan Department of Corrections, *Annual Report,* 1937–38; and from a special series in the *Ann Arbor News,* 22–23 April 1940.

unwieldy for safe management. Its capacity was three or four times
what most experts, even at the time, considered optimal,[3] and its
oversized population, as prison progressives lamented, made effective classification or rehabilitation impossible. "Little wonder that
scandals, escapes, and riots have plagued the history of this mon-
strous institution," intoned Arthur Wood in 1954, echoing almost
verbatim the findings of an official report on the riot of 1952.[4] In the
1960s efforts were made greatly to reduce the population; in the 1970s
structural renovations were begun to break up the institution into
smaller units that could operate as separate, self-contained prisons
under separate administrations. Yet even today Department of Corrections officials hate the State Prison of Southern Michigan at Jackson; it is a place where careers are wrecked (as well as made), a white
elephant, "overly large" and "poorly designed."[5]

Why did they build it so big? We cannot answer this question
with any certainty. No one living remembers, and the archival record
of the 1920s is almost entirely silent on the matter. The surviving
papers of Alex J. Groesbeck, the governor who initiated construction
and closely followed its progress, contain no discussion of plans.
Indeed, the official record suggests no internal planning at all during
the initial stages of construction. The Prison Commission minutes
contain scant evidence of any discussion of the project; there is no
indication that the state Administrative Board, which was a sort of
cabinet overseeing purchases and expenditures, or the state legislature, which in the 1920s met for only a few months every other year,

---

3. The Wickersham Commission felt that eight hundred units was ideal, while
Austin MacCormick, an expert working for the Osborne Association, usually said that
a capacity of fifteen hundred was optimal. See U.S. National Commission on Law
Observance and Enforcement, no. 9: "Report on Penal Institutions, Probation and
Parole (Washington, D.C., 23 June 1931), 234; and Osborne Association, *Handbook of
American Prisons and Reformatories*, vol. 1 (New York, 1931).

4. Arthur Evans Wood was then a University of Michigan sociology professor
and, during the late 1920s, head of the Michigan parole system. He wrote the introduction for a "Study of Penal Facilities for the State of Michigan" prepared by Chester Clark
and Associates in February 1954, at the Michigan State Archives, Lansing.

5. Letter, Warden Ralph Benson to Russell Searl, 17 December 1946, box 8,
Combined Recommendations of Investigation, 1940–48 (Assistant Director, Prisons
File), State Archives; Ragen-Curran Report on the State Prison of Southern Michigan,
April 1954, ibid., box 6; C. J. Clark and Associates, "Study of Penal Facilities of the State
of Michigan," February 1954; Report of Special Committee on Prison Disturbances to
Governor William Milliken, 4 August 1981; interview with William Kime, Michigan
Department of Corrections, February 1979.

gave the matter of a new prison more than passing attention. No original blueprints survive, nor does it appear that proper books were kept on the project before 1926. Yet, clearly, between 1920 and 1925 decisions were taken, contracts were let, and work was undertaken to build a huge new prison with a capacity well over five thousand inmates on a site just down the road from the old facility at Jackson.

Gaps in the record may, of course, result from sloppy office procedure or the destruction of files, or from laziness or bad luck on the part of the researcher. But it is equally possible that certain acts or decisions were not considered important enough to record or were buried in other routines and practices. Since history cannot be built entirely upon a foundation of absent evidence, we must try to infer and deduce what we can from what is available. This procedure will not yield definite causal explanations, but it will open up a number of parallel stories whose conjuncture bear upon the decision to build the new prison. In this way we will be able to explore several dimensions of carceral practice in the 1920s. Together these will allow us to see how deeply embedded the prison was in contemporary systems of power, not just formally or analytically but in terms of everyday routines and social relations. Ultimately, it becomes apparent, in this case at least, that the silence of the archives faithfully records the tacit, face-to-face, and verbal world of personal relations and patronage transactions that constituted political practice in the state of Michigan in the 1920s. Constructing a huge new prison was an integral part of—not simply a reflection of but a constitutive element in—the construction of power relations in the state.

Booze and Crime

Numbers are a logical place to begin. An in-house history of Jackson prison, composed by an anonymous chronicler in 1928, presents the following account of how the prison grew so large:

> In 1920 the state legislature authorized the State Prison Commissioner to submit a report on the requirements and plans of a new prison. At first, an institution accommodating 1500 prisoners was planned, with expansion possibilities to take care of 1,000 additional men in the future, but later, on account of the rapid increase in the prison population, it was decided to change the

plans so as to accommodate 5180 prisoners. Due to a revision in the plans at this time [1928] it will be possible to accommodate 100 more, making a total accommodation for 5280 prisoners.[6]

This statement captures both the formlessness of decision making and the almost continuous upward creep in capacity that marked the early phases of construction. It also suggests a commonsense explanation for building a huge new institution: more prisoners.

During the first half of the 1920s Michigan, like the rest of the nation, experienced a "crime wave," made more visible and alarming by sensational press reports. With the rise in crime went an equally dramatic, if more uneven, increase in the number of people sent to prison; the adult male population in the state's three main institutions—Jackson, Ionia, and Marquette—more than doubled between 1920 and 1926, rising from 2,192 to 4,675. In 1927 the Michigan system was among the most overcrowded in the nation.[7]

To some extent these increases reflect the extraordinary rise in the state's population during the first quarter of the twentieth century. Especially in Detroit, hometown for nine out of ten state prisoners, the explosive growth of the automobile industry doubled the population between 1910 and 1920 and increased it by half again before 1930. Many of the newcomers were single males under twenty-five, often living in rooming houses and hotels and depending on bars, bawdy houses, and one another's companionship for entertainment. Perhaps more worrisome to civic groups and urban elites was the fact that, by 1925, over half the city's population was foreign-born or black.[8] These shifts in the age and complexion of the state's population are undoubtedly reflected in the increasing rate of incarceration in Michigan; the proportion of the state's population that went to prison doubled between 1918 and 1929.

But behind this figure—and indeed behind the general fear of

---

6. *The Michigan State Prison, Jackson, 1837–1928* (State Prison Industries, 1928), 59–60.

7. Wickersham Commission, report no. 9, 232.

8. The foreign-born population of Detroit doubled between 1910 and 1920, and by 1925 it constituted nearly half of Detroit's population of 1,242,044. The black population of the city remained far smaller but showed a dramatic increase of over 600 percent between 1910 and 1920, when it stood at 35,097. During the 1920s African Americans made up about 6.5 percent of Detroit's population and constituted about 17 percent of the state's prison population.

crime and the patterns of imprisonment in the 1920s—lay prohibition. Michigan banned the sale of liquor as of May 1918, nearly two years before the rest of the nation joined the wagon under the Eighteenth Amendment.[9] Miraculously, it seemed for a time that Billy Sunday had been right, that banning "God's worst enemy" would "turn our prisons into factories and our jails into storehouses and corncribs."[10] The press reported improved productivity, increased bank savings, and a dramatic fall in crime rates. As the number of arrests and convictions continued to decline through 1918 and 1919, Detroit's mayor, James Couzens, proclaimed himself a belated convert to temperance and postponed a planned expansion of the city police force. But this tide was soon to turn. Whereas in 1918 1,275 people were arrested in Detroit on liquor law violations, by 1925 the figure ran over 27,000. Ten people from Detroit were sent to Jackson prison on liquor convictions in 1919; by 1922 the number was up to 149, and two years later it reached 350.[11] By 1921 the smuggling of booze on the Detroit River and Lake St. Clair was in full swing, and in 1922 the governor sent the state police to occupy the downriver community of Ecorse and crack down on a purported flood of liquor bound mainly for Detroit. By 1923 the *Detroit News* estimated that there were ten thousand blind pigs in the city, and two years later the federal administrator assigned to enforce prohibition in Michigan declared Detroit "the wettest city I have been assigned to . . . nowhere else is the law so openly violated as it is here."[12] Indeed, it was estimated that the smuggling, production, and sale of illegal liquor had become Detroit's second largest and most profitable commercial activity, exceeded only by the manufacture of automobiles.

Prohibition was, of course, a politician's nightmare. It was one of those morally charged valence issues that permitted indisputably antagonistic points of view and demanded choices. Most elected officials outside of Detroit rode with the temperance movement into the early 1920s, because it commanded the votes. While the emotional

9. Larry Englemann, *Intemperance: The Lost War against Liquor* (New York: Free Press, 1979), is, despite its general title, an account of prohibition in Michigan.

10. Quoted in ibid., xi.

11. Based on tabulations from surviving entry logs at Jackson prison for 1919–26, State Archives.

12. *Detroit News*, 3 November 1925; Englemann, *Intemperance*, 125–26.

core of prohibition arose from nativist religiosity and rural, small-town values, its political success in the state was built on the bridgeheads it established in the cities, especially Detroit, among middle-class Protestants (many of whose pastors became vocal champions of temperance) and among industrial and civic leaders who were attracted to the anti-saloon cause as part of their pursuit of other goals, such as electoral reform, higher productivity and better labor control, the "Americanization" of foreigners, or the containment of the criminal and moral "looseness" associated with the war era. Civic associations, industrial managers, and an upscale pastorate formed a phalanx of righteousness inside the sinful city, promoting a vigorous, if rather nostalgic, moralism as a bulwark of order against the harrowing instability of the Fordist boomtown.

While elite opinion in Detroit initially coalesced in support of prohibition, however, the crime wave it engendered soon placed strains upon this consensus. For many, the lawlessness and disrespect for authority that seemed to accompany prohibition proved far more alarming than drunkardness. "Dry" advocates were, of course, reluctant to admit that temperance produced crime, fearing that a costly and unpopular policy of repression would undermine the cause of prohibition itself. They preferred to treat the crime wave as evidence of a hopefully fading recalcitrance among the wicked, the inebriated, or the foreign-born and to criticize police and enforcement agencies for irresolution in the application of sanctions. Public administrators and police officials knew better, and it was in these circles that doubts about, even outright opposition to, prohibition tended to arise. Yet, whatever their skepticism, the political credibility and professional pride of police and city officials depended upon the maintenance of good order, and they were only too willing to demand additional resources for the enforcement of laws they knew would be broken. This produced an odd world of rhetorical posturing, in which those who wanted to suppress drink were reluctant to fund enforcement and those who doubted the law could be enforced called for more funds. These contradictions produced periodic outbursts of debate between critics and defenders of prohibition, which, though generally unedifying, even ritualistic, tended to frame the terms and conditions of political survival for those holding electoral office in the prohibition era. And it is here that we may begin to frame the context of timing for the decision to build a new prison at Jackson.

One of the first and most dramatic of these periodic debates over prohibition was played out in the pages of the Detroit newspapers during September 1923.[13] Prompted by a highly pessimistic federal report on the enforcement of prohibition, the *Detroit News* launched a sensational, weeklong investigation of local crime and liquor law violations. Day after day readers were treated to front-page stories of smuggling and rum-running, of blind pigs and shady roadhouses, of gang warfare and hired gunmen, of corrupted officials and private debaucheries—all presented with a naive wonderment of first revelations; figures like the "bootlegger" and expressions like "a ride on the river," which bulked large in these reports and later became familiar staples of American movies, were still new and bewildering to the average reader in 1923, and at week's end the *News* concluded its introduction to this "underworld" with dire warnings about the "moral breakdown threatening the very existence of American free institutions."

The revelations provoked immediate and widespread debate. On the second day of the series, police commissioner Frank Croul took occasion to attack prohibition itself, contending that the reports made public what he had long known—that his police officers were locked in a lethal war with well-armed gangsters and bootleggers that they could never win, even with ten thousand additional patrolmen, because "no law is workable that has the majority of the people against it." Croul was soon joined by others in law enforcement, the sheriff of Wayne County, the chief probation officer of the Detroit Juvenile Court, the Wayne County health commissioner, and Roy Vandercook, head of the state police, who summed up the general position succinctly: "We could not enforce the Prohibition Law in Michigan if we had a standing army."[14]

The enemies of drink were quick to respond. On 9 September P. N. Holsaple, head of the Michigan Anti-Saloon League and longtime leader of the temperance movement, denounced Croul as a defeatist and called for his resignation. Insisting that "the greater number of violators of the prohibition law are foreigners" who "came to America with the understanding that it is a free country" and took this ideal rather too literally, Holsaple argued that, if the laws of the

---

13. What follows is drawn from the *Detroit News*, 7–17 September 1923; and from a senior seminar essay on the subject by Patrick Staiger, "The Detroit News and the Shift in Elite Consensus over Prohibition in 1923," in my possession.

14. *Detroit News*, 8 and 12 September 1923.

land were not enforced more rigorously or if public officials openly admitted their inability to enforce the law, rampant disrespect for authority and social order would be the inevitable result. Ministers from across Detroit joined in, supported by resolutions from various temperance organizations and religious groups. On Sunday, 17 September, the pulpits of the city rang with resounding reaffirmations of the prohibitionist creed and calls for Croul's resignation.[15]

Before this mobilized wrath of the righteous, critics of prohibition beat a hasty retreat. George Walters, Wayne County sheriff, insisted he was not discussing the merits of prohibition, only the problems of enforcement, and Croul told reporters, "I'm not going to resign, but I'm through talking about prohibition." Yet, while Croul's effort to turn the crime wave into a debate over the viability of prohibition had in this case been blocked by a show of popular sentiment, the champions of temperance had also shifted their ground during the skirmish. The conviction, widespread in the early 1920s, that continued liquor law violations were a residual problem that would recede before the triumphal advance of "dry" sentiment, could not be sustained in the face of the *News'* reports. "Isn't it about time we faced the facts?" declared the Rev. Edgar Dewitt Jones. "Disrespect for law and a new species of anarchy is abroad in the land."[16] This was a novel and alarming situation that had to be addressed, not by attacks on law enforcement officials but by wholehearted support for their efforts; this was the position taken by an ad hoc Committee of Eleven, representing various civic and religious groups in Wayne County, in circulating a self-critical appraisal of the sweeping claims and dubious statistics heretofore employed in support of prohibition and calling a meeting at the Anti-Saloon League offices in the Kresge Building to reaffirm public support for the police. Holsaple, who was present, issued a statement several days later commending the *Detroit News* investigation on the grounds that, while painting a dismal picture, it would serve to awaken the champions of temperance, "many of [whom] are visionary and didn't dream that conditions such as are described in the newspapers exist."[17] A new sobriety was evident in

---

15. The sermons were fully reported in the *Detroit News* on 18 September 1923.

16. *Detroit News*, 10 September 1923. Jones went on to be a member of the state Corrections Commission during the 1940s.

17. A year and a half later Holsaple was reported to be an enthusiastic booster of

anti-saloon rhetoric, and this led to a fuller appreciation of the difficult work of law enforcement.

It was here, in support of stricter enforcement, that common
ground was found and the rift in elite consensus at least partially and
temporarily repaired. Whatever one's view of prohibition itself, it was
apparent to all leaders of opinion that the crime and widespread
disrespect for law that prohibition engendered posed a serious threat
to social order and elite authority. Retreating from the pros and cons
of prohibition to the high ground of law and order, politicians could
take a firm stand *for* social order rather than *against* drink and reframe
the terms of elite agreement around a commitment to uphold, both
symbolically and practically, the authority of the law. Unlike prohibition, strict law enforcement did not admit of two points of view, and
politicians, whether they believed in sobriety or not, could usually
agree on the importance of showing workers, foreigners, and low-
lifes that those in authority were prepared to defend their capacity to
govern.

A new get-tough attitude was soon apparent. In December 1923
the state police occupied Hamtramck in a dramatic and highly publicized move to close down the liquor traffic and end corruption in
that Polish suburb; the mayor was hauled before Governor Groesbeck
for a hearing in Lansing, and city government was largely supplanted
by state supervisors. Early the next year Police Commissioner Croul,
having abandoned his critique of prohibition, reemerged with a con-
troversial and constitutionally dubious enforcement strategy, called
the "tip-over raid"; when "morally certain" that a place was violating
liquor laws, police would enter without warrant and smash it up,
again and again, with the aim of harassing bootleggers and blind pig
operators until they gave up and went out of business.[18] As repeated
raids by police brought so-called frequenters before judges who were,
for their part, increasingly inclined to punish with jail terms instead
of fines, the number of people arrested and sent to prison on liquor
law violations began a steady rise in 1924, one that was to continue

the state police under its commissioner of Public Safety, Harry Jackson, because of
several spectacular liquor raids, especially in Hamtramck. The budget of the state
police had more than doubled since 1919 (*Detroit News*, 3 February 1925). Harry Jackson
went on to become warden of Jackson prison in 1925.

18. See Englemann, *Intemperance*, 128–29.

until the repeal of prohibition (see table 1).[19] In that same year Michigan officials commenced construction of a huge new prison at Jackson, concrete symbol of their fresh resolve to demonstrate the state's capacity to uphold the law and punish wrongdoers.

Outside of Detroit, however, crime and prohibition did not figure prominently in state politics during the early 1920s. Although there seems to have been a broad consensus among state officials that additional prison capacity would be needed sometime in the future, there were no signs of urgency. In 1921 the legislature commissioned a study of needs and options, and by the following year the Prison Commission had settled on a plan to build a new prison for 1,500 to 2,000 men somewhere in the Upper Peninsula (UP).[20] A number of possible sites came under consideration, as county officials and local politicians rushed to offer free site development and to sing the praises of the labor market in their area.[21] For a time Keweenaw County was a leading contender because it had numerous rock quarries for prisoners to work in and plenty of free land to offer the state. But Groesbeck was besieged by many other bids and competing lobbies, and he complained to an associate early in 1923 that he felt under pressure to move "too fast" on the new prison project.[22]

Throughout his first term in office (1921–22) Groesbeck was, in fact, content to handle the pressures of prison overcrowding with tools long available to governors. He sought, first, to improve the system's absorptive capacity by adding beds and dormitory space to existing state institutions (especially at Ionia, where a bad fire in October 1921 made extensive renovation and rebuilding necessary anyway) and by distributing inmates on short terms to various road camps around the state (a move that enabled Jackson prison, in particular, to take far more inmates on its rolls than its cell capacity would allow). Until these measures were in place, however, Groesbeck tried to reduce new commitments to the three penitentiaries by encourag-

---

19. *Detroit News*, 7 January 1926, which also reports a beer famine in the city.

20. *Detroit News*, 1 February 1922.

21. The papers of Alex Groesbeck contain much of this material: Records of the Executive Office, 1921–26, box 22, file 24, State Archives. It is striking that no one expressed opposition to the prison being located in the Upper Peninsula or voiced fear about it being in their neighborhood.

22. Letter, Groesbeck to W. H. Wallace, 25 January 1923, Groesbeck Papers, box 30, file 1.

TABLE 1. Populations of Jackson Prison and All Michigan Prisons by Year (Commitments and Total Populations)

Year	Commitments to Jackson Prison	Total Population of Jackson Prison	Total Commitments to Michigan Prisons	Total Population of Michigan Prisons	Commitments in Michigan (per 100,000 Population)	Inmates in Michigan (per 100,000 Population)
1916	326	1,073	993	2,347	29.8	70.0
1917	560	1,080	1,295	2,309	38.0	67.9
1918	409	1,289	898	2,455	25.5	70.0
1919	383	1,225	1,148	2,530	32.0	71.0
1920	682	1,200	1,664	2,275	45.3	62.0
1921	915	1,312	2,279	3,092	60.5	81.5
1922	971	1,681	2,093	3,352	53.5	85.8
1923	1,023	2,013	2,039	4,030	50.8	100.5
1924	1,295	1,983	2,775	3,588	67.0	86.8
1925	1,162	2,215	3,108	4,292	73.0	100.7
1926	1,628	2,350	3,459	4,944	79.0	113.0
1927	1,772	2,782	3,789	5,537	84.3	123.0
1928	2,113	3,430	4,239	6,833	92.0	148.5
1929	1,960	3,935	3,907	7,053	83.0	149.0
1930	2,491	4,418	4,343	7,711	90.0	159.0
1931	1,992	5,086	3,759	8,136	76.0	165.0
1932	1,468	5,690	3,328	8,995	65.0	175.0
1933	1,429	5,611	2,820	8,689	56.0	172.0
1934	1,408	5,215	2,699	7,703	53.0	151.3
1935	1,357	5,128	2,747	7,487	54.0	147.0

Source: Michigan State Prisons: Statistical Report, comp. Gilbert Haigh (statistician) (Lansing: State Welfare Department, 1936), 9, 11.

ing judges around the state to hold petty offenders in county jails and work camps until more space was available in state institutions.[23] But this had little effect, because, as one judge wrote, "the good people of my community demand that all liquor violators be sent to prison."[24] New commitments were in fact higher in both 1921 and 1922. State institutions became dangerously overcrowded. The old facility at Jackson, built in the middle of the nineteenth century, exceeded its capacity of 1,250 during 1920 and by 1923 carried more than 2,000 inmates on the daily count. As the prison population reached record levels, Groesbeck came under strong pressure from his wardens—"I am doing all in my power to prevent . . . any trouble at this institution, but I need help from you in this line"[25]—and turned to a third expedient: venting pressures inside by letting more prisoners out. A larger than usual number of short-term prisoners were paroled early in 1923.[26]

The state parole system had been completely overhauled in 1921, as Groesbeck moved to reduce the powers of local judges and centralize supervision over parole and probation officers in the field. The new Commissioner of Pardons and Paroles, a political appointee, oversaw the process, but in key respects parole became the provenance of the governor, who frequently sat in on parole hearings and received recommendations directly from the wardens.[27] Although parole had long been used to regulate population levels in state prisons, Groesbeck's decision to increase paroles in 1923 proved extremely unpopular with crime-conscious voters, while the new centralized procedures increased his visibility in the parole process and made

23. Groesbeck Papers, box 1, file 15, circular letter of 22 December 1921 and other correspondence. The new building and additions at Ionia were ready for occupancy by March 1922.

24. Ibid., Judge Clarence Browne to Groesbeck, 31 December 1921.

25. Letter, Harry Hulbert to Groesbeck, 9 December 1922, Groesbeck Papers, box 22, file 9.

26. See data in *Report of the Commission of Pardons and Paroles for the Years 1927 and 1928* (Arthur Wood, commissioner) (Lansing, 1929). The number of paroles jumped from 1,205 in 1922 to 1,846 in 1923. Whereas there were 922 more new commitments than paroles in 1922, the figure was down to 125 in 1923. The effects can be seen in the prison population figures for 1924.

27. See Frank Woodford, *Alex J. Groesbeck: Portrait of a Public Man* (Detroit: Wayne State University Press, 1962), 169; the Groesbeck Papers (box 21, file 23) contain the hearings Groesbeck conducted personally during 1923. Box 94, file 4, contains correspondence between the governor and his commissioner of pardons and paroles, Fred Janette.

him more vulnerable to attack. Groesbeck seems to have concluded during the legislative session in the spring of 1923 that the parole device was no longer at his disposal to relieve overcrowding. Over the next three years, especially in his reelection campaigns of 1924 and 1926, he took an increasingly hard line on furloughs and paroles: "There are going to be fewer men released from Michigan prisons," he promised the press. Not only were guidelines stiffened, but the governor impatiently dismissed the appeals of his wardens for some relief of overcrowding through early release, even turning against the traditional practice of granting sentimental pardons at Christmas and on national holidays. By the middle of the decade state officials were routinely claiming that the dramatic increase in the state's prison population was largely due to the governor's stinginess with parole, and, indeed, at no time between 1920 and 1932 did the number of paroles exceed the number of new commitments.[28]

As more people were sent to prison and fewer got out, pressures increased for additional prison space. It was during the spring of 1923 that the Prison Commission abandoned the Upper Peninsula as a site for the new prison and decided, instead, to build it at Jackson, just down the road from the old prison. The most compelling reason appears to have been the ready supply of cheap prison labor for the project. A request was made of the legislature for $400,000 to acquire and prepare a site. At this point they were still thinking in terms of a 1,500- to 2,000-man unit, and still there was no sense of great urgency. A year later the prison commissioner from Jackson County, Mark Merriman, was worrying that the money allocated by the legislature for "starting a new prison at Jackson" had not been fully spent and might revert to the general fund at the end of the fiscal year unless it could be used up.[29] Work finally began in June 1924, with the warden at Jackson, Harry Hulbert, assuming the newly created post

---

28. See Groesbeck Papers, box 94, file 1, Prison Commission Correspondence, 1925; undated memo by William Porter, chairman, developing a comparison of Groesbeck's parole record with that of his predecessors, for press release. Also box 94, file 5, a press release in December 1925 from Fred Janette's office: "Prison population in this state has been growing rapidly since 1921 because prisoners are not being released as rapidly as in the years preceding." This point was reiterated in a letter to William Hopp, chaplain at Jackson, 30 December 1925 (box 94, file 5). See also *Detroit News*, 1 February 1922; 13 December 1925; 6 January 1926.

29. Groesbeck Papers, box 49, file 9, State Prison Commission, Merriman to Groesbeck, 7 June 1924.

of superintendent of construction. By the time the legislature convened in the spring of 1925, the project had begun to grow, first to
2,400 capacity and then, by the fall, to a "general plan" for a
5,000-man facility.[30] Even then no final plans were submitted, no cost
estimates were tendered, and no bids were compared. The legislature
appropriated $1 million, half for 1925 fiscal year, half for 1926, but the
full dimensions of the project do not seem to have been understood.
In 1926, during a special session of the legislature, Groesbeck asked
for more money, estimating that the total cost of the project would be
$6 million.[31] There was general shock a year later, when the new
governor, Fred Green, reckoned that the cost of completing the structure then under way would be in excess of $12 million.[32]

In general, then, we may conclude that the decision to build a
new prison was in step with the tough enforcement policy that
emerged in 1924, and the growing size of the projected facility was
roughly in step with the rapid increase in the number sent to prison
after 1924. Yet, this tells us very little, only that a new prison would
not have been built without a crime wave and a political consensus to
crush it. It frames a context and suggests a commonsense causality.
The huge new facility may be taken as a symbolic or ideological statement of the state's determination to defend its authority in the face
of growing disrespect for the law and to absorb the consequences of
that determination with expanded prison capacity. But as a practical
matter, the new facility was big enough to hold the entire inmate
population of the state of Michigan in 1925, with room to spare, and
it could easily contain three times the number of prisoners as were
then crammed into the old buildings at Jackson. It thus anticipated
a prison population and a rate of growth far in excess of anything so
far experienced in an exceptionally crime-conscious decade. There
is, however, no indication in the record that state officials engaged in
the kind of policy planning that might have informed such an antici-
pation. The slack and inchoate process of decision making that gave
rise to it and the way the project kept getting bigger suggest that

---

30. *Detroit News,* 27 September 1925. Hulbert submitted sketch plans, without
estimates, to the Prison Commission in May 1925. See Groesbeck Papers, box 94, file 1,
Minutes of the Prison Commission, 26 May 1925.

31. *Detroit News,* 27 January 1926.

32. Report of Harry Conrad, chief engineer of H. G. Christman Co., to Governor
Fred Green, 1 February 1927, as communicated to the State Senate, 17 March 1927
(*Journal of the Senate* [1927]: 316–24).

something more than public fear of crime or a rising prison population were at work in the construction of this oversized facility. Two additional lines of explanation are worth pursuing here, one having to do with political patronage and the organization of state politics in Michigan during the 1920s, the other having to do with the related matter of the uses of inmate labor and the organization of prison life itself.

Patronage and the Politics of Prison Construction

Like other states in the North after the Civil War, Michigan was virtually a one-party state until the New Deal. Nomination by the Republican Party was, for all intents and purposes, a guarantee of election. Occasionally, a split in Republican ranks allowed a Democrat to slip into the governor's mansion, most notably in 1912 and 1914, but the Democrats almost never got elected to subordinate state offices, and they won control of the state legislature (which until 1913 chose U.S. senators) only once in the eighty years between 1852 and 1932. As late as the 1920s, there were elections in which not a single Democratic candidate won anywhere in the state. For decades Republicans controlled federal patronage, postmasterships, and customs houses along the lakefronts as well as the policies and patronage of Lansing. Politics in the state was organized through the party, and the rules of political survival were largely determined by the way party relations and procedures channeled competition.

At the end of the nineteenth century the Michigan Republican Party was dominated by U.S. Senator James McMillan, a railroad and shipping magnate from Detroit who built a statewide party "machine" that effectively managed political transactions for over fifteen years. This organization was based on a tripartite alliance among railroad and utility interests in Detroit, who supplied money for the election campaigns of state legislators and local officials; timber and mining operators in the Upper Peninsula, who controlled large blocks of immigrant votes and traditionally laid claim to the lieutenant governor's slot; and the post commanders of the Grand Army of the Republic, who provided the local cadres that got out the vote and received their rewards in the form of pensions and postmasterships.[33] Like

---

33. Marie Heyda, "Senator James McMillan and the Flowering of the Spoils

state machines throughout the country in this period, the McMillan organization was maintained through personal contacts and correspondence, in a continuous transaction of small favors and courtesies, underwritten by interest brokering and lubricated by money. Although the senator's personal ascendancy did not go unopposed—as, most notably, when Hazen Pingree twice won the governorship in the 1890s[34]—he was able to establish and maintain a coherent political framework for competition over state offices and the distribution of state and federal patronage.

After McMillan's death in 1902 his party organization muddled along, increasingly strained by the rivalry of his heirs, and was finally shattered in the bitter feud between Taft and Roosevelt at the national level. This breach rumbled on in state party ranks throughout the 1920s, finding renewed expression in the intramural feud between Alex Groesbeck, a Taftite party regular who had enjoyed cordial ties with McMillan's son, and Fred Green, a youthful admirer of Pingree and a leading Roosevelt partisan in 1912. But, while rival lineages continued to shape political alignments, changes in the rules of political combat worked to revamp political practices in the party. Two progressive Republican governors, Fred Warner and Chase Osborn, followed by a brief Democratic incumbency (1913–17), produced a legacy of reforms that reconfigured the terrain of postwar politics. Indeed, many of the characteristics of party practice in the 1920s may be seen as solutions to the problems of political organization and competition left over by the changes of the Progressive Era. In particular, the adoption of an open primary system for the selection of gubernatorial candidates made it much harder to control internally the nomination process; at the same time, the popular election of U.S. senators broke the close structural synapses that existed in McMillan's day between federal patronage and party organization in the state legislature. Statewide party machines became much harder to sustain. The last attempt to build one came in 1918, when Truman Newberry spent upwards of $500,000 running against Henry Ford in the sena-

System," *Michigan History* 54 (Fall 1970); David Rothman, *Politics and Power: The United States Senate, 1869–1901* (Cambridge: Harvard University Press, 1966), 164–66, 176–78; Mary Dearing, *Veterans in Politics: The Story of the GAR* (Baton Rouge: Louisiana State University Press, 1952), 460 ff.

34. See Melvin Holli, *Reform in Detroit: Hazen S. Pingree and Urban Politics* (New York: Oxford University Press, 1969).

torial primary and assembled in the process what many considered the most comprehensive political organization ever seen in the state. Before he could take his seat, however, Newberry and about a hundred of his operatives were indicted under the Federal Corrupt Practices Act, and, although he was eventually exonerated by the Supreme Court, many of his cronies were convicted, and the bad press that attended the affair ruined his career. He resigned in 1922.

By then the Republican Party, though still in undisputed control of state offices, had lost all internal coherence, becoming "a series of groupings around personalities who, although essentially agreed on what government should do, differed only as to which of them should have the power and the accompanying perquisites of doing it."[35] None of the governors elected between 1920 and 1932, all Republicans, could claim to control a statewide party organization. Each had to construct ad hoc political alliances around some formula that linked Wayne County, which had a third of the state's population and commensurate weight in party conventions, with enough outstate county support to win nomination. This was no easy task, especially in view of the wide gulf in outlook between urban and rural voters over such issues as prohibition. Groesbeck managed to win the governorship in 1920 because his close friend and constant companion, James Haggerty, controlled the Wayne County caucus at the state convention and had developed some key alliances in populous counties such as Genesee, Oakland, and Kent. In winning reelection in 1922 and 1924, Groesbeck usually carried the Upper Peninsula but regularly lost counties in the heartland of the state; he never had secure organizational control over the party, and, especially after 1924, he was beset with ambitious rivals and challengers. Indeed, Groesbeck lost a bitter primary fight in 1926 after a private falling out with Haggerty, ostensibly over appointments at the state fair, prompted the latter to swing the Wayne County delegation to Groesbeck's longtime rival, Fred Green, the thirteen-term mayor of Ionia. With some standing in western counties, Green developed a tentative alliance, through Haggerty, with Detroit mayor John Smith and enjoyed some enthusiastic boosting from Spanish-American War veterans associations around the state. But, though he was able,

---

35. Stephen B. and Vera H. Sarasohn, *Political Party Patterns in Michigan* (Detroit: Wayne State University Press, 1957), 25.

briefly, to unify the anti-Groesbeck forces and win election in 1926, and reelection in 1928, Green had even less success than Groesbeck in consolidating a solid, statewide base within the Republican Party.[36]

Lacking firm organizational control of the party that controlled state politics, Republican governors in the 1920s came to rely increasingly upon the state apparatus to consolidate a political base. Patronage—jobs, contracts, access, and favors—had always been the glue of political loyalties, but during the 1920s long-standing practices became more competitive and centrally controlled, thus increasingly critical in linking up supporters, rewarding friends, punishing enemies, and gaining influence over local and county caucuses. While this shift in the organization of power, from party machine to state apparatus, certainly reflected the more open, inchoate nature of competition within the Republican Party after the collapse of the McMillan machine and the failure of the Newberry restoration, it also captured two other, new features of the political landscape in the 1920s: the booming economy of the state and the growing influence of the popular media. Ballooning state revenues, borne along by the tremendous expansion of the auto industry, supplied the governor with the resources to accomplish great things. By spending millions of "new" dollars on public buildings, highways, and other internal improvements, he could promote a media image of himself as the "master builder of Michigan," doing the people's business in the common interest while, at the same time, dramatically expanding the store of partible resources available for patronage distribution. The organization and allocation of patronage rewards remained a personal and rather private affair, involving direct transactions among politicians and their supporters, but the existence of these relations was no longer denied or sequestered in back rooms. Patronage politics was covered in the press as the way those in the know got things done. In some respects a more affluent and well-heeled spoilsmanship was simply dressed up and re-presented in new buildings, roads, bridges, and state services as the proceeds of modern and efficient government. Whenever one of these projects got done, it provided occasion for the rituals and speeches that played so well in the newspapers and publicized politicians in service to the people.

Alex Groesbeck was one of the architects and most successful

---

36. Ibid., 21–22; and Woodford, *Groesbeck*.

practitioners of the "new politics" of the 1920s. He built his political career upon a carefully nurtured reputation as the can-do champion of good government, an apostle of the modern principles of efficiency, competence, and accountability. His tenure was marked by a restless renovation of state government and a tendency to use state resources for his personal political aggrandizement. His central complaint was that the decentralized structure of state government—over one hundred distinct units and departments, many run by boards or commissions that were appointed to staggered terms that exceeded the governor's own—was not only wasteful and inefficient, diffusing authority, rendering jurisdictions amorphous and accountability impossible, but made it almost impossible for elected officials to gain operational control of the state apparatus.[37] His solution was to create an Administrative Board, modeled on a corporate board of directors. Pushed through the legislature in the spring of 1921 with the support of civic reform groups and the latest studies by political scientists at the University of Michigan and the Detroit Bureau of Governmental Research, this seven-man board, made up of the principal elected officials of the state (the Secretary of State, the State Treasurer, the Auditor General, the Attorney General, the Highway Commissioner, and the Superintendent of Public Instruction) with the governor in the chair wielding veto powers, was designed to exercise "supervisory control over the functions and activities of all administrative departments, boards, commissions, and officers of the state, and of all state institutions."[38]

This move effectively centralized the management of state administration, budgeting, purchasing, and contracting. It gave Groesbeck much closer control over appointments, promotions, salaries, and other personnel decisions in the state bureaucracy, and it placed appointment to all state boards and commissions at his disposal. It also offered greater executive leverage over contracts for highway construction and other public building projects, and it opened more direct access to the whole phalanx of state purchasing agents who

37. See his first inaugural address, 6 January 1921, in George Fuller, ed., *Messages of the Governors of Michigan* (Lansing, 1927), 4:775–88.

38. Quoted from the public act, in Woodford, *Groesbeck*, 136. The only, and standard, account of the creation of the Administrative Board is George Benson and Edward Litchfield, *The State Administrative Board in Michigan*, Michigan Governmental Studies, no. 1 (Ann Arbor: University of Michigan Press, 1938); see also Lent D. Upson, "State Reorganization in Michigan," *American Political Science Review* 15 (1921).

bought the supplies and equipment used in state operations—coal, lumber, machinery, automobiles, tires, gasoline, uniforms, food, paper, typewriters, paint, cement, asphalt, and (later) liquor. In effect, a nineteenth-century spoils system, which had functioned through scores of appointed officials, commissioners, and placemen gaining segmented access to bits of the state, feeding off the resources of autonomous elements in a decentralized system of authority, got turned on its head. Groesbeck's reform not only ended the perceived abuses of delegated authority and rendered state agencies more accountable to their political superiors; it also greatly expanded the capacity of the governor to act. And by providing him with more effective control over the distribution of patronage, the reform enhanced his ability to organize through action a coherent network of political support around the state.

Since centralizing control over patronage was also an aspect of reforming state administration and rendering it more effective, spoilsmanship could take on the public face of good government. Modernizing Michigan and organizing power went hand in hand. The highway program was the richest plum. Whatever explains it— the lure of the road, the mystique of the automobile, the pressure of highway lobbies, or the clout of car manufacturers—building and improving highways was *the* major political issue of the 1920s. Unlike prohibition, no one opposed it, and there was no difficulty finding money to spend on it. A $50 million state bond issue for road construction was floated in 1921 and largely spent by 1924. Thereafter, a two-cent gasoline tax, coupled with a weight levy, generated over $5 million a year for highway construction, a figure now supplemented by federal matching grants. In all, during Groesbeck's six years in office, over six thousand miles of trunk and county roads received concrete surfaces, another three thousand miles of highway were added to the system, and some two hundred and forty bridges were built around Michigan.

Such an enormous public project entailed contracts, purchases, and jobs all over the state. The papers of Frank Fitzgerald, whom Groesbeck appointed both business manager in the Highway Department and (not incidentally) secretary of the Republican State Central Committee, provide a detailed picture of the many favors and attentions, all quite legal, that were dispensed through the highway program.[39] The careful cultivation of local notables, the negotiations with contractors in every county, the decisions about where to lay a new road or which section of old highway to pave next, the hiring of a college-bound son of a friend for the summer, the purchase of stamps from small-town post offices that needed sales in order to maintain federal classification, and the annual round of county road builders' association meetings—all facilitated the construction of a state highway system while cementing the ties of political reciprocity. Local party notables were extremely sensitive to highway matters and competed with one another for funds not only because many were in the road building business themselves but also because road building was good for business, especially the kind of commercial and real estate development that, along with the law, were mainstays of small-town Republican livelihoods.

The governor took an active, personal interest in these relations. He routinely reviewed contracts and estimates, working closely with the highway commission in setting routes and schedules, and he regularly roared off in one of his powerful motorcars on inspection tours around the state, giving simultaneous expression to his love of speed and surprise. No detail was too small to escape his attention, and it was said, especially in his later years, that not a mile of highway was completed anywhere in the state that the governor had not personally seen. And nearly every mile paved (or left unpaved) registered some obscure political fact; wrote one supporter, after the election of 1924, concerning a two-mile stretch of road south of St. Louis, Michigan, where several of the governor's local opponents happened to live: "Now Governor, can much be gained by rewarding [your] enemies too quickly after bad behavior? . . . I am sure, just at the present time, it is poor policy to reward such ungrateful citizens with a thousand dollars worth of new pavement."[40] When confronted with a county contractor he disliked or by local labor costs he thought too high, Groesbeck was quite prepared to bypass them with gangs of prisoners, working on contract to the state out of temporary road

39. Fitzgerald Papers, boxes 1–2, Michigan Historical Collections, Bentley Library, Ann Arbor, Michigan.

40. Groesbeck Papers, box 76, file 2: Aldrich to Groesbeck, 12 July 1925. Box 107, files 1–2 (Highway Matters, 1926), is full of letters regarding paving contracts in various counties.

camps, to build his highways and bridges more cheaply.[41] When he became frustrated by the high cost of cement, he canceled contracts with private producers and leased the Chelsea Cement Plant; finding that, with the use of prison labor, he could produce concrete at great savings while committing total output to highway projects, he then had the state buy the plant and go directly into the cement business.[42] Not a few inmates gained parole after coming under the governor's watchful eye. To be sure, restless supervision and high-handed interventions earned Groesbeck many enemies and the nickname "little Mussolini," a term that, in the 1920s, described a dictator and a bully but also betokened a grudging respect for hard drive and acknowledged results. People wanted paved roads; Groesbeck got the job done. "The one thing uppermost in the minds of Michigan voters today is the question of paved roads," lamented Fred Green, while running against Groesbeck in 1926; "in spite of Groesbeck's methods and his personal unpopularity, the people are willing to vote for him because he stands in their minds as being the one man who is willing and able to give paved highways."[43]

Compared to road building, the construction of a new prison lacked glamour, but, in a period of hardening opinion on law and order, the expansion of prison capacity certainly had public sanction, and it was not without patronage possibilities. Indeed, in most respects the operation of the prison system shared with the highway program the dual aspects of public service and spoilsmanship that characterized Michigan politics in the 1920s. Groesbeck's administra-

---

41. The exact number employed varied annually and seasonally. Between 100 and 220 prisoners were used in winter projects; from 350 to 500 were used in summer. See Groesbeck Papers, box 29, file 13, letter to Frank X. Martel, 9 August 1923, and to George Sloaim, 8 September 1923; box 118, file 7, Prison Commission Correspondence, 1926; *Detroit News*, 31 January 1926; Executive Office Correspondence, 1927–30, Fred Green Papers, box 16, file 6: State Prison (Jackson), memorandum (n.d.) from the summer of 1927, reporting that about 300 inmates had been deployed for road work and another 170 were at work in the Chelsea Cement plant.

42. See *Detroit News*, 15 February 1925. Negotiations for such a lease actually began in 1922 (Groesbeck Papers, box 21, file 16: letters between state senator Bayard Davis and Groesbeck, 20 and 24 April, 22 May 1922). There was talk, in 1926, of selling the plant again (box 118, file 7; and box 119, file 1: Prison Commission Correspondence, 1926), but no decision was taken. In 1927 the Green administration conducted a highly critical assessment of the Chelsea operation and sold the plant (Fuller, *Messages of the Governors*, 4:891–911).

43. Green to Chase Osborn, 21 April 1926. The Chase Osborn Papers, box 59, Michigan Historical Collections, Bentley Library, Ann Arbor, Michigan.

tive reform did little to centralize daily operations in the prison system, because the three main institutions were scattered across the state and well rooted in the political economies of their respective counties. But Groesbeck did gain closer control over the five-man Prison Commission, which served at the governor's pleasure and exercised supervisory responsibilities over the whole system, and he revamped the administration of parole under a new Commissioner of Pardons and Paroles, whose appointment was also in the governor's gift. At the next level the governor named the wardens of state institutions and had a hand in the selection of regional parole supervisors. At lower levels, both in principle and in practice, every employee of the system, down to the guards in the cell blocks and the probation officers in the field, were subject to demotion or dismissal at the governor's command and without recourse to civil service protection. After every election, there was a check on loyalties and a purge. The personnel shake-up that followed Green's takeover in 1927, or even Groesbeck's narrow reelection victory in 1924, was comprehensive and conducted on an openly political basis, registering both the seismic intensity of the bitter political feud between these two men and the political importance of using state appointments and spending to build organizational support.[44]

Appointment to the Prison Commission was by no means a sinecure or an invitation to inactivity. The five-member board[45] presided over a rapidly expanding system; the number of employees and the annual budget of the state prison administration grew steadily throughout the 1920s.[46] In overseeing the various prisons and satellite

---

44. Correspondence regarding job seeking, referrals, and thanks can be found in Executive Office, 1927–30, Papers of Fred Green, box 176, file 5; box 192, file 2. Much of what we know about the internal operation of Jackson prison in this period comes from affidavits that were collected and witnessed by former employees at the prison who had been displaced for personal or political reasons. This material is collected in the Attorney General's Records, Criminal Justice Division, Investigations of SPSM, 1927–47, box 1, files 1 and 3, State Archives, Lansing. See, for example, statements by Arthur Briggs, a former guard (19 June 1926); and by Edward Gougeon, a carpenter on the new prison site, who was fired "for political reasons" in December 1926 (5 March 1927); and by Charles Cole, let go in July 1926, because "I was a little bit too much of a Green supporter."

45. The usual practice was to appoint one member from Detroit, one from Lansing, and one as "resident" commissioner for each of the three prisons—from Jackson County, the Houghton–Marquette area, and the Kalamazoo–Ingham County area.

46. The total budget for state prisons rose from under one million dollars in 1919 to over four million in 1928 (*Michigan State Prisons, Statistical Reports*, 13).

camps, the commissioners gathered regularly, at Lansing or at one of the main penitentiaries, often with the governor in attendance, to deal with an array of mundane matters—arrangements for spring planting, plans for reroofing a utility building, the repair of kitchen steaming equipment, the best way to soften water or handle a report of the state health examiner, new regulations on discipline or security, and provision of coal reserves for the winter, as well as contracts or bids on supplies, spare parts, repairs, and construction. The list was long, routine, and unnoteworthy.[47] What is noteworthy, but unfortunately, at this distance, largely invisible, were the elaborate networks of personal connection and referral embedded in these deliberations. Without the informal lore that informed routine decisions, names and connections no longer resonate with us or carry much significance. It is only at moments of turnover and upheaval that the now-buried connections surface, and we can see, or at least sense, the interpenetration of public service and private interest.

"We called the Governor . . . in regard to the insurance on the new Prison plant," wrote Jackson Country Republican chairman, A. D. McBurney, to the secretary of Fred Green, the newly elected governor, in the spring of 1927.

> It is our opinion that this should be carried as a Builder's Risk, rather than the way it is now carried. Mr. Foster [an emissary of the governor] has not as yet grasped our situation in regard to McKone. McKone and Finch own the Wright Agency here. Mr. McKone was in charge of the Groesbeck campaign in this County and their methods we really do not care to comment on as anything we might say would be too hot for the paper or the typist to handle. In November [right after the election], [Harry] Hulbert [the former warden, in charge of construction at the new site] wrote [Kennedy] Potter [Groesbeck's chairman of the State Republican Committee in 1926 and a Jackson businessman] suggesting that all the insurance be handled by McKone. . . . [Since the election] McKone has placed every obstacle possible in [our] way and is making the statement that regardless of what our pleasure

---

47. The minutes of the Prison Commission are not collected prior to the 1930s but may be found scattered in the files of the Executive Office. See, for example, Groesbeck Papers, box 117, file 5. Correspondence concerning routine commission business may also be found in Groesbeck Papers, box 94, file, 2; box 118, file 5.

in the matter is, or the Governor's pleasure in the matter is . . . they are going to have a part of the insurance, and indications are that Hulburt is working to that end, and from all the facts, as we know them here, we are bitterly opposed to McKone's further interest in any capacity.[48]

At the same time, the president of the Union National Bank in the Upper Peninsula was writing urgently to the new governor begging him not to move the Marquette prison accounts to the First National Bank.[49] The fact that Alton Roberts, Groesbeck's member of the Prison Commission from the UP, "opposed you so strenuously in the campaign" should not be held against the bank, he averred, as Roberts had been "removed from the Presidency a short time ago." If the prison accounts had gone to the Union Bank in the first place because Roberts was its president, this should not cause the new governor to overlook the many of his faithful supporters who were presently depositors. In referring the letter to his (entirely new) Prison Commission, Green asked that they split the prison accounts between the two banks. Alterations and adjustments of this kind proceeded throughout Green's first term in office. A year after his inauguration the accountant at Jackson prison was replaced, because Green had made a promise during the primary that the job would go to one of "the Bay County boys," and, after some wrangling, the "boys" had come up with a name. The Prison Commission assured State Treasurer Frank McKay, in whose gift the appointment was held, that they "would be glad to make the change any time."[50]

These were overtly political transactions, made to reward supporters and to assert control over state agencies. Patronage appointments established hierarchical lines of obligation and reciprocity and opened avenues of extension as new incumbents used the resources of their offices to bind and reward their own clients and friends. The basic relations thus created were continuously coated in a multitude of routine courtesies and reciprocal favors that reenacted the bonds of

48. Letter, McBurney to Howard Lawrence, 23 February 1927, Fred Green Papers, box 16, file 6, Correspondence, Jackson prison.

49. Green Papers, box 16, file 5, Prison Commission: copy of letter, S. A. Chamberlain to Fred Green, 27 May 1927.

50. Letter, Frank McKay to Howard Lawrence, 27 June 1928, Green Papers, Correspondence, 1928, box 69, file 5.

condescension and deference in small, everyday ways. All wardens knew to whom they owed their appointment, and they expressed this knowledge in small favors for the commissioners in their area—inmate gardeners, house repairs, free gasoline and tune-ups, preferments for friends, presents of turkeys and hams at holidays.

At Jackson prison large quantities of beef, pork, and chicken flowed to the warden's house to be passed along to friends in the county or used to entertain visiting dignitaries; the prison steward remembered a party once given in honor of Governor Groesbeck, in which 45 inmate waiters served up steaks to 370 guests while the prison band played waltzes.[51] Cases of canned goods from the cannery were routinely shipped out to William Porter, chairman of the commission ("ok'd by the Warden"), Lt. Governor George Welsh ("Warden's instructions"), Charles DeLand, the secretary of state, or B. E. Brower, the state senator from Jackson.[52] On the warden's orders a prime bull was purchased from a local farmer who also happened to be a relative of Mark Merriman, the resident commissioner. Chairman William Porter could, in turn, recommend a "good man" for the plumbing contract at the new prison,[53] or his colleague on the commission, Frank Eamans, a Detroit organizer for Groesbeck and attorney for the First National Bank, which handled prison industry accounts, could urge Hulbert to give special consideration to a particular ironworks in awarding contracts for cell construction.[54] When Porter sought a wedding gift for his daughter and asked the warden at Ionia to "give me the bottom price that you can make me for one table, one buffet, one china cabinet, and six dining chairs,"[55] he did

51. Testimony by M. E. Brogan, 21 December 1926. Attorney General Investigations, box 1, file 1.

52. Attorney General Investigations, box 1, file 5. Copies of shipping records from the cannery for 1924.

53. Affidavits by prisoners to V. A. Loomis, Department of Public Safety, Attorney General Investigations, box 1, file 3. There was much talk among prisoners about the poor quality of the pipe used in the plumbing (many felt the fixtures were "seconds"); the steam fitter used on the project was an employee of Prison Commissioner Charles Blaney, of Kalamazoo. See "Miscellaneous Memorandum," n.d., in ibid.

54. Groesbeck Papers, box 118, file 5: Porter to Hulbert, 27 January 1926; box 94, file 2: Eaman to the Prison Commission, 20 October 1925. It was a widely held view in prison circles that Hulbert was kept on, despite scandals and personal difficulties, because "he was Eaman's man" (Attorney General Investigations, box 1, file 4: Report by V. A. Loomis of the State Police [n.d., 1927]).

55. Letter, Porter to Charles Shean, 12 October 1926, Groesbeck Papers, box 118, file 7, Prison Commission.

nothing illegal or improper. These were routine transactions, not subject to much comment, and, while the interlocking relationships thus formed were loose and susceptible to all sorts of trimming and hedging, they did serve to restate and reinforce ties of obligation and political allegiance, cultivating networks that would become available at election time in organizing support for their governor and benefactor.

"Quite a few calls are coming in from various clubs throughout the small towns," reported Harry Hulbert in 1922. "I have covered Hillsdale, Dowagiac, Coldwater, Tecumseh, Concord, and a number of other such towns of that size," and "do not be afraid to ask if I can be of service to you . . . thru this coming election."[56] As this boosterism makes evident, wardens in this era were not solely, nor even primarily, prison managers. They got their jobs through political connections and kept them by using the resources made available by their jobs to promote their mentor's political interest. They did this in several ways: they hired their friends as guards and prison officials ("There are times when it seems they are trying to hire enough officers here to elect a governor");[57] they rewarded local supporters and attracted new retainers by a calculated allocation of supply orders and contracts for the prison; as prominent and well-paid public servants, they played the role of local VIPs, much in demand as after-dinner speakers or to chair civic committees; and they used these connections and clients to organize county politics, attending party caucuses and state conventions and getting out the vote on election day. This was modest power in ordinary times, involving perhaps no more than a few hundred people and extending only as far as the county line. And it could never achieve total control over local politics, for the very process of doling out jobs and contracts involved firings and exclusions as well, and around each state prison there gathered cadres of former employees anxious for a chance to return and available for rival organization. But in the rough-and-tumble of primary campaigns, and especially in the bitter feud between Groesbeck and Green, the use of state patronage to secure three outstate counties was not an insignificant contribution to success.

---

56. Letter, Harry Hulbert to Alex Groesbeck, 19 June 1922. Groesbeck Papers, box 22, file 9: Prisons, Jackson State Prison.

57. Attorney General Investigations, box 1, file 1: letter from "the Committee of Jackson Prison," n.d. (but probably 1926).

The building of a new prison at Jackson, of course, opened up expanded vistas. Like the highway program, the prison project was big enough to draw suppliers and contractors from around the state and made the process of sorting out the deserving and catering to special interests considerably more complex. As important, the construction dramatically increased the flow of spoils and the density of patronage obligations in Jackson County. Hulbert, an engineer by training, took the title of Director of Construction (the salary of which, on top of his pay as warden and as superintendent of prison industries, made him, briefly, the second highest paid official in the state),[58] and he clung to this post even after he was removed as the warden in 1925. "All buildings were laid out and designed under [his] personal supervision. All materials and supplies, specialties and staples were purchased on his specification."[59] He had absolute control over hiring and subcontracting. Everyone wanting a piece of the action beat a path to Hulbert's door.

As construction got under way, jobs flowed out through Jackson County, carrying along many of Hulbert's friends and dependents as well as a large number of former sheriffs, city employees, and even complete strangers. The head superintendent at the site, a Mr. Heiderman, "must have been a particular friend of the warden; the reason he was there, it wasn't that he knew anything."[60] Apparently, Hulbert had told him to "go down there and look wise," but most of the inmates working on the project believed "he couldn't build a wood box unless he had a drawing and a foreman over him."[61] His assistant, Douglass Faulds, a baker by trade, was "a pal of Hulbert's, [who had] no duties other than acting as companion."[62] A former deputy sheriff in charge of the sand shed did "nothing more than roast his shines before a fire," while a former city manager from Jackson served as a "stock chaser," whose precise duties no one un-

---

58. *Detroit News*, 21 January 1925. The highest-paid state official was the manager of the Michigan State Fair, a post that was in the gift of Groesbeck's main ally in Wayne County, John Haggerty.

59. Report from Harry Conrad, chief engineer, H. G. Christman Co., to Fred Green, 1 February 1927; communicated to the legislature in Fuller, *Messages of Governors*, 918.

60. Affidavit by Guy Cronkhite, 11 April 1927, Attorney General Investigations, box 1 file 3.

61. Affidavit from William Holland, 11 April 1927, ibid.

62. Affidavit from Bruce McNabb, 28 January 1927, ibid.

derstood.[63] Several people familiar with the construction project reckoned that over half the "free" employees at the site were cronies of the warden.

"The engineering force didn't know where they were at; it was one day one thing, and another day another."[64] Not surprisingly, mistakes were made. Many who worked on the project reported that the site was poorly drained and swampy and that the buildings were improperly seated.[65] Water bubbled up in trenches and seeped around newly laid footings; walls settled and cracked. The main wall on the south side of the prison sank over a foot, and additional courses of brick and mortar had to be added to level it off again. Great cracks appeared in Cell Block 1, and the doors of the cell units had to be rehung as settling skewed the openings. Coping with such problems naturally involved a lot of redoing and covering up. Cracked floors had to be torn out and relaid; footings poured in sub-zero temperatures had to be recast; corners had to be braced and reinforced against sinkage; roof beams had to be reset after settling threw them out of line. Hulbert was forever rushing from one crisis to the next, always exasperated, often, seemingly, a bit desperate. Though he was "the only person having a full and complete knowledge of all details of the entire job,"[66] it was clear that, with incomplete blueprints and incompetent subordinates, he could not effectively manage such a large undertaking. The project had a kind of headless momentum of its own.

Waste was endemic. "Lumber was ordered in prodigious quantities, carload after carload, but the records are of no practical value to indicate where it was all used or how."[67] Reports from prison workers indicate that extraordinary amounts of usable lumber was simply burned. Cement sacks, left out in the rain, hardened; tile unloaded too hastily broke and ended up in a landfill; high-quality washed

---

63. Statement from Harry Vickers, 25 January 1927, ibid.

64. Affidavit of John Clancy, 23 January 1926, Attorney General Investigations, box 1, file 1.

65. What follows is gleaned from reports by V. A. Loomis of the state police to William Galbraith, assistant attorney general, dated 7 February 1927, Attorney General Investigations, box 1, file 3.

66. Report of Harry L. Conrad, chief engineer for H. G. Christman Co., to Fred Green, 1 February 1927, passed to the state legislature and reprinted in Fuller, *Messages of Governors*, 912–19; quote on 918.

67. Ibid.

gravel was used to fill holes; endless problems with improper mix-
tures of cement spoiled floors and footings. Without systematic accounting records, it is impossible to get an accurate estimate of the
scale of wastage, and, in any case, it is clear that a lot of juggling and
fudging was going on, as Hulbert covered his tracks, rationalized the
waste, and tried to keep the many suppliers who besieged him well
plied with orders. There were numerous reports of arranged contracts: paint and varnish had to come from Barry Brothers, on
Hulbert's orders, so the head painter had to arrange his sample tests
accordingly; all brushes and trowels had to come from a particular
hardware supplier, and fault had to be found with any other, less
costly offers; no one questioned the quality or the sack weights of
cement from the Chelsea plant. In the summer of 1925 "someone
woke up to the fact that a large amount of material had been used in
the construction of the new prison and there was no record of it,"[68]
but an audit begun in the fall took over a year to establish some order
in the books.

     And through it all, the project kept growing. "No complete plans
with specifications are available. . . . The building plans and details
have been developed on the job by the architectural designer and
engineer as the progress of the project necessitated."[69] A new building here, an extension there, extra rooms in this building, more space
in the coal yard. "It was kind of a joke between us fellows," testified
John DeLair, a foreman, "when we started a new job we would have
to change it five or six times before Hulbert would make up his mind
what he wanted."[70] Several inmates noted that a change in plans
often followed one of Groesbeck's many visits to the site; M. E. Bor-
gan remembered a visit in June 1926, when the governor and Hulbert
walked the grounds, and "the next thing that appeared . . . was the
plans for taking in ten acres more of ground to enlarge the site. . . .
Three hundred feet of this wall had already been poured . . . all of
which had to be torn down, destroyed, and thrown away."[71] For
several months there was considerable confusion about which of sev-

---

68. Attorney General Investigations, box 1, file 3: "Graft in the Construction of
the New Prison, 1927," a "Miscellaneous Memorandum," n.d.
     69. Ibid.
     70. Statement to Gailbraith, 11 April 1927, Attorney General Investigations, box
1, file 3.
     71. Affidavit of M. E. Brogan, 21 December 1926, in ibid, box 1 file 1.

eral sets of drawings was operative. With no approved plans or budget, there was no external check on this kind of creeping enlargement of the project. Whether from whim or the incompetence of supervisors, the need to accommodate pressures for jobs or to allocate contracts among the supplicants who congregated around the project—or even to use up the abundant materials that accumulated at the construction site—there were powerful internal dynamics of growth embedded in the process of building the new prison. If the fear of crime or the get-tough policies of authority made it possible to build a new prison, the mundane, everyday operations of patronage, through which state agencies did the people's business, made it easy to build a big prison.

We may, of course, wonder if patronage practices took on a shadier, even criminal, edge when they came in contact with a prison, and we will have occasion to pursue this possibility in due course. But we must first consider the political context in which this construction took place. For most of the graft, incompetence, and runaway growth for which we have evidence occurred during 1925 and 1926, under the direction of Harry Hulbert. This was Groesbeck's third term in office, an embattled and unhappy time for the governor, which ended with his defeat in one of the bitterest primary battles of the era. There is considerable indication that, faced with new rivals and mounting competition during these years, Groesbeck revved up his patronage machine and drove it for broke.

The pressures began building immediately after his successful reelection in the fall of 1924. Fred Green, recently defeated in his primary challenge to Groesbeck, was reported to be teaming up with Albert Sleeper, a former governor from Bay City whom Groesbeck has supplanted in 1920, and John Smith, newly elected mayor of Detroit and a rival of Groesbeck's main operative in Wayne County, John Haggerty.[72] Though "still in a formative stage," this combination was expected to try and "establish" itself at the state Republican convention in February 1925. For Groesbeck the threat suddenly became more menacing in January, when Calvin Coolidge nominated Charles Beecher Warren of Michigan as U.S. Attorney General.[73] This was a personal blow to Groesbeck, who disliked Warren and entertained

---

72. *Detroit News*, 11 January 1925.

73. This story is followed in the press, see esp. *Detroit News*, 11–13 January and 3 March 1925; and Woodford, *Groesbeck*, 239–41.

hopes of himself being elevated to a Cabinet office, but it also presented a serious challenge to Groesbeck's control of the state convention, since Warren was from Bay City and a close ally of Albert Sleeper, and, if he were to become attorney general, he would be in a position to establish a new conduit of federal patronage into the state party that would feed a combination hostile to the governor. Instantly, the pickets were thrown up and maneuvering began.

Groesbeck pulled out all the stops in Washington to block the Warren appointment; his main allies were Senator James Couzens, whom Groesbeck had appointed as Newberry's replacement in 1922,[74] and Vice President Charles Dawes, whom Groesbeck had supported at the 1924 national convention against a challenge by Herbert Hoover, strongly backed by Charles Warren. But at home the Green-Sleeper-Smith combination, counting on Warren's appointment, moved to attack Groesbeck's political base in the state.[75] Their friends in the legislature went after Harry Hulbert, accusing him of mismanaging Prison Industry accounts and forcing the governor to order an audit; when this audit revealed omissions and imbalances, Groesbeck felt compelled, over the objections of his prison commissioners, to fire Hulbert in order to forestall a legislative investigation into prison management. Everyone agreed not to infer wrongdoing, and Groesbeck issued a strong statement insisting that "he had found not the slightest evidence of graft" and, as a token of continuing confidence in the warden, asking Hulbert to stay on as director of construction for the new prison. But around Jackson County it was clear to seasoned observers that damage had been done to Groesbeck's position.

In a raucous battle at the state convention in February 1925[76] Groesbeck forces beat back challenges from the opposition axis, and Kennedy Potter, a prominent businessman in Jackson County and former owner of the Chelsea Cement Company, was elected party chairman. A close ally of the governor, his nomination was at least partly calculated to restore Groesbeck's position in Jackson County.

74. John Smith, who was lining up with Green and Sleeper, had been a Newberry operative in Polish communities in Detroit and had been among those indicted with him; Couzens was not only disliked by the Newberry loyalists in the state but, in turn, detested Warren.

75. This may be followed in *Detroit News*, 21, 27, and 28 January and 2, 4, and 5 February 1925.

76. *Detroit News*, 25, 26, and 27 February 1925; Woodford, *Groesbeck*, 241.

But many of the people who rallied to the governor at the convention and supported Potter's election were not entirely disinterested: Charles DeLand, the Secretary of State, was from Jackson County, an old friend of Potter and now openly bidding for the governorship, while Mark McKee of Mount Clemens was a prominent figure in the Michigan Veterans of Foreign Wars (VFW), in which Potter was also active, and seemed, in supporting Potter, to be intent upon advancing his own protégé, Wilbur Brucker, to higher office.[77] Thus even in winning, Groesbeck was fostering new rebellions.

In the autumn of 1925 came the break with Haggerty. This dramatic falling out, which has never been adequately explained,[78] was triggered by a dispute over appointments at the state fair, on whose supervisory commission Haggerty had a seat, but the rift clearly went deeper. Haggerty was scrambling to fend off a challenge in Detroit from the dynamic newcomer, John Smith, and, in doing so, he was employing tactics that put Groesbeck, who depended on Haggerty's control of Wayne County but who also needed outstate support to retain state office, at odds with party faithful outside Detroit. It was also a personal estrangement: two bachelors who had been inseparable friends—who had dined together every day, taken vacations together, and kept adjoining offices in Detroit—ceased to speak to each other or even to acknowledge the other in passing. Whatever the causes, the effects of the breach were immediate. The moment the Groesbeck-Haggerty combination broke down, everything was up for grabs. Groesbeck, without his ally, no longer controlled Wayne County, upon which renomination depended; Haggerty, for his part, was extremely vulnerable without his mentor and moved quickly to mend fences with Smith. These shifts stirred a revolt on the Administrative Board. None of Groesbeck's colleagues were prepared to ride a downfall with him, and some, like Charles DeLand and State Treasurer Frank McKay, saw opportunity in the governor's discomfiture. In the spring of 1926 they staged an insurrection: while Groesbeck was on vacation in Mexico, they demanded a statement of accounts from the Highway Department and then declared that the fund showed five million dollars in deficits and imbalances.[79] A furious

77. *Detroit News*, 27 February and 3 March 1925.

78. See the account in Woodford, *Groesbeck*, 241–45.

79. *Detroit News*, 31 March and 1, 8, 9, and 10 April 1926; Woodford, *Groesbeck*, 246–47.

Groesbeck stormed back to town, threatening to impeach the insurgents and calling for a showdown. In an ugly, highly publicized series of meetings, conducted before a large, often unruly, audience of highway boosters and contractors, Groesbeck presented his figures, cross-examined McKay's, and forced one retraction after another.[80] The insurgents were cowed into submission, but the revolt created an indelible appearance of fiscal mismanagement and raised new complaints, especially in newspapers already critical of the governor, that he was an increasingly high-handed and dictatorial force in Michigan politics that ought to be curbed. In effect, the primary campaign of 1926 was already on.

There is little doubt that in the six months between March and September 1926, Groesbeck pulled every string and called in every debt in his bid to win renomination. Though he had friends and supporters in all corners of the state, many were coming under serious challenge from the Green forces, and not a few were switching sides. But, as reports of desertions poured in,[81] the State Prison Commission and the Highway Department remained staunch adherents of the governor's cause, and Groesbeck made sure that both had plenty of money to work with. The legislature, called into specials session in March, voted additional funds for road and prison construction; indeed, part of Groesbeck's subsequent conflict with the Administrative Board over highway accounts had to do with his decision to spend in 1926 monies appropriated for 1927. After beating back the insurgencies on the board, a triumphant Groesbeck vowed: "Notwithstanding such pin-pricking tactics and regardless of them, there will be put on this year a highway building program worthy of Michigan."[82]

In a similar way the prison project got a boost. "It might be well for us to get in touch with [the governor]," Hulbert wrote commission chairman, William Porter, "and see just exactly how far he wants us to go. We can shape ourselves for almost anything he wants us to do,

---

80. *Detroit News*, 14, 16, and 21 April 1926.

81. For example, in Kent County (Grand Rapids) Groesbeck's longtime ally, George Welsh, was locked in a tough battle with state treasurer Frank McKay for control of the country caucus, and James Quinian, an old Groesbeck ally, whom the governor backed in his successful run for the state senate in 1924, was reported lining up with the Green (McKay) forces. See *Detroit News*, 25 April 1926. Similar stories from around the state appeared throughout the summer.

82. *Detroit News*, 8 April 1926.

and we can work out figures very quickly, showing just what costs would be."[83] Porter agreed that it was time for action, but he also worried that with "the wolves" jumping all over Groesbeck, "ready at any time when they thought they could start something," it was also necessary to maintain control: "I do not feel that this is any time for the Commission or any other friend of the Governor to take any action that might in any way reflect on him."[84] Indeed, a circular letter had already gone out to all wardens warning them that the governor expected all operations to stay within budget through the election.[85] Still, the chairman felt it was essential to develop campaign support for Groesbeck in "every township and ward," and he urged Hulbert to get to work firming up his county organization, putting out "propaganda," feeling out "the sentiment," and preparing to "see that the vote is got out" on primary day.[86] This dual effort, to keep the lid on any scandalous possibilities that his enemies might exploit and, at the same time, to shore up local support—especially urgent in outstate counties now that Groesbeck's control of the Wayne County caucus was in doubt—found a clear reflection in Hulbert's own free-wheeling conduct at the construction site that summer. His wide-ranging disbursal of jobs and contracts and his concurrent, if rather clumsy, efforts to cover his waste and rationalize his mistakes were fully in step with the marching orders of his boss.

It was ultimately for naught. In the September primary Groesbeck lost Wayne County by 121 votes and, with it, the nomination. "We have met the enemy and we are theirs," Porter wrote his colleague in the UP, Alton Roberts, "I notice that you were the only member of the Prison Commission who carried his county for Governor Groesbeck. Lansing city [Porter's own base] was for him alright, but the farmer vote swamped us."[87] To Hulbert, who carried the city of Jackson but narrowly lost the county, he wrote: "If you would go [to the state convention, where the rest of the slate was to be selected] and nominate your friend John Haggerty for Secretary of State, you

83. Letter, Hulbert to Porter, 10 March 1926. Groesbeck Papers, box 118, file 5, Prison Commission.
84. Letters, Porter to Charles Blaney, and to "A.T." (probably Alton Roberts), 1 April 1926, ibid., box 118, file 7.
85. Circular of 20 March 1926; letter, Porter to Charles Blaney, 20 March 1926, ibid.
86. Letter, Porter to Hulbert, 29 June 1926, ibid., box 118, file 4.
87. Letter, Porter to Roberts, 15 September 1926, ibid., Prison Commission.

might possibly get a job as janitor or something in the office after he was elected."[88] But the warden at Marquette was more realistic: "We sure got ours and we are in discard. I presume that those of us who carried our home city or county will need to begin looking for another job about the 1st of January."[89] And so they were, all of them, swept away—except for the new warden at Jackson prison, Harry Jackson, who had been appointed by Groesbeck the year before, when Hulbert had come under attack. Just how close Harry Jackson came to losing his job is not clear,[90] but a number of factors worked in his favor: he was close to Frank Fitzgerald at the Highway Department and through him, apparently, in touch with State Treasurer Frank McKay, who backed Green and emerged on the winning side; also Harry Jackson was a member of the United Spanish-American War Veterans association, in which Green was also prominent, and they organized a letter-writing campaign in support of "our beloved comrade," which apparently salvaged the warden's job. For his part Harry Jackson was most assiduous in making room for Green supporters in the administrative and duty rosters of the prison.[91]

In completing this rather digressive excursion into the partisan frays of the mid-1920s, we do well to highlight one or two features of the story. This political system was not a fixed premodern order, a realm of presumably "traditional" politics, whose laws of motion were settled and routinized and whose contours were only gradually being erased by the onward march of progress. It was an embattled, continuously evolving political practice defined by the specific character of the Michigan political economy in the 1920s. Moreover, Groesbeck's management of patronage affairs in 1925–26, and the way these practices affected Harry Hulbert and shaped the construction of a new prison at Jackson, constituted a particular moment in the evolution of a partisan system that was, itself, short-lived and never stable. In this sense the new prison at Jackson was born of conjunctures, none permanent or abiding. There were, as we shall see in the next section, other, more systemic forces at work in shaping the new edifice, but without the specific conjuncture of politics in the mid-

---

88. Letter, Porter to Hulbert, 21 September 1926, ibid.
89. Letter, James Corgan to Porter, 22 September 1926, ibid.
90. See correspondence in Green Papers, box 16, file 6, State Prison (Jackson).
91. Ibid.; and box 142, file 3, prison (Jackson) correspondence for 1928–29.

1920s, these would have taken other forms and found expression in other ways.

Second, we should emphasize that the instabilities of the state patronage order in the 1920s were inherent. The system was embattled, not because there were any discernible "reform" forces pressing upon its space nor because the economic resources necessary to fuel patronage relations were undergoing constriction but because patronage relations posed specific problems in securing obedience and preempting opposition. The contradictions came in several parts. In the first place, as Hulbert's career makes clear, even Groesbeck's most loyal boosters were not really under his control. There were huge gaps in the synapses of command and accountability. Indeed, paradoxically, the more resources Groesbeck could distribute to appointees lower down in the state apparatus, the more likely they were to develop independent operations of their own. Thus while the governor had control of more resources than any of his predecessors and deployed these more actively in his personal political interest, his largesse tended to create independent satraps lower down in the system whose agendas and capacity for autonomous action increased as the patronage resources in the governor's gift grew more plentiful.

The more Groesbeck sought to centralize the levers of patronage in the governor's office, the more he fueled factional infighting and rivalries at the center of the state apparatus. The Administrative Board, whose creation was in principle designed to tighten administrative control, tended also to expand the resources and jurisdictions of secondary state administrators, all of whom, as elected officials in their own right, nursing political ambitions and developing clienteles of their own, found it difficult to forgo the enhanced opportunities to build personal empires within the burgeoning state apparatus. Thus even as the governor became more dominant—and domineering—the members of his Administrative Board became more rebellious. Things tended to get out of control, both at the center and lower down in the departments and agencies of government, while the centralization of patronage operations in the governor's hands tended also to make him more visible and hence more vulnerable to accusation and blame by all those who were cut out, excluded, or injured in the scrambles for spoils. Colleagues and potential heirs on the Administrative Board were only too willing to exploit these slights and humiliations in lining up combinations of opponents. Ultimately, what Groesbeck discovered was that even a freewheeling expansive patronage system was built upon exclusivity, limited access, and privileged connection and thus remained, however generous or powerful, vulnerable to attack from coalitions of losers.

The Dream of an Industrial Penitentiary

But why was only one prison built? Patronage may help account for the construction of a larger, more expensive prison, but it might have made more sense, from the standpoint of spreading the rewards, to build several, smaller institutions around the state, maximizing patronage possibilities by distributing jobs and contracts in several counties. As we have seen, Groesbeck initially considered other sites, especially in the Upper Peninsula, but he finally settled on Jackson because of the ready availability of prison labor. This represented a significant savings to the state and a boon for his hard-pressed warden. With a rapidly expanding prison population, Harry Hulbert could expect to employ as many as five hundred of his inmates on the new construction project, while the use of prison labor, at a cost of about seventy-five cents a day, enabled the state to contract itself for the construction work at costs well below that of private contractors. This, however, was only the surface aspect of a more complex story that takes us inside the walls of Jackson prison.

Work was always at the core of the penitentiary and the carceral principles it represented. The metaphors and modalities of labor were everywhere—in the explanations for criminal behavior, in the organization and routine of the prison, in the criteria for parole, in the measures of success (both disciplinary and rehabilitative), indeed in the very point of incarceration itself. Work was punitive, a form of punishment (sentences at "hard labor" continued to be made long after the rock piles and even ordinary jobs were gone from Jackson); work was a key device for organizing and controlling inmate populations (idleness was universally treated as a threat to institutional security); work was an instrument for inculcating self-discipline in the wayward and self-esteem in the marginal (a hard day's labor was the measure of the man); and work was the guiding purpose and (hopefully) the main result of a passage in prison:

The bulk of the men in our prisons are there because they were never taught to work systematically, and to put the best that is in them to work; that is, they never became efficient workers. They are not savers but spenders. If we are to correct this fault in those men—this infirmity—we have got to teach them in the prison the things for want of which they got into the prisons—that is, industry and thrift.[92]

To work was normal; to be sent to prison was to be corrected or normalized by work, to work.

If anything, the belief that prisoners should work became stronger with time. If we follow Rothman, the Jacksonians who invented the penitentiary felt that prisons should serve as models for the rest of society, places in which order, sobriety, devotion, and steady work were upheld against the evil and wayward instincts of those remanded to custody. By taking wrongdoers out of society, where indolence and intemperance reigned, "the progress of corruption is arrested; no additional contamination can be received or communicated," and the carceral effort to instill self-discipline and regularity could proceed uninterrupted. Work was an important part of this effort, but so too was reflection (silence), repentance (Bible readings), and pain (corporal punishments). The idea (never realized) was to create an improved model of ordinary society, so perfect in its austerity that, as one advocate wrote, "could we all be put on prison fare, for the space of two or three generations, the world would ultimately be the better for it."[93]

Two generations later progressive reformers reversed this equation: prisons, they argued, should be made more like real communities on the outside. In part this reflected a growing disillusionment with the disciplinary regimes that developed behind the walls. In Michigan a scandal over methods of punishment at Jackson in the 1870s[94] and the exertions of an unusually progressive warden in the

---

92. Warden James Russell of Marquette, testifying before the Senate Committee on Education and Labor, 22 March 1916. *Hearings before the Committee on Education and Labor*, U.S. Senate, 64th Congress, pt. 2, 27.

93. David Rothman, *The Discovery of the Asylum* (Boston: Little, Brown, 1971), 84–85.

94. Extensive, rather gruesome testimony was collected by a special legislative committee, in *Testimony Taken in an Investigation before a Joint Committee of the Michigan Legislature of 1875 Touching on the Administration of the Affairs of the State Prison at Jackson* (Lansing, 1875).

1880s[95] combined to banish the water treatment, wooden horse, wire cap, iron collar, foot clogs, whipping cross, and other bizarre elements of custodial dressage. But this critique of prevailing practices was closely tied to a revisioning of the carceral process and its relationship to industrial society. A growing confidence in the effectiveness of industrial discipline as the foundation of social order imparted to prison managers a surer sense that the purpose of incarceration should be to tame and channel criminal energies into productive work.[96] Since most prisoners eventually got out, it made sense to entertain the idea (again, never realized) that prison should be a preparation for release, in which ne'er-do-wells and misfits learned a trade and acquired the habits of steady work. The more perfectly prison society replicated the ways of the free world, the better chance prisoners would have of a successful reentry. In this perspective the traditional "make-work" schemes (treadmills, rock smashing, coal piles) by which prison authorities had kept their charges busy and out of trouble seemed useless, even counterproductive.

> You never saw a man in prison breaking rock with a hammer that would look up at you as you passed by with any degree of self-contentment in his work [Warden Nathan Simpson of Jackson prison told a Senate committee in 1916]. Why is that? It is because every man wants his labor and his activities along any industrial line to count for something to somebody.[97]

As this statement suggests, what underwent revision was not the universal belief in the beneficial effects of work in prison but, rather, the place of prison labor within carceral practice as a whole. Prison work was to be made productive in the fullest, modern sense of the word. Prisoners should not only make useful things, this utility being measured by the profits commanded from market sales, but the income from prison production should be applied to the support and upkeep of prisoners. During the 1880s upwards of 400 inmates at

---

95. Warden W. F. Hatch (1885–91) was an early and persuasive critic of striped uniforms and lockstep marching and an advocate of the indeterminate sentence and inmate classification (which he wanted to base on head measurements).

96. The best account of general progressive thinking in penology is David Rothman's *Conscience and Convenience*.

97. Hearings, Committee on Education and Labor, 22 March 1916, 34.

Jackson (in a total population of 750 to 800) were employed by contractors at a per diem rate, and the income from this work was sufficient in good years to cover the operating costs of the institution.[98] A survey of the state prison system at the end of the century[99] recommended a general expansion of contract work, both to keep up with the rising costs of the institution and to insure that prisoners had "useful" and "productive" work to do. The benefits seemed obvious: to save the taxpayers money and to return to society prisoners who had learned a "sense of duty to support one's self" through hard work.

In Michigan, however, innovations in prison work were blocked by a peculiar provision of the state constitution of 1850 that prohibited teaching inmates "mechanical trades."[100] Thus, when make-work and disciplinary drudgery fell out of favor, the only kind of productive labor that could be readily expanded in state prisons was piecework on contract in unskilled trades—rolling cigars, making certain kinds of brushes and brooms, and producing "parts" (spokes for wagon wheels, tongues and tops for shoes, linings for garments) to be assembled elsewhere—since these activities did not violate the law or incur the hostility of free labor. While these were profitable enterprises, they did not go very far toward the kind of rehabilitative labor that progressives believed would train prisoners for eventual re-inclusion in free society. By the turn of the century, however, the growing friction between constitutional limitations, on the one hand, and the rising population and growing operating costs of prison, on the other, created openings for experimentation. In 1907, after careful comparisons with other states and a study of what supplies Michigan farmers had to import from out-of-state, the Board of Control started up a

98. See the Annual Reports of the Inspectors of the State Prison, for 1880, 1890, and 1900, in the Michigan State Library, Lansing. It appears (though the data are very patchy) that Jackson prison supported itself in 1880, more or less broke even by the end of the decade (carrying a surplus on account of about a thousand dollars in 1890), but then began to fall short by the turn of the century.

99. Orlando Barnes. *The Prison System of Michigan; an Account of the Penal and Penitentiary System and Institutions of the State of Michigan* (Lansing, 1899), 16–21.

100. Section 3, Article 18, announced that "no mechanical trade shall hereafter be taught to convicts in the State Prison of this State except the manufacture of those articles of which the chief supply for home consumption is imported from other states or countries." Interpreting this provision, the state supreme court in 1906 maintained that the manufacture of "ordinary goods" for sale constituted the teaching of a mechanical trade.

factory at Jackson to manufacture binder twine; this facility, entirely owned by the state and operated on state account, showed an immediate profit. At the same time, the legislature moved to eliminate, through constitutional amendment, all legal restrictions on the production of "ordinary goods"; when this passed in April 1907, the way was clear for a rapid expansion of contract industries as well. This opened two possible paths of development: an extension of contract labor along established lines, in which private sector entrepreneurs came into the prison and employed inmate workers at fixed rates paid to the state, or a further elaboration of the binder twine model, in which the state owned and managed industrial operations using prison labor.

In the debate that ensued between advocates of both models, the contract system had the obvious advantage of bringing experienced entrepreneurs into the prison, while a state-run system, subject to a constant politicized turnover of administration, could not hope to hire or long retain managers who were able to organize production and sales efficiently. On the other hand, contract production gave at least the appearance of unfair advantage to private capitalists who were able to obtain state contracts, exploit cheap prison labor, and thereby gain market advantage over "free world" competitors; production on state account, whether competitive in the marketplace or not, always bore the stamp of tax relief and public benefit, if only because income earned was retained by the state, not carted off as profits by private entrepreneurs. Perhaps most persuasive to forward-thinking prison managers, however, was the fact that prison contacts tended to foster undercapitalized and technically backward businesses, while state-owned industries could be, at least theoretically, more up-to-date and modern, thus tailored to the needs of inmate "uplift" and rehabilitation. A lengthy report prepared for the legislature in 1909 by the Michigan Board of Prison Industries aired these conflicting views and, based on a comparison of profits and a survey of prison production in other states, came down decisively in favor of state-owned prison industries.[101] The legislature responded by banning all new contracts after 1912; private entrepreneurs operat-

---

101. "Report of the Board of Prison Industries of Michigan" addressed to the state legislature in 1909. Copy in the Michigan State Library, Lansing.

ing plants in state prisons were told that their contacts would not be renewed when they expired. The state went into business for itself.

> Now, the policy of the Michigan State's prison [Warden Simpson told a Senate committee in 1916] is to follow, just as soon as the contracts are out, a plan that will diversify all of the industries in the institution, along lines of practical, useful, profitable work that will train men to go outside and make a living.[102]

In shaping this outcome, the need for revenue had neatly dovetailed with the recommendations of progressive penology. Within a decade an entirely new vision of the penitentiary had begun to take shape. The basic equation was clearly articulated by the Board of Industries in its 1909 report: "The old idea of prison management," it said,

> was to pound, beat, and by brute force and torture, over-whelm and coerce the prisoner into submission, obedience and the performance of unsatisfactory and undesirable labor. They were confined in dark dungeons, worked in stone quarries, and at labor of such a nature that only the cheapest, poorest and most illiterate free laborer would engage in. It is demonstrated beyond successful contradiction today that these old methods were wrong and not productive of proper results.[103]

In the new approach the "primary purpose" of imprisonment was to punish, but, once a person was incarcerated, "the aim of the State should be to reform and release him a better citizen." This additional claim upon the penalty, beyond the sentence, became the domain of "elevation" and "uplift," the process that raised the downtrodden to dignity again and restored the outcast to society as a useful and productive citizen. At the core of this transformation was work—work that was neither useless nor "effeminate" (a swipe at sewing, cigar rolling, and other "feminized" sweated trades) but steady and sound, capable of teaching inmates useful trades and preparing them "for

102. U.S. Senate Hearings, Committee on Education and Labor, 22 March 1916, pt. 2, 35.
103. Board of Industries, 9.

earning good and substantial wages when they are released." At the same time, there was no contradiction in demanding that prison work "yield a substantial profit." Indeed, the key pivot of the new vision of penology was precisely the link that could be made between the promise of relieving "the burden of taxation" and the equally tantalizing pledge to return prisoners to society able "to secure remunerative employment." Warden Simpson wound up his testimony before Congress with an eloquent plug for the combined benefits of uplift and self-sufficiency:

> success in a reformatory way and in the way of rebuilding men and returning them to society depends wholly upon useful and instructive labor, and your useful and instructive and profitable labor, if properly managed, will also be paying and self-supporting, and if the two worked together in the same field, then the same field that makes your prison self-supporting is the best field in the world and the only field, in my judgement, in which you can reform men.[104]

The move, in pursuit of profits and uplift, toward a fuller industrialization of the prison entailed a transformation of the disciplinary regime inside. In the first place the introduction of machine technology and mass production techniques behind the walls displaced older practices of lockstep marching, striped uniforms, and vicious corporal punishment. While direct physical violence was by no means abolished, control of the body through pain, drill, and silence became less crucial as a tool of institutional management. The regimented forms of carceral dressage associated with lockstep shuffles and the silent system gave way, gradually and partially, to the comparatively less rigid routines of the factory floor and machine-paced discipline. The prison became noisier and more unruly. At the same time, getting a full day's work out of inmate labor power presented novel custodial challenges. Since convicts were not easily cowed by the threat of the sack, various tiers of incentives and disincentives had to be elaborated. Physical segregation, in the hole, on bread and water, with occasional beatings, coupled perhaps with a loss of privileges, a less

---

104. U.S. Senate Hearings, Committee on Education and Labor, 22 March 1916, pt. 2, 48.

desirable work assignment, or a cell transfer—all threats residing in the guard's power to write a "ticket"—were soon adapted to the problem of disciplining inmate-workers to productive labor.

Of far greater importance in the new dispositions of discipline, however, were innovations in parole and conditional release. Indeed, the expanded use of parole, together with the adoption in 1902 of indeterminate sentencing,[105] which conferred power to the parole function, went hand in hand with the transformation of the prison labor system after the turn of the century. Groesbeck's reorganization of parole in 1921 was the last in a series of measures designed to "fine-tune" the process of conditional release, bringing it all under a state director of pardons and paroles who oversaw a system of field supervision designed to continue surveillance of those let out. As a good work record became essential to an inmate's prospects of getting out, the technologies of control inside the "big house" came increasingly to revolve around some interplay of work routines and the dream of release. Conformity was won, less with the whip than with the threat of interminable incarceration, and it was measured or gauged, less by acts of submission than by evidence of cooperation. Ultimately, release was won, not by endurance—that is, holding out over a given stretch of time against oppressive authorities—but by figuring out how to get along with the keepers and winning their endorsement for early release. Thus the industrialization of the prison not only reconfigured everyday routines inside; it multiplied the incentives for collusive understandings between keeper and kept, as prisoners explored openings for "conning" their masters, and custodians sought ways of turning the new requirements for parole into means of insuring docility and cooperation among the inmates.

As parole was adapted to an elaborating system of labor discipline and industrial production inside, and productive work was tied to an ideology of rehabilitation and re-inclusion, a continuous and coherent account evolved of what was being done to felons, after conviction, by those responsible for the state's punishment system. It was a no-nonsense account, full of hard-headed appeals to discipline and labor yet permitting a progressive, even optimistic tone; the promise of "uplift"-on-the-cheap, of saving the taxpayers money

---

105. Marvin Zalman, "The Rise and Fall of the Indeterminate Sentence" *Wayne Law Review* 24, no. 1 (November 1977): 45–94.

while producing positive results, was politically irresistible. It could be buttered up into pufferies:

> We do not care to have our institution termed a prison. We prefer to have it called a corrective institution, to be treated more like you would a sanitarium. If a man goes there with a crooked spine, the sanitarium will treat him and correct it. If a man comes to our institution with a crooked mind, we try to correct that mind. We find that nothing else but intelligent well-directed industry will bring a result.[106]

It could just as easily be reduced to the hardtack problems of policy planning and implementation, carrying

> the burden of solving the problem for the State in deciding upon rational prison industries that will work out beneficial industrial training for the men, have a proper relationship to the working world outside, and, if possible, place the institution on a self-sustaining basis, relieving to some extent the burden of taxation.[107]

Either way, what was done to people in prison had less and less to do with what got them there in the first place; on top of retribution for past deeds were laid demands for change and measures for future conduct. The "work of reform" began with "the breaking of old habits of vice, of drink, of dope, and of indolence" and proceeded to "the forming of habits of industry and right living." By working, prisoners not only acquired new behaviors, associated with sobriety, regularity, application, and diligence, but, in the bargain, they produced useful and marketable goods that, when sold, brought income to the prison, enabling it feed and clothe its charges, and self-respect to prisoner-workers, allowing them to see their hard labor amount to something. The new acquisitions of pride and self-respect, once firmly implanted

---

106. Edward Frensdorf, chairman of the Board of Control at Jackson, before the Senate Committee, U.S. Senate Hearings, Committee on Education and Labor, 14 March 1916, pt. 1, 14–15.

107. Warden Nathan Simpson, in a memorandum on "Prison Industries" prepared by the Joint Prison and Affiliated Boards of Michigan for the state legislature, under the title "Proposed Prison Legislation, Present Laws in Force, and Reasons Why Changes Are Desirable" (1912), 34. Michigan State Library, Lansing.

by a prison regimen, could then be tested in "real-world" conditions under the continuing supervision of parole to insure that the changes were genuine and permanent and to assure the public that the system was working.

By 1915 the main questions facing Michigan prison managers had less to do with ideological direction than with practical choices: "What are the proper industries to establish in our penal institutions?" The Board of Prison Industries, which posed this question in 1909, had no answers. It recommended that the state take over industries already established under contract, look into expanding the binder twine facility at Jackson, and perhaps add furniture making, which seemed to do well at Ionia. While it rejected roadwork and other construction projects as involving "a class of labor" beneath the rehabilitative intentions of the prison, it had few positive ideas. The legislature proceeded to abolish contract labor without, Simpson later complained, providing "industries to take its place or money to install or inaugurate such industries." Indeed, the testimony of Michigan prison officials before the U.S. Senate committee in 1916 suggests that they were all scrambling to improvise solutions that would keep inmates busy and cover their costs. Simpson, who was a farmer, preached the virtues of agriculture; he persuaded the state to lease, then purchase, several large tracts of land adjacent to the prison, and in 1912 he established a commercial cannery on the prison farms that was soon selling vegetables under the brand name "Home Grown." Hulbert, as we shall see, preferred machine production and poured energy and money into developing a textile mill and expanding binder twine production. It is perhaps not the least of the ironies surrounding progressive penology that a movement to bring the prison into the modern age should embrace forms of industrial production that would steer inmates into the most backward, least dynamic sectors of the wage labor market.[108] But the logic of this development was clear. Prisons had an abundance of labor and little capital. "The ideal prison industry must require the minimum of material and the maximum of labor, thus to employ the entire prison population with the least

---

108. Estelle Freedman, in *Their Sisters' Keepers*, notes a similar feature of the women's prison reform movement in the nineteenth century: progressive women, entering professions and demanding reformed institutions for women, run by women, developed programs within these prisons that steered "their girls" into domestic service and other preindustrial pursuits.

expenditure."[109] The goal was useful training and uplift, to be sure, but it was also to turn a profit. And, indeed, the Jackson facility was able to cover its expenses in 1914, 1916, and 1917 with a mixture of income from the sale of its prison-made goods and the payments due under the remaining contracts in the prison.

> Now, that means that every bit of expense, even to the upkeep of the prison, is paid by the prisoners. Hence, I say that the prisoner does pay for his board, and does pay for his lodging, and does pay for his clothing, and does pay for his medicine and hospital treatment, and does pay for the schooling that he gets.[110]

In rendering a coherent account of themselves to the public, this ultimately was what mattered, and it was the restless pursuit of profits and profitability that was to characterize Harry Hulbert's management of the prison during the 1920s.

Finally, in establishing the context for Hulbert's career at Jackson, we must stress again the conjunctural nature of the moment. In some respects Michigan prison industries took a singular path in this period. While several states well known for their progressive penal practices, such as New York, New Jersey, and California, shifted from private contracting and leasing systems to the much more restrictive practice of producing solely for state use, withdrawing entirely from the open market and from interstate commerce, Michigan, along with Illinois and several other midwestern states, went into business for itself. The state bought machinery and equipment, operated plants using inmate labor, and produced goods for sale, competitively, on the open market. While this attracted the almost continuous opposition of business and labor associations, it remained a viable option and an expanding possibility throughout the 1920s. By combining profit with uplift, prison managers were able to fend off critics by appealing to the higher goal of reformation and the practical promise of self-sufficiency. This path of development in prison industries only lasted for about fifteen years. In the 1930s, the Depression made it increasingly difficult to defend the offsetting good of rehabilitation

---

109. Simpson, "Proposed Prison Legislation," 36.
110. Simpson, in the Senate hearings, 22 March 1916, 43.

against the pressure of the unemployed in the free labor market. Already in 1929, the Wickersham Commission renounced the linkage between profit and uplift, arguing that state account production was "essentially a system of State industry . . . in direct competition with private industry," which made it some hybrid of socialism and totalitarianism, "not . . . desirable or consistent with our economic institutions."[111] Federal legislation in 1929, the Hawes-Cooper Act, banned prison-made goods from interstate commerce after 1935, and in that year Michigan moved to implement the federal statute by limiting prison-made goods to state use only.[112]

It was in this context of brief but comparative latitude that Harry Hulbert's career flourished. He was intimately involved in the transformation of the Michigan prison labor system. Indeed, his appointment as warden came in 1918, at the behest of Alex Groesbeck, then the Attorney General, when an investigation revealed that the acting warden at Jackson, Edward Frensdorf, who was a Democrat, had held onto his post after the Republicans resumed the governorship in 1917, in part by allowing several lucrative contracts for chair manufacturing in the prison to be continued despite legislative prohibitions. One of the companies concerned was the Ypsilanti Reed Furniture Company, whose principal owner was Fred Green, then a member of the Republican Central Committee, and the extension had apparently been arranged with the full knowledge of then-governor Albert Sleeper, whom Groesbeck hoped to supplant.[113] Although it took several years to get Green and other residual contractors out of the state prisons—the last contract at Jackson lapsed in 1923—Hulbert was already looking ahead; in fact, the rising population and operational costs of his institution forced him to expand industrial production in any and every way possible. He proved instrumental in piloting the

---

111. U.S. National Commission on Law Observance and Enforcement, no. 9: "Report on Penal Institutions, Probation and Parole," 94.

112. This was the Munshaw-Frey Act of 1935. On the history of prison labor in the nineteenth century, see Glen A. Gildemeister, *Prison Labor and Convict Competition with Free Workers in Industrializing America, 1840–1890* (New York: Garland, 1987); and Howard Gill, "The Prison Labor Problem," *Annals of the American Academy of Political Science* 157 (1931): 83–101; for comparative data, see U.S. Bureau of Labor Statistics, *Convict Labor in 1923*, bull. 372 (Washington, D.C.: Government Printing Office, 1925); there is useful comparative material in *Proceedings of the American Prison Association*, 56th sess., 1926, 158–59. On prison industries in Michigan, see Woodford, *Groesbeck*, 166–67; Jackson, *Michigan State Prison*, 55–56.

113. Woodford, *Groesbeck*, 104; *Detroit News*, 18 April 1926.

shift to state management and in steering state-run industries at Jackson toward the free market. But he was also pivotal in adapting the new and expanded uses of prison labor to evolving strategies for controlling an overcrowded institution. In this sense Hulbert was a transitional figure, an experimenter whose innovations ultimately ran up a dead end.

Hulbert's basic techniques of prison management mixed old-fashioned force with a creative manipulation of jobs and placement opportunities. With few legal or administrative constraints on his authority, the warden had almost unlimited recourse to physical force. And Hulbert was, by all accounts, a mean and unstable man, given to violent outbursts of temper. He kept the whole prison, inmates and employees alike, on edge and off balance with his brawling, capricious, weirdly charismatic style. He freely used his fists, billy clubs, and sticks on prisoners, and the bullpen at Jackson was notorious for producing broken bones. Several prisoners died in the early 1920s, ostensibly suicides, but under mysterious circumstances; Lewis White, who was stabbed in the heart and had his throat slit from ear to ear, was said to have committed suicide, while Brownie Herbot's death was ruled a suicide by hanging, although his wrist was broken and the coroner's report indicated no strangulation.[114] Many inmates, as well as prison employees, commented on Hulbert's penchant for picking fights with anyone who crossed him. "I have licked a good many men in the west," he railed at a foreman on the farm, "and I won't take that from you."[115] Several witnesses reported how he beat up a seventy-five-year-old prisoner for mumbling.[116] This sort of physical violence went hand in hand with small, often stupid, demonstrations of authority: John Clancy told how Hulbert ordered a large store of onions and potatoes to be dumped because a

114. Statement by W. E. Bailey, 26 February 1925, and related material in Attorney General Investigations, box 1, file 4. J. Glenn Toner, on a life sentence, died in the bullpen in 1926, ostensibly of a heart attack, although other inmates heard him screaming a lot. Toner seems to have been involved in a "Committee of Jackson Prison," which sent letters to public officials about conditions in the prison. See anonymous letters (n.d.) to the Pathfinders of America, Attorney General Investigations, box 1, file 1.

115. Affidavit from John Clancey, 23 January 1925, ibid.

116. "Is that old son-of-a-bitch talking back at me? Bring him out here, the old family-fucking son-of-a-bitch, and I will knock his cock stiff while it is nice and cool." Statement by Clifford Jackson (26 January 1925) in ibid. Confirmed by John Clancey in ibid.

few had rotted; when the order was not carried out, the warden returned in a rage: "I am the warden of the state prison. The statues of the state of Michigan says that the warden is the head of this institution. I told you a week ago I wanted those potatoes dumped and I want to know why in hell you haven't dumped them."[117] Similar reports appeared later at the construction site, when Hulbert ordered lumber burned and cement thrown away. All this may betoken character disorder, but there was also a certain charismatic method in Hulbert's behavior: power was expressed in his capacity to give and enforce outrageous orders. At the Chelsea Cement Plant, Superintendent Griffiths, who indulged in quite similar kinds of physical (and it seems, also, sexual) abuse of prisoners and subordinates, defined the terms of authority succinctly: "It is my personality that runs this place, and I am going to run it."[118]

Yet, though physical intimidation remained a powerful weapon in Hulbert's arsenal of control, he also came to rely more heavily on work, on the manipulation of jobs and the possibilities of parole through work, to manage a burgeoning prison population. This was an inescapable consequence of the move to recenter the carceral regime around industrial production. The older panoptic techniques of isolation, silence, the precise monitoring of movement, and the compartmentalization of the body in daily routine gave way in the industrial era to the relative sociability of the factory floor, where massed hands concealed a lot of unsanctioned activity and the need for collective effort made individual surveillance less intimate. The warden and his deputies came to rely on more indirect forms of leverage, over jobs and cell placements inside the prison and assignments to work details outside; recalcitrants and troublemakers could be punished with hard labor and seamy tasks; collaborators could be rewarded and cooperation encouraged with easy or lucrative assignments. Behind these sanctions lay the promise of parole, the ultimate incentive in the warden's gift. With the elaboration of parole procedures, a new terrain took shape in which the warden could play "middleman" between the governor and his commissioner of parole, on the one hand, and prisoners, on the other. Hulbert worked hard to develop the possibilities of this position, needling Groesbeck for more le-

117. Ibid.
118. Quoted in a report to Fred Green from the attorney general's office and transmitted to the legislature, 14 February 1927. In Fuller, *Messages of Governors*, 901.

niency in letting men go and flaunting his connections with the governor before the inmate population in an effort to make work and self-discipline mean something to inmates anxious to get out.

However, if work was to be made an effective instrument of control, two corollary requirements had also to be met. First, the number and diversity of jobs had to be continually expanded. Hulbert was relentless in his efforts to expand the job opportunities he had to deploy: when Groesbeck needed prisoners to work the highways, Hulbert eagerly volunteered his charges and committed money to construct temporary camps; when a new prison came under consideration, Hulbert convinced his boss that the state could save money and he could solve control problems by employing inmate labor on the project. The warden's letters to the governor were full of wide-eyed visions about expanded production and employment prospects. "Perhaps you are familiar with the fact that there are a large number of things that could be made that would be good sellers on the market," wrote Hulbert in one letter, pressing the case for a new textile plant; and on another occasion: "I am endeavoring to start two more additional industries, having started five in the last year."[119] While leaving no stone unturned in his restless rummaging for jobs, Hulbert still needed to insure, in the second place, that the perks and payoffs of work were obvious and plentiful—if not directly in wages, then informally, in the possibilities jobs offered for an improvement in the quality of life inside or for an early release. Hulbert was, in fact, surprisingly lax in the supervision of workers on the job; as we shall see, prisoners (and guards) felt free to take enormous liberties in expanding and exploiting the informal opportunities afforded by their job placements. And they were encouraged in these illicit activities by an administration that needed inmate cooperation in keeping the vast institution peaceful, in meeting production goals and sustaining profit margins, and in presenting to the public a plausible account of how the carceral regime produced uplift and reformation in even the most hardened criminals.

By the mid-1920s Hulbert could boast that over 75 percent of the prisoners at Jackson were gainfully employed, half of them on projects outside the prison walls. The mainstay of prison industry at Jackson was the binder twine plant, originally established in 1907 as

---

119. Letter, Hulbert to Groesbeck, 26 May 1922, ibid.

an experiment in state-account production. A new mixture of sisal, manila, and hemp made the quality of Jackson twine extremely competitive in the early 1920s, and Hulbert ran the plant "night and day" to produce 14 million pounds a year. Most of this was sold out of state, through agents and consignments across the northwest, and, while there was significant annual variation, profits averaged around $90,000 a year.[120] Hulbert expanded the brush shop, producing over fifty kinds of brushes and brooms for sale to hardware stores and wholesale suppliers; he started up a tombstone and marker shop, expanded production in the chair factory to over three hundred kinds of furniture, and added a cot factory, manufacturing the steel frames for folding beds. He developed an aluminum stamping operation, making utensils for sale to institutions across the country; he started up a brick and tile works at Onondaga and took over control of the Chelsea Cement Plant, which with the boom in highway construction was earning a profit of $180,000 by 1925;[121] he expanded the output of the cannery, marketing over four hundred thousand cans of vegetables a year to groceries and institutions, and added a cider works that made vinegar for commercial sale. Under Hulbert's hand Michigan took a lead in that new, now universal staple of prison production, the manufacture of license plates and road signs for the state; he invested over $60,000 in new stamping and enameling equipment, and, while output was largely for "state use" in Michigan, he stood ready to take orders from states as far away as Vermont. But it was the textile plant upon which Hulbert lavished most hope, attention, and capital. After a visit to Pennsylvania in 1922, Hulbert convinced his

---

120. The boast that production was running "night and day" is from a report on prison industries by Hulbert to the Prison Commission, 27 November 1922 (Groesbeck Papers, box 119, file 3); the profit estimate is drawn from a memo by the State Prison Commission to Groesbeck, 27 December 1926 (ibid., box 118, file 3), which is a general review of the entire administration. There is considerable correspondence on the technical operations of the binder twine plant in box 119, files 1–2.

As will become apparent, all Hulbert's accounting reports are suspect. His report of binder twine operations shows a profit of $127,000 in 1921; a loss of $6,000 in 1922 and of $3,600 in 1923; a profit of $44,800 in 1924, a profit of $146,000 in 1925, and a profit of $90,000 in 1926—for a net profit over five years of just under $400,000.

All profit estimates in Hulbert's day did *not* include the cost of feeding and housing the work force. Thus, when Hulbert's successor, Harry Jackson, computed the profits for 1925, he deducted $92,000 for "inmate maintenance" (Report of the Warden, 19 October 1925, box 94, file 9: Jackson Prison, Binder Twine, 1925).

121. *Detroit News*, 15 February 1925.

superiors of the potential for making cotton cloth and turning out shirts, sheets, toweling, and other staples both for state institutions and for sale on the open market. He even explored the possibility of a direct trade between Michigan and prison systems in the South that raised cotton with convict labor, exchanging raw materials for finished goods.[122] By the end of his tenure Hulbert had invested nearly $150,000 in plant and equipment for textile production.

In all of this Hulbert was quite in step with national trends. Binder twine, textiles, and license plates emerged, along with commercial farming, as the leading lines of prison production across the country by the early 1920s.[123] Hulbert took to attending national conferences as an expert on prison industry, extolling—at times rather incoherently—the innovations and successes of the Michigan system.[124] As he described them, the problems he faced were familiar ones to his colleagues in the American Prison Association: finding product lines that did not compete too openly with local or state industries but for which there was a good market; developing operations that did not require complex machinery or skilled labor; and establishing a method of bookkeeping that covered the cost of materials and equipment, provided for the upkeep of the labor force, and paid some sort of wage to inmate workers as well as salaries to supervisors, guards, and sales staff—without dissolving all profits into overhead. There were tricky trade-offs here, which Hulbert, for the most part, finessed with various kinds of accounting fraud and legerdemain. His "main thought," he said, was "to put inside of prison walls factories that would be a profit to the state."[125]

---

122. This plan is reported, along with a detailed review of the equipment needed for starting a plant, in Hulbert's memorandum to the Prison Commission, 27 November 1922, Groesbeck Papers, box 119, file 3.

123. Gill, "Prison Labor Problem," 85.

124. For example, *Proceedings, American Prison Association*, Annual Congress, 1922. At the session on Prison Industries, at which Hulbert was the main speaker (66–70), the warden delivered himself of the following: "I am compelled to keep 500 and more prisoners outside of the walls, and any Warden who has 500 prisoners outside the walls has to work overtime in mind, body and soul for the keeping of these men, so thus we have at Jackson one of the largest industries which I struggle to advance every day, and as yet, I do not believe we have even got the roof on, and that factory is a factory that every State institution in the world should have one like and every institution has one if the Warden in the front office has a heart and a soul, and that is a factory of *rebuilding man*. The subject is a broad one."

125. Ibid., 66.

But there was a good deal more: "My dear Governor," he wrote in making his case for a textile plant,

> there is a great possibility of expansion in this industry and at any time that you want to talk with me, I would be very glad to go over the situation with you as I think we can put Michigan's prison industries on the map so that when you leave office the state will look up to you as doing something that no other Governor ever did.[126]

What Hulbert had in mind was to insure that Jackson prison was able to pay for itself. As we have seen, the dream of self-sufficiency was widely shared among early advocates of prison industrialization in the 1920s; their model was the Minnesota State Prison at Stillwater, which was the other leading producer of prison-made binder twine in the country, as well as of farm equipment, and which made claims of profitability that were legendary in the profession, though never adequately documented.[127] There was nothing particularly outrageous in Hulbert's ambition; Jackson prison had managed to cover expenses from industrial profits off and on for years and, most recently, during Simpson's wartime administration. The trick that Hulbert had to turn was to sustain a rapid expansion of profits in step with a burgeoning inmate population. Groesbeck was apparently always skeptical of Hulbert's lavish promotions and blatant ambitions, but he had no reason to refuse Hulbert enough leeway to chase his dream of a self-sustaining penitentiary. In 1921 the governor struck a deal with his warden: the state would provide $300,000 from the General Fund for operating Jackson prison in each of the next four years (1922–25), and

---

126. Letter, Hulbert to Groesbeck, 9 December 1922, Groesbeck Papers, box 22, file 9.

127. Gill, "Prison Labor Problem," 97–98. Advocates of progressive penology, such as Gill, wondered if Stillwater taught useful skills in its industry, but the claim that it earned enough from its industries to cover upkeep and support of the prison, while paying prison workers a wage, seems to have been generally accepted. The claims were presented to the Congress, in the U.S. Senate Hearings before the Committee on Education and Labor, on 19 January 1916, by Ralph Wheelock of the Minnesota Board of Control. The example of Stillwater was repeatedly invoked at professional meetings in the 1920s and again in the Wickersham Commission report, in which a case was made for the "exceptional" circumstances that made Minnesota one of the few profitable success stories (84 ff.).

Hulbert agreed to meet the balance of operational expenses from the profits of prison industries.[128]

This gave Hulbert, briefly, in 1922, 1923, and 1924, a virtual carte blanche to pursue his dreams. His superiors on the commission, knowing that he had the governor's endorsement, made him head of Michigan Prison Industries in 1923, a post that doubled his income and expanded his powers, and they approved all the equipment purchases and improvements of facilities that the warden recommended. There was no sign in these years of an impending move to a new prison, as Hulbert invested $450,000 in developing the plant and equipment of the old prison facility, actually spending more on industrial buildings than on additional dormitories for the growing inmate population. And there was a general inclination in Lansing to ignore a rising chorus of complaints about Hulbert's energetic efforts to boost sales. A former warden of Stillwater prison was hired as sales manager for binder twine, earning $25,000 a year in salary and commissions to develop markets out of state. Although the man was clearly an "expert" in the field, not a few Michigan Republicans felt they had been cut out of a lucrative post. More troublesome was the grumbling of businessmen around the state as they ran across the new competitor in town: food and hardware wholesalers complained that Prison Industry salesmen were undercutting their markups by going straight to retailers with lower prices; grocers complained that some competitors were being allowed to carry extensive credit (including the husband of one of Hulbert's secretaries, who opened a grocery in Jackson on what amounted to a subsidy from prison industries); two hardware stores in one small town protested that they had both been given "exclusive" rights to prison-made utensils and brushes on condition that they place a large order.[129] There was nothing illegal in any of this: the state was in business, and good business often involved deals at the expense of loyal taxpayers and Republican voters. Thus, when Mack and Company of Ann Arbor made inquiries about furniture prices from Prison Industries, in connection with a big sale to a

---

128. There is no surviving document on this transaction from 1921, but it was frequently referred to by Hulbert's successor, Harry Jackson (see, e.g., Report to the Prison Commission, 23 February 1927, in Executive Records, Groesbeck Papers, box 118, file 3), and summarized by the Prison Commission in its review of the Groesbeck administration (ibid., 27 December 1926, 11–12).

129. These and other sales practices were detailed in an undated memo by Robert Reece (Attorney General Investigations, box 1, file 1).

fraternity house, and then found that a salesman from the prison had gone straight to the fraternity house and sold the furniture at a better price, Mack and Company could not complain about the business practices of Prison Industries, but it could insist, through political channels, that the prison keep out of its business.

Hulbert's business antics were the result not only of his personal ambition and braggadocio but of his deal with the governor. Ultimately, this proved his undoing. While his efforts to foster jobs made him, in the eyes of the Prison Commission, an ideal warden—"the discipline of the prison has been excellent. No outbreaks, mutinies or riots have occurred"[130]—his financial arrangement with Groesbeck forced him into a heedless expansion, committing more and more resources to prison industry in order to boost output and sales. Yet he could never keep up with his obligations. The rapid increase in prison population after 1922 drove up the annual cost of maintenance, from $675,000 in 1922 to $840,000 in 1925. At the same time, Hulbert poured nearly $300,000 into new equipment and another $150,000 into structures for his expanding industries. Perhaps inevitably, start-up delays plagued the textile plant, which lost $63,000 in its first three years of operation, while a statewide boycott of bricklayers, responding to appeals from private manufacturers, brought production at the Onondaga facility to a standstill in 1925. Hulbert met his obligations in 1922, but, thereafter, industries at Jackson failed to come up with its share of operating costs until 1926, when it paid $148,000 against an accrued deficit to the General Fund that now totaled over $1.3 million.[131] This was the biggest operating debt the prison had ever sustained.

Hulbert's financial difficulties angered the governor, who wrote the resident commissioner at Jackson, Mark Merriman, that "the business end of this institution has not been properly looked after."[132] Under political pressure from his enemies, as we have seen, Groesbeck was forced to conduct an audit of prison industry books. What the accountants found was a "real mess," and, while nothing was ever said officially or publicly, Robert Davidson, the accountant

---

130. Summary report, 27 December 1926, Executive Records, Groesbeck Papers, box 118, file 3.

131. All these figures are from the summary report (ibid).

132. Letter, Groesbeck to Merriman, 26 November 1924, Groesbeck Papers, box 49, file 9.

in charge, attributed the mess to a "willful manipulation" of the accounts.[133] After meetings with the auditors in Detroit and several
heated exchanges with Hulbert, Groesbeck let his warden know that
"his resignation was looked for."[134] The governor was engaged in a
salvage operation, trying, as we saw, to protect his political position
against the sniping of his enemies; by removing Hulbert as warden,
he prevented a legislative investigation or legal proceedings and
probably salvaged Hulbert's reputation.[135] But the warden had himself also been engaged in a cover-up; he had launched an ambitious
expansion of prison industries and promised great profits, yet he was
unable to meet his obligations under the operating agreement with
the governor. Trying to show a profit while explaining his inability to
pay forced the warden to "cook" his books, and in a prison it was not
hard to find experts skilled in juggling accounts and fixing the books.
The inmate in charge of industrial records, an accountant by profession and a convicted embezzler, could of course explain the elaborate
ploys of double bookkeeping—twine sent out on consignment was
designated "sold" and entered as profit, the nonexistent cash was
entered as accounts relievable or unpaid, and merchandise recovered
from the jobber was then logged as inventory on hand—but, on
balance, he had to admit "the whole accounting system was a fraud
and a delusion."[136]

Always running just ahead of the game, Hulbert carved out a
good career for himself and made his contribution to three Groesbeck
electoral victories. When he finally tripped up, it was not because the
goal itself was discredited but because Groesbeck had lost faith in
Hulbert's methods, or, more exactly, was no longer able to shield
those methods from hostile scrutiny. Locked in a close primary fight,

133. This in an affidavit by Robert Reece, dated January 1925 (Attorney General
Investigations, box 1, file 5), reporting a conversation with Robert Davidson.

134. *Detroit News*, 21 January 1925.

135. The widely held belief around the prison was that Hulbert was, in the end,
protected by Frank Eamons, a Detroit attorney, who was a member of the Prison
Commission and important to Groesbeck in his battle with Smith for control of Wayne
County.

136. Statement by Roy Beebee, 3 August 1926, Attorney General Investigations,
box 1, file 1; the details were further spelled out and corroborated by the testimony of
the prison bookkeeper, Harold DeWitt, to William Galbraith, in ibid., dated 18 March
1927.

the governor had to avoid the taint of corruption or waste. But he still needed Hulbert and so transferred him down the road to the new prison project that the warden had begun in 1924 largely as an extension of his efforts to keep his retainers and charges fully employed. The scale of this project, and its annual budget, was a good deal larger than Prison Industries, and, while Hulbert took a cut in salary when he gave up his posts as warden and director of Industries, he had, as we saw, ample scope in the construction project for his restless energies and ambitions. From what we know of his activities on the site, Hulbert did not slow down or change his habits in the least. His instincts for empire building were fully engaged on the building project and quite in step with, and of use to, Groesbeck in his battle for political survival during 1925–26.

Yet, while Hulbert's conduct at the new construction site expressed both his continuing personal ambitions and his determination to serve his longtime political mentor, his drive to build a bigger and better prison may have also been an effort to solve the problems of profitability that he had encountered at the old prison and that had wrecked his deal with Groesbeck. Hulbert forged ahead with his dream of a completely industrialized, self-sufficient penitentiary. Indeed, to his way of thinking the failure to meet his obligations under the pact with Groesbeck had been due entirely to the rapid rise in the operational costs of the old prison. The growing number of inmates had strained the capacity of the old facility and had forced him to distribute his population to the farms, dormitory annexes, road camps, and factories outside the walls, thus greatly increasing the costs of guarding and feeding his charges. Moreover, the effort to expand productive facilities and jobs within the old main prison had run up against limitations of space and antiquated structures, raising at every turn the start-up costs for new operations. Even with these impediments to success, and despite the rigidities of his deal with Groesbeck, Hulbert could claim that Prison Industries had managed to make a total profit of nearly one million dollars under his direction and, from these proceeds, to finance entirely the purchase of new plant and equipment for expansion. Such a return from an old, dilapidated prison gave fair promise that a new prison might be able to sustain itself, provided enough land, labor, and machinery could be brought together and used effectively. There was no necessary limit to the size of such an operation. Indeed, in an era when Henry Ford was achieving notable efficiencies and highly publicized economies of scale at his mammoth new River Rouge plant, it was not difficult for Hulbert to conclude that a larger facility and greater concentration of men and equipment might serve the ends of economy and even, eventually, of self-sufficiency. Reasoning in this way made the grandiose seem practicable.

It was also politically persuasive. We may consider Hulbert foolish or blindly ambitious to commit himself to creating a self-supporting, industrial prison. But, ultimately, as the terms of his deal with Groesbeck make clear, he never claimed that the prison did, or even would, pay for itself, only that it ought to try. It was (if the word is not too solemn to apply to Harry Hulbert) his aspiration to make the prison a productive enterprise, and it was this that resonated politically. His goal was entirely in step with the role of punishment in the prohibition era. What, after all, was prohibition all about, if not to salvage and harness the energies of labor for production, to steer the shiftless into the orderly and disciplined ways of industrial life? What better use could prison make of the rising number of convicted bootleggers and mobsters, tavern keepers and moonshiners, than to put them to productive work? Correction or reformation was not the crux of the matter here, although Hulbert could talk a progressive line when called upon; at issue was the creation of a carceral practice that affirmed, through punishment, the social priorities of sobriety and industrial discipline and anchored the legitimacy of authority not in the policing of drunkards but in the construction of orderly and productive institutions capable of serving the people with efficiency and the most up-to-date methods. Cost-effective and businesslike administration were the perennial slogans of Groesbeck's campaigns.

The new prison at Jackson was thus, in many ways, a monument to Harry Hulbert's persistent ambition and Alex Groesbeck's needs of the moment. The dreams of self-sufficiency, which served so well the ideology of punishment under prohibition and which seem to embody the presumptive links between profit and uplift, and the requirements of patronage, which continually expanded outward the networks of obligation necessary to sustain competition for power at the center, joined to fashion this white elephant of corrections. Even the fiercest critics of Hulbert and Groesbeck had to admit that "the taxpayers of Michigan need not fear faulty design, workmanship, or construction, as the work built to date is superfine."[137] It was easy enough to complain that the single-man cells with hot-and-cold running water and "push button control vitreous china water closets" sported "more conveniences than in the rooms of some of our finest hotels." And the terrazzo floors and glazed brick walls seemed unnecessarily ostentatious for a penitentiary. Yet critics waxed wistful before the enormous walls that, however grandiose, would "be admired by those who know a beautiful piece of work when they see it." Ambition and self-aggrandizement had combined with the calculations of patronage and the pressures of political competition to produce high quality from great waste. As with some great enterprise of the ancien régime, the corruption that surrounded the construction of the new prison reflected, on the one hand, the expanding resources of the state and, on the other, the inadequacy of its institutional apparatus to control or manage the tasks it had undertaken. Graft and venality filled the gaps of incomplete state formation, and, while Fred Green might attack the corruption of the Groesbeck administration and Harry Jackson might shake his head at the heedless and highhanded ways of Harry Hulbert, the epigoni were not essentially different from their predecessors, reapplying the same appeals for efficiency and administrative accountability and replaying the same rules of political combat with, perhaps, a little more caution and a little less flamboyance.

Patronage inside the Industrial Prison

Prisons are secret places. The public is, lamented one prisoner, "utterly void of all knowledge as to what is being done in their name inside prison walls."[138] In fact, the walls faced two ways, keeping the prisoners in and shutting the public out. Their main purpose was to establish and maintain the separation, the physical and social divide, between the universe of the prison and the world outside. Theorists and managers of prisons have always insisted that this enforced segregation was, at once, a form of therapy for criminals and of protection for the public. The less the public knew about prisons, or the

---

137. Report of Harry Conrad to Fred Green, 1 February 1927, in Fuller, *Messages of Governors*, 4:912–19.
138. Letter from "The Committee of Jackson Prison," n.d., to J. W. Wright (Pathfinders of America), Attorney General Investigations, box 1, file 1.

more that enforced social distance allowed the manipulation of mediated images about the criminal and his fate, the more imprisonment could be used to terrorize and deter; wrote one circuit judge in 1922, "to my mind, the prison should be inaccessible to the public, nothing should be known of its workings and among criminals generally it should be regarded as equal to, or worse than, a death sentence."[139]

We may wonder just how separate the prison world really was, even in the heyday of the "big house," and we may debate the deterrent effects of imprisonment upon would-be criminals, but enforced social distance served both the practical needs of prison management and the larger intent of incarceration in the industrial penitentiary. When Harry Hulbert enforced an oath of secrecy on new employees, he was less interested in striking fear in the hearts of the guilty than in making sure that "the public is kept in ignorance of what is going on Prison Property."[140] And this was less because the public would regard what he was doing as improper than because public scrutiny, in whatever form, would constrict his autonomy as warden. And it was this autonomy that was fundamental. Without it he would be less able to run the institution in the brawling manner he preferred or to use his position as warden so blatantly for political purposes. Nor would he be able to enforce that claim to an excess of penalty beyond the sentence so central to a rehabilitative discipline; social distance imposed a firm distinction between what was done to inmates after incarceration and the criminal acts that landed them in prison in the first place.

For historians the practical effect of contemporary ignorance is that we know precious little about life inside Jackson prison during the 1920s. What information comes to us is fragmentary and, at this distance, unverifiable. In fact, the bulk of material in the state archives was collected by a certain Robert Reece, onetime employee at the prison, who either resigned or was fired in the early 1920s and spent the next several years trying to ruin Harry Hulbert. Reece was convinced that it was possible to buy a parole from Jackson prison, and it was upon this "pardons mill," as he preferred to call it, that he focused his attention. With the energy and determination of the

---

139. Charles Collingwood to C. A. Blaney, 17 March 1922, Executive Office, Groesbeck Papers, box 22, file 3.

140. Affidavit by J. J. Aldred, 29 January 1927, Attorney General Investigations, box 1, file 3.

wronged or the self-righteous, he built a case against Hulbert and, more particularly, against the prison chaplain, William Hopp. He interviewed former prisoners, collected sworn statements, and tried to interest the courts in undertaking a formal investigation. Apparently, sometime in 1925, a preliminary grand jury hearing was held on the question of parole peddling, but it led nowhere; according to one of Reece's informants,[141] the Jackson attorney who was called to testify, and who was widely believed to have a hand in the "pardons mill," laughed it off: "You are on the right track," he said, "there is plenty of it, but you can't get it."

But Reece did not give up. Along the way, at first incidentally and then more systematically, he began to amass material on other matters, such as brutality at the prison, official corruption, and the sale of drugs. As his investigation branched out, he made trips to Chicago to track down and interview parolees who, at greater distance, might be more willing to talk.[142] He also gained an important ally in the editor of the *Jackson News*; the paper circulated a citizens' petition in 1925 to initiate grand jury proceedings. In January 1926 Circuit Judge Benjamin Williams was moved to constitute himself as a one-man grand jury to investigate waste and corruption at the prison.[143] We do not know if there were political motives behind this probe or what became of it, but during the summer of 1926 Reece made several unsuccessful efforts to publicize his findings. The chairman of the Prison Commission alerted Hulbert: "Our mutual friend Reece came here a few days ago and went to the Lansing State Journal, spent several hours with them and tried to get them to come out with a lot of the slush that he has been peddling for a number of years."[144] Happily, "Carl Sheil of the Journal came to me this morning and said he had simply refused to print anything that Reece had given him." Later, in Chicago, Reece turned over evidence he had collected on the prison

---

141. Letter from G. Elmer McArthur to Reece, 11 December 1926, ibid., box 1, file 1.

142. A "Digest of Interviews, Conversations etc. Held during Many Successive Visits to Chicago" is included in ibid., box 1, file 1, n.d.

143. *Detroit News*, 2 May 1926. Apparently, local citizens were less annoyed with Harry Hulbert's administration of the prison than with Jackson County sheriff, Warren Stoddard, who was a close friend and political ally of Hulbert's. Stoddard operated an extortion racket on bootleggers transporting liquor from Detroit to Chicago. See Englemann, *Intemperance*, 152.

144. William Porter to Harry Hulbert, 8 June 1926, Groesbeck Papers, box 118, file 4.

"dope trade" to federal authorities, but when a representative of the Narcotics Bureau confronted Groesbeck with it, the governor "laughed the matter off" and told the emissary that "Reece was crazy." In July Hopp filed charges of slander against Reece. By then, with the primary in full swing and Groesbeck's political fortunes on the line, Reece had become a political menace, and Fred Green, who was naturally interested in anything that might discredit his enemy, openly welcomed Reece's investigation. After the election Green assigned an assistant attorney general to develop the evidence, and Reece turned over all his files to the state. The inquiry soon fizzled, as Groesbeck's appointees were swept from office and the whole point of an exposé was lost; but Reece's documents found their way into the state archives, and there remain the only opening through which we can hear, however faintly, the voices of inmates.

The material Reece gathered is, of course, doubly suspect. He was, himself, on a rather peculiar personal campaign against "the whole administration," and his reports suggest a rather narrow, moral, straight-laced man, undoubtedly honest but also obsessed with his mission and, we may surmise, rather easily fooled. Moreover, his main sources of information were paroled prisoners. This is not a prima facie reason to disbelieve them. But they were not speaking for themselves; they were responding to questions put by Reece, and what they said was then crammed, again by Reece, into a stilted format that bore all the marks of a non-lawyer trying to compose a document that would carry legal weight. Moreover, there was no reason why parolees should want to talk to Reece; he carried no official title or sanction, and he could offer neither reward nor protection for those who cooperated with him.[145] For the most part those who talked to Reece shared with him a desire to "get back" at the prison and its warden. A comradeship of grievance would not necessarily produce falsehood—and there is no reason to construe fabrica-

---

145. At least one of his informants, a Roy Beebe, whom he interviewed in Chicago, subsequently wrote to Reece demanding the return of all statements and affidavits. Beebe indicated that he had been threatened by Emory Lyon, a parole supervisor in Chicago. In "Digest of Interviews" Reece claimed that Beebe subsequently telephoned him to indicate that, in demanding the documents back, he was not taking back anything he had said. See Beebe's letter of 21 August 1926, Attorney General's Investigations, box 1, file 1.

tion—but it certainly could be selective and mutually self-reinforcing in what it chose to remember or to record.

This said, we need not therefore discount the reports. If a large number of former prisoners tell of similar, or the same, practices and remember the same events, we may take it to be, at the very least, their truth and fruitfully place it in the context of what we otherwise know. This is particularly the case if we bear in mind that prisoners in the 1920s were only beginning to learn the new rules for parole or conditional release, and the game must have appeared somewhat mysterious. Explaining exactly how someone got out of prison when the procedures were as yet unclear and decisions in individual cases were made entirely in secret could easily produce stories of a "pardons mill"—indeed, the very term they all used suggests the vagueness of the process in prisoners' (and Reece's) minds, for parole was not a pardon, while an executive pardon had in the past been about the only way to gain release before the expiration of the full sentence.

Moreover, the kind of stories prisoners told involved, as we shall see, cash and connections. For such stories to have currency, and especially to enjoy widespread credence, there must have been a lot of money circulating in the prison and lots of opportunities for inmates to earn it; further, there must have been a "culture of corruption"—guards know to be on the take, officials reputed to be "available," outside "doormen" ready to open the parole gates for a fee—in short, ways of doing and getting things through informal and illegal networks. That such avenues were open, or at least accessible, at any time should not surprise us, but in the 1920s the context in which the prison was located proved peculiarly conducive to the sort of activities described by Reece's informants. Harry Hulbert was himself a freewheeling patronage master who was relying more heavily upon work and job placements to control the prison; not only was the state economy booming, but the prison world itself was rapidly expanding, generating surpluses of all kinds that, however marginal, were available for illicit accumulation. We must attempt to see the sale of paroles and drugs as the deviant end of a whole network of otherwise "normal" relations inside the prison, just as these relations were, in their turn, both an extension of and a constituent element in the routine political relations of the state.

Were paroles for sale? It is impossible to say. The prisoners certainly thought so. What is clear is that money was taken by several officials in exchange for a promise of parole, and on many occasions, though not all, release soon followed. "The truth is that when a prisoner announced that his friends have been able to raise some money, we know he will leave us in a short while."[146] Said Roy Beebe, "If you want to be paroled, work for Chaplain Hopp."[147] He was at the center of most of the stories. A seedy Lutheran cleric from Detroit who, according to prison gossip, had lost his pastorate after sleeping with a parishioner, Hopp was widely regarded as a dissolute and immoral man. Many inmates were convinced that he pursued and seduced their wives, and it was widely said that he owned controlling interest in a Detroit whorehouse.[148] Hopp apparently kept close tabs on prisoners with money, regularly checking inmate accounts to see if anyone showed signs of affluence[149] and approaching wives and other relatives with offers of services in exchange for cash. When Roy Daniels showed six hundred dollars in his account, Hopp approached his wife with a proposition for parole, at five hundred dollars; Ms. Daniels haggled him down, and her husband got his parole for three hundred dollars. Blackie Henderson's wife, reputedly a "madam" in Detroit who saw Hopp regularly, sold a ring for twelve hundred dollars to get her man released.[150] The price Hopp quoted varied according to capacity to pay and other considerations; he seems to have been a rank opportunist, using what openings were made available through his job to milk prisoners for whatever he could get.

Exactly how Hopp secured paroles for his clients is not clear. As chaplain, he was ostensibly a friend and confidant of inmates, and his good word presumably carried weight with the governor. Moreover,

---

146. Letter from "Committee on Jackson Prison, n.d., in ibid., box 1, file 1. Another prisoner told Reece: "Since I have been here, hundreds of men receiving sentences ranging from 10 to 20, 15 to 30, 20 to 40, and life have left here on a governor's parole after doing only a small fraction of the minimum imposed by the courts—in some cases doing only a few months. And many of these men . . . have told me that they were buying their way out."

147. Beebe's supplementary testimony, 2 August 1926, in ibid.

148. This latter "fact" was confirmed to Reece by the Detroit Police Department (DPD); see letter from Sgt. George Ludwig of the DPD to R. W. Reece, 26 November 1924, ibid., box 1, file 1. Hopp owned the Liberty Hotel, which was at 400 Congress Avenue at the corner of Brush, and was well-known by the police as a haven for bootleggers and "dopers."

149. Statement by Leslie Welford, 20 July 1926, in ibid.

150. Statements by Daniels, 11 June 1926, and Henderson, 9 June 1926, in ibid.

he and Hulbert were reportedly "as thick as thieves"[151] and frequently made joint recommendations for parole. According to one inmate, Hulbert boasted about Blackie Henderson's parole that "there is a fifty-fifty split in this for me,"[152] and it is not inconceivable that Hopp, whose appointment was in the warden's gift, shared proceeds with him on a regular basis. It also appears that there were other, rival conduits for purchasing release: a Senator Riopelle from Detroit would use his contacts for a fee and had "never double-crossed anyone," while Bernie Brower, the state senator from Jackson, was a close friend of Fred Janette, the parole commissioner in Lansing, and occasionally took money to arrange paroles.[153] In securing parole for Arthur Henderson, Brower reportedly got $850 in installments from the prisoner's wife; Hopp urgently pressed them both to learn how much Brower was charging for his services, and at least one of these interrogations took place in the presence of Hulbert's successor, Harry Jackson.[154] In each of these cases the statements of inmates cannot be independently verified, but recurrent patterns are plain. In a period when, on the one hand, paroles were not easy to secure and the support of influential figures imperative and, on the other, the practices of job placement under patronage made it normal and acceptable for incumbents to "develop" the possibilities of their position, it would hardly be surprising if, at least on some occasions, certain officials exchanged their endorsement of parole for cash.

The sale of paroles indicates a general availability of contraband cash. Although Chaplain Hopp apparently worked the "outside networks" for income, it is also clear that a lot of money was circulating inside the prison and that one had to have a good deal of it on account to get the chaplain's attention. The money circulating behind the walls came in through the "underground passage" in the pockets of guards. These couriers, who usually took 25 to 40 percent off the top for their services, dealt only with particular prisoners, the so-called go-betweens, who in turn did business, for a further cut, with other

---

151. Statement of Winton Herbert, n.d., in ibid.

152. James Rogers statement, 15 June 1926, in ibid.

153. Statements of Arthur Henderson, 27 December 1926, and of John Carson, 17 January 1927, in ibid.

154. Arthur Henderson statement, 27 December 1926, in ibid.

inmates.[155] Cash was mainly used inside to sustain gambling and to buy drugs. The prison was "infested with dope and drugs," mostly cocaine and morphine.[156] According to prison reports, there were three main conduits: the binder twine plant, where supervisor John Kline would sell just about "anything" to prison workers; the Inmate Store, run by Hulbert's brother-in-law, E. D. Deane, which was supposed to sell soap, groceries, and other amenities but apparently added drugs, syringes, and droppers to its inventory; and Chaplain Hopp, whose weekly Sunday visits to his flock also resupplied his clerks for their dope runs through the institution.[157] Charlie Morono knew at least seventy-five active addicts in prison, and Roy Daniels claimed to have made three regular buys a week and to have sustained his habit from the proceeds of his gambling ring.[158] But cash could also be used to purchase work and cell assignments from the deputies, to establish internal trade in contraband or loan-sharking, and to secure passes for "outside" details in Jackson or even Detroit.

The circulation of cash went hand in hand with a quite extraordinary movement of goods. Jackson prison in the 1920s was wide open. The dispersal of prisoners at various, often temporary job sites, working in close proximity with free labor and under the supervision of venial guards, made it difficult, if not impossible, to prevent collusion. When W. A. Hunter took charge of the Ypsilanti Road Camp, he reported that "inmates were allowed to come and go as they pleased and were allowed to have all the money they wished."[159] There was plenty of liquor and drugs in the camp, and prisoners were in the habit of "going down the road" for food from the local grocery or visits with local acquaintances. There was also a considerable traffic in state property. "The fact is," wrote one prisoner, "that half the people within a radius of 10 miles of a road camp are supplied with gas, oil, tires, auto parts, flour, sugar, coffee, hams, army blankets, etc. from

---

155. Roy Beebe, 2 August 1926; Eugene Baker, 2 August 1926; Winton Herbert, n.d., in ibid.

156. William Dooley statement, 26 November 1926, in ibid. Dooley considered Jackson the worst institution he had seen in eighteen years of "prison experience."

157. Statements of George Bennett, 20 April 1927; Roy Beebe, 2 August 1926; John Trigg, 24 June 1926; Homer Trotter, 28 June 1926; and James Rogers, 15 June 1926, in ibid.

158. Charles Morono statement, n.d.; Roy Daniels, 11 June 1926, in ibid.

159. Report of Hunter to Harry Jackson, 28 January 1926, Groesbeck Papers, box 119, file 3.

state supplies. These are sold through officers and free men working in collusion with convicts."[160] Not only did large amounts of prison goods and property simply disappear from the farms and the road camps, flowing into the outside world with the help of prisoners and guards, but contraband of all kinds got behind the walls and circulated through the entrepreneurial networks of inmates inside. Movement in and out of the old main prison was only loosely monitored; prisoners came and went, and outside contractors and their employees had routine access to the institution. The flow of drugs, liquor, food, tools and utensils, sheets, blankets, pictures, dirty magazines, and cash was continuous, and, as contacts, messages, deliveries, and visitors moved back and forth across the forbidden zone, guards were routinely paid to serve as intermediaries or to look the other way as prisoners conducted their business. This continuous current of contraband into and through the prison, and the differential ability of various inmates to control both the movement and the dispersal of goods inside, fostered hierarchies and alliances among prisoners that were, in turn, attached to the custodial staff by complex patterns of reciprocity and dependency. Access conferred and confirmed power.

With everything for sale, from necessities to luxuries to jobs, even release, inmates were pushed into a kind of primitive accumulation, devising schemes to turn a profit and defensive alliances to protect advantages. An internal cash economy established the imperatives of survival and the everyday preoccupations of prisoners and forced them into collaborative collusion with the custodians. Since street money was at once essential to life inside and yet a form of contraband, its accumulation was inevitably subjected to informal "taxation" by guards, who had the power to conduct shakedowns and cell searches at any time—and often did so as a form of extortion. Prison staff were thus both instrumental and parasitic to the economic life of prisoners, providing essential services, taking cuts from profits, and wielding the powers of discipline and punishment that could be used with calculation to insure custodial access to and control over inmate enterprise. At the same time, the petty profiteering of prison guards and civilian employees bound them more securely to

160. Letter from "Committee for Jackson prison," n.d., Attorney General Investigations, box 1, file 1.

the warden, who not only provided them with jobs but was usually able to protect them, through his political connections, as they exploited the opportunities provided by their positions. Inmates and custodians alike thus developed a stake in the system, using each other to tap the resources made available by a permissive warden and a rapidly expanding prison society. Far from discouraging such activities, Hulbert probably considered the petty graft of his subordinates as a form of flattery and often took a cut for himself. In all events what was important was that the flow of contraband and the expanding horizons of opportunity at the prison organized life behind the walls and nourished hierarchies of mutual interdependency among keepers and kept that were, ultimately, tied to the warden himself.

We may note here the new instrumentalities of carceral control that Hulbert was engineering: the manipulation of work and parole. As warden and head of Prison Industries—and, after 1924, chief of construction at the new site—Hulbert exercised almost unchallenged authority over the distribution of all prison jobs for civilian employees and inmates alike. Custodial staff and the "free" labor force employed in maintenance work and construction served at the warden's pleasure; not only did he control hiring and firing, promotion and demotion, but he also set the pay scales and could thus manipulate the rewards structure in more subtle ways. And if a guard's hope for advancement lay entirely at the warden's discretion, so did a prisoner's dream of release. This was the most powerful incentive in the warden's gift. Under the new administrative procedures established by Groesbeck, the governor and his parole commissioner usually granted paroles on the direct recommendation of the warden, and, in a period when parole was becoming more difficult to obtain, the advocacy of the warden (or his chaplain) was indispensable to a prisoner's hopes. If the threat of the sack kept the civilian staff compliant, the threat of prolonged incarceration and the hope of "promotion" to the free world fostered caution and obedience among all but the most long-term inmates.

Inside the institution, moreover, a good work record was not only a prerequisite to a parole recommendation, but particular job assignments, especially outside the walls, were often crucial for the conduct of illicit prison business. For those without hope of parole, the warden's control over job and cell assignments could place them at the critical junctions and entrepôts of prison society and, in effect, invest them with social power. Giving his favorites positions of leverage enabled the warden, in turn, to monitor and control the activities of other prisoners. As the jobs and employment opportunities in the prison expanded, and especially as outside details multiplied, Harry Hulbert was able to rely more heavily upon his command of jobs to control the prison and insure his personal ascendancy over keepers and kept alike.

It is important to emphasize, however, that the reorganization of the prison around industrial labor in the 1920s was anything but a move to consolidate panoptic discipline in Foucault's sense. Not only did the congregate labor of the shop floor produce new arenas of inmate sociability, but the workplace in prison was actually less closely monitored, movement less regulated, and spaces less closely ordered than the cell block–home. It is striking how quickly the workplaces of the prison became sites of other activities, unassociated with the labor process or production. It was in prison industries and the numerous work sites outside the walls that illicit activities were concentrated—the stills, the stashes of contraband, the drug dealing, the sources of supply, the business negotiations and peace conferences, as well as the fights. It was in the movement to and from the workplaces, in the unmonitored halls, passageways, and paths across the yard or out into the fields and road camps, that plans were laid, information exchanged, goods and weapons passed. The industrial prison offered rapidly expanding opportunities for pilfering—tools, utensils, clothing, canned goods, the spare parts and raw materials of contraband weapons and possessions. Moreover, in their effort to maximize output and win inmate collaboration in the productive process, prison managers under Hulbert's direction tacitly permitted a proliferation of illicit activities and winked at the compromises of carceral discipline that followed as inmates took advantage of available opportunities.

We may think of all this as the "tolerated illegalities" of the industrial prison. While the scope of such activity may have been greater at Jackson than in other penitentiaries of the day, the fact of this widespread and full-blown inmate self-activity indicates how far the industrial prison expanded openings for inmates to take and organize parallel spaces and to construct networks of exchange and remuneration beyond effective surveillance or custodial supervision. These activities were not oppositional in the sense of challenging work processes or conditions of labor; there is no hint of trade unionism nor, certainly, of confronting authorities directly. Hulbert's control of the prison was never in question. Rather, inmate effort focused on the creation and reproduction of counter-events, carried on among themselves in the name of sustaining or improving the quality of their lives. This prison version of *Eigensinn* produced the parallel worlds behind the walls that mimicked, tested, and evaded the formal structures of custody. These were the social constructions that Clemmer and other sociologists of the prison then discovered and studied.

The fact that these illegalities were so broadly tolerated suggests, in turn, that prison authorities, whatever their public rhetoric about the aims of punishment, were less concerned with the consistent and unbroken application of discipline than with appearances. It was less important that prisoners actually stepped up to the mark, learned regular work habits, and reformed themselves than that they seemed to do so. In exchange for the appearance of compliance in a smooth-running institution, moreover, prison officials were prepared to cut a little slack and give prisoners space to pursue parallel agendas. This was, as we saw, a gritty, uneven, continuously tested and contested standoff, and, from within Foucault's self-sustaining logic, the *effects* added up to the reproduction of domination, in that it did not much matter whether someone pretended to conform or really meant to. But the fact that prisoners were not so much reformed as invited to appear so does point to a certain "lie" at the heart of discipline. Prisons were no doubt expressions of the disciplinary intent and character of the well-ordered, industrial society, but they also embodied the lie of noncompletion, of partial compliance, of cynical, self-interested, and resigned consent that also continued, in the same moment, to express resistance, noncompliance, and a refusal to cave in or be overwhelmed. Everyone inside Jackson prison knew this. On the outside appearances were kept. The prison thus sustained, in the lie of compliance, an illusion that discipline was in place. If this suggests that, pace Foucault, the microcircuits of power in free society that organize consent, internalize self-judgment, and render the disciplined speechless are, in fact, deeply flawed and incomplete—even, perhaps, an elaborate confidence trick—it may also amplify the implications of our insistence that, in prison at least, the objects of discipline are, at once, both compliant and complaining, outwardly conformist and inwardly subversive.

The Symmetry of Practices

None of this meant that the industrial penitentiary of the 1920s was a failure. Its internal regime, forged at the intersection between the imperatives of custodial order and the possibilities of inmate self-activity, kept prisoners in line and sustained the appearance of reformation. In effect, Hulbert reproduced behind the walls the terms of his own survival outside. All the essential elements of a patronage order—access to jobs and, through jobs, to resources, the creation of reciprocal networks of deference and obligation through differentials of access, the enforcement of hierarchy through informal and face-to-face undertakings, the absolute lack of guarantees or protection, coupled with the ever-present risk of exclusion from privilege or denial of access—were imported into the prison and deployed there as instruments of internal control. What Hulbert did inside replicated practices that he had learned outside and upon which his career depended. The boundary between political and penal practices was neither distinct nor very meaningful. Moreover, the traffic between the two worlds was by no means entirely one-way. To be sure, the warden got his job and kept it by playing according to certain political rules; his subordinates and charges in the prison got their jobs and kept them through an elaboration of these same practices behind the walls. The social relations of hierarchy and deference inside the prison replicated political relations outside. But, conversely, prison practices underwrote the system that produced it. The warden used his office, the resources and powers that came to him through appointment, to further his own career, which also meant rendering himself useful, even indispensable, to his mentor. In this way he underwrote and, on election day, quite literally worked to reproduce the position of his political boss. Running the prison was thus not merely an extension of particular political relations and practices; it was a constitutive element in their maintenance and reproduction.

At all levels patronage turned upon differentials of power that rested upon, and at the same time made possible, differentials of access. Carceral practices proved infinitely fungible with political patronage, because the prison was built upon hierarchies of inequality within an economy of relative scarcity, in which the effectiveness of authority depended upon the collusion of the subordinate. The differentials among inmates, as well as between the kept and their keepers, were of degree, not of kind. There was a marked continuity of behavior between the criminal and the noncriminal, as custody tended to shade over into what it was keeping and inmates co-opted guards to their entrepreneurial activities. Ultimately, the differences between "us" and "them," good and bad, criminal and noncriminal, were constituted by and through the process of punishment itself, in the constant engagement, the face-to-face arrangements, and the tense interplay of co-optation and threat that were the basic relations between keeper and kept around which prison society cohered. And the same applied on up the line: the differences between a guard and a deputy, a deputy and the warden, the warden and a prison commissioner, the prison commission and the governor, while they added up to immense distinctions in power and prestige, were built upon small differentials of place and access and upon the mundane, entirely reciprocal transactions of favor and obligation across these small gradations.

This was no meritocracy; the very lack of established procedures for placement and promotion facilitated a face-to-face world of signal and contact in which the rules were well-known but remained unwritten. Transactions were conducted with a "secret" knowledge of potential rewards and implicit threat. This secrecy reflected the fact that the informal relations of patronage promoted a gap between the real and the supposed worlds of power, as a substantive capacity to govern was constructed inside the formal constitutional order. This capacity could only survive as invisible and informal relations. The potential for exposure conditioned prisoners as much as politicians and imposed on them all a basic, reciprocal discretion. To lay bare the synapses of patronage was to subject them to public scrutiny; to scrutinize was to codify, and to codify was, ultimately, to define standards and practices too closely for the system to operate effectively. Thus, between the governor and his wardens, between the warden and his guards, between the guards and the prisoners, there were deep understandings as well as differentials of power. The need to cover and be covered established rules of restraint and conditioned the way superiors supervised subordinates and underlings co-opted those who watched over them. And a remarkably expansive, freewheeling system of power remained, at the same time, extremely reticent and self-effacing.

Chapter 3

Scandals, Probes, and Purges: The Politics of Reform

On 23 November 1944 Joseph Medley, a prisoner at Jackson serving a thirty-to-sixty-year sentence for armed robbery, went to town on an "outside detail" to deposit eight hundred dollars that had been collected from inmates in a war bonds drive. Accompanied by an officer, Lt. Howard Freeland, he went first to the home of Joseph Porrier, the civilian employee who managed inmate accounts, where he changed into street clothes; he and the lieutenant then went to breakfast at a local restaurant and afterward drove over to the bank, where Medley left Freeland waiting in a car and went to make his deposit. He never came back. Later arrested in Washington, D.C., and charged with several robberies and the murder of a woman, Medley was eventually tried, convicted, and executed.

It was his escape, not his fate, that raised a political storm in Michigan. Prison officials in Lansing immediately launched an investigation. As rumors surfaced that Medley's trip to town was only the tip of an iceberg and media attention began driving a public outcry, Michigan Attorney General John Dethmers, sensing a brightening political spotlight, stepped in and took over the official inquiry. Shouldering prison administrators aside, he soon broadened the scope of questions to include all aspects of operations at the State Prison of Southern Michigan.

Meanwhile, on 11 January 1945, along a lonely stretch of the M-99 near Springport, State Senator Warren Hooper, driving down from Lansing to his home in Albion, was pulled to the side of the road and shot three times in what looked like a gangland slaying. Special Prosecutor Kim Sigler, who was leading a grand jury probe into bribery and corruption among state legislators, immediately went before newsmen and announced that Hooper had been scheduled to testify only two days later as a star witness in his developing case against Frank McKay, longtime political eminence and patronage master of the Republican Party. The implication was that McKay had bought himself immunity by hiring some professional killers. In the underworld of Detroit and among journalists covering the story, confused and imprecise rumors circulated that this was an "inside" job, carried off by Jackson inmates connected to Detroit's notorious Purple Gang. In June Sigler's grand jury indicted four Detroit hoodlums for "conspiracy to commit murder" (no one admitted to doing it, but several were accused to plotting it); one of those charged was Mike Selig, a former inmate at Jackson, who had once been the warden's houseboy and driver. Was it possible that someone in the Detroit underworld had arranged with Warden Harry Jackson or one of his deputies to let convicted gangsters out of prison long enough to commit murder?[1]

On 24 July 1945, while Sigler's conspiracy trial against the four Detroit hoodlums was in full swing, the attorney general released the findings of his probe into Jackson prison. It was a media bombshell: "Parties, Gambling, Rackets in Prison," screamed the headlines; "A 'Cupid's Club' for Lovelorn Inmates"; "Widespread Sex Perversion in the State Prison."[2] In all thirty charges of negligence and malfeasance were laid against the warden and his staff, painting an alarming picture of a prison run by inmate "big shots" and their thoroughly corrupted keepers. Joseph Medley was identified as one of these "kingpins," as was Henry Luks, Sigler's chief witness against the four conspirators in the Hooper murder case. These revelations, and the convoluted connections between prison officials, corrupt politicians, and underworld figures that they suggested, ruined Warden Harry Jackson. He was instantly suspended along with seven of his subordinates, including the deputy warden and assistant deputy. The world's

---

1. The story of the Hooper murder is told in fine whodunit style by Bruce Rubenstein and Lawrence Ziewacz, *Three Bullets Sealed His Lips* (E. Lansing: Michigan State University Press, 1987). See also a report by Joseph Sheridan, the original investigator in the case, to State Police Chief Donald Leonard, 17 April 1945, and supplementary assessments two years later, 27 January and 19 December 1947. The Leonard Papers, box 18, the Hooper Case Files: Statements and Depositions, Michigan Historical Collections (MHC), Bentley Library, University of Michigan. The full case files of the investigation are in the Michigan State Police, Administrative Records, 1917–79: The Hooper Murder Investigation, boxes 1–12, at the State Archives in Lansing, Michigan.

2. *Detroit News*, 24 and 25 July 1945; *New York Times*, 25 July 1945.

largest penitentiary was caught in the eye of a swirling, public scandal, by far the worst in its checkered history. Yet, as one witness recalled, "they made a big deal of it, because somebody wanted to make a big deal of it."[3]

The Politics of Scandal

People love a good scandal. The sense of being present at the unraveling of a great secret; the stream of revelations and new exposés that make each day a potential new beginning; the careful examination of details that, however carelessly handled or distorted, may lead to yet more hidden goings-on or illuminate still unseen connections; and the ever-growing parade of nefarious characters, with now and then, the delectable appearance of a familiar face—all these aspects of an unfolding scandal give it power and public appeal. Political scandals play with reputations and therefore presume an audience; they attract attention like mafia murders and sell newspapers. Spread out in the press before mass witnesses, they flourish in arenas where public images and reputations are made and unmade in mediated, not direct, ways and where a public discourse is shaped in slogans, broadcast appeals, and the illusionary intimacy that media politics fosters between leaders and followers. In this sense the politics of scandal represents the polar opposite of patronage politics, which, as we have seen, depended upon mutual discretion and implicit face-to-face understandings among those with access and in the know. The very foundation of a good scandal is that it makes visible what was otherwise not seen, framing it in established formulas, even criminalizing it, and thus rendering it for public judgment.

Yet scandals are not really about what is exposed. They have broader cultural and political dimensions beyond what everyone is looking at. Exposé can destroy careers and tarnish a good name. But for those doing the exposing, scandal is an opportunity to make a reputation and command public attention. It is a way of exercising power, hence of practicing politics. Those who are good at it become popular heroes, white knights who stand in as society's surrogates in the battle against the dark forces lurking in unseen places. The goals

---

3. Interview with George Kropp, at that time a junior clerk in the Lansing office and later the warden at Jackson (May 1979).

of such champions are implicitly shared, their feats applauded, their motives rarely examined. Moreover, the process of exposing and reporting scandalous activities can call into question old and established practices; it can revise prevailing definitions of corruption or malfeasance; it can redefine (or reaffirm) the boundaries of sanctioned behavior and legitimize calls for reform. Scandal, in short, is a way of changing the rules by evoking "higher" values; the production of scandal is also an indication that rules are being contested or rewritten.

Historians must approach scandal with caution. Obviously, whenever "the cover is ripped off" to reveal otherwise hidden activities, usable evidence comes to the surface. But anyone piggybacking on the thousands of pages of transcript generated by Dethmers's probe into Jackson prison in hopes of gaining glimpses of life behind the walls is bound to be disappointed. The attorney general knew nothing about prisons. The deputy he assigned to the case and the team of state police officers he used to conduct interviews were intent upon building a case against prison officials; they were not interested in how the prison worked, nor were they engaged in a sociology of the informal networks and arrangements that bound prisoners together and made the social life of the prison cohere. Their inquiry tended to veer off after any hint of "sex perversion and degeneracy," to explore in detail reports of "wild weekend parties with women," and to find much of interest along the "booze trail" between O'Larry's Bar on Detroit's westside and the State Prison of Southern Michigan.[4] This was not a criminal investigation, only an effort to establish grounds for dismissal, but careers and reputations were on the line. Moreover, collecting evidence of malfeasance or misconduct encouraged a good deal of moral posturing, head wagging, and finger shaking, and the hidden agendas embedded in the exposure of wrongdoing were legion.

The report that John Dethmers released in July 1945, after numerous leaks and well-publicized delays, was certainly explosive.[5] It came in four installments, accompanied by a series of press confer-

---

4. This was the official designation (SPSM was its acronym) for the prison after 1937.

5. Report of Investigation of SPSM, 1945, Attorney General Investigations of SPSM, 1921–1947, box 2, State Archives, Lansing, Michigan; *Detroit News* and *Detroit Free Press*, 24, 25, and 26 July 1945; *New York Times*, 25 July 1945; *Newsweek*, 6 August 1945.

ences in which Dethmers underscored the most shocking revelations and his role in uncovering them. He spoke of widespread gambling and bookmaking at the prison, openly operated by inmates, some of them carrying around large amounts of cash; he reported heavy drinking at the prison, both homemade "hootch" and "spud juice" but also brand-name whiskey brought in from Detroit by members of the staff; and he told of times when the warden and some of his closest associates had been seen drunk inside the prison. He claimed that homosexuality (though he used the vaguer and somehow more titillating term "sex perversion") ran unchecked in the prison, especially in the "love nests" of the gymnasium, and he told how inmates could, for a fee, arrange to have sex with female visitors at the prison hospital (Dethmers even had pictures of the setup, a hospital bed with ward curtains drawn around it). Certain inmate "big shots" were found to have spent long evenings carousing at Deputy D. C. Pettit's house; Dethmers produced a photograph showing a group of notorious criminals, including Joseph Medley, neatly dressed in white shirts and lounging in the deputy's red roadster. He claimed that these same "big shots" had been given the run of the prison and allowed to control cell assignments, job placements, and the coveted outside details. Specifying names and citing incidents, Dethmers told of how prisoners, dressed in civilian clothes and driving in prison cars in the company of prison officials, had made trips to Jackson and Detroit to frequent houses of prostitution, hang out in local bars, attend ballgames, and visit with family and friends. And he hinted darkly that it was "within the realm of human possibility" that dangerous killers incarcerated at Jackson had been let out long enough to murder Senator Warren Hooper.[6]

Of course, many people not in prison gamble, drink, and have sex. That prisoners tried, or even succeeded, in doing these things might have seemed only natural and, in itself, inconsequential; what made it scandalous was that prison officials had apparently colluded in the inmates' pursuit of forbidden pleasures. More alarming, especially in the context of the Medley escape, were the outside details. Prisoners were definitely not supposed to be let out, and the idea that good citizens might have been rubbing elbows with convicted murderers cheering the Tigers at Brigg's Stadium was somewhat chilling.

---

6. *Detroit News*, 25 July 1945.

But what was probably most damning to the warden's career and good name was the suggestion that he had coddled criminals, that he and his subordinates had let them "run the joint" and do as they pleased. Joseph Medley's comment, which Dethmers highlighted, that Jackson was nothing but a "damned playhouse," cut to the heart of Harry Jackson's administration and made him look weak. The attorney general's report painted a picture of an old warden, tired and out of touch, unwilling to conduct regular tours of inspection and not really in control of his institution. This impression of general incompetence, and the implication that the keepers did not have charge of the kept, effectively erased the long, enviable record of peace and good order at the prison that Harry Jackson had compiled over a twenty-year career as warden.

In addition to citations of misconduct and malfeasance, the attorney general's report also accused the warden and his associates of insubordination. They had resisted orders from above and had been surly and disrespectful of their superiors in Lansing. Garrett Heyns, the director of the department, and Ross Pascoe, the head of the parole board, both testified that they had been aware of the situation at Jackson and had urged the warden to change his ways, but to no avail.

> I was looking for some kind of an opening [Heyns told investigators][7] which would lead to this thing, to present it to the Commission and get a good sized investigation. There were a number of these things that have been brought to my attention. Then when this Medley escape business came up there was my chance.

Harry Jackson had defied superior authority and resisted direct instructions. "It is very apparent," read Dethmers's final report, "that some of the officials at the Southern Michigan Prison do not believe in the new 'modern' prison philosophy."[8] Harry Jackson was "the chief stumbling block . . . to proper administration" and set a bad example for his subordinates. Indeed, the main charges against the Classifications Director, H. C. (Chuck) Watson, who was suspended along with

---

7. Heyns's testimony is in Attorney General Investigation, box 2, bk. 28.
8. Attorney General's Final Report, 92.

the warden, was his "hostile" and "argumentative attitude" and his "vicious" attacks on departmental superiors:

> one of the most damaging facts against this witness is the fact that the kind of testimony he gave, which was punctuated with "God damn it" and "What the hell," is . . . completely out of line with the entire program and policy as laid down by the Corrections Commission and its Executive Director.[9]

The report concluded by making an explicit connection between the charges of malfeasance against officials at SPSM and their apparent opposition to progressive principles in penology:

> Certainly when inmates can visit the homes of prison officials on an even social basis, drink intoxicating liquors, go downtown, drink in taverns, visit houses of prostitution, go to Detroit, stopping at the best hotels, use chickens and farm produce to pay cabs from Jackson and as pay in exchange for the service of prostitutes, using state and private cars for the purpose of driving to known hangouts of Detroit hoodlums to bring back whiskey for prison officials, when inmates know that homosexuality is carried on openly, when the inmates find that they have to pay another inmate . . . for a choice cell or a soft job, they must stop and wonder about the sincerity of the program which proposes to make them good citizens.[10]

In short, Harry Jackson and his colleagues were not only negligent managers; they were also reactionaries, and their refusal to cooperate with progressive agendas in penology undermined the coherence of rehabilitational programs and the plausibility of the narrative of correction that their superiors in Lansing were trying to articulate.

It is difficult to escape the impression that Dethmers's report was carefully prepared to trap the warden. When Harry Jackson first appeared to answer questions in May 1945, he was caught squarely between a dog and a lamppost.[11] If he denied knowledge of what was

---

9. Ibid., 44.
10. Ibid, 92.
11. His testimony to investigators is in Attorney General Investigations, box 2, bk. 26.

going on, he appeared incompetent; if he admitted knowledge but dismissed the revelations as inconsequential or not new, he appeared irresponsible, if not complicit in wrongdoing. He blustered and argued, claiming plots and conspiracies against him and citing the austerities of wartime resources and the impossibilities of getting good help, but he found it difficult to defend himself. The case against him was convincing—but of what? Was it a "big deal," or did "somebody want to make a big deal of it"? Was the evidence developed by the attorney general's investigation anything new, or was he, as Dethmers himself declared, "ripping the cover off" old and established practices? Was this the internal patronage order of the 1920s, now being reevaluated, or had the system evolved into something altogether different and more criminal? Had Harry Jackson and his principal deputy, D. C. Pettit—who between them had over a half-century of experience at Jackson prison—suddenly become incompetent, or had the ground shifted beneath them, placing old practices under a new light? And what was this "modern" prison philosophy that became the leitmotif of judgment against Harry Jackson? How had a progressive warden of the 1920s, recognized as an efficient manager of the most modern industrial prison in the country, suddenly been rendered old-fashioned and out of touch; how could a veteran administrator known for his toughness be charged with coddling convicts? And, if all this was not new or newly discovered in the summer of 1945, what made for a scandal at that particular moment? What conjuncture of factors lent a particular interpretative color to the evidence turned up by the attorney general's investigation?

To begin answering these questions, we must first recognize that established benchmarks of interpretation were in motion in the summer of 1945 and that the way John Dethmers framed his questions is not the most helpful for historical understanding. Without proposing a heresy, we should in this instance be less interested in the facts— what actually happened and how we know it happened—than in the contexts—the parallel and convergent stories that surrounded and enveloped the facts, conditioned them, and framed historical interpretations of them. Dethmers's team of investigators were prison "outsiders," only vaguely acquainted with the everyday life of SPSM. Yet it was precisely this ignorance of prison society that enabled them to take the conduct and activities they discovered going on behind the walls, detach these from their quotidian contexts, and reframe them in scandalous interpretations. By reclaiming the context for the facts, we may understand better not only the events that made for scandal but also the reasons scandal was made of them.

Thus we may recognize that, whatever else it was, the scandal that precipitated Harry Jackson's downfall was not an isolated or purely personal disaster. It paralleled and was a concomitant event in the collapse of Frank McKay's political fortunes, which was in turn part of the upheaval that tore the Republican Party apart and destroyed its monopoly on power. The old manipulator and patronage master of the party was in legal trouble throughout the 1940s and under indictment by 1945. His principal pursuer and the main beneficiary of his downfall was special prosecutor Kim Sigler, who was appointed to investigate corruption in the state legislature and soon focused his inquiries on Frank McKay. In a scattershot of indictments against Detroit hoodlums and gangsters, small-time politicians and state legislators, Sigler sought to develop a full-court press on his quarry, aiming to turn the casual corruption of patronage relations into more diabolical and legally convincing charges of kickbacks, bribery, and malfeasance. His erratic but media-sensitive swirl of allegations, rumors, hearings, and charges enabled Sigler not only to suggest the existence of a vast and nefarious conspiracy behind the scenes but also to keep his name before the public and promote an image of himself as the incorruptible white knight of reform.

During the summer and fall of 1945 Sigler's pursuit of McKay competed for headlines with Dethmers's investigations at Jackson prison, and the two rapidly emerged as the main rivals for leadership in the Republican Party and principal contenders for the gubernatorial nomination in the upcoming primaries of 1946. While Sigler proved more adept at nursing his scandals and developing their installments, Dethmers had the richer sensations to reveal and was periodically able to blow Sigler off the front page. But both were using scandal as a vehicle to higher office. Indeed, if we extend the contention of the previous chapter, that patronage politics found its expression inside the prison through the organization of inmate society and systems of control behind the walls, we will be inclined to see the scandals that rocked SPSM in 1945 as part and parcel of a broader reconstruction of the terms of political combat in the state. Scandal was a tool of that combat, its victims and its authors participants in that struggle.

Finally, we need to recognize that the *way* the old-timers were chased from the scene, on the front pages of the papers and in dramatic news conferences, registers the new importance of image making, media coverage, and reform rhetoric in the practice of state politics. Gaining public notice and currying popular favor by crusading against the evildoings of establishment figures who had themselves once commanded vast public approval suggests not only that a generational turnover was under way but that settled benchmarks in the practices of power were being overturned as well. In vying with each other for the leadership of the Republican Party by combining to tar two prominent "old guard" Republicans, Sigler and Dethmers were experimenting with new ideologies of reform and the rhetorical possibilities of scandal to win public attention and mobilize voter support. The scandal over Jackson prison, like the pursuit of McKay for corruption, framed a new language of "clean government" and shaped new practices of media image making, crusading zeal, and exposé that became increasingly central to Republican politics in the era of the New Deal and in the face of a sustained Democratic challenge. Once again we find the state prison playing its part in a larger political drama, reflecting, but also contributing to, the reconstruction of political practices and power relations in the state. In exploring these changes, moreover, we will be able to see more clearly how the formulation of viable rhetorics and the alignment of practices in coherent narratives helped determine which practices survived and flourished and which were allowed to wither and be discarded.

Frank McKay

We first encountered Frank McKay as State Treasurer in the 1920s, when he led the Administrative Board revolt against Groesbeck in the spring of 1926 and, in defeat, engineered the desertion of many party leaders to Fred Green in the fall primary. Already he displayed a penchant for "backroom" politicking and a formidable capacity for operating the internal networks of party power. These were skills he had honed in his years as assignment clerk for the circuit court in Grand Rapids, where he had been responsible for assembling jury panels, granting exemptions, approving excuses, and writing the paychecks and where, as a marginal player in all major trials, he had made the acquaintance of the leading lawyers and judges of the Kent County area. Through these networks of contacts and acquaintances,

McKay was able—for the duties of his job were never onerous—to pursue several business sidelines, on county time and telephone, and to make quite a lot of money.[12] Almost inevitably, a political career blossomed, first as a delegate to county and state conventions then as a candidate himself and, finally, as a powerful officeholder dispensing patronage among his friends and connections throughout the Kent County area. McKay served two more terms as state treasurer under Fred Green, chairing the powerful highway and finance committees of the Administrative Board, and then he "retired." During the 1930s he held no public office. Yet he dominated Republican politics. He did this by parlaying a vast statewide network of friends and allies, connected by reciprocal ties of favor and obligation, into an unchallengeable personal ascendancy over party conventions and the mechanisms by which the party distributed power.

These conventions were not occasional or ceremonial affairs, but annual gatherings of party regulars, and we should pay attention to the details of party conclaves if we are to understand McKay's informal ascendancy. Every two years there were statewide elections. The law provided that the candidates for governor and lieutenant governor would be selected in a primary, but the rest of the slate (secretary of state, treasurer, auditor general, and attorney general) was chosen in a party convention. Thus every other year there were primary elections in the summer, followed by a statewide party convention in the fall to fill out the ticket and lay plans for the November ballot. In presidential election years, moreover, there was also a spring convention to select delegates to the national Republican conclave—a matter of considerable internal interest, since the state delegation to the national convention elected the two national committee members from Michigan, who had an important hand in the distribution of federal patronage in the state. Finally, in odd years there were spring elections to select various regents and judges, and in every fourth year the highway commissioner and superintendent of public instruction. These elections also required a statewide convention of the party, usually in February.[13] Thus an ordinary sequence of conventions

---

12. On these, quite classic beginnings, see Z. Z. Lydens, ed. *The Story of Grand Rapids* (Grand Rapids: Kregel Publications, 1966), 93–95.

13. For Detroiter there was an additional election, in November of odd years, to select a mayor; these were ostensibly nonpartisan events, but many Republican activists were involved.

would, for example, run: February 1935, April 1936, September 1936, and February 1937.

These state conventions, which met for one or two days, usually in Detroit or Grand Rapids, were, however, only the tip of a much larger system of party activity. The thousand or so delegates to the state conventions represented eighty-three counties in the state, each of which held local conventions several weeks prior to a state conclave to select their delegates. Often these county conventions grew out of precinct meetings or canvasses, in which would-be delegates collected the required number of signatures for selection to the county convention. The frequency of state conventions meant a fairly continuous round of political activities for party regulars throughout the state and ample opportunity for personal and political infighting. Any number of factions might be operating at the county level at any given time: the party apparatus in each county had a steering committee that was periodically reelected; the local members of the state legislature often had county organizers and partisans; there might also be opposition factions to legislative incumbents that turned out for county conventions to cause trouble; and the picture could also be further complicated by the presence of friends and organizers working for the area U.S. congressman. The possible permutations of alliance and conflict at the local level were thus endless and had as much to do with personalities as with issues.

Yet, while these eddies and currents were always present and potentially disruptive, matters were ordinarily under fairly tight control. Local party leaders, who were often businessmen and notables of the locality, typically held sway over local party machinery for long periods of time. Legislators who got reelected with some regularity developed close ties with these local party activists, and both looked to Lansing for favors and patronage to cement local positions—county road contracts, a new bridge, liquor licenses, supply orders, state institutions in the area, minor clerkships or local offices, preferment or recognition at state conventions, perhaps even appointment to a state commission or board, and so on. These "spoils" shored up county organizations and stabilized the control of local notables, many of whom regularly attended the state conventions to renew acquaintances and firm up alliances. Ultimately, the base of local power was in the county organizations, but the point of local power was to secure statewide combinations, or blocs, that could elect candi-

dates to office and insure, in return, a continuing flow of state patronage to the localities.

Frank McKay's power rested on his ability to organize this internal party process. He cultivated contacts in every locality, wined and
dined county delegations, paid the bills of local candidates, made the
contacts and assisted small-town politicians with the wider contacts
and connections that insured them a hometown significance, and
built alliances among regulars that could be delivered in the conventions to candidates of his choice. His key allies in the 1930s were two
other county "bosses": Edward Barnard, a labor lawyer with close
ties, through Frank Martel, to the Detroit and Wayne County American
Federation of Labor (AFL), who emerged from the wreckage of the
Groesbeck-Green wars of the 1920s in control of the Wayne County
Republican organization and solidified this position with a network of
Republican clubs throughout Detroit; and William McKeighan, a five-
term mayor of Flint in the 1920s with, reputedly, extensive underworld connections and the dominant figure in the Genesee County
Republican organization.[14] This tripartite alliance of Wayne, Genesee,
and Kent Counties controlled three-quarters of the votes needed for
any nomination at the state convention; McKay's statewide contacts
could easily supply the rest.[15] Thus, while his control over the outcome of state primaries, which nominated the governor and his running mate, remained indirect, depending on his organizational connections and ability to turn out regular voters in primary elections,
McKay's ability literally to dictate the slate of Republican candidates
running for the lesser elective offices of state administration was un-
surpassed. Moreover, these candidates, once elected, had numerous
offices, contracts, and other favors in their gift, and McKay was not
only in a position to influence how "his men" in office distributed
these spoils, but, through his contacts with local activists across the
state, he was in constant touch with a large pool of supplicants whom
he could recommend for preferment. By helping people, McKay insured that people needing help came to him, and, in this way, he

---

14. These figures and their alliance with McKay is outlined in Sarasohn, *Political
Party Patterns*, 26–30.

15. According to a calculation by Frank Fitzgerald in 1930, it took 694 votes (out
of 1,387 delegates) to secure a nomination; Wayne alone had 383, Kent 81, and Genesee
62—the largest three counties, which together managed 526 of the total needed
(Fitzgerald Papers, box 1, memorandum [n.d., probably May] 1930, MHC, Ann Arbor).

extended the favors he could collect at convention time. "Friends," he commented in response to a question about his success, "no leader in either politics or business is any stronger than his friends make him."[16]

McKay's critics—and among them, none were more vociferous than the two leading Detroit newspapers—regarded his personal ascendancy within the Republican Party as rather sinister:

> Frank McKay does not control the membership of the Republican Party of Michigan, but he controls its machinery. He can deliver no elections; but he can deliver caucuses, conventions, and legislatures. He can do this because the bulk of the men who make up caucuses, conventions, and legislatures are small and weak men. They can be bullwhipped into line by threats, or lured in by sugared promises. They are ambitious men, and McKay can satisfy or destroy their ambitions through his control of conventions and party machinery.[17]

Though quite accurate in substance, this sort of criticism had the perverse effect of strengthening loyalty to McKay among party regulars, who did not like to be considered small or weak. To local and country politicians a party engineer like McKay was valuable precisely because he could pull together statewide coalitions that won elections and insured a broadly organized dispersal of patronage. He offered a certain predictability, regular rewards, and stabilized control over routine political activity. The truly ambitious might chafe at McKay's manipulative hand, but the ordinary and locally ambitious politicos tended to support him because he provided the necessary mediation, the transactional grease, that held the party together.

McKay always regarded himself as a party man. On those few occasions when he spoke about his life in politics, he made it clear that his primary loyalty was to the party worker, not the officeholder.

> To the worker goes some consideration. I don't mean exactly, "to the victor goes the spoils," but the fellow who works should get

---

16. *Michigan Times*, 31 March 1944.
17. *Detroit News*, 27 Nov. 1940.

some consideration back from the party. If he is eligible for aposi-
tion or has some merchandise to sell, everything being equal, he
should be given consideration and not ruled out just because he
had been active in politics."[18]

He had nothing but contempt for those "self-righteous good government men" who wanted to get politics out of government by detach-
ing government from politics and, as he saw the matter, vesting it in
elite hands. McKay prided himself on being one of the boys, and he
liked to throw big parties at state conventions and sit among his pals.
It was his painstaking cultivation of party regulars and his solicitous
attention to their needs that made McKay an indispensable "insider."
In his kind of direct and instrumental politics the rules were clear:
loyalty and service got rewarded. "Yes," he wrote to a delegate from
Flint after the 1938 convention, "good old Genesee never wavered a
bit and went down the line 100 percent with a smile. Surely the boss
[Frank Fitzgerald] should appreciate this and not forget this loyalty at
the proper time."[19] Fitzgerald in turn left it to McKay to select the
precise rewards to give to particular individuals, declaring, "I have
always found Frank McKay to be a fair, square fellow."[20]

McKay became immensely wealthy from his political works. Indeed, as the hardest-working "fellow who works," he did not hesitate
to put himself "in the way of favors" as compensation. Around Grand
Rapids his business dealings were legendary and labyrinthine. He
had fingers in real estate (and behind the scenes, influence on property tax assessments), banking (he sold surety bonds to banks wanting city and state deposits, and he owned a bank building, which he
redubbed McKay Tower), newspapers (he owned the *Michigan Times*),
meat and food supplies (local restaurants, aware of his influence with
city inspectors, bought from his wholesale firm), tires (he supplied
the state in such amplitude that the Murphy administration was left
holding a warehouse of surplus tires), road building, lumber, stocks

---

18. Interview, *Michigan Times*, 31 March 1944.

19. Copy of letter, McKay to Franklin, 14 October 1938, Wilbur Brucker Papers,
MHC, Ann Arbor, box 3.

20. He added, "He has been a good friend of mine for a number of years and not
in one single instance do I recall any happening which would cause me to lose faith in
his honesty and integrity" (Fitzgerald to Chase Osborn, 27 November 1935, Fitzgerald
PP, box 15).

and bonds (he was once indicted for fraudulent bids on municipal bonds), and untold other, silent partnerships.[21]

His most notorious business dealings, however, had to do with the liquor trade. When prohibition was abolished, the state took charge of bulk liquor purchases and retailing licenses, placing both operations under the supervision of the Liquor Control Commission (LCC). This three-man commission, and its secretary, who in fact did most of the day-to-day purchasing and licensing, were all political appointees and, during both Fitzgerald administrations, were all "McKay men." Getting access to the LCC, and especially to its secretary, was essential for liquor companies hoping to sell products in Michigan. McKay could provide that access. He proved especially receptive to representatives of those companies he considered loyal supporters of the Republican Party, favoring Hiram Walker, Schenley's, Mohawk, and Arrow, while regarding Seagram's and Calvert's as "Democratic" companies to be placed at the end of the line. Salesmen from favored companies would approach McKay, who, in turn, would call the LCC secretary on a private line to urge consideration. Not surprisingly, several of McKay's pals got jobs as liquor salesmen solely because they knew "the old man." McKay took a consideration for his pains, sometimes a dollar for every case of liquor sold, sometimes a percentage of the salesman's commission. Later estimates of the "cut" he received during 1939–40 ranged as high as a half-million dollars, and, again, his activities left the state loaded up with an inventory of little-known brands.[22]

It was primarily because of his liquor dealings that McKay got a shady reputation. He certainly knew important Detroit gangsters, who had monopolized the illegal liquor trade before 1933 and thereafter moved into legitimate sales and distribution. Several of the salesmen who approached him had gang connections, and two of McKay's bodyguards in the late 1930s were formerly associated with the Pur-

---

21. A recitation, from a critical standpoint, of McKay's many business dealings can be found in Interviews with Willard B. VerMeulen (26 January 1980) and Dorothy Judd (27 January 1980) conducted by Gerard Soapes, in the Gerald R. Ford Library, Ann Arbor, Michigan.

22. This information is largely gleaned from the newspaper clippings in two scrapbooks covering his federal (1941) and state (1946) trials on these dealings (McKay Papers, MHC, Ann Arbor). Sidney Fine discusses what the Murphy administration found wrong with state purchasing and liquor controls in *Frank Murphy: The New Deal Years* (Chicago: University of Chicago Press, 1979), 392–99.

ple Gang, thus providing plausible connections between "the boss" and those who apparently did the Hooper murder. Yet, though he was twice indicted for corrupting state officials, he was never convicted, because it was never proved that any state employee ever took a bribe from him or a cut of the profits. The most that could be shown in court was that McKay reminded political appointees that their positions in state service depended upon Republican electoral success and that it therefore made sense to give consideration to those companies and sales representatives who supported the party. Since everyone on the LCC knew that McKay had considerable influence over who got political appointments, a word from the boss was, in fact, sufficient to close most deals. McKay remained a private citizen representing private interests in their dealings with the state, and while state officials often owed their jobs to his influence, the implicit understanding seems to have been that they should enjoy the perks of their office while McKay made the money. McKay himself seems to have regarded the profiteering as a necessary analogue of his political activity: "I always played politics hard. We gave appointments to those who were loyal. That's the way you stay on top and those are the rules of the game. But I never took anything from the state. . . . Why should I have? I was doing pretty well for myself outside of politics."[23]

In fact, however, McKay's dominant role in the Republican Party during the 1930s reflected a systemic crisis in patronage politics brought on by the Depression. Economic collapse radically altered the flush conditions of boom and expansion that had sustained the development of state-based patronage empires in the 1920s. This did not produce an instant or total collapse of spoils, to be sure; indeed, insofar as patronage politics involved inexpensive acts of courtesy and consideration, economic recession changed very little: when Frank Fitzgerald ran for reelection as governor in 1936, his renomination petition went out on state stationery over the signature of Leslie Kefgen, a member of his Prison Commission; the Kalamazoo Country chairman canvassed his workers on Prison Industry stationery; and Harry Jackson covered the postage for sixty-five hundred mailings to Detroit police and firemen on the warden's account at the

23. Quoted in Rubenstein and Ziewacz, *Three Bullets,* 5.

prison.[24] But from a wider perspective the Depression radically altered the terrain of politics in the state. Economic collapse quickly squeezed state revenues and, by shrinking both budget and administration as well as the scale of projects the state could undertake, sharply reduced the number of jobs and contracts that were available for political use. At the same time, the need for jobs—any job—and the number of beleaguered people seeking offices and favors from elected officials increased dramatically. Demand grew as supply constricted.

Each new governor in the period was greeted on inauguration by a siege of supplicants and an endless flow of letters coupling tales of woe with pleas for work. All incumbents complained that patronage matters took too much of their time; "I have endured," an exasperated Fitzgerald told listeners at the St. Joseph county fair in 1935, "almost nine months of an existence made burdensome by favor-hunters snapping at my heels, awakening me from my sleep, and taking up time in my office that should rightly be devoted to constructive work."[25] All were forced to delegate much of the routine distribution of spoils to trusted subordinates: William Comstock (1933–35) turned things over to Horatio Abbott and Alfred Debo, who scandalized even hardened "pros" with their blatant display of partisan appointments; Fitzgerald (1935–37) left matters in the hands of Frank McKay, who was quieter and more effective; Frank Murphy (1937–39) tried to look another way and earned the enmity of party regulars for neglecting patronage matters; Fitzgerald, returning to office in 1939, allowed McKay another run. These were all ad hoc responses to a pervasive, and worsening, problem:

> I have never in my life gone through anything like this [wrote Paul Tara, who handled patronage matters in Detroit for the newly elected Governor Fitzgerald in 1935], and I think that you are the only one who really can appreciate what it has cost me in mental distress. It seems to me that everybody, just everybody, either wants something from the state or wants to sell something to the state. Job hunters in themselves are bad enough, but aside

---

24. Fitzgerald Papers, box 17: circular dated 22 June 1936; Neil Verburg's letter, 30 June 1936; Harry Jackson's contribution is noted in a summary of campaign postage contributions, dated 4 November 1936, in box 19.

25. Quoted in Fine, *Frank Murphy*, 374. Comstock reportedly divided his day in half, between state business and patronage matters.

from that I have been approached by people who are most insistent that I use my influence with this, that or the other thing, always believing that if they can get my backing they can accomplish the thing that they are after. They feel that if they can get to you they will get what they want, and if they can't get to you I am the next best bet, and I have been called upon to use my influence for passes to theaters, ball games, reductions in railroad rates, free airplane rides, and to sell the state rubber goods, optical goods, electrical goods, plumbing goods and every known commodity; I was even called upon to sell fish to the state, but the liquor situation of course is by far the worst. . . . I could not begin to recite the things that I am asked to do and expected to do and how peeved people get at me if I don't do them. So you see I am always in the middle.[26]

Squabbling over shrinking spoils often got very personal. When feelings were hurt, apologies had to be made and compensations found. "Of course, the patronage problem is a difficult one to handle," wrote Fitzgerald to Jim Driver, a party regular who had alerted the governor to the injured feelings of a mutual friend, "and of course you understand that the Governor cannot keep touch with all those who may or may not be on the payroll."[27] And, of course, not everyone could be satisfied, and the number of people turned away or neglected inevitably swelled the ranks of the rejected, the excluded, and the disgruntled.

Aside from the reduction in the material rewards of office, the Depression also brought new competitors into the field seeking shares of the shrinking pie. McKay's growing influence in Republican ranks clearly registered the psephological presence of Democrats, who began getting elected to state office in significant numbers after 1932. Democratic governors rode Franklin Roosevelt's coattails to power in 1932 (Comstock), 1936 (Murphy), and 1940 (Van Wagoner), although in each case the Democratic Party remained too weak and fractious to insure reelection in the off-year campaigns of 1934 (Fitzgerald), 1938 (Fitzgerald), and 1942 (Kelly); in Roosevelt's last

---

26. Paul Tara to Frank Fitzgerald, 10 June 1935, Fitzgerald Papers, box 15. There are other letters from Tara that summer on related patronage matters: see letters, 2 August and 22 August 1935, ibid.

27. Letter, 4 April 1936, Fitzgerald Papers, box 17.

campaign in 1944 the Republicans managed to reelect their incumbent, despite the national victory of the Democrats. This almost continuous rotation of office between the two parties was a new and quite unfamiliar situation for both. Republicans lost their monopoly on office; Democrats suddenly found themselves in office. In effect, they were changing places every two years throughout the decade, and, by prevailing custom, every employee of the state was liable to change with them. This revolving door created a tremendous upheaval in state personnel after every election, adding to the press of applicants and to the difficulties faced by each new administration in making an equitable distribution of appointments. The turmoil that patronage turnovers caused in the continuity and efficiency of state government, not to mention the headaches it produced for each new governor, had effects in two divergent directions. On the one hand, it produced pressures for change in both parties; reform currents mounted campaigns to provide civil service protection for state employees and to limit the number of jobs in administration available for patronage distribution. At the same time, however, the crisis of patronage fostered continuous experimentation by party professionals, in a muddled and not always consistent effort to adjust prevailing practices to the new terrain of two-party competition and rotating appointments.

The most notable of these adjustments was the emergence in the 1930s of the so-called political boss, or strongman.[28] With fewer jobs and contracts to dispense, it became necessary for officeholders of both parties to husband resources and distribute them more carefully. Thus the Depression, in limiting the scope of patronage possibilities, also tended to promote a centralization of control over patronage distribution. At the same time, especially among Republicans, who were quite unaccustomed to competition in the field, the need to contain factional infighting and unite the party faithful for partisan combat against the Democrats enhanced the role of internal brokerage and promoted the rise of in-house specialists such as McKay, Barnard, and McKeighen, who were able to reduce bickering and soothe bitter feelings with a more systematic allocation of available

---

28. The main secondary study of this phenomenon is in Sarasohn, *Political Party Patterns*, 24–36.

spoils. Finally, the constant rotation of offices between the two parties tended, within each party, to disrupt internal relations of favor and obligation and, again, to give scope to party professionals who could tend to the continuities and respond to the personal needs of party activists. Some, such as Debo and Abbott in the Comstock administration or Frank Tara in Fitzgerald's first administration, were merely powerful assistants to the governor who gathered patronage into their hands as a service to their leader. Others, such as the Democrat Murray Van Wagoner, who was elected to a four-year term as highway commissioner in 1933 and reelected in 1937, enjoyed sufficient longevity in office and access to a broad enough spectrum of jobs and contracts to build a political machine in the Groesbeck style, merging patronage with public service; this was an autonomous, personal satrapy, not beholden to anyone else, and it proved powerful enough to lift Van Wagoner to the governorship in 1940. Still others represented a new breed of the behind-the-scenes patronage manager who, without formal office, pulled strings and gathered the traces together in more invisible, quasi-private networks of power.

Frank McKay was the master practitioner of this latter model of eminence in the 1930s. Yet McKay was actually operating at the outer limits of patronage politics. The general narrowing of spoils opportunities and the new terrain of two-party competition meant, first of all, that McKay's patronage operations became more preoccupied with healing internal divisions and uniting Republicans against their common enemy. He was patently serving the interest of one party and its regulars, and his efforts to scavenge, hoard, and distribute scarce spoils thus had a more overtly partisan appearance than they had in the 1920s, when Republicans had also been, automatically, the party of government. This meant that increasingly the central pivot of patronage lay within party organization, not in state administration. In mending rifts within his party, McKay was actually severing the intimate links that had been forged in the 1920s between public service and private interest and turning the distribution of state offices and contracts to the service of a discrete and now permanent political machine. Patronage became more private and secretive, while the exclusionary aspects of its practice became more sharply etched to public view. This laid McKay open to attack, both from Republicans who did not enjoy his favor and from Democrats who could combine denunciations of McKay's machine politics with calls for civil service reform. Frank Murphy made "McKayism" a central theme of his campaign for governor in 1936, promising to rid the state "of sinister influences and of selfish men seeking their own advantage at the expense of the public interest."[29] When Murphy won, it was clear, even to Republican regulars, that McKay was becoming something of an electoral liability.

The problem was not simply partisan attacks, however. McKay's instrumental brand of politics failed to attract people at the level of principles or beliefs. The party under McKay could hardly stand *for* anything—other than the successful control of state offices. Yet Republicans were now facing a new kind of political challenge, a politics of ideology, which demanded something more than instrumental answers. Roosevelt, and Murphy after him, were hostile in principle to patronage politics, or, rather, they understood its instrumentality differently. They were intent on building a party through new mobilizations, and their focus was on blocs or categories of voters—ethnics, workers, blacks, women, and so on—and on the kinds of programs and appeals that would attract them. This politics of mobilization and new participation threatened to explode the very foundations of patronage politics, and it challenged those schooled in the older arts to develop more inclusive and broadly attractive responses. Not only was McKay unable to proffer such responses, but many in the Republican Party concluded that the best way to contend with the appeal of the New Deal was to take up a program and ideology of reform directed against McKay and the patronage masters. Fitzgerald was already edging in this direction during the election campaign of 1936, telling a confidant that "my hope for the Republican party . . . [is] a broad, progressive program that will attract the rank and file of our people."[30] In this vein the governor embraced a liberal, "new dealish" platform, including the principle of civil service reform, and he played the possibilities of a new rhetoric, attacking Murphy as a placeman of the Roosevelt administration, which, he declared, "used the tremendous power of its patronage, purchased with billions of dollars of the taxpayers' money, to thrust a handpicked candidate upon the people of Michigan."[31] Fitzgerald's defeat in 1936, along

29. Fine, *Frank Murphy*, 231; see also 239, 242–43.
30. Fitzgerald to DeFoe, 17 April 1936, Fitzgerald Papers, box 17.
31. Fine, *Frank Murphy*, 343.

with the general washout of Republican candidates nationally, may be taken as the beginning of a long quest by that party for an adequate political counterpoise to the seemingly inexhaustible electoral appeal of the New Deal.

The Murphy administration in Michigan, one of the "little New Deals" that filtered down to the states from the Roosevelt victory train, was high-minded, reformist, and of mixed success. We need not review the full record here.[32] But among Murphy's legislative and administrative initiatives, few were more important nor certainly, for our purposes, more consequential than civil service reform. The problem of patronage politics and the putative solution for it—to "get politics out of government"—had already been mapped out for him by the report of a Civil Service Study Commission which Fitzgerald had appointed in 1936. Murphy took up this lead with the enthusiastic backing of a broad-based citizens' association already engaged in an active lobbying campaign and made civil service reform his main legislative priority.[33] Weathering a stormy and convoluted passage through the Michigan legislature, Murphy's measure established a merit system for hiring and promotion in all state agencies and blanketed in most of the state's sixteen thousand employees through written examinations administered by a bipartisan civil service commission.

Few party professionals liked the reform, and opinions varied about Murphy's motives. There was undeniably a strong element of idealism and civic conviction at work, especially among the intellectual and academic experts who worked up the plan. The Michigan law became a model of its kind, widely consulted by other states trying to establish a merit system. The faith in professional standing as established by examinations and credentials that underwrote the measure was widely shared by reformers and civic activists, among whose number Murphy certainly counted himself. Many Republicans, of course, regarded the reform as a cynical fraud promoted by

32. Sidney Fine (ibid.) has said about all there is to say about Murphy's New Deal years. His judgment on the Murphy administration is detailed, comprehensive, judicious, and deftly balanced in Murphy's favor.

33. The Michigan Merit System Association was formed in April 1936, under the chair of William Lovett, to greet the report of the commission, issued in July (*Report of the Civil Service Study Commission* [Lansing, 1936]). The commission was chaired by UM political science professor James Pollock. For a discussion of its findings, see Fine, *Frank Murphy*, 374–77.

Democrats who, having placed their partisans in many state offices, were now intent on covenanting them permanently with civil service protection. On the face of it the Democratic Party, as the perennial loser in Michigan politics, had every reason, while in office, to try to insure that its supporters held onto their posts when the party was turned out again.

In fact, however, this criticism of Murphy's motives fell between the two stools of the Democratic Party. For his part Murphy's principled attitude toward appointments—"I do not intend to follow county committee recommendations in selecting state hospital superintendents"[34]—expressed a personal commitment to qualifications over connections. But this stance deeply angered regular party workers. Dissident Democrats found a friend in Murray Van Wagoner, who emerged as Murphy's main antagonist for party leadership and whose Highway Department disposed of a large campaign fund to help local candidates. Van Wagoner was known to be cool toward the New Deal, although he made savvy use of Work Projects Administration (WPA) money in the Highway Department, and he was distant from, if not hostile to, Murphy. His views on civil service reform were studiedly ambiguous,[35] although his protégé, Edward Fry, who was state Democratic chairman and undoubtedly represented the views of county activists, was openly contemptuous: "Those charged with the administration of departments and the forming of policies should be Democrats when the Democratic party is in power and Republicans when the Republican party wins."[36] In this view Murphy's victory made patronage spoils available to the Democratic Party, and they should be used aggressively in the partisan interest. When Murphy turned his back on these labors, Van Wagoner drew away from him. It was widely believed that Van Wagoner's neutrality during the gubernatorial election of 1938 cost Murphy his reelection.[37]

---

34. Quoted in ibid., 276.

35. Although Van Wagoner seems to have been influential in getting legislation through the Senate (see ibid., 384), he told interviewers many years later that he was always opposed to civil service ("because it was anything but civil") but concluded that it would not seriously affect the operation of the highway department, since most of the jobs it had to offer were short-term, summer work, or under federal programs and thus did not fall within the ambit of civil service (interview, April 1985).

36. *Detroit Free Press*, 10 June 1938.

37. Fine, *Frank Murphy*, 481–528; Samuel McSeveney, "The Michigan Gubernatorial Campaign of 1938," *Michigan History* 45, no. 2 (June 1961): 97–127.

Ultimately, civil service reform was less an effort, as Republicans suspected, of lodging Democrats permanently in state offices than it was an aspect of ongoing debates among Democrats over how to translate their stunning national successes into gains for the party at the state and local levels. The practical problem was to convert votes for Roosevelt every four years into sustained support for Democrats in the more frequent and less interesting state elections. Murphy, following the lead of the New Deal, tried to use incumbency to mobilize mass support. He tended, therefore, to focus on broadening the appeal of the party through programs and initiatives that attracted new cadres of activists and new blocs of voters to the standard. But for all of his success, especially in building support among organized labor and in sharpening the ideological distinctiveness of the Democratic Party, Murphy paid too little attention to the nuts and bolts of party building and paid for his neglect in the defeat of 1938. For his part Van Wagoner regarded Roosevelt's national successes, and the coattail effect his victories had in Michigan, as a signal opportunity for local Democrats to take hold of the state apparatus and use its resources and patronage to build a permanent statewide organization. The point was not to replicate the New Deal in Michigan. Indeed, Van Wagoner was not especially close to labor; he did not feel comfortable with the New Deal's social agenda or with its more ideological brand of politics. He was preoccupied, instead, with translating electoral success into an organizational base for party regulars. After Murphy's disappointing performance in 1938, the party relied heavily on Van Wagoner's "highway machine" to reclaim the governorship in 1940. But a patronage machine that depended on FDR's appeal yet refused to espouse his New Deal agenda also proved rickety. The Democrats failed to reelect Van Wagoner in 1944 or to carry Michigan in Roosevelt's last campaign, and by 1946 the party was in such disarray that Van Wagoner's third try for the governor's office proved a joke.

So long as the old regulars resisted the intrusion of new forces and the broadening of the party, they could maintain their hold upon the party apparatus, but the party continued to lose elections. It took a postwar revolt against this old guard, led by a younger cadre of liberals with experience in New Deal and wartime Washington, to revive the party's chances, and even then it was only the conjuncture of these developments inside the state Democratic Party, with the

move by the United Automobile Workers (UAW), under the pressure
of Taft-Hartley legislation and the onset of the cold war, toward closer
affiliation with the state Democratic Party, that enabled the insurgency to forge a new liberal-labor alliance that carried G. Mennen
Williams to victory in 1948 and in five successive elections.[38]

Republicans were on a parallel, if obverse, trajectory. While for
Democrats the political problem was how to replicate national successes on the state and local level, the political conundrum facing
Republicans was more intricate: how to devise from state-level practice the elements of a national comeback strategy that would effectively answer Roosevelt's continuing appeal. At first, party regulars in
Michigan were inclined to regard the national Democratic juggernaut
as an ephemeral phenomenon whose moment would pass. After
Roosevelt's first reelection and Murphy's victory in 1936, McKay
wrote Fitzgerald: "Apparently the country has temporarily at least
gone completely socialistic, [but] we are all badly in need of rest, so
we'll coast a while and then set about to repair the damage. When we
regain our perspective and build up our forces we will again be in
power."[39] In this vein many Republicans flatly opposed Murphy's
civil service reform because of the barriers it erected to their eventual
return to power.[40] When the party swept back into office in 1938,
many of its leaders were determined to roll back the Murphy reforms.
"There is no excuse for keeping on the public payroll men and
women who helped the Democratic cause," announced Republican
state chairman, James Thompson,[41] and the legislature proceeded to
enact the so-called "ripper bill," which drastically cut appropriations
for the Civil Service Commission and removed over nine thousand
state jobs, mainly at the supervisory and salaried level, from civil
service protection. The opportunities of patronage politics thus reopened, McKay had another innings.

But McKay underestimated how permanently the New Deal—
even such mundane changes as civil service—was altering the political
landscape in Michigan. Fitzgerald, always a cautious politician, had

---

38. These developments have been studied by Martin Halpern, *UAW Politics in
the Cold War Era* (Albany, N.Y.: State University of New York Press, 1988); and undergraduates in the Residential College at the University of Michigan, *The Transformation of
Michigan Politics in the 1940s*, SFRC Monograph no. 11 (1985).
39. McKay to Fitzgerald, 5 November 1936, Fitzgerald Papers, box 19.
40. See Fine, *Frank Murphy*, 380.
41. James K. Pollack Papers, box 5, folder 14, MHC, Ann Arbor.

already drawn a different lesson from his defeat in 1936: Republicans, he felt, needed a more positive program, "something more than the condemnation of the other fellow's ideas."[42] Meeting the New Deal halfway meant, among other things, supporting civil service reform, cooperating with labor, and accepting a positive role for the state in such areas as welfare and social services. Accordingly, over the next several years Fitzgerald took an increasingly progressive stance, carving out an ideological space of moderate, or "responsible," reformism, which Republican militants would later denounce as "me-too-ism." After Fitzgerald's sudden death in 1939, this current in the party became associated with Harry Kelly, who beat Van Wagoner in 1942 and won reelection in 1944. By the mid-1940s Kelly had became part of a new cadre of Republican leaders across the nation—Thomas Dewey in New York, Earl Warren in California, James Bricker in Ohio, Harold Stassen in Minnesota—all energetic state governors seeking to parlay local and regional success into national political careers.

While the current of moderate reformism was dominant in the party during the years of wartime bipartisanship and later became the base of support for Eisenhower in states like Michigan, it was continuously contested by a more militant brand of Republicanism that sought to define an ideological position of implacable opposition to the New Deal. This rejectionist front within the party denounced Roosevelt and all his works as wasteful, corrupting, overbearing, in service of special interests, and, in all, un-American, "socialistic," even "godless." Such a position could, of course, draw on old Republican themes of good government, managerial competence, balanced budgets, and efficiency. But it was also predicated upon the conviction that only by drawing a clear line, implacably rejecting all collaboration with the New Deal, could the party mobilize effectively against the Democrats. Implied in this current, then, was a presumption of innocence, that the Republican Party was pure, uncorrupted, and public spirited. To sustain such a position required, first and foremost, purging the party not only of its moderate New Deal fellow travelers but also of its patronage bosses and corrupt politicians. Paradoxically, then, the most virulently anti–New Deal elements of the party in Michigan turned out to be Frank McKay's most dangerous enemies.

---

42. Fitzgerald to John Beukema, 16 November 1936, Fitzgerald Papers, box 19.

Initially, this current centered around the so-called Grosse Pointe crowd, who found a spokesman in Wilbur Brucker, a former governor and old Hooverite. Brucker successfully challenged James Couzens in the 1936 Republican Senate primary, largely on the grounds that Couzens had sold out to the New Deal, and then went on to lose the general election to a Democrat. Widely regarded among party regulars and McKay allies as a windbag and a bull in the china shop, Brucker was well connected in Detroit, a good organizer, and a very effective fund-raiser for the party. In the early 1940s he led a group of affluent, civic-minded conservatives in building a precinct organization in Detroit to challenge Edward Bernard, McKay's main ally in the city, and then expanded the anti-boss front to the state level by campaigning against McKay himself at party conventions. This hard-right reform current was partially contained by wartime bipartisanship but burst loose in the party at the end of the world war, with the destruction of Frank McKay and the rise of Kim Sigler's brand of "exposé politics"; after a rocky career it blended into the broader anticommunist themes around which Republican leaders such as Robert Taft sought, in the late 1940s, to build an ideological answer and countermobilization to the seemingly unbeatable Democrats.

Thus in both major parties during the 1940s, rival factions contested with one another over how best to do battle with the other. No faction was able to prevail for long or to establish stable positions. While the infighting tended to weaken the electoral effectiveness of each party, insuring a continuous rotation of office, and while both parties tended to oscillate between unfurling the flags of ideological principle and seeking the grounds of pragmatic accommodation, the trajectory of both parties during the 1940s was toward new terms of political combat. The Democrats stumbled toward a fuller alliance with labor and a firmer identification with the themes of the New Deal, especially as these were reformulated by Truman in the context of the cold war; the Republicans, in seeking a riposte to the continuing national appeal of the Democrats, moved through experiments in reform-minded exposé politics to a full-throated ideological anticommunism. While we must follow this process in greater detail to reveal its ramifications, we may here essay a preliminary point that emerges clearly: the general trajectories of development in both the Democratic and Republican Parties, toward ideological combat based on programmatic appeals and mass mobilizations, left diminished space for patronage politics, and its main practitioners, men like Frank McKay, found themselves slowly but inexorably squeezed out over the course of the decade. The implications of this general movement for the prison system proved enormous.

Civil Service in the Prison System

It was the intention of the Murphy administration to reform Michigan prisons. Everyone was aware that the Depression had shut down Prison Industries and brought mass unemployment to prisoners. This had seriously undermined prevailing control strategies. Facing sharp budget cutbacks, the Prison Commission ended construction on the new prison in 1934, declaring it finished; when the new facility was occupied, the old one was closed. All jobs associated with the building project vanished, as did numerous jobs in factories and plants at the old prison. The Chelsea Cement Plant was also dismantled. At the same time, rising unemployment on the outside made it impossible, especially for Democratic administrations, to use prison labor on the few remaining highway projects that the state could afford; the road camps were closed or turned over to federal works agencies. In 1935, when federal bans on prison-made goods in interstate commerce went into effect, the state legislature formally restricted the output of prison industry to "state use."[43] A year later only 500 of Jackson's 5,500 inmates had jobs.[44] Hulbert's dream of a self-sufficient, industrial prison had evaporated.

It was also widely recognized that the rapidly revolving patronage door created by two-party competition after 1932 played havoc with the continuity of prison personnel, especially at the higher levels of administration, and imposed additional strains upon custodial routines. As the Democrats rotated out in 1934, many solemnly pointed

---

43. This was the Munshaw-Frey Act of 1935.

44. In the next two years the Murphy administration got the figure up to 790, but 250 jobs were then lost again by 1940. See *Michigan Correctional System*, First Biennial Report, 1937–38 (Lansing, 1939), 59, 62–65, 84–85; *Detroit News*, 2 February 1940. Said a guard, retiring in 1937, "I don't believe there is much difference between the convict of the present day and the one who was here when I first started working [in 1911]. The question of occupation, however, is important. Nowadays, inmates have nothing to do" (*Jackson Citizen-Patriot*, 20 March 1937).

to the politicization of appointments as "one of the chief difficulties in [prison] management,"[45] and Republicans were heard to echo these sentiments two years later. A report prepared in 1934 by the Osborne Association, a national prison reform group, worried about inmate idleness and the disciplinary problems it posed but concluded that the greatest threat to the security of the institution lay in the way politics contaminated administration. When appointments were determined by "political patronage, not professional competence," wrote these experts, it placed "this, the largest prison in the United States, under the direction of a prison commission and warden entirely without previous experience in the difficult and hazardous business of administering a prison."[46] Their call, which Murphy took up, was to get politics out of the prison.

Immediately after the elections of 1936, Arthur Wood, a University of Michigan social work professor and former commissioner of paroles, convened an informal group of academics to shape a new order. This effort was then taken up by the new governor, who formed a select commission to draft legislation that would place Michigan prisons on a "scientific" basis.[47] The plan, which sailed through the legislature in the spring of 1937, sought to integrate the "interdependent phases of correctional work" by consolidating punishment, probation, and parole into a "unified" Department of Corrections.[48] The director of this department, overseeing three assistant directors running bureaus for prisons, paroles, and probation, was appointed by, and answerable to, a new Corrections Commission, made up of five members selected by the governor for staggered terms, which by law, had to be bipartisan in composition. The wardens of the several state institutions were subordinated to this new executive apparatus.

---

45. Warden Peter Gray, leaving Jackson, quoted in *Detroit News*, 12 December 1934. George Kropp said, in an interview, that "Gray didn't know anything more about the prison the day he left it than the day he arrived" (May 1979).

46. *New York Times*, 29 November 1934; excerpts from this report were included in a later report by the association, penned by its executive director, Austin MacCormick (1940 *Survey of Michigan Penal Institutions* [New York: Osborne Association, 1940], 43–44).

47. The story of this committee, which was chaired by Caroline Parker, is told in Fine, *Frank Murphy*, 425–26; the transcript of the committee's meetings are in the Hilmer Gellein Papers, box 1, at MHC, Ann Arbor. Gellein, once a court stenographer for Murphy, was secretary of the committee and went on to become the state's first director of corrections.

48. Osborne Association, *1940 Survey*, 8.

As important, the legislation created an autonomous, three-person parole board, with a full-time support staff, which was charged with regularizing procedures and supervising the process of conditional release. The reformers hoped all employees in what they now called the "corrections system," including officers in Lansing and wardens and their deputies at the prisons, would soon come under civil service protection. Their aim was to foster career paths in the system and a greater professionalization of the service. In all, the reform legislation was quite in step with the best thinking in American penology at the time, and the Osborne Association hailed the new order as "one of the best administrative structures for the control and management of prisons and prison industries, pardons and paroles, and probation ever established by any American governmental unit."[49]

Hyperbole flowed faster than change. Despite reform measures, turnover in top administration continued. Indeed, the Murphy administration itself installed a slate of reform-minded Democrat appointees (Hilmer Gellein as director of the department, Joel Moore at Jackson, Garrett Heyns at Ionia, and Marvin Coon at Marquette) to replace Republicans.[50] As the reform warden at Jackson, Moore began by firing fifteen employees and hiring thirty-seven others, most of them Democrats laid off in 1935 by the Fitzgerald administration; although Moore and Gellein insisted they were not playing politics with positions, there seems to have been local feeling around Jackson County to the contrary.[51] Undoubtedly, most older line guards and long-term employees at the prison remained personally loyal to Harry Jackson, welcomed his return as warden when the Republicans swept Democratic administrators aside in 1939, and stood behind him thereafter. In fact, greater continuity is to be found in this personal loyalty than in the workings of the merit system. For while all employees at the prison passed under civil service protection during 1938, many were removed again the following year, when returning Republicans passed the "ripper act," which eliminated civil service protection for top and middle echelons of state and prison administration. A vig-

---

49. Ibid.
50. The Jackson prison staff threw a big going-away party for Harry Jackson. Former Governor Fitzgerald came, along with all the Republican bigwigs of Jackson County, and they gave the warden a watch (*Jackson Citizen Patriot*, 12 and 14 March 1937).
51. *Jackson Citizen Patriot*, 16 July 1937.

orous campaign by citizens' groups then got the merit issue on the ballot as a constitutional amendment in 1940, and, when this passed, civil service was restored. But it was not until 1942 that most prison employees were once again protected.

In 1940 the State Corrections Committee, a citizens' lobby composed of the leading lights of prison reform in the Murphy administration, who were engaged in a rear-guard action against the Republican backlash of 1939–40, invited Austin MacCormick back for another tour of Michigan prisons. He found little changed; Michigan prisons had, after all, "not been removed from the field of partisan politics," had "not been placed under expert leadership," and were still run by men whose "jobs are not dependent on efficiency and integrity alone but on political considerations."[52] MacCormick missed no opportunity to bemoan Republican efforts to undo the laudable progress of reform in Michigan corrections; "politicized penology" was, he argued, undermining discipline and threatening institutional security. He cited as evidence reports of discontent and indiscipline in the state prisons and a spate of escape attempts at Jackson and Marquette during 1939; these, he claimed, indicated that only mismanagement and incompetence could follow from the appointment of unprofessional and politically well-connected amateurs to prison administration.[53]

This report was itself a partisan document, and while the contention that politics created disciplinary problems in prisons made for good polemics and was in harmony with prevailing reform opinion, it was not well-founded. There was in fact no evidence that the contin-

---

52. Osborne Association, *1940 Survey,* 45. MacCormick reviewed his findings and the rationale for his recommendations in the *New Bulletin,* vol. 11, of the Osborne Association (December 1940).

53. In September 1939 several prisoners at Marquette kidnapped the warden, Marvin Coon, and several members of the parole board, including its chairman, Ross Pascoe, and took them on a terrifying chase across the Upper Peninsula. In November six inmates broke out of Jackson, killing chief inspector Fred Boucher, the fifth-ranking official at the prison, as they went; Harry Jackson, who was having a shave in the prison barbershop at the time, supervised the recapture, pistol in hand and soap on his face, and he had the prisoners beaten so badly that the press was not allowed to photograph them when they appeared at an inquest the next day. See Ike Wood, *One Hundred Years at Hard Labor: A History of Marquette State Prison* (Au Train, Mich.: KA-ED Publishing Company, 1985), 239–44. A sensationalized account of the Jackson prison break is to be found in Levant Vandervoort, "Black Sunday," *True Detective Mysteries* (May 1940). See also *Detroit News,* 6 and 8 November 1939.

uous, politicized rotation of officials did serious harm to the operation of Michigan prisons. Several of Murphy's appointees who were removed in 1939 by the returning Republicans were no more experienced or qualified in prison management than their replacements; Garrett Heyns, a schoolteacher by trade, had run unsuccessfully for Congress on the Democratic ticket in 1936, before Murphy picked him as Warden at Ionia, and Marvin Coon was a businessman with close ties to the Democratic organization in the UP, who had served on the state Liquor Control Commission in the Comstock administration, before Murphy made him warden of Marquette.[54] Joel Moore, Murphy's appointment as warden of Jackson, was undoubtedly qualified by his experience in federal probations, but he was replaced in 1939 by the Republican Harry Jackson, who, however well connected politically, was also the most experienced prison manager in the state.[55] There is no question that Ernest Haeckel, the Republican replacement for Hilmer Gellein as department director in 1939, "wasn't in any way qualified"—"hell, he couldn't even spell prison"[56]—but it is doubtful that his amiable incompetence fostered disorder behind the walls. He certainly conducted no purge in the ranks. Indeed, while MacCormick could show that, in all, 177 positions in the prison system had been withdrawn from civil service protection by the "ripper act"—62 of these at Jackson—only 13 of these "declassified" people were actually removed during 1939.[57] This was hardly the upheaval in administration that could foster escape attempts and the other signs of inmate unrest to which MacCormick alluded.

From the point of view of prisoners at Jackson, in fact, it was the policy priorities and ideological commitments of Murphy's reform warden, Joel Moore, that proved most disruptive of settled routines inside. "I did not like the system that was in vogue here when I came to the prison," Moore told the press, "and I am going to put in my own system."[58] In particular, he cracked down on inmate mobility:

---

54. Interview with Robert Northrup, May 1979; editorials concerning the Coon appointment, May 1937, Murphy Papers, box 56. The Republicans later replaced Coon with Simon Anderson, owner of an ice company in the Upper Peninsula and no more qualified than Coon for the job; he later failed the civil service exam and was let go.

55. MacCormick acknowledged this without conceding the principle at stake (Osborne Association, *1940 Survey*, 48).

56. Comments by George Kropp, May 1979.

57. Osborne Association, *1940 Survey*, 49.

58. *Jackson Citizen Patriot*, 23 April 1937.

Appalling was the looseness of the control of "inside" and "outside" men [he reported].[59] Contacts and contraband flowed easily through the west and main gates and the south traffic gates and even at times through the east railroad gates. "Picture men," who domiciled "inside" but whose maintenance work was both inside and outside the walls passed freely. Outside "trustees" domiciled in 16-block or 10-block or in a farm house passed in and out quite freely on various errands. "Front House" inmate employees passed freely through the main gates several times each day. Outsiders drove trucks and even private cars through the traffic gates.

Moore imposed a strict separation between "inside" and "outside," making the walls more salient and monitoring passage more closely; he suspended public tours of the prison and tightened up visiting privileges. While we have no direct evidence of the impact of these measures upon prisoners, we may surmise that they were not popular; coming on top of the tremendous loss of jobs and of the access to contraband that these jobs had afforded, Moore's crackdown on internal movement imposed a new and severe austerity upon the informal economy of the prison.

At the same time, moreover, Moore changed disciplinary procedures. The use of physical force—beatings, clubbings, and whippings—was sharply restricted, and the "bull pen" was abolished as "worse than useless, detrimental to a prison aiming at rehabilitation." In its place the warden substituted segregation, "a more perfect seclusion," as the principal means of disciplining recalcitrants.[60] Although eliminating physical brutality was in keeping with the precepts of progressive penology, the move was not popular among guards, many of whom felt that Moore was depriving them of their right to discretionary violence, the ultimate recourse of custodial authority. The restrictions on movement and the diminution of material affluence created tensions among inmates and between the kept and their keepers that prison guards felt less able to control, either through the incentives of venial opportunity or threats of unrestricted physical

---

59. Michigan Correctional System (MCS), *First Biennial Report*, 1937–38, 55. The *Detroit News* gave echo to Moore's concern about looseness of discipline and the dangers posed by free movement (13 March 1937).

60. Ibid., 54.

violence. We may also assume that numerous informal arrangements between custodians and prisoners were disrupted by Moore's interventions. The conditions for profitable collusion between prisoners and guards changed, promoting a common sense of grievance against the new regime. Undoubtedly some of Moore's personnel turnover *was* politically motivated—not in replacing Republicans with Democrats but in gaining ascendancy over the internal operations of the prison.

From this perspective it was not the rollback of civil service in 1939, but the return of Harry Jackson that drew clear battle lines within the new Department of Corrections. The veteran warden, having spent the Murphy years managing "goon squads" for Harry Bennett at Ford Motor Company, swept aside the innovations of "pansy penology," restoring harsh physical discipline, including the "glory hole," in which prisoners were suspended on cell doors for long periods and frequently beaten. With the renewal of harsh punishment, however, came a relaxation of internal controls over inmate movement and enterprise. Internal patronage practices, which Harry Jackson had helped innovate in the 1920s, were revived and, as we shall see, allowed to run amok. At the same time, Harry Jackson aligned himself with inmates and custodians against the new administrative overlords in Lansing and the independent parole board. In his view it was not incompetent political appointments but interference by reform-minded ideologues that crippled prison management and made control of the institution difficult. This reading of the problem—that a crisis of control arose from trying to change things, not from the practices being changed—placed the warden squarely athwart the reform initiatives coming from above and turned him into the champion and leading defender of unreformed practices. The rotation of Joel Moore and Harry Jackson between 1937 and 1939 was thus something more than a sign of continuing partisan interference; it also defined a new terrain of struggle that was to dominate prison politics in the 1940s. In shaping this terrain, we need to take account of the long-term, indirect impact of the Murphy reforms and to understand that to take politics out of prisons was itself a political act that had the perverse effect of politicizing every aspect of prison life.

What the Murphy reforms did was to redistribute the field of power, or, more precisely, to redistribute positions within that field from which power could be exercised. In this way relations of power were slowly but permanently altered. We may sketch this process in several dimensions. Structurally, the reforms of 1937 severely restricted the governor's ability to interfere in the operation of the prison system, by placing his statutory powers over pardons and paroles in the hands of an independent parole board and by interposing a bipartisan corrections commission between the chief executive and the wardens. On the other hand, the departmental structure greatly restricted the autonomy of prison wardens, by subordinating them to closer administrative supervision from Lansing and thereby blocking their traditional direct access to the governor's office. The lines of political patronage within the system were thus short-circuited.

In addition, the creation of an independent parole board robbed the warden of his most powerful incentive, the promise of release. When a board, not the warden, determined the conditions of release, the warden's ability to organize the rewards structure inside was compromised. A potential rival, an alternative center of power, was inserted into the prison. Similarly, civil service stripped the warden of his powers to hire, fire, and promote guards by establishing an alternative structure for selection and promotion that rivaled the warden's patronage. Moreover, this weakening of the warden's internal authority was accompanied by his increasing accountability to external executive controls. Structurally, a director responsible for the operation of an entire department could no longer tolerate independent satraps in the system. In order to protect himself politically, the director had to have a voice, if only as a veto, in the day-to-day, internal operation of the various institutions in his charge. Thus, in developing a sphere of executive authority, officials in the department found that they could not dismantle patronage relations at the state level without pursuing the process down the line through lower levels of administration. Supervisors simply could not allow the wardens to run the prisons according to practices and codes that they themselves had eschewed or were legally forbidden to use. Dismantling patronage prompted ever deeper and more extensive interventions into the operations of the prison and required further and ever more permanent curtailments of the wardens' traditional autonomy. Inevitably, this involved the Department of Corrections in the internal problems of day-to-day prison management and, most difficult, in an uncharted quest for new mechanisms of internal control. With a warden sympathetic to the enterprise of change, such as Joel Moore, this process produced rubs and disagreements but no serious collisions; with Harry Jackson, who was frankly hostile to change, it came to open warfare. Thus the centralization of power fostered an ongoing, rolling transformation of custodial techniques and a profound reordering of life and rewards inside the prison—all of it accomplished through a grinding, attritional struggle within prison administration.

Such a top-down revamping of the prison could not be accomplished in silence. New practices and procedures entailed a new rhetoric. The articulation of a replacement for patronage politics in the management and internal operation of the prison took time to take shape and was shaped by intense struggle. But what was eventually codified into the "individualized treatment model" of corrections during the 1950s was already anticipated in the ideological iterations of prison reformers in the late 1930s. Again the contrast between Joel Moore and Harry Jackson is instructive. Moore spoke of placing "corrections" on a "scientific basis" under the management of "experts." This implied a very definite view of the purposes of punishment, and nowhere was this new agenda more clearly formulated than in the operation of the Classification Board established at Jackson under the reform administration.[61] "What's wrong or defective in the inmate and WHY and WHAT TO DO about it both by prison and inmate are subjects of expert and prolonged study by the classification committee, directed by the prison psychiatrist," reported Moore. The idea was to test and evaluate each new prisoner, upon commitment, "with a view to determine what best will serve to correct tendencies toward crime."[62] By exploring life histories and examining psychological profiles, the board was supposed to determine "just what queer mental kink has caused criminal tendencies." The "classification machinery" would produce a program, the right mix of work, education, and counseling, to correct these aberrations. Since the reform or rehabilitation of prisoners could not be accomplished by "negative" or coercive pressure, it was thought necessary to gain ascendancy over those in correction by other, largely mental means, and this involved

---

61. The new classification system is outlined by Moore, in ibid., 55–56; and in Osborne Association, *1940 Survey*, 25–28.

62. *Detroit Times*, 14 February 1937.

playing, with increasingly nuanced variations, upon the theme of conditional release and tying the behavior of prisoners in incarceration to their central preoccupation, getting out. The reform ideology, in short, delineated a new avenue to freedom through treatment to parole that was full of new rules and pitfalls, involving new stratagems and games, insisting on new terminologies and rhetorics. This "alternative" program inside the prison developed alongside, and in competition with, the older structures of custody and control, co-opting its essential means and joining these to a more comprehensive and intrusive practice that, literally, invaded the minds of inmates and played with their destinies.

The inauguration of a "new penology" did not mean, however, that politics was taken out of prisons or that prison was withdrawn from politics. Far from being eliminated, politics in prison assumed new forms. Since civil service rules made it impossible for one party to throw the other out, rival factions had to learn to coexist or fight it out within the confines of the department and the rules of bureaucratic order. Cliques and factions blossomed during the 1940s, precisely because Democrats and Republicans could no longer fight over the prison and instead had to enter it, sublimating their partisan rivalries into more byzantine institutional tussles. As these factions and cliques adopted policies and assumed ideological identities, making allies and enemies and maneuvering for position and leverage, the nature and meaning of political combat was transformed. The new terms of competition and of survival took over, distributing positions and aligning forces in new ways. What we see in Michigan prisons during the 1940s is not simply the working out of the implications and ramifications of reform or the struggles aroused by the extrapolation of these top-down changes into entrenched echelons lower down but also, more important, the recomposition of politics itself. The prison system became a locus of experiments in the uses of scandal and the politics of exposé, which, in turn, made political careers and shaped the trajectories of political change in the state. Once again, albeit in a new way, we find the prison being made by, and at the same time participating in the making of, Michigan politics; and here, when practices were in crisis and transition, we see more clearly the role of ideas in forging a coherent account of carceral practice.

The Department of Corrections versus the Warden at Jackson

Departmental infighting was enlivened by strong personalities. Harry Jackson, a burly, outspoken man of vast experience, ran his prison according to his own lights, which, if somewhat old-fashioned by the emerging standards of the 1940s, were based upon an intimate knowledge of the institution and an expansive confidence in his own abilities. In 1940 he had been warden at Jackson for twelve years, over three separate terms, under six governors. Although his principal benefactor in state politics, Frank Fitzgerald, had recently died, he remained well connected in Republican circles and on good terms with the party fixer, Frank McKay. As a prison manager, he was highly regarded in law enforcement and legislative circles as well as by outside reform groups like the Osborne Association. Compared to his predecessor, Harry Hulbert, Harry Jackson was a professional in the prison business: he was a careful manager of the institution, keeping his books balanced and his political connections well-heeled; he was unfailingly considerate toward his subordinates, earning their loyalty by being a good boss; while quite capable of harsh discipline, even brutality, he was no brawler, preferring orderly procedures and a regular chain of command; and on the surface at least he was responsive to progressive agendas in penology, developing programs for guard training, education, and classification at the prison. Yet his expertise remained that of experience and common sense, not of education or formal training; he was always contemptuous of Democratic reformers, and he was not about to allow inexperienced bureaucrats in Lansing to define the duties of a job he had held since they were in high school or to tell him how to run a prison he himself had built.

This attitude placed him on line for a confrontation with his departmental overlords. The battle was delayed as long as the amiable Ernest Haeckel was director, but the election of a Democratic governor, Murray Van Wagoner, in November 1940 and the appointment of Garrett Heyns as director of the Corrections Department at the end of the year brought matters to a head. Heyns was from western Michigan and had a wide circle of contacts and supporters among Republicans and Democrats in the Holland and Grand Rapids area. Murphy made him warden at Ionia, and thus he became associated with the reform cadre of 1937, even though he had no experience in prison work, was neither a penal ideologue nor a New Dealer, and enjoyed anything but cordial relations with Murphy's corrections director, Hilmer Gellein. Politically, he seems to have been closer to the Van Wagoner wing of the party, and it was the latter's victory in 1940 that brought Heyns to the top in state corrections. Although he supported civil service reform and the new organization of the prison system, his political instincts were entirely compatible with older, patronage practices: he developed strong cross-party alliances in Lansing and remained on good terms with Frank McKay; within the prison system, moreover, he was careful to cultivate allies and retainers, bringing out of western Michigan and the Ionia institution a long list of protégés, including Gus Harrison and William Bannon, who were to dominate Michigan corrections in the 1950s. By nature Heyns was not a fighter, and he would probably have sought accommodation with Harry Jackson if the old warden had been more forthcoming. But he was also a savvy politician, cautious yet ambitious. And it was undoubtedly considerations of bureaucratic survival, rather than high principle, that pushed Heyns into conflict with Harry Jackson.

The ideological fire for this showdown came from A. Ross Pascoe, known in prison circles as "Mr. Parole" and among prisoners as "the blowtorch."[63] A University of Michigan Law School graduate, who moved directly to a position with the commissioner of pardons and paroles (Pasoce's father was a member of the Prison Commission during the Green administration), Pascoe made himself an expert in the field of parole. He was a deputy commissioner by 1935 and, though a staunch Republican, took an active role in shaping the parole provisions of the 1937 reform act. Thereafter, he served on the parole board continuously, in 1939 becoming assistant director for the Bureau of Pardons and Paroles in the department and chairman of the three-man parole board. From then until his death in 1954, Pascoe shaped parole policy in the state.

His principles were, by the standards of the day, entirely "modern": punishment, properly administered, could work for the reformation and rehabilitation of criminals. This, in his view, required

---

63. Interview with William Kime, April 1979.

three things: an end to political influence and patronage in prison management and the delegation of correctional tasks to experts trained and committed to professional standards; the enforcement of strict discipline and uniform rules of procedures inside the prison, so that all inmates were treated alike without special favors or consideration; and, finally, the grounding of parole upon scientific foundations, in which an impartial panel of experts reviewed individual performance, measured it against that of other inmates, past and present, and made a determination about future prospects for adjustment in the free world. An extremely hard-working civil servant, enormously proud of the detailed dossiers he compiled on each prisoner and fundamentally contemptuous of any attempt by prison inmates or officials to interfere in his work or to influence his conclusions, Pascoe was, by all accounts,[64] a highly principled man, who strongly disapproved of political patronage and the ad hoc, hands-on style of prison management that Harry Jackson embodied. While Heyns entered the fray with Harry Jackson reluctantly, Pascoe joined in with relish.

Harry Jackson was well entrenched and not easily ousted. Whatever might appear the chain of authority in the new organizational chart of Michigan corrections, the warden ran an institution with over five hundred state employees, many of whom, though now under civil service protection, were personally attached or beholden to him. The central office in Lansing employed only about twenty people, and not only were they all, including the director, paid less than the warden and his deputies, but they had little day-to-day access to the prison. While he was perhaps no longer the "independent Czar" of yore,[65] Harry Jackson had claim to a venerable and much-used tradition of personal autonomy that could only be eroded through sustained pressure. The director in Lansing was in no position to undertake such initiatives. Moreover, once Harry Jackson passed under civil service in the fall of 1941, he could only be removed for incompetence or malfeasance. The first was difficult to establish in view of his long experience in prison work; the second required a redefinition of corruption in that the prevailing norms that governed internal operations and upheld the warden's autonomy had been standard practices

64. Based on interviews with Robert Northrup, George Kropp, and William Kime, April–May 1979.

65. See *Detroit News*, 31 October 1941.

in the system for over a generation. All of this seems to have been apparent to Garrett Heyns, who handled his wardens gingerly and fended off crude attempts in 1941 to embarrass Harry Jackson politically.[66]

Ross Pascoe's power was of a different sort and more directly dangerous to the warden. Board members had routine access to the prison. They talked with prisoners privately, and their records were confidential. Since the board controlled the powerful promise of release, it was not difficult for its members to elicit information from inmates about internal operations at the prison. Over the years Pascoe and his colleagues developed an extensive dossier on Harry Jackson's administration. There was nothing very subtle about their intelligence gathering. In one of the few transcripts of a parole hearing available in the state archives, we find Pascoe quizzing an inmate, Glenn Davis, about cell block procedures, outside details, and personnel matters—none of it especially relevant to a parole proceeding.[67] We may gain the flavor of this line of questioning from the following sample:

> *Pascoe:* What else do you know that we ought to know? A. I know there is a lot of feuding going on around here between the Deputy [G. I. Francis] and [the Assistant Deputy] D. C. Pettit.
> *[Parole board member Gerald] Bush:* What is the reason for the feud as you know it? A. The average fellow inside the walls here knows Pettit has quite a lot more power than Francis has. Naturally he resents it because he has the better job.
> *Bush:* Why and how does Pettit have more power than Francis? A. He made all the assignments. He took care of all outside placements. . . .
> *Pascoe:* Is there an opinion the warden will O.K. anything that Pettit is willing to do? A. In most cases, yes. . . .
> *Bush:* Have you any reason to believe that Pettit profited in any way from the details that he was in a position to sign and the assignments that he could make? A. Yes. I would say that. He had Mike Selik working for him as house boy. Because we

---

66. Both Pascoe and Van Wagoner tried to use press reports of improper use of inmate labor on private homes to lever Jackson out of his job. See *Detroit News,* 30 September, 1, 4, 28, and 29 October, and 1 November 1941.

67. Attorney General, Criminal Investigation Division, box 1, file 14: Parole Hearing, 8 February 1945.

know Mike said all the time he was out there his cellar was always stocked up with good whiskey.

"Why are you willing to tell us these things?" Bush asked at the end of this exchange. "I want to get out of here" was the honest response. "These parole board members would hold hearings in the prison," recalled George Kropp, "and then they'd come back and one after another would come in carrying stories to the Director about something at Jackson." It was thus no great stretch of effort to have a word or two with a news reporter and to use the resulting story to embarrass the warden and to put pressure on the director for remedial action against him.

Bureaucratic maneuvers and turf fights went on almost continuously inside the Department of Corrections during the war years. Gradually, on several fronts, Harry Jackson lost ground. This long, attritional rear-guard action forms the context in which we can best understand the internal procedures and control strategies that the warden came to depend on in defending his position in the institution.

Prison Industries had languished during the 1930s. Joel Moore, who had believed with all prison progressives in the rehabilitative powers of work—"when a man is permitted to produce things with his hands while in prison, he gets a confidence in himself and a pride of accomplishment which helps restore him [as] a useful citizen again"[68]—had ended up plugging hobby crafts as a means of rehabilitative training, for lack of anything more germane. But during the war prison production enjoyed a sudden resurgence, making everything from clothes and mattress covers to assault boats for the navy and turning out an expanding line of canned goods for the armed services.[69] In the peak years of 1943 and 1944 over 90 percent of the prison population was gainfully employed and the textile mills were again operating twenty-four hours a day.[70] But, while prisoners worked in record numbers, the warden no longer controlled these

68. *Jackson Citizen Patriot*, 28 March 1937.

69. Summaries may be found in *Detroit News*, 8 April 1942 and 9 April 1944 as well as in the *Ann Arbor News*, 19 June and 10 November 1942. We will reserve full discussion of Prison Industries in the war for later, when it came under investigation in 1947.

70. Testimony of G. I. Francis before the Civil Service Commission, 9 April 1946, Attorney General, Criminal Investigations, box 10.

jobs. Under the 1937 reorganization Prison Industries had come under the Bureau of Prisons in Lansing. During 1937 and 1938 Joel Moore had combined the posts of warden at Jackson and assistant director of the Bureau of Prisons, thus maintaining the administrative link between the main prison and its industries that dated back to Harry Hulbert's regime. But Heyns enforced a separation in 1940 by taking charge of Prison Industries himself and placing a number of his men as managers and supervisors of production at the prison.[71] The industries at Jackson became known as "Heyns's territory," not part of the warden's gift and thus not available for venial use. Not only did the warden lose exclusive control over this area of the institution, but his enemies gained routine access to the prison and to information from prisoners working in the plants.

At the same time, wartime pressures combined with civil service to weaken the warden's leverage over the custodial staff. Many guards left the prison for military service or jobs in war industries, where the pay was better; new recruits were hard to find and were, in Harry Jackson's opinion, "the poorest that I have ever had since I have been there."[72] Duty rosters were consistently understrength during the war; in 1937 there had been 424 guards for 4,307 prisoners; by 1942 the same number of guards were managing 5,410 prisoners, and thereafter the number of guards fell, to 383 by 1945, while the number of inmates held constant.[73] There were 47 vacant positions at the end of the war, and the median age of the custodian force was nearly fifty years of age (there were ten guards over seventy).[74] At the same time, moreover, the warden's ability to discipline his custodial staff ebbed

---

71. One of these, William Burke, went on to the War Production Board and, upon his return, was appointed assistant director for the Bureau of Prisons. Both he and Fred Munnell at Jackson were very critical of Harry Jackson. See their statements, n.d., in Attorney General Investigations, box 1, file 11.

72. Harry Jackson, testimony, 31 May 1945, Attorney General Investigations, box 2, bk. 26. This was a view of prison guards widely shared by prisoners: see the testimony of James Buchannan, 20 March 1945, ibid., box 2, bk. 2.

73. Ibid., box 1, file 13: Personnel: Guard-Prisoner Ratios. Corrections Commission minutes give skeletal evidence of Harry Jackson's recurrent concern about security: on 22 September 1943 he reported that the custodial staff was short fifty guards and that there was a lot of pressure for overtime pay; on 20 December 1944 he asked for ninety new positions; on 12 April 1945 he indicated that he was still fifty men under staff; and on 7 June 1945 he was authorized to pay overtime rates recommended by the Civil Service Commission.

74. Ibid., box 1, file 13: Breakdown of Guard Force, 1 March 1945.

during the war years, in part because everyone had access to better-paying jobs elsewhere, in part because civil service gave enhanced protection to those who stayed on the job, and in part because the guards organized a union, and the wartime labor shortage increased the leverage of the union in protecting their rights and improving their pay.

If the old tools of the warden's management were weakening, moreover, splits in the ranks of the managers further compromised Harry Jackson's authority inside the prison. As we heard one inmate tell the parole board, the deputy and assistant deputy warden hated each other. Thanks to civil service placement, George I. Francis, the education director, had been promoted in 1941 to deputy warden, the number 2 spot in the prison, ahead of D. C. Pettit, a twenty-year veteran and longtime protégé of the warden. Yet, as assistant deputy, Pettit remained Harry Jackson's chief ally and instrument in the daily operations of the prison, while Francis was deliberately bypassed and excluded. Pettit had been an employee at the prison, more or less continuously, since 1919, and he was extremely popular among prisoners and staff—"a real individual, very knowledgeable, very capable," as Kropp recalled. Charles Watson, the head of classification, believed Pettit was "the only man who knew his business" and credited him, not Harry Jackson, with keeping the lid on the institution during the war years. There were reports that Pettit drank heavily and even rumors that he was addicted to morphine, but he was also courteous, approachable, and unpretentious, and it was said that he knew every prisoner by name. He was also extremely loyal to Harry Jackson, whom he had known since 1925.[75] Francis, by contrast, was a relative newcomer to the prison, brought on in the mid-1930s to administer the new educational programs and promoted, as the old-timers would have it, because of brains, not experience. A sharp, abrasive personality, he chafed at the limitations that the Jackson-Pettit axis imposed on his authority and reacted vindictively. The growing feud between the two deputies split the institutional staff. When Vernon Fox arrived at the prison in 1942, he found their animosity pervading everything: "G. I. never spoke a civil word to me, and D. C. never spoke a harsh one, probably because Chuck Watson,

75. Jackson *Citizen Patriot*, 1 May 1937; 30 March 1938; Statement by Charles Watson, 18 April 1945, Attorney General Investigations, box 1, file 13; Report of the Attorney General, 19 June 1945, in box 1, file 11.

my boss, supported the warden with D. C. The inmates supported
D. C. because he was humane and courteous to everybody, while
G. I. was caustic and personally ambitious."[76] Since Pettit clearly had
the support of "the old man," Francis aligned himself with the views
of the parole board and the Lansing office. Prison staff who disliked
Pettit or Harry Jackson or who were employed in "reformed" areas of
the prison, such as psychiatric and educational services, or in Prison
Industries, lined up behind Francis. The deputy lunched every day
with his allies; the assistant deputy had his henchmen over for drinks
at his house in the evening. The factions drew their legitimacy and
boundaries from the feuding between Harry Jackson and the department. In this way the bureaucratic power struggle penetrated the
walls and invaded the once-autonomous space of the warden.

It was in the area of paroles, however, that Harry Jackson felt the
most direct and dramatic challenge to his control of the institution.
Pascoe's ideological stance, that parole policy should be guided by
"scientific principles," meant in practice a sharp drop in the number
of prisoners released. During the Depression paroles had been widely
used as an institutional device for controlling idleness among prisoners. The economic crisis and, above all, the end of Prohibition had,
of course, brought an immediate fall in both the number and rate of
new commitments and in the overall population of the prison (see
table 1, chap. 2). The count at Jackson (both old and new facilities)
peaked in 1932, at 5,690; already new commitments, both to Jackson
and to the Michigan system as a whole, were nearly 1,000 below what
they had been in 1930.[77] But, while the fall in new commitments
helped to relieve overcrowding and the completion of the new facility
at Jackson in 1934 greatly expanded the state's overall capacity, both
Democratic and Republican administrations in this period were inclined to accelerate the number and rate of paroles quite dramatically.
Between 1932 and 1936 the average number of paroles granted each
year was five hundred more than in the previous five years; after 1931
paroles exceeded new commitments in every year until 1937. The

---

76. Vernon Fox. *Violence behind Bars* (New York: Vantage Press, 1956), 76.
77. *Michigan State Prisons, Statistical Report,* (Lansing, 1936), 9, 11. New commitments to Jackson in 1930 ran at 2,491 but dropped to 1,468 in 1932; state totals in the
same period were 4,343 and 3,328. The rate of commitment per 100,000 in the state
population dropped from 90 in 1930 to 65 in 1932 and continued to fall to 54 in 1935.

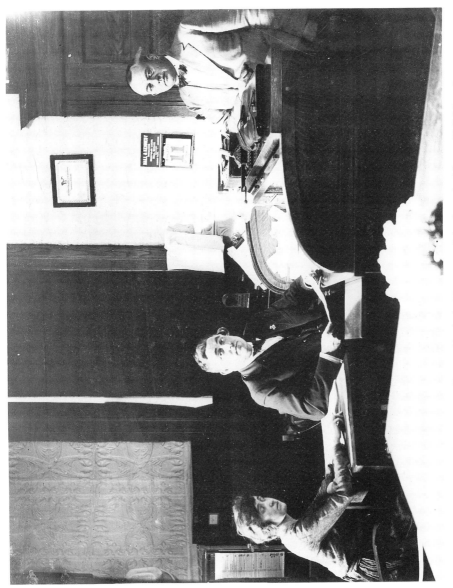

Fig. 1. Warden Harry Hulbert at his desk. (Courtesy of the State Archives of Michigan.)

Fig. 2. Governor Alex Groesbeck at his desk. (Courtesy of the State Archives of Michigan.)

Fig. 3. Frank McKay. (Courtesy of the State Archives of Michigan.)

Fig. 4. Governor Kim Sigler. (Courtesy of the State Archives of Michigan.)

Fig. 5. Warden Harry Jackson. (Courtesy of the State Archives of Michigan.)

Fig. 6. Inmate "big shots" in Deputy Pettit's red roadster. Joseph Medley is standing at the far left; next to him is Henry Luks. Raymond Fox is at the wheel. (Courtesy of the State Archives of Michigan.)

Fig. 7. The State Prison of Southern Michigan. (Courtesy of the State Archives of Michigan.)

population at Jackson fell by nearly 1,000 between 1932 and 1936, standing at 4,799 in that year—well below its capacity.

With the arrival of Pascoe and the independent parole board in 1937, however, these trends were instantly reversed. In the first five years of its operation the board reduced the annual average of paroles by nearly nine hundred, bringing it not only below the elevated levels of the Depression era but well below the averages maintained in the late 1920s.[78] Even with lower commitments the population of the prison began to rise again, reaching 5,400 by 1940. As the war produced shortages of custodians and reduced the ratio of guards to inmates, Harry Jackson urged the parole board to release more men. Pascoe refused to cooperate; paroles were not available to solve institutional problems. The average annual parole figure remained resolutely the same, as the chorus of grumbling and complaint among inmates rose.

Behind these managerial tensions lay issues of substance. In Harry Jackson's opinion, "a person is sent to prison as punishment and not for punishment."[79] If a prisoner kept a clean record, he should be given "good time" credit and released on the warden's recommendation at the expiration of his minimum sentence; if he amassed misconduct reports, he should serve the added forfeitures of good time and then be released. The point of indeterminate sentences, in this view, was to give the warden some leverage over an inmate's conduct while in prison. Pascoe's view of the indeterminacy of incarceration was quite different. "The Parole Board definitely rejects the 'cash and carry' philosophy of crime and imprisonment—so much time for a crime—a debt to society therefore paid—freedom to re-engage in crime once more on a similar quid pro quo basis."[80] The point of imprisonment was correction, and the decision to release a prisoner was based on evidence of correction. Moreover, "the Parole

---

78. The average number of paroles for 1927–31 was 2,508; the average for 1932–36 was 3,012; the average for 1937–1941 was 2,166. Computed from figures in Hilmer Gellein Papers, box 1; and the Third Biennial Report of the State Department of Corrections, for 1941–42, *Corrections in Wartime* (Lansing, 1943), 96.

79. Memorandum, Harry Jackson to John Dethmers, n.d. (May 1945), Attorney General Investigations, box 1, file 11.

80. These and other statements from Pascoe were made in January 1945 in response to press criticism of parole procedures ("Parole Indictment and Responses, 1945," included in Noel Fox's *Survey of Michigan Corrections*, 20 June 1949, G. Mennen Williams Papers, box 14).

Board would be stupid in the extreme to believe that a pattern of criminal behavior established over a period of 20 years can and is, inevitably, reconstructed by a relatively brief exposure to the corrective processes of Jackson prison."[81] Indeed, the strong presumption of the board was that no inmate was rehabilitated after serving his minimum sentence; rather, the expiration of the minimum provided an occasion to review the file and lay down the steps an inmate would have to take in order to secure release short of his maximum. Indeterminacy was a device for securing the transformation, not merely the compliance, of a prisoner. "The Board could not function if it did not believe wholeheartedly in the possibility of reformation and vocational-social rehabilitation."

Little wonder, then, that Harry Jackson soon convinced himself that deserving men were being held beyond their due, that many parolees were being returned to the prison on minor or technical violations, and that his staff was being made to cope with the anger and demoralization caused among prisoners by the parole board's autocratic and stingy ways.

> There are approximately one thousand men in the State Prison of Southern Michigan, [he wrote in 1945] who alone have served their minimum terms as predetermined by the courts and have been arbitrarily passed by the Parole Board to serve indefinite periods, most of them to their maximum terms. The majority have maintained good institutional records. The warden recommended parole at the minimum expiration. Neither prison officials nor inmates know why they were passed.[82]

Pascoe's response to this kind of accusation was delphic: "We cannot apply a precise actuarial yardstick to a human being," he averred; still, he could assure critics, "the reasons for passing an individual may not be known to him, but the Board is able to cite its reasons in every instance."[83] The parole board, said Harry Jackson, was "a dirty bunch of sons-of-bitches."[84]

---

81. Ibid.

82. Memorandum, Harry Jackson to Attorney General John Dethmers, n.d. (May 1945), Attorney General Investigations, box 1, file 11.

83. "Parole Indictment and Responses," Noel Fox's *Survey of Michigan Corrections*, G. Mennen Williams Papers, box 14.

84. Quoted from testimony given by an inmate Hull, n.d., Attorney General Investigations, box 1, file 14.

Pascoe's appeal to "scientific" standards amounted to a preclusive claim of monopoly over release. When Harry Jackson railed against the parole board's "autocratic" and "star chamber" proceedings, he was not concerned primarily with whether injustices were being done but, rather, with his own exclusion from the process. By cauterizing itself against "outside" influences, the parole board effectively preempted the warden's ultimate payoff inside—the promise of release—and compromised his ability to organize society behind the walls. As Harry Jackson complained in 1945, "prison officials have no authority to grant rewards for good work or conduct, thus have lost control over prisoners."[85] "To elaborate: the warden's recommendations for men appearing for parole consideration were often held up to ridicule or ignored. As a result, many inmates were penalized for working in certain programs and assignments, and many of them preferred not to have a favorable recommendation from the warden."[86] This, Jackson argued, was not only personally humiliating, undermining his prestige among inmates, but it "created discord and made discipline difficult," jeopardizing his control over the institution.

The warden's preference was to take parole authority out of the hands of the independent board and vest it, instead, in a three-man panel, made up of one member of the parole board, the warden of the institution, sitting as chairman, and the record clerk of the prison, who would be responsible, instead of the parole board, for maintaining case files and corresponding with sentencing judges.[87] Yet such alternative suggestions—indeed, all complaints from the warden— went unheeded. The support that Pascoe could muster in Lansing was impressive, and he had no trouble defending his autonomy against Harry Jackson's counterattacks. The routine administration of parole required a statewide network of local parole officers, often working in conjunction with county sheriffs departments, and board members were in regular correspondence with prosecutors and judges around the state, most of them locally powerful figures and many of them politically influential. This enhanced Pascoe's bureau-

---

85. Memorandum, Harry Jackson to Attorney General John Dethmers, n.d. (May 1945), Attorney General Investigations, box 1, file 11.

86. Letter, Harry Jackson to Members of the Michigan Legislature, 20 March 1948, Donald Leonard Papers, box 19: Prison Investigations, 1947.

87. This alternative, along with several other proposals, were included in Harry Jackson' memorandum to the attorney general, n.d. (May 1945).

cratic clout and made Harry Jackson's complaint only part hyperbole: "With their control of patronage in the Corrections Department which covers all counties in the state, and their control over the lives of all prisoners committed to Corrections Department control, they have one of the strongest political machines in the State of Michigan"[88]—in fact, "more power and authority than the old Czars of Russia."[89]

The embattled warden felt increasingly hemmed in by the encroachments of the department and the high-minded indifference of the parole board. The problems of control that confronted him did not stem from overcrowding or unemployment, for the prison population was below capacity and war production provided many prisoners with industrial jobs. Rather, his difficulties flowed from the organizational changes that weakened his capacity to organize an internal rewards structure around job placements and recommendations for release. Harry Jackson read these changes negatively, as stripping him of the resources and tools that, heretofore, had enabled him to maintain institutional security. Pascoe's view was the inverse, seeing the changes as only the first tentative steps of progress toward a new penology that would eventually displace the warden's ways. Yet, while the department and parole board had succeeded in invading the autonomy of the warden and weakening his power, they had not established principles of internal order that were sufficiently effective or comprehensive to supplant the established system of control. The warden was thus caught in transitional contradictions that he could not resolve but that he had to absorb in the course of running his prison on a day-to-day basis.

The Carceral Regime of Harry Jackson

In trying to determine how Harry Jackson "kept the lid on," it is important to bear in mind that most of the evidence we have about life inside the prison during this period was gathered in an effort to destroy Harry Jackson.[90] While it is undoubtedly a partial and selec-

---

88. Ibid.

89. Ibid.

90. Preliminary material is in Attorney General Investigations, box 1, file 11, while information assembled in the course of formal hearings is now deposited in thirty bound volumes of transcripts in box 2 of ibid. The affidavits collected by the attorney

tive picture, full of slants and distortions, we will use it, gingerly and with reservations duly noted, to suggest the kind of social order that emerged behind the walls during the war. What we can see, if only in glimpses and patches, makes logical and human sense. Harry Jackson, stripped of his former command over custodial jobs and inmate placements, denied control over prison industries, unable to manipulate the promise of release, and pressured by departmental supervision and parole board intrusions, fell back on the resources at hand. In effect, he defended his ground by extending and elaborating the old system of patronage rewards—stretching it and overworking it in an effort to salvage it. Graft, petty venality, payoffs, and rip-offs—all of which had characterized the organization of internal order in the 1920s—flourished and proliferated in the 1940s. The system spread out and grew denser. To compensate for his loss of control over release, the warden provided his prisoners with new venial incentives to make life inside agreeable and to promote inmate cooperation; to secure the loyalty of a custodial staff he could no longer appoint or dismiss, he condoned petty graft and allowed opportunities for parasitical plunder to proliferate. And to maintain the ties between keeper and kept that protected the informal understandings and corrupt collusions around which prison society cohered and institutional control was maintained, Harry Jackson presided over the emergence of a network of inmate "big shots," who acted as enforcers in the system, collaborating with the keepers in exchange for special favors and privileges. To defend his position Harry Jackson strained the old order to its limits before it came crashing down around him in the spring of 1945.

Rather than try to assemble snippets and bits from affidavits and testimony into a composite (and probably false) picture of the whole, let us consider for a moment the story of inmate Weaver, #52970.[91] It

---

general's office were mainly done by Lt. James Sheridan of the state police and S. J. Gilman of the parole board. Gilman came to the Department of Corrections as part of a WPA project to reorganize prison records; then, taking a job with the department, he became involved in setting up civil service procedures and moved from there to work for the parole board, conducting investigations and preliminary hearings (Kropp interview, May 1979).

91. Weaver's is one of the more comprehensive and detailed of the many reports of interviews that Sheridan and Gilman collected for the attorney general. They are to be found in Attorney General Investigations, box 1, file 11. They were collected sometime in May 1945.

appears on three, single-spaced, typewritten pages that are, obviously, the condensation of a longer interview, which may actually have taken place at Marquette, where Weaver was transferred in September 1944, or perhaps in Lansing. The story has been reassembled by Weaver's interrogators into a continuous narrative with some semblance of chronological continuity, and, while the sequence could easily be rearranged, there is a consistent theme upon which Weaver's tale hangs: his need to accumulate one hundred dollars.

Charles Weaver was a professional thief from Grand Rapids who had two brief convictions during the Depression, for "receiving stolen property" in 1932 and for "possession of burglary tools" in 1934. When he came to Jackson in March 1942 on his third sentence, this one a ten-to-fifteen-year stretch for breaking and entering, he was approaching forty and had a wife and son.[92] He arrived with fifteen dollars in his pocket and was assigned to a job in the laundry, an extremely hot and unpleasant place reserved for new arrivals. He did not like the work. Having been to Jackson before, he knew the ropes and went immediately to a Captain Goodell to see about a transfer. Goodell inquired about Weaver's cash assets and sent him to the assistant deputy warden, D. C. Pettit:

> [Weaver] told D. C. he wanted to get out of the laundry and D.C. asked, "how much money have you got?" Weaver said that he had fifteen dollars. Pettit said that he could put him in the kitchen, which was done. Incidentally, Weaver asked D. C. how he could get out on the farms. D. C. said, "I'll have to look at your card." When D. C. discovered [Weaver] had a ten year minimum and very little time in, D. C. said, "I couldn't go to the old man with less than a hundred dollars." Weaver didn't have the hundred dollars at the time so he couldn't go out on the farm. After he worked in the kitchen for a while, Nick Ross went to D. C. Pettit for free to see whether Weaver could be transferred to one of the farms. D. C. told Nick Ross: "you tell Weaver if he wants to go out on the farm he knows how to get there."

Weaver set about accumulating the necessary fee.

Acquiring one hundred dollars was not easy. He had to get in-

---

92. He weighed two hundred pounds and had brown hair and blue eyes. What little we know about Weaver can be pieced together from his testimony and from his "card" (there are actually three of them) now deposited at the State Archives.

volved in illegal activities. Apparently, his post in the kitchen made Weaver useful to the liquor makers in the prison, because he had access to the sugar they needed.

> Sharp, an officer, and Ansley, an inmate, were making hootch. They had a still in the cannery. In fact, they had the hootch concession over in the cannery. [Officers] Emerson and Greening told Weaver that they had orders from Warden Jackson not to knock Sharp's still in the cannery. . . . Weaver and Ansley were friends. They wanted Weaver to come in with them on the hootch business and I [Gilman?] guess that Weaver did in some small degree. Incidentally, Sharp steals sugar for the still and in this connection Weaver tells about sugar going out of the kitchen to the Warden and others in hundred pound bags, lots and lots of it, that Officer Engelgau got suspicious about the sugar shortage, talked about it and very promptly found himself transferred to the Textile Mill. The hootch that was made in the cannery was sold for twenty dollars a gallon. Sharp's house won't stand a shakedown. It is full of prison-made materials of all sorts, shirts, canned goods and the like.

Apparently Ansley was in the habit of consuming quantities of the product, for he was often drunk on the yard; after several warnings, he was sent to the bull pen, and apparently some move was made to ship him to Marquette.

> Officer Greening was under the impression that Ansley had plenty of money so Greening told Weaver that if Ansley was to stay away from Marquette it would cost plenty. Some of the money was to go to Greening and most of it to D. C. Although Weaver was nearly broke at the time, he finally offered twenty-five dollars. Greening wanted more but he finally took the twenty-five dollars and Ansley was released from the bull pen.

Weaver, however, was back to square one, no closer to the farm and again without money. Meanwhile,

> Deputy [Warden G. I.] Francis tried to fire Sharp, found he couldn't fire him, so transferred him to 16 Block. Sharp very definitely didn't like working in 16 Block, took the matter up with

Warden Jackson and Warden Jackson ordered him re-instated in his old job back in the cannery. When he got back, however, the liquor business had got too hot and he and Ansley opened up a book. They went along pretty well for a while but Sharp was dragging down too much, they got hit pretty badly and went broke. They came to Weaver for a loan.

Weaver saw a new opportunity. He arranged for his wife to deliver forty dollars to Officer Sharp in a poolroom in Jackson, while he scraped together another twenty dollars on the inside. Altogether, he advanced Sharp and Ansley sixty dollars,

> with the understanding that in a few months they would pay him back a hundred dollars and then it was Weaver's plan with the hundred dollars to go to D. C. and get a farm placement. Unfortunately for Weaver's plans, Ansley got knocked off by Kaminski. Kaminski and Francis questioned Ansley and Ansley said the money and tickets [for bookmaking] found on him belonged to Weaver. Weaver was called in. He wouldn't talk and he suddenly found himself in the bull pen bound for Marquette. While he was in the bull pen awaiting transfer to Marquette, he talked with Officer Greening, asked Greening how he could get off from the Marquette transfer. Greening said that he'd have to take that up with D. C. Greening talked with D. C. and came back to Weaver laughing to beat hell with this message: "D. C. says that the price on them tickets is the same as out to the farm."

With this cruel joke at the prisoner's expense, the report ends, and inmate Weaver disappears from view. We may remark on his irrepressible entrepreneurial energies and shake our heads at the loyalty he evinced for such a shiftless and treacherous friend. But personal qualities aside, Weaver was in most respects a very ordinary prisoner of his day. He was clearly a small-time operator, not a dangerous person, and the story he told was exceptional only in the richness of its detail, not in its substance.

The "thieves' code" dominated the big house penitentiary, and ordinarily thieves did not talk.[93] For some reason Weaver talked

---

93. See John Irwin, *Prisons in Turmoil,* for a discussion of the centrality of thieves' culture in the prisons of the 1920s and 1930s.

freely—we don't know why—and for some reason his interrogators let him ramble, recording his odyssey in considerable detail. They then digested his remarks and reproduced them in the form of an affidavit; we thus represent what Weaver represented to listeners who, in turn, re-presented what they were told to their superiors. They were clearly interested in anything that might reflect badly on Harry Jackson's administration of the prison. They were especially intent on identifying corrupt guards ("Sharp's house won't stand a shakedown") and to mark moments in the story when the warden makes a personal appearance; they were also careful to name the officers who, like lone knights placing obstacles in the path of evil, broke into the story and tried to disrupt its course ("Francis tried to fire Sharp"—"Ansley got knocked off by Kaminski"—"Officer Engelgau got suspicious . . . talked about it . . . found himself transferred"). In shaping Weaver's story for the record, the investigators do not seem surprised by reports of inmates gambling, drinking, or stealing chickens; this was to be expected of prisoners, and there is no word of censure for them in this document. What earns their contempt is the corruption of officers, who, they imply, ought to be different. Besides D. C. Pettit and Harry Jackson, seven officers (and only four prisoners) are mentioned by name as being engaged in illegal activities. The moral tone that suffuses the treatment of details makes transparent the authors' agenda: they are concerned primarily with the boundaries of proper custodial behavior, and they reshaped Weaver's information into a narrative about what was, or ought to have been, appropriate, permissible, and professional conduct on the part of custodians. It is in this sense a company document.

Setting judgments aside, however, we can catch glimpses, in the incidental details, of how Harry Jackson ran his prison. We can see many indications of a highly commercialized, cash-conscious world, in which material goods and human actions are for sale and charitable acts ("Nick Ross went to D. C. Pettit for free") merit mention. Everyone is preoccupied with money, looking for ways to make it, following its movement around the institution, and ready to pounce on any sign of its accumulation. Prisoners help one another and steal from one another; guards move in and out, as facilitators and predators; D. C. Pettit has a hand in everything, and, at a distance, the "old man" is aware of, condones, and apparently takes a cut from the activities of his subordinates. For the inmates clear boundaries are in force. Corruption has its rules of silence, and illegalities require discretion; hence, Ansley ended up in the bull pen bound for Marquette because he drank too much too often and thus exposed his still and his association with Officer Sharp too openly. On the ground in the prison there were dense thickets of custom and a pervasive need for caution. Everything may have been negotiable, but there were also clear rules and deep inequalities.

The personal rivalry between G. I. Francis and D. C. Pettit suffuses Weaver's narrative. The deputy and his allies seem determined to disrupt Pettit's operations, while the latter moves to protect his men from interference. Officer Engelgau, who is here depicted as a "good guy" for reporting the theft of sugar, gets transferred to the Textile Plant, a dirty and unpleasant post but also part of Prison Industries, known as "Heyns territory"; Officer Sharp, presented here as a thoroughly corrupt custodian, has only to speak with the warden to get back his old job and venial connections. There are good guards and bad guards everywhere, as the prison pits the honest against the wicked—at least in the official re-telling of Weaver's tale. But from Weaver's own point of view, it is apparent that the feuds among the keepers only added an unwelcome element of capriciousness to the uncertainties of prison life. G. I. Francis and his supporters appear in his story not as a comprehensive system of rules or boundaries but as random interventions that strike unexpectedly, like accidents or bad luck, and send settled arrangements into disarray. Those who, to Weaver's interrogators, appeared as champions of the new order, struggling against the benighted reign of the old, appeared to Weaver and other prisoners as loose cannons, to be watched for and avoided. When Kaminski "knocked off" Ansley and confiscated his money, it turned out he was not looking for a cut in the action but for a change in the rules. He represented a new, mysterious contingency; Ansley apparently had no idea how to neutralize it, so he "ratted" on Weaver and left our protagonist in the bull pen bound for Marquette.

This was the battle among prison managers as it was experienced by the prisoners. Ultimately, what was most disconcerting to them was not that the rules were changing but that they were in dispute and hence difficult to read. Harry Jackson and D. C. Pettit were still able to defend their regime against the intruders. There were limits to how far Francis could go, especially with the guards: he could not fire Sharp, nor could he protect Engelgau. But these limits were less ap-

parent in his dealings with prisoners, for here his rights to reprimand, punish, or transfer inmates were grounded in his status as a
custodian, the deputy warden, not in his role as a carrier of the new
penology. Pettit could not protect Weaver from the deputy warden's
discipline, or at least he was not willing to try without substantial
remuneration. Thus the battle between the department and the warden, as it went behind the walls in the form of a feud or turf fight
between Francis and Pettit, made life more capricious and unpredictable for prisoners—indeed, it tended to be played out at their expense. The grumbling and discontent that arose among prisoners
reached the ears of Harry Jackson, who heard it as a threat to institutional discipline and good order and translated this information into
denunciations of the parole board and the Department of Corrections
for compromising his capacity to control the institution—a position
that, without irony, many inmates endorsed.

Except for its more vivid detail, Weaver's story is not substantially
different from dozens of others that came out of Jackson prison in the
mid-1940s. Certainly the evidence that surfaced in the 1945 investigation—of bookmaking, loan sharking, gambling, bootlegging, contraband smuggling, and outright stealing—bore out D. C. Pettit's remark
that "there is more crime in prison than outside of prison."[94] The
diversity of "hustles" and "scams" by which inmates tried to make
life tolerable or accumulate a little working capital within a society of
scarcity was truly extraordinary. Some of these activities were entirely
legal, such as the operation of candy, tobacco, pencil, handkerchief,
and other concessions, which inmates bought and sold from one
another,[95] or the sale of hobby crafts and canaries. Joel Moore and
Harry Jackson had promoted arts and crafts after the Munshaw Act
foreclosed sale of prison-made goods on the open market in 1935.
Hundreds of prisoners became involved in such activities as leather
tooling and jewelry making, fashioning goods that were sold in a
small shop at the prison gate to visitors and passersby or were exchanged among inmates as a form of currency. Some prisoners became hobby craft entrepreneurs, hiring others as subcontractors, often at wages higher than those paid by prison industry. In 1944 the

94. Pascoe testimony, 27 March 1945, Attorney General Investigations, box 2,
bk. 7.

95. Material on concessions may be found in ibid., box 2, bk. 18.

profits for arts and crafts totaled over forty-three thousand dollars, and one inmate earned five thousand dollars in personal income.[96] Raising canaries for sale in the roadside store and making cages for their keep also turned into a thriving business under Harry Jackson; Weaver's story tells of an officer named Oakley who carried birds out of the prison for sale in pet stores.

Other activities were illegal but widely tolerated, such as the operation of pawn shops that held personal items for inmates as security against loans and bets or the widespread traffic in chickens from the poultry farm. According to inmate Briggs, thousands of chickens were unaccounted for:

> more than $1600 worth of chickens went off the farm [in the year he worked there]. Briggs collected the money and split with Morris Glover [the farm foreman]. Briggs believes that Morris Glover, in turn, split with Pettit. Chicken orders often did not go through the farm office so no record of these transactions was ever made. Briggs says that Mrs. Jackson and Warden Harry Jackson got a lot more chickens than they could possibly use themselves. . . . Briggs says further that Officer Larson whose wife apparently ran the kitchen at the Country club bought chickens from Briggs, at eighteen cents per pound dressed, and paid the inmate. The inmate Briggs kept most of the money although he would split some with Glover.[97]

When confronted with this testimony, Morris Glover denied any impropriety, insisting that he was only following established practice in dispensing chickens to prison officials and implying that keeping track of the comings and goings of chickens and inmates was beyond his ken.

> He admits that he was giving a chicken away "here and there." He cannot account for the loss of 4000 chickens in the last three and one-half years, but speaks in generalities. He claims that

---

96. Auditor General's File, Special Audit of SPSM, 1947, Arts and Craft Statement, December 1947.

97. Affidavit on Briggs, n.d., Attorney General Investigations, box 1, file 11.

many died, many were stolen by inmates while working on the farm. He says some were stolen by other people who would drive to the chicken farm at night and then be handed out some chickens by inmates who were supposed to be watchmen at night. He says on one occasion a truck load of inmates were taken from his farm to Sixteen Block to attend a show at night and somebody pulled an unexpected shakedown on this truck load and much contraband was found including cooked chickens, raw chickens, eggs, etc. He states that was the first shakedown he could remember in his tenure as superintendent of this chicken farm.[98]

Other moneymaking activities were reasonably harmless, though they seem to have shocked the attorney general and made for vivid headlines:

Baxter testifies that an inmate can get into the hospital for one dollar. The nurse gets the one dollar and signs the inmate in. If the inmate wants to stay in the hospital long enough to receive visits, the inmate builds up his temperature so that the Doctor will believe it's a real illness. Visitors to the hospital are brought over by officers from the Hall Office and for five bucks most of the officers will take a walk. The Doctors are not in on the racket. If the visitor pretends to be the inmate's wife, while the officer has taken a walk, the wife, real or pretended, will take care of the inmate.[99]

But the really big money was in gambling and bookmaking, together with the loan-sharking that sustained these enterprises. One "bookie" told a dissident guard that "he could pick up a thousand dollars in ten minutes," and several inmates spoke of crap games with several hundred dollars on the table.[100] The center of gambling was in the gym, but on holidays and Sundays prisoners would set up "concessions" for gambling in the yard, sometimes paying a guard for

---

98. Affidavit on interviews with Morris Glover, among other things, dated 22 May 1945, ibid.

99. Affidavit by Baxter, n.d., ibid.

100. Alfred Fingel, in testimony before the Civil Service Commission (Attorney General, Criminal Files, box 10, 9 April 1946) and in personal interview (May 1979).

early "unlock" so they could get their blankets down at the best spots.[101] Numbers runners kept book all over the prison, and, while there was a lot of turnover in the business, several inmates reckoned there were, at any given time, eight to ten bookmaking operations going inside the walls. Some inmates who accumulated large sums became bankers, carrying around rolls of $500 and $800 to lend to others at 25 to 30 percent interest.[102] In Weaver's story we discover that: "Archie Hyatt was the inmate who loaned money to men operating handbooks. If you operated a book and didn't get your capital from Hyatt, D. C. knocked you off because Hyatt was D. C.'s connection on booking on the farm."

Here, indeed, was the stuff of scandal. As one inmate observed, "The shit will rise," and, while we must assume that the attorney general's investigators skimmed the cream of scandal from their interviews and, in re-presenting it to their superiors, sought to churn their evidence into a firm case against Harry Jackson, the record they left will support several general observations. In the first place keepers and kept were clearly locked in an elaborate game of antagonistic collaboration. Forced to cohabit in a crude and unequal intimacy, guards and prisoners arrived at a point of mutual dependency and mutual exploitation—using each other in the fullest sense. At every turn guards participated in the entrepreneurial activities of their charges, facilitating it but also plundering it. For every officer, like Sharp, who was directly involved in illegal business and, perhaps, "dragging down too much," there were others who were more casually corrupt, "killing a charge" for a few dollars or looking the other way in return for a tip. A number of guards were involved in smuggling contraband into the prison; Weaver speaks of Officer Penny as "a petty chiseler" who was, nevertheless, "a main connection on money" through whom "a good many inmates receive money from outside." Others were engaged in smuggling prison goods out; chickens, canned foods, gasoline, even canaries were reportedly car-

---

101. Weaver speaks of these "concessions" in a way that suggests a double meaning: on the one hand, they were "open for business," like so many blackjack tables in a casino, but it is also clear, on the other hand, that guards made special concessions with the rules on holidays, allowing prisoners to gamble openly and for high stakes in a way that would not be allowed on a typical weekday.

102. Testimony of James Buchannan, 20 March 1945, Attorney General Investigations, box 2, bk. 2.

ried off by guards on their way home. A few guards were aggressively greedy, using their custodial power to extort money from inmates. Since all cash inside was contraband, it was subject to confis-
cation whenever a guard decided to conduct a shakedown. General
institutional shakedowns were almost unknown during Harry Jackson's tenure, but informal shakedowns of individuals—or threats of
shakedown as a means of extorting a cut—were daily, almost continuous, occurrences. Clearly, inmates with money attracted attention,
and when entrepreneurial success attracted guards leveraging a cut, it
was not easy to "get ahead." But, if this sort of parasitical extraction
by custodians constantly threatened to cancel out inmate gains, the
reverse imperative also applied: the system could not long remain
lucrative for guards unless prisoners were allowed to develop and
pursue their entrepreneurial opportunities. Official profiteering required inmate enterprise that, in turn, depended on the tolerance and
forbearance of custodians. The difference here between criminals and
their keepers was one of degree, not of kind.

Yet, while pervasive, this symbiotic crookedness was not the core
of internal order. For what is noteworthy, in the second place, is the
extent to which the whole thing seems to have been organized. The
central figure in all the stories is D. C. Pettit. His office was the hub of
prison life. The assistant deputy controlled all inmate placements
within the institution. While the Classification Committee made initial job assignments, usually in the least desirable positions in the
laundry or textile mill, all changes in placement as well as any move
to the farms or trusty division were controlled through Pettit's office.
So were cell assignments: prisoners who wanted to get away from
enemies, move closer to friends or lovers, establish residence near a
concession, or gain access to a cell block for numbers running or other
illegal activities had to make these arrangements at the deputy's office. Both job and cell assignment could, of course, be turned to
lucrative use: one inmate paid twenty-five dollars for the job of hall
boy on a gallery in a cell block and then made that much every week
serving as lookout for craps games and carrying money for inmates
who did not enjoy his unrestricted movement in the building. Disciplinary reports also went through Pettit's office, as did all appeals to
have "tickets" suppressed. As Pascoe's conservative parole policy began to take effect, Pettit could insure the clean record so necessary for

an appearance before the board. And, finally, through Pettit's office prisoners could arrange "vacations" from prison—the outside details that took them on trips to Jackson, Detroit, and other destinations for a day, even overnight. For twenty dollars one could purchase a trip to a whorehouse in Jackson: ten went to Pettit's office for distribution between the deputy and his clerks; five went to tip the officer who chaperoned the excursion; and five more paid for the services and silence of the brothel. All of this could be arranged, for a consideration, through Pettit's office, making it a sort of central clearinghouse or exchange mart that organized access to the good things of prison life and, in the process, set the prices. These transactions, in turn, served to organize the conduct of ordinary inmates, like Weaver, setting the imperatives of their daily existence and channeling their energies into "productive" activities that Pettit could monitor, regulate, and expropriate. "D. C. knows everything that goes on in the institution," reported one prisoner. "How does he find it out?" he was asked. "Through the system that has developed."[103]

The "system" involved a good deal more than a transaction of services and favors through Pettit's office, however. His control over placement, movement, and residence enabled Pettit to locate "his men" all over the institution and protect them against interlopers and competitors. If Archie Hyatt was "D. C.'s connection on booking on the farm," we may be sure that Pettit had similar connections on bookmaking, lending, and gambling in all the cell blocks; if Sharp and Ansley "had the hootch concession over in the cannery," there were other, equally profitable operations in the power plant and on the Dalton Farm. Many of the activities Pettit organized behind the walls were illegal (gambling, bookmaking, loan-sharking) or illicit tampering with ordinary housekeeping routines (cell changes, passes, and details), but even legal activities could be organized for illicit profit: Bing LaBady was Pettit's "pay-off man" in Arts and Crafts, to whom prisoners engaged in hobby craft had to turn for scarce materials, passes to move about the institution in the conduct of their business, or details to town to buy supplies.[104]

---

103. Bob Johnson, testimony, 27 March 1945, ibid., box 1, file 14.

104. LaBady was also a close friend of Joseph Medley, which is why his activities were recorded in a memo by Victor Anderson, n.d. (1947), in an interrogation of James Stiel about the Medley escape. In the Leonard Papers, box 19, Investigation of SPSM, 1947, Testimony (1).

Pettit's power was thus a compound one: he could provide access to lucrative arenas, and, preclusively, he could insure monopoly in those arenas. His retainers, in turn, depended on his favor and supplied him with a steady flow of information and a network of enforcers—not to mention a substantial cut of the take. Undoubtedly, each of Pettit's "boys" had his own retinue of followers among the prisoners, although these connections are now virtually impossible to reconstruct. Through extended linkages of patronage and reciprocal obligation, Pettit was able to reach down into prison society and shape an internal rewards structure, supplementing custodial force with a wide range of economic incentives and penalties that kept people in line and framed the options of everyday life.

Pettit was indeed a real presence in the prison—far more accessible than the warden and on familiar terms with many inmates. But this was not his personal domain. Crucial to his control of institutional life was a cadre of old-time, long-term inmates who worked as clerks and office assistants throughout the prison. The most powerful of these clerks congregated in Pettit's office. These were the "big shots" who had practical, day-to-day charge of allocating the favors in the assistant deputy warden's gift. Vernon Fox tells how, as a newcomer to the prison in 1942, he tried to get a cell change for his clerk through normal channels, but he found that "cell-change cards would be misplaced, misfiled, get lost, or evaporate," until he got the message, that the clerk in Pettit's office who controlled cell assignments was waiting for some consideration.[105] The clerk in question was Raymond Fox, who, along with Joseph Medley, was the most powerful of the "big shots" in Pettit's office. But there were perhaps a dozen others who controlled fiefdoms or monopolized particular "rackets" in the prison—Mike Biagini, Chester (Big Moe) Jurczyszyn, Philip Keywell, Ray Bernstein, John Mocheri, Bing Labady, and, until his release, Mike Selig. Some, like Fox and Medley, were "loners" whose power was built upon a career in prison; they were tough, "stir-savvy" and incarcerated for long terms—the sort of "old cons" Pettit could rely on to build internal organizations while feathering their own nests. Others, like Keywell, Bernstein, and Selig, were members of Detroit's powerful Purple Gang, who, while in prison, maintained close ties and "business" associations with gang members outside. "A

---

105. Fox, *Violence Behind Bars*, 76.

man is convicted in Detroit, we'll say. He belongs to a certain group. That group makes arrangements before he arrives and before he is out of quarantine he has a job with details within the institution or privileges that some men fight for for ten years."[106] Pettit seems to have used gangsters, less for organizational work in the prison than as enforcers, and he clearly made a trade of status inside for favors outside; Selig's brother, Chuck, owned O'Larry's Bar in Detroit, which ran "a tab" on the deputy and his cronies and kept them well supplied with liquor.[107]

Allies and, as often, rivals, the "big shots"—also called, suggestively, "the politicians"—divided and redivided the available pickings, organized satrapies of retainers and enforcers, and collaborated with Pettit in keeping the rest of the prison in line. "It was just a racket where the little fellow pays off the bigger fellow and the big fellow can have what he wants."[108] The "king pins" locked together in the upper tier of 15 Block, which was known in those days as "aristocrats' row"; they were free to roam the institution and, changing into civilian clothes, to leave for an afternoon at the bars or the ballgame in Detroit. Every now and then Pettit had them all over to his house for a party or up to his lake cottage for a weekend of merrymaking. A fistfight between Medley and Raymond Fox, in Pettit's basement bar, became a legend among prisoners. A photograph of nine "big shots" lounging in the deputy's red roadster became famous when it was published in the press. Pettit always insisted that the nine were only turned out, in white shirts and ties, to serve the

---

106. Bob Johnson's testimony, 27 March 1945, Attorney General Investigations, box 1, file 14.

107. O'Larry's Bar on Dexter Avenue in Detroit was the focus of much attention as the "liquor source" for prisoners. It was co-owned by Mike Selig's brother, Chuck, and Harry Fleisher, a well-known hoodlum in Detroit and leader of the Purple Gang. The bar was a favorite meeting place and watering hole for ex-convicts, paroled prisoners, and inmates from SPSM in town on outside details. D. C. Pettit and other prison officials also dropped by when in the city, and there were several reports of caseloads of liquor being picked up for shipment to the prison—on occasion by high officials in the prison. And it was in O'Larry's that the conspiracy to kill Senator Hooper was supposedly hatched. A summary of some of these associations is to be found in a Memorandum to Commissioner Donald Leonard, 2 February 1947, in the Leonard Papers, box 19, Case Files: Miscellanea (3).

108. Testimony of Bob Johnson, 27 March 1945 Attorney General Investigations, box 1, file 14.

buffet at his son "Pinkie's" wedding. In fact, this ambiguity—whether they were servants or comrades of the deputy warden—was precisely the point in question.[109]

The "big shots" had immense prestige in the prison, not only because they had access and clout as Pettit's clerks and were showered with various tokens of favor for loyal service but also because they enjoyed, quite openly, a certain reprieve from the rigors of prison. Betty Furstenberg, a waitress at O'Larry's Bar, told investigators how an inmate would turn up, accompanied by Walter Wilson, chief inspector of the guards, or Richard Riley, the athletic director of the prison, and load a prison car with whiskey, cigarettes, cakes, bologna, canned fruit, Saunders candy, and sardines—"the boys at the prison did not like sardines which were packed in tomato sauce, they had to be packed in oil"—for delivery to Jackson; apparently, the liquor would go to Pettit, Wilson, and Riley, all known for their heavy drinking, while the food would be distributed among the "big shots."[110]

But it was not only their access to scarce commodities that marked the class privilege of the "big shots"; they also enjoyed a relative immunity from custodial authority. Ordinary guards did not dare interfere with "big shot" activities; as one put it, "the rules don't seem to apply."[111] Some felt intimidated:

> *Q.* Did you ever have any reason to feel that because you weren't playing ball with Pettit . . . that there might be some reprisal against you?
>
> *A.* I did, yes, sir.
>
> *Q.* Well, what kind of reprisal would you expect?
>
> *A.* Well, they could—they could either get you demoted or fired, or pretty near anything they wanted to do.[112]

---

109. It was this same red roadster that figured prominently in the Hooper murder case, as several witnesses claimed to have seen it on the M-99 highway the night that the senator was shot.

110. Testimony of Elizabeth Furstenberg, 9 March (April?) 1945, box 1, file 11 (the interview took place on 7 April and was reported by Capt. Harold Mulbar of the state police). Furstenberg was interviewed again in February 1947; see Leonard Papers, box 19, Case Files: Miscellaneous (3).

111. Testimony of N. W. Shafter, Attorney General Investigations, box 2, bk. 4.

112. Testimony of Howard Freeland, ibid., box 2, bk. 1.

Some guards got frustrated and later cooperated with investiga-tors.[113] But others found that they could use their custodial powers to leverage a cut and thus profit from the activities of the inmates. Pettit sanctioned the activities of his cronies, but he also affirmed the right of guards to draw a parasitical share. He apparently had an ally in Walter Wilson, the chief inspector of guards, who not only had charge of the custodial staff but, through his office clerks, maintained close links with incarcerated members of the Purple Gang, whom he used as an official "goon squad" in the prison.[114] Alongside the formal order of custody stood a parallel, informal order for inmate control. "Big shot politicians" with protection from the warden or his deputy, were able to confer small, and no doubt diminishing, degrees of autonomy upon whole retinues of runners, operatives, and enforcers who, interacting in daily collusion with line guards and shop fore-men, ran the prison.

How new was all of this? It is anybody's guess. Something very much like this must have gone on in the 1920s, although the evidenti-ary traces are too faint to say for certain. Much of what emerged from the 1945 investigation and got roundly condemned was precisely what patronage relations became, when adapted to the conditions of prison. The informal, face-to-face, and venial nature of the internal order had long been characteristic of Jackson prison; Harry Jackson had, after all, been in charge since the mid-1920s, and Pettit had been around even longer. It is therefore quite possible that the investiga-tion of 1945 merely ripped the cover from old, deeply entrenched practices—in which case, we must look outside the prison, to the world of politics and popular morality, to understand why it was, now and of a sudden, so scandalous.

Before doing this, however, we might consider for a moment the possibility that the internal system of the 1940s, while adhering to the

---

113. Al Fingel was one, and he told of others (interview, May 1979).

114. Wilson's role in the Pettit organization remains obscure, largely because investigators were not interested in the internal order of the prison but in the illegal activities of custodians; thus, they documented Wilson's visits to O'Larry's Bar in the company of inmates, his heavy drinking, and his willingness to take gifts of liquor, but they did not study seriously his relationship to Keywell and Bernstein. The suggestions here, that Wilson's big shots handled enforcement in the prison, are based on scattered bits of information included in a report by Walter Williams and Murray Young to Donald Leonard, 2 February 1947, Leonard Papers, box 19, Case Files: Miscellaneous (3).

basic forms of patronage practice inside, was different from, or had undergone alterations since, the 1920s. Identifying new elements or twists and understanding how the internal order had evolved over twenty years in response to changing circumstances are important not only in underscoring, again, that prisons are not static institutions, however massive and unalterable they may appear, but also in locating the conjuncture of forces that, in 1945, brought about a very rapid, and for Harry Jackson quite devastating, shift in the definitions of corruption and the boundary lines of what was tolerable.

With this in mind we may note that the stories and affidavits of inmates make almost no mention of drugs in the prison. Drugs had been commonplace in the 1920s, and addicts had no difficulty supporting a habit while incarcerated. By the 1940s, however, this lively traffic in cocaine and morphine seems to have been largely suppressed. Silence in the record betokens an absence that is further confirmed by passing remarks that drugs and other "outside" goods were harder to come by than in the past.[115] The blurred boundaries and casual interactions that had characterized the road camps and construction site were things of the past; the Depression had brought the expansive, freewheeling industrial operations to a screeching halt; Joel Moore had imposed firmer control on movement between inside and outside. In all, the impression left by inmate testimony in the 1940s is that traffic with the outside world had been much diminished; the flow of contraband was more constricted, and the internal economy was more paultry and less affluent. The social status of "big shots" was expressed in their access to sardines.

The organization of inmate opportunities and entrepreneurial activities was more closely monitored and centrally controlled, and Harry Jackson and D. C. Pettit kept much closer tabs on inmate activities and managed the resources moving through the prison economy much more carefully than Harry Hulbert had done. In part this reflected the impact of the Depression upon the decentralized internal economy of the 1920s; shrinking resources had to be more carefully husbanded. But the tighter management also reflected the way

---

115. See, for example, testimony of James Buchannan, ibid., box 2, bk. 2, pointing to the heavy "doping" as being "in 1930 and 1931, when they were building that place and it was pretty open"; and of Ross Pascoe, box 2, bk. 7, maintaining that "at present time there isn't any dope traffic."

changes in patronage practices at the state level had altered these relations inside the prison. As far as I can tell, there were no "big shots" in the prison of the 1920s; the phenomenon seems to have been a new or in any case, a far more salient feature of the prison in the 1940s. It was clearly related to the growing role and significance of inmate clerks and office workers at SPSM, whose numbers grew with Depression-era cutbacks and wartime shortages of custodial and clerical staff and the general shrinkage of civilian employees that accompanied the collapse of industrial operations. These inmate clerks came to handle and mishandle much of the quotidian routine and paper traffic in the institution, and they were able, through these nodal points, to facilitate a much tighter, more centralized supervision of inmate activities. Many clerks were (or became) "big shots" themselves or were their loyal lieutenants. Their emergence as power brokers was the result of fierce, now invisible, power struggles among inmates, as they adapted the spaces of self-activity and the networks of power vouchsafed in the industrial prison to the new conditions of idleness and diminished opportunity. Those few who emerged on top of these reorganized power relations could, by virtue of their clout inside, make themselves useful to hard-pressed authorities. The "big shot" phenomenon was thus the product of a momentary conjuncture between the receding capacity of the warden to organize reward structures inside and the struggles among inmates to control the more limited opportunities of prison life. This created the conditions for a new collusive symbiosis of keeper and kept, in which the spaces of inmate self-activity steadily expanded and prisoners were able, in effect, to colonize the administration of the institution. As increasingly pivotal power brokers, the "big shots" at Jackson were thus the precise analogue of the "bosses" that appeared in Michigan politics in the same period; the Depression-era constriction of patronage opportunities set off scrambles for power that produced the "fixers," capable of centralizing control over the distribution of scarce resources and of turning these capacities into the practices that sustained patronage relations in straitened and changing circumstances.

Yet it would be misleading, despite appearances, to conclude that the cons really ran the joint. If we listen to the stories of the small-time operators, like inmate Weaver, we encounter a more complicated, multivalent struggle that was stamped by deep inequalities and highly stratified relations of power. What appeared to outsiders as collusion between custody and criminals seems to have been, for most prisoners, an ever-shifting, capricious zone of contestation, in which the everyday struggles to get by and make life agreeable grated against the formal rules and the venal demands of corrupt authorities, on the one hand, and against the accumulated privileges and the trip wires of informal power laid down by powerful inmate rings, on the other. Ordinary prisoners were caught in the double grip of official and unofficial power, whose collaboration, even interpenetration, was becoming ever deeper. We have no idea how voluntary their participation was or how much violence and intimidation was deployed to insure compliance, for, as custody retreated and inmate spaces expanded, the need for discretion and silence grew as well. Defiance was pointless—indeed, the collusion between Pettit and the "big shots" dissolved the distinctions between the official regime and oppositional practices and thus vitiated the grounds for meaningful resistance. It was in no one's interest to reveal how far the social order of the prison had come to rest upon the self-activity of inmates and the systematic corruption of custodial discipline. Instead, prisoners were positively encouraged to enter into activities that, in a formal sense, were oppositional, or counter-correctional, but were, in the blurred crossovers of Jackson prison, officially promoted. The rules that hemmed in individual inmates, shaping their prospects and aspirations, as well as the sanctions that disciplined and channeled their energies, were forged in an ever more overt collusion between prison "big shots" and corrupted officials, in which the real hidden transcript was the shared knowledge that the compliance of prisoners was purchased through an explicit criminalization of authority.

This growing gap between appearance and reality could not be concealed forever, and here we may observe, finally, the fatal weakness of this carceral regime. The expression that Harry Jackson and his compatriots typically used in defending their actions—"we kept the lid on"[116]—had a double meaning. On the one hand, it was a

---

116. This was the term used by Harry Jackson in his letter to the attorney general and by Charles Watson in testimony, 18 April 1945, box 1, file 13. Richard Riley, who was in charge of the gym, acknowledged in testimony (ibid.) that, while he might have been drunk at times, and often absent, allowing his inmate clerks to punch the clock for him: "What of it. The Prison is still here." And Jackson also maintained that, in spite of everything, "that place is going along pretty good over there" (testimony, 31 May 1945, box 2, bk. 26).

public boast that the peace and order of the institution had been maintained in the face of wartime shortages of staff and the widespread discontent of inmates, especially with parole procedures; on the other hand, it was a "private" affirmation of their determination to be discrete about how control was insured. In the rapidly changing external context of the 1940s, in which the patronage relations that had organized politics were being overturned or radically foreshortened, the continued operation of the internal system at Jackson prison required not only the silent understandings of mutual discretion but absolute secrecy as well. Indiscretions were not as easy to cover up or bury as they had been in the 1920s, and there was little room for mistakes; no publicity was admissible. To the degree that the "cons ran the joint," it became necessary that their masters adopt the "convict's code" of silence.

Yet here, obviously, Harry Jackson and D. C. Pettit were playing with fire. For prisoners—however much they might collaborate, however well the internal rewards guaranteed their cooperation—were ultimately unwilling colleagues, whose participation was not voluntary and whose main preoccupation was to get out. This, as we have seen, made the parole board extremely dangerous to the warden, because prisoners might, at any time, tell all in a bid for release. It also meant that Pettit had continually to add sweeteners to keep the "big shots" happy, while they, for their part, exercised powerful leverage over their masters and were able repeatedly to ratchet upward the terms of their cooperation. And it meant, finally, that the boundary between keeper and kept, and between noncriminal and criminal activity, became increasingly fuzzy. As standards of corrections on the outside changed, prescribing a more rigorous separation between prisoner and custodian, prison managers at Jackson came to rely more completely on the older, face-to-face modalities of patronage, promoting an ever denser interpenetration of keeper and kept. By almost any measure Pettit "went over" to the cons, in the sense that his mode of operation and even his style of life was more and more like that of his charges: he caroused with his "big shot" pals and knew their families; if we accept the circumstantial evidence that later emerged, his role in the Hooper murder was nothing less than criminal. The closer the collusion, moreover, the greater the risk of an explosion, for prisoners, especially those serving life terms, had less to lose in withdrawing cooperation than did Harry Jackson or D. C. Pettit. When

Joseph Medley walked away from the bank in Jackson and went on a murder spree, he was exercising his capacity not only for self-destruction but for bringing the big house down on his keepers' heads. When the ensuing investigation revealed the extent to which the fiction of compliance was maintained through the corruption of authority, the prison's capacity to produce usable delinquents evaporated, and the entire disciplinary project was called into question.

The Downfall of Harry Jackson

Medley's escape was the occasion, not the cause, of Harry Jackson's downfall. Nor can the crisis that overtook the warden in March 1945 be treated simply as an extension of departmental infighting. Heyns was candidly "looking for some kind of opening" to displace the warden, and Pascoe was almost certainly peddling stories of laxity and mismanagement in the press;[117] at one point the Corrections Commission had to order prison officials to cease their backbiting in public.[118] But it is not enough to monitor the pressures placed on Harry Jackson by his superiors and rivals in Lansing and to observe how he fell back on more and more unsavory practices to salvage his position—setting himself up for a decapitating blow. For, ultimately, what went on inside the prison rarely occasioned comment, let alone serious political fallout. What made the warden vulnerable and what gave political salience to conditions behind the walls were the changing terms of Republican politics outside. Indeed, it was the parallel and quite analogous collapse of Frank McKay's fortunes that forged the essential prerequisite for Harry Jackson's demise in 1945.

From the death of Frank Fitzgerald, his political ally and protector, in 1939, to his final ouster as party strongman, in 1944, Frank McKay was engaged in a long rear-guard action against reform currents within the Republican Party. The campaign against the "boss" was spearheaded by the radical, or ideological, right wing of the party

---

117. The tale that made the widest rounds was that of Chris Schumacher, a prisoner carried to Detroit in a prison car to promote a song he had written, called "Count the Stars in the Window," and afterward allowed to spend the weekend with his wife at home (*Detroit News* 18 February 1945; and retold 20 March 1945).

118. Minutes of the Corrections Committee, 16 February 1945; *Detroit News,* 18 February 1945. A summary of the "charges" leveled by Warden Jackson at the parole board and Pascoe's responses was assembled sometime in January 1945 for the Corrections Commission; this exchange was later reproduced in Noel Fox's *Survey,* 1949.

and led by former governor Wilbur Brucker. Their aim initially was to build a grassroots insurgency against Edward Barnard, the boss of Wayne County and McKay's principal ally in Detroit. By taking to the streets, ringing doorbells, leaving literature, and holding precinct meetings, they hoped to draw "the better sort" into political activity and, in Brucker's words, by "cleaning out the machine politics from their malignant control of Party affairs, make way for a new leadership."[119] Allied after 1942 with a grassroots anti-McKay group in Grand Rapids called the "Home Front,"[120] the campaign against "bossism" steadily expanded its leverage in party affairs, especially in organizational, financial, and platform committees and on the state Central Committee; it succeeded in electing a national committeewoman allied to Brucker, in reorganizing the Wayne County caucus to undercut Barnard's machine, in redirecting control of campaign financing from the national committee (controlled by McKay) to an independent party finance chairman, and in electing to that position a Flint auto dealer and reform ally, Arthur Summerfield. Perhaps its most visible triumph came in 1942, with the ouster of state party chairman, Les Butler, "that stooge of the McKay-Barnard-McKeighan crowd," in favor of John Dethmers, an outstate Republican from Holland with a reputation for neutrality.[121]

The rapid advance of reform within the party must, of course, be seen in its larger, political context. Roosevelt's reelection for a third term in 1940 not only appeared to give the Democrats a permanent lock on the White House but brought them back to power in Lansing as well. This double defeat gave Republican insurgents such as Brucker and the Home Front a convincing case for an internal purge of the party. The call for a resolute, no-nonsense attack on "bossism" made political sense in 1941–42; the Van Wagoner administration was

---

119. Brucker to E. F. Steffan, 12 March 1942, Brucker Papers, box 3.

120. The best sources are interviews with principals, Dorothy Judd and Willard VerMeulen (Gerald R. Ford Library). Ford's father was associated with the "Home Front" group; aside from McKay, one of their main targets was Congressman Bartel Jonckman, whom young Gerald Ford unseated in 1948 (interview with Stanton Todd, another activist in the group, April 1985).

121. These efforts are more fully described in SFRC, *The Transformation of Michigan Politics*, 41–50. The quote is from Brucker, to Ray Young, 14 February 1942, Brucker Papers, box 3; see also correspondence with Walter Greis, 14 May 1941, John Dethmers, 8 October 1941; and various newspaper clippings in box 3. See also *Grand Rapids Press*, 18 December 1943.

itself a patronage hungry (but clearly Democratic) machine, and Republicans could plausibly contend that a thorough housecleaning of their own ranks would enable them to paint the Democrats with the brush of corruption and offer Republicans as the champions in the favorite slogan of the day, "of good clean government."[122] Not surprisingly, the campaign against McKay went into high gear during 1941–42.

The return of Republicans to power in Lansing in 1943 made the radicals' campaign for a party purge more problematic. But Brucker did not let up. When a grand jury (with Kim Sigler as special prosecutor) was impaneled in 1943 to investigate bribery in the state legislature, reformers found new reasons to insist that the party extract itself from the pervasive aura of corruption and called for the selection of a national committeeman who "stands against bossism, for good clean government, and who, in his official capacity, would fight for the elimination of any McKayism in the state government."[123] McKay, in turn, refused to budge. He was determined not to step aside, he told Vandenberg,[124] dismissing the attack on him as an "elite conspiracy" put up by a "meager handful of Wayne County moneybags."[125] To demonstrate the extent of his support in the party, he stood for reelection as national committeeman in 1944.

This deepening, seemingly unbridgeable polarization within the party alarmed many regulars. McKay may have been a growing embarrassment, but for many Brucker was a wrecker, who threatened to destroy the party in his effort to reform it. These more moderate elements constituted an emergent third current in the party, which found a leader in Governor Harry Kelly (elected in 1942 and reelected in 1944). A protégé of Frank Fitzgerald, Kelly had gotten his start in politics as the Detroit manager of the Liquor Control Commission and then been picked by the party bosses as secretary of state;[126] he was of Irish-Catholic background and had little in common with the Grosse

---

122. See exchange of letters, Brucker and Hale Brake, 31 December 1941 and 4 January 1942, Brucker Papers, box 3.

123. Statement by Henry Sheldon, *Grand Rapids Press*, 13 January 1944.

124. This in response to Vandenberg's suggestion that he "do the big thing" and retire (Vandenberg to McKay, 27 February 1944, and exchange of letters, 17 and 20 April 1944, McKay Papers, box 1).

125. McKay interview, *Grand Rapids Herald*, 19 March 1944.

126. Biographical material on Kelly is hard to come by. This is drawn from the *Ann Arbor News*, 26 June 1954.

Pointe "club." As a world war veteran who had lost a leg in France, he enjoyed a wide following in VFW posts around the state and thus had the basis of an independent statewide network. Though originally a patronage placeman, Kelly was neither a close friend of McKay nor a zealous champion of reform, and, as governor, his natural instincts were to contain factional infighting in the party and bend the rival currents to his leadership. With appeals to party unity, Kelly moved in 1943–44 to arrest the polarization by rejuvenating the middle ground of moderate reformism that Fitzgerald had originally culti- vated. Brucker resisted his efforts, claiming that appeals to harmony provided a screen behind which McKay could regroup his forces: "It is simply impossible to have harmony without letting that gang con- trol everything."[127] But Kelly's position was a distinct one; as his ally, U.S. Senator Homer Ferguson, put it, in calling for McKay's retire- ment, "I am not a reformer, but I stand for good clean government and I don't see how you can have that with McKay."[128]

During 1944, in the run-up to the national convention and fall elections, Kelly moved decisively and with considerable finesse to resolve the infighting and establish his personal control over the party.[129] On the eve of county conventions the governor called pub- licly for McKay's removal; then, at the district and county conven- tions in Wayne County, he turned around and aligned himself with McKay's old allies and cronies against the reform candidates of Brucker's Precinct Organization. By thus insuring that neither side held sway in the state convention or on the delegation sent to the national conclave in Chicago, Kelly emerged in control of both. McKay lost his bid for reelection as national committeeman by a nar- row margin—a vote made even narrower by Kelly's maneuvers to cancel out the rival factions. It is clear that many of McKay's enemies

127. Letter to Ray Young, 19 March 1942, Brucker Papers, box 3.
128. *Grand Rapids Press*, 16 February 1944.
129. The ground for these maneuvers was extremely complex: in March eighty- three counties, along with the five congressional districts in Wayne County, held con- ventions to elect twelve hundred delegates to the state convention. In April, before this convention met, delegates formed into caucuses for the seventeen Michigan congres- sional districts, and each selected two delegates to the national Republican Convention in Chicago that summer; these thirty-four delegates were then joined by seven mem- bers-at-large, appointed by the governor, to elect the national committeeman and committeewoman. Essentially, Kelly sought to control both the national delegation and the state convention. The details are developed in SFRC, *The Transformation of Michigan Politics*, 41–50; and, more generally, in Sarasohn, *Political Party Patterns*, 36–37.

in outstate counties, who had no connection with the Detroit reform movement or distrusted its elitist leadership, rallied to the governor's centrist position, but it is also apparent that many old cronies and beneficiaries of McKay's favor found in Kelly's middle ground a way to hedge their bets and abandon the old boss gracefully, in the name of party unity and without going over to his enemies in the reform movement. At the same time, reformers were put on notice not to embitter the air needlessly or to press the fight to open civil war.[130] By deftly breaking McKay's hold on the party organization while denying Brucker the fruits of victory, Kelly restored the current of moderate reformism to dominance in the state Republican Party.

Kelly's intervention was apparently in service of his own national ambitions. He was among a group of state governors vying for leadership roles in the party on the basis of what might be called "constructive engagement" with the New Deal, and he seems to have hoped that, if a Republican won in 1944, he might be in line for a Cabinet appointment or, should Vandenberg move up, to a Senate seat.[131] But the effect of his intervention and the elimination of McKay was to shift the center of gravity within the state Republican Party and to reset the stage of state politics. In the fall, when the Dewey ticket went down to defeat, Kelly found the door of personal advancement effectively closed, and, while he himself easily won reelection, his political future seemed in doubt. Would-be heirs, looking ahead to 1946 or 1948, began jockeying for position. By the spring of 1945 rumors were abroad that Kelly would retire in 1946,[132] and, when in July the governor announced that he would be stepping down, a "free-for-all" ensued.[133] The scramble of the epigoni was chaotic because, with McKay's machine now in total disarray, they were all would-be captains without armies or organizational bases. As relative newcomers without deep support, they quickly came to rely on press exposure and media images to make headway. It did not take long for

---

130. See *Detroit Free Press*, 12, 20 and 21 March and 20 April 1944; *Grand Rapids Press*, 9, 20, and 21 March 1944.

131. To insure this latter prospect, Kelly engineered the downfall of his lieutenant governor, Eugene Keyes, at the state convention in April 1944. By persuading the auditor general, Vernon Brown, to accept the second spot, Kelly made sure that, if Vandenberg took Cabinet office and he resigned his governorship, a close ally would be in the line of succession to appoint him to Vandenberg's Senate seat.

132. See, for example, *Ann Arbor News*, 5 and 12 May 1945.

133. *Detroit Free Press*, 13 July 1945.

them to notice that denouncing the "bosses" and exposing their corruption was an effective way of gaining notoriety.

The leading contenders for party leadership, John Dethmers and Kim Sigler, both made their names and a case for their elevation to higher officer during 1945 by appearing in the media as exposers of scandal and scourges of corruption. Of the two Dethmers was closer to the moderate center of the party, a former state chairman who had responded to Kelly's mediation efforts in 1944 and taken a place on his ticket as attorney general. He was taciturn, upright, and sober—the polar opposite of the dapper, talkative, and flamboyant Kim Sigler, who had built a base for himself as the special prosecutor leading the grand jury inquiry into legislative corruption. Highly ambitious, careless of details, but adroit in the pursuit of the main chance, Sigler had managed, by the fall of 1944, to put dozens of lawmakers under indictment and to win favorable press attention as "Sir Kim," the white knight of "good, clean government."

> You have no conception [he wrote a friend] of the extent to which graft has run rampant in the legislative halls, the various departments of government within our state government, and elsewhere within our state's life as it has been centered here in Lansing.[134]

In the middle of it all he saw Frank McKay:

> You spoke of Frank McKay and some of the other "big shots." Don't worry, Old Top, I have my heavy artillery constantly trained on it, and some of these days, I expect to blow them out of the water. It may take some time and there may be a number of other indictments in the meantime, but you can rest assured that I am going to give them all I've got, and the funny thing about it . . . is that they all know it.[135]

His single-minded crusade was inspired, in part, by the belief that, if he could put Frank McKay behind bars, he could put himself in the governor's chair or even, following Dewey's "gang-busting" trajec-

---

134. Sigler to William Cook, 24 January 1944, William and Marshall Cook Papers, box 5, MHC, Ann Arbor.

135. Sigler to Cook, 9 May 1944, ibid.

tory, on the road to the White House.[136] Thus nearly a decade after Frank Murphy first made "McKayism" a centerpiece of political sloganeering and in the same months that Kelly shattered the remnants of McKay's party machine, Kim Sigler began to beat the same, now nearly dead, horse. In December 1944, just as Dethmers won office as attorney general, Sigler secured indictments against McKay and several others for buying legislators' votes in an effort to block the installation of "totalizers," which computed betting odds at Detroit racetracks. It was this case that, according to Sigler, was wrecked a few weeks later when Senator Hooper was murdered on the highway to Albion. As the special prosecutor stepped before news reporters with these sensational revelations (which some lawyers felt violated the secrecy of the grand jury), the attorney general stepped into the growing limelight of scandal at Jackson prison and took charge of that investigation. Over the next several months, as Sigler hounded McKay and Dethmers pursued Harry Jackson, the two competed for headlines and hurled charges at each other in what was, for all practical purposes, the opening salvo of the 1946 gubernatorial race.

At the time what attracted most attention were the tantalizing suggestions of a link between the scandals at Jackson and the murder of Senator Warren Hooper in January 1945. Hooper himself was a person of little consequence, a petty grafter who had taken money from any number of shady associates. A native of California, who had played the stock market and lost everything in the crash, he had abandoned his first wife and taken up journalism. Bouncing from job to job before landing a position with the *Albion Evening Recorder*, he married a local music teacher and, losing his job at the paper, used her money to buy a service station. In 1938, drawing on business connections, he ran for the state legislature, winning, some believed, because he shared a surname with a popular senator from a neighboring district. Once elected he sold his gas station and tried to live on the three-dollar per diem he got when the legislature was in session. He was more than usually susceptible to money offerings from interested parties.[137] And it was only his standing as a state senator that gave his killing some sensational zest. In fact, what lifted it from the footnotes was the combined significance lent to his murder by Kim

---

136. Sigler's ambitions are discussed at length in Rubenstein and Ziewacz, *Three Bullets.*

137. Ibid., 15–16.

Sigler's investigation of political corruption and John Dethmers's probe into the affairs of Jackson prison—and the fact that these two men happened to be rivals for the gubernatorial nomination of the Republican Party. Both men used the Hooper case for their own purposes, although this did not result in a solution to Hooper's murder, which remains a mystery to this day.

It is fairly clear,[138] and was apparent to investigators at the time, that the murder was engineered by the Purple Gang in Detroit, booze dealers during Prohibition and deeply involved in illegal gambling during the 1930s. Two ex-convicts, Sam Abramowitz and Henry Luks, admitted under grant of immunity that they had been approached by other gangsters with a contract to kill Hooper but had backed out after "casing" the job and finding the problems of "setup" and escape too complex; they identified Purple Gang big shots Harry and Sam Fleisher, along with Mike Selig and Pete Mahoney, as the ones who propositioned them. When Sigler's grand jury brought charges against these four for conspiring to commit the murder, they denied everything and accused Abramowitz and Luks of the killing. The trial in the summer of 1945 turned on these charges and counter-charges. But what seems more likely to have happened is that the Fleisher brothers tried to get Abramowitz and Luks to do the hit and, when they backed out, considered doing it themselves but, feeling conspicuous out in the rural reaches of Calhoun and Jackson Counties or fearing that gang operations in Detroit might be disrupted if they were arrested, took the matter to gang leaders Ray Bernstein and Philip Keywell, imprisoned at Jackson since 1931. Much circumstantial evidence suggests that the latter two arranged an outside detail and, using two automobiles (one of which may have been D. C. Pettit's red roadster), and a gun smuggled into the prison from O'Larry's Bar in Detroit, drove up the road to the junction with M-99, shot Hooper, and returned to prison with the best alibi in the world.

Were Harry Jackson or his deputy, D. C. Pettit, involved? There was never proof, and the evidence remained sketchy and contradictory. But for Dethmers it was only necessary to hint at a connection between the murder and the prison to seal his contention that outside details constituted a scandalous malpractice in prison administration and a demonstrable danger to the public. For Kim Sigler, on the other

---

138. Based on Rubenstein and Ziewacz's plausible account (ibid.).

hand, the problems posed by the Hooper case were more complex. The special prosecutor was not interested in the prison scandal, except insofar as it gave Dethmers the spotlight and competed for headlines with his own investigations. His aim was always to prove that Frank McKay, the main target of his elaborate probe, had instigated the killing. Again the chains of association were highly circumstantial and never proved. First, Sigler claimed that Hooper was the key witness against McKay. It was never revealed precisely what Sigler expected Hooper to say on the stand, and not a few critics pointed out that the Purple Gang had reasons, independent of McKay, to be interested in gambling legislation concerning Detroit racetracks. If, as was very likely, Hooper himself had taken bribes and faced criminal prosecution, he might easily have been induced, under grant of immunity, to make—or invent—corrupt connections with McKay, whom everyone knew was Sigler's main target. Informed observers understood that "Hooper, admittedly . . . a bribes craftsman . . . having been cornered, was quick to see that his one way out was to involve some 'big name' man, known through connection with public affairs."[139] Thus when Hooper was murdered, Sigler instantly concluded that McKay, fearing Hooper's testimony, had put up the money for the hit; again, he needed someone to "finger" his man. It was for this reason, some have argued,[140] that Sigler refused to follow the many leads pointing to Bernstein and Keywell in Jackson prison and focused, instead, upon the Fleisher brothers. Hardened criminals already serving life sentences were not likely to reveal any links to McKay under prosecutorial threats from Sigler, whereas hoodlums on the street could be hounded with the specter of imprisonment to reveal, or make, the connection to McKay that Sigler wanted. Thus he charged the four gangsters in Detroit with "conspiracy" to commit the Hooper murder, and, when this did not produce revelations, he added further charges of robbery against them, piling up the prospect of interminable incarceration.

As he pursued McKay, Sigler kept a weather eye on Dethmers's investigation, less for the material it was generating than for the publicity it was bringing his rival. The two men studiously avoided helping each another: Dethmers refused to explore connections be-

---

139. This point was made by the *Lansing State Digest*, 20 June 1945.
140. This is one of the main contention of Rubenstein and Ziewacz's book *Three Bullets*.

tween Harry Jackson and Frank McKay, though there were several suggestive possibilities, nor did he go further into D. C. Pettit's relations with Bernstein and Keywell, despite numerous (admittedly contradictory) rumors circulating among (admittedly unreliable) prisoners that Pettit's roadster had been the getaway car; for his part Sigler refused to follow the many, strong leads in the Hooper killing that pointed to Bernstein and Keywell, lest he lose his chance to implicate McKay and add richness to the scandal at Jackson that Dethmers was already mining. In July the two collided head-on. Sigler was furious when Dethmers released his report on the prison; he was convinced that the attorney general's gratuitous but public suggestion that Hooper's murderers were already prisoners at Jackson not only undercut his case against the four gangsters for conspiracy but also spoiled his chance of implicating McKay. In a rage Sigler subpoenaed the attorney general to appear at the trial, and in a moment of high drama the public was entertained by the spectacle of the two rivals yelling at each other.

> [Sigler] "Didn't it occur to you that the statement in the press that the Hooper murder may have been committed by someone in that prison might take the heat off the four defendants?
> "No, and I don't think so now.
> "Didn't it occur to you that by distributing that picture of Henry Luks, one of the state's top witnesses, in the company of murderers and rapists, you would be doing the people of Michigan irreparable harm?
> "No."[141]

Sigler's main concern was to discredit Dethmers, not to debate his findings. One sharp exchange in the courtroom signaled the political stakes involved and the understanding both protagonists had of the new style of media combat:

> *Sigler:* "Didn't you release the prison scandal reports in installments in order to spread the publicity out over a longer period?"

---

141. From the transcripts, as quoted in ibid., 131.

Dethmers: "No, if I were going to spread it out, I could have released it weeks apart and got more publicity."[142]

In a statement to the bench after Dethmers left, Sigler made a tortured summary of associations:

Your Honor, I submit that when the attorney general uses the press for an opening campaign statement, it is pretty bad. . . . If anything happens to this case as far as the People are concerned, no one but Dethmers will be to blame. Dethmers was the leading light in the Republican party when Frank D. McKay was boss. Jackson Prison has been rotten for years, but it wasn't until . . . your humble servant got close to them that they did anything. Then this attorney general—this former bedfellow of Frank D. McKay—got busy. It is ridiculous for him to say that his report has to be issued at this time. Politicians like him want to see [my] grand jury fail, but it will not. In September we are going to do our best to put that crooked political boss McKay where he belongs.[143]

Over the next six months the political struggle escalated. Dethmers won praise for the care and skill with which he built the state's case against Harry Jackson and maintained it against an inevitable round of appeals, but Sigler proved more adroit at keeping his name in the headlines, milking each new revelation for its sinister possibilities while promising yet more sensations to come. As a producer of news, Sigler simply outclassed Dethmers. But he also seemed oblivious of the political enemies he was making. Loyalists of Governor Kelly were offended by his wild swings, especially his habit of seeing "a bedfellow of Frank McKay" in every political opponent, and party regulars were alarmed by his broadening attacks on political insiders, the "Lansing clique," which included, at least by implication, everyone in elective office. As moderate forces in the Republican Party coalesced to protect Dethmers and derail Sigler's investigation, Judge John Simpson suddenly and quite unexpectedly dismissed Sigler's much-publicized case against Frank McKay on the grounds

---

142. Ibid.
143. Ibid., 131–32.

that "in the entire evidence presented in the case there is no testimony that the defendants did one single criminal act as we know the term."[144] There was no case. Republican leaders in the legislature immediately launched an investigation into the rather large expense accounts Sigler's office had run up during its pursuit of McKay. In the face of adverse publicity Judge Louis Coash, who had succeeded Leland Carr as the one-man presiding officer of the special grand jury, closed down the special prosecutor's investigation. Sigler was out of a job, and with enough of a cloud over his head to cast a shadow on his gleaming reputation as the scourge of corruption. But, like a true performer, Sigler saw the dramatic possibilities of the moment; muttering that the unseen hand of Frank McKay was at work, he went before a news conference and announced that he was running for governor to "clean up the whole smelly mess."[145] His response to setback was to turn the tables and expand the crusade.

Scandal and Reform: Words and Practices

Early in 1946 the main beneficiaries of McKay's downfall collided head-on. Both factions battling for control of the party had long and well-established anti-McKay credentials, with Sigler finding support among the more "radical" reformers around Brucker and the Home Front and Dethmers drawing his support from the centrist current of moderate reformism around Governor Kelly and party regulars. As the lines of debate within the Republican Party shifted toward a more ideological delineation of positions, between an implacable hostility to the New Deal and a constructive engagement with its legacy, the factions dividing the party along new cleavages now converged to render the old guard irrelevant. In their combined, but uneven, assaults on Frank McKay and Harry Jackson, the scourges of corruption enunciated, by implication as well as intention, new standards of behavior and a new language of politics. As this "reform world" congealed, it produced a rapid shift in the definitions of corruption, recasting old practices in new contexts and displacing those who had once commanded respect and attention. This was not only a redefini-

---

144. *Grand Rapids Herald*, 15 February 1946.
145. *Detroit News*, 17 March 1946.

tion of rules or a shift in practices; the field of power was itself recon-figured.

Thus repositioned, Harry Jackson was easily picked off. The net-work of connections and associations that had enveloped and pro-tected him dissolved, leaving him isolated. As the internal order of his prison fell increasingly out of sync with the evolving language and relations of power in the state, scandal could be made of everyday operations, because the warden could be detached from his context, from the world he had made and that had made him, and his actions could be re-presented as outmoded and corrupt within a political arena that was itself being rapidly remade. Scandal arose from—indeed was made possible by—the gaps that opened up between the rhetorical world of state politics and the internal order of the main state prison. The continuum of practices that had once linked the prison to its political environment was ruptured; the narrative of industrial redemption that had once provided a coherent account of carceral practices and their relationship to socially desirable goals no longer carried conviction. As power relations shifted on him, Harry Jackson became, as it were, unconnected. When he appeared before the Civil Service Commission, which reviewed, and subsequently upheld, his dismissal,[146] he found no one was listening to him; tried-and-true phrases echoed back, and everything he said was turned against him. State investigators carefully laid out the official guide-lines and procedures that marked the warden's deviations and, in rehearsing their findings against him, explicitly refused any connec-tion between his internal regime at the prison and official policy or professional practices. His superiors disowned him; his colleagues abandoned him; no politician stepped up to defend him. The warden was denied avenues of excuse or blame; he was rendered, quite liter-ally, speechless.

Unable to refute the evidence against their client, Harry Jackson's lawyers sought instead to destroy the credibility of inmate wit-nesses—to show that they were nothing but "an array of sexual psy-

---

146. Civil Service Commission, Michigan Corrections Commission vs. Harry Jack-son, box 10, at the State Archives. The hearings, which paraded out many of the witnesses interviewed the previous year, received a lot of press coverage. See *Detroit News* 23 March, 6, 9, 12, 13, 20, 23, 26, and 27 April 1946; the *Ann Arbor News* gave the story extensive coverage over the same period. Final rulings were made on 7 May 1946. See *Detroit News* of that day; *Ann Arbor News*, 8 May 1946.

chopaths, degenerates, syphilitics, and egocentric men whom the warden had punished" and who were now seeking their revenge. Prisoners called to the stand and subjected to a hostile review of their criminal careers and character tried to defend themselves by maligning the warden, and they wound up confirming the state's case against him. Scandal turned worlds inside upside down. For the most damning charge against Harry Jackson's regime was always that the keepers had become, in practice, no different from the kept. They had stolen from and depended on one another, in a mutually corrupting relationship that had sustained institutional order and organized life inside. Now, on the witness stand, denials by both inmates and the warden drove a wedge between these erstwhile collaborators, forcing them into positions where they had no choice but to attack each other. In the process all the tacit arrangements and silent undertakings that had tempered antagonisms and soothed anger were ripped apart, and the essential hostility between those with the keys and those locked up was laid bare. This estrangement within the prison between keeper and kept was the product of scandal, not its cause, and it was upon this gap, or rupture, inside that the foundations of a reform regime had to be laid in the wake of Harry Jackson's downfall.

The scandal of 1945 was not produced by a shift in practices alone. To be sure, the attempt to abolish patronage relations in state politics during the late 1930s enforced a shift in practices on down the line. When Harry Jackson resisted these changes, mobilizing, as it were, the last possibilities of a patronage regime behind the walls, he had to be eliminated if reform penology was to become politically viable in state administration. In this sense Jackson's dismissal broke up one of the last vestiges of patronage politics in the state. Yet in a larger sense the warden's downfall was occasioned by a crisis of meaning as well as practices. The collapse of industrial penology in the Depression snapped the sentences that had been spun around the carceral project in the 1920s. There was no longer a coherent account of what prisons were doing, to whom, or with what effect by the early 1940s—only a variety of essays, formulations of words, that collided with, and contradicted one another. As a reform regime took shape in Lansing and found its ideological voice in Ross Pascoe, it could not easily overturn Harry Jackson's operation, not only because the warden dug in behind the walls and civil service protection but also because the iterations of a reform penology did not, in fact, explain what was being done inside Jackson prison, nor did it elaborate a fully convincing program for the control and reformation of prisoners. Conversely, Harry Jackson's answers to his superiors in the early 1940s still sounded like superior wisdom, or at least the voice of experience. It took a more multifaceted shift in power relations to displace Harry Jackson and to silence his line in penology. Even then, in 1945, nothing definitive was solved. The new order at the prison had to overhaul the old warden's internal control regime, but it had also to attach convincingly its new practices inside with a public account of what incarceration was for and what results were being produced by it, for the new penology to fully cohere. This took eight years, and a major riot, to accomplish.

Chapter 4

Uniform Discipline and Individual Treatment: The New Model of Corrections and the Jackson Riot of 1952

Early in the evening of Sunday, 20 April 1952, a young inmate on the fourth gallery of 15 Block persuaded a rookie guard of the same age to open his cell door after final lockdown. He said he wanted to pass a shoe box to a prisoner in another cell. The shoe box concealed a knife. Quickly overpowered and relieved of his keys, the guard was locked in the opened cell, and the prisoner proceeded to release two older inmates whom he idolized, Earl Ward and "Crazy" Jack Hyatt. Slipping down the narrow stairway to the ground floor, these three made hostages of the other guards on duty in the building (one got away) and then released 185 prisoners. Unsure what to do next, everyone milled about in the hallways and galleries, whooping and yelling, breaking furniture and toilets, and unhinging cell doors. There were several rapes (the newspapers spoke of "sex orgies"), and some old scores were settled in savage beatings. Throughout the night sounds of defiant rejoicing and aimless pleasures drifted through the institution.[1]

---

1. The fullest account of the 1952 riot is provided by John Bartlow Martin, *Break Down the Walls* (New York: Ballantine Books, 1954), chap. 8. This is largely based on contemporary news accounts and a long report in the *Saturday Evening Post*, 6 June 1953. Vernon Fox provided his rendition of events in a memoir, *Violence behind Bars* (New York: Vantage Press, 1956), 86–144.

Archival material, including a Governor's Special Commission of Investigation Report and a full investigation by the attorney general's office, are to be found in the G. Mennen Williams Papers, box 83, MHC, Ann Arbor; and in the Attorney General, Criminal Law, Investigations of SPSM, boxes 5–6, at the State Archives, Lansing,

Already the most serious crisis of custodial control in the prison's history, the insurrection proved especially dangerous because, in the late 1940s, 15 Block had been made over into the segregation, or disciplinary, unit. The building was set apart in the yard, which insured maximum security but also made it possible, once the prisoners had gained control of the block, to fortify and defend it. Behind the barricades were some of the most dangerous inmates in the Michigan system—institutional misfits and rebels, "psychopaths" and "crazies," killers and hardened "lifers" who had little to lose in defying authority. Also housed in this unit were those in need of special protection, youngsters and homosexuals, who might be preyed upon, along with stool pigeons and sex offenders, who might be targets of reprisal. Quite a few inmates who were released that evening were already serving life sentences without hope of parole (the maximum penalty allowed under state law), and there was no fate worse than segregation in the punishment cells of 15 Block to intimidate them. Now they were loose and armed, and they held four hostages.

None of the officials at Jackson prison had ever faced a situation like this. The warden, Julian Frisbie, had been appointed in 1948, straight from a career in the Marine Corps, where he had once had charge of the Naval Disciplinary Barracks at Portsmouth, New Hampshire, responsible for AWOLs and other insubordinates. Neither he nor his immediate superior in Lansing, Corrections Commissioner Earnest Brooks, had any idea how to quell a riot: "I didn't know what

---

Michigan. Additional information about the course of events in the riot is to be found in the Department of Corrections, Bureau of Correctional Facilities, SPSM, box 1, at the State Archives; and in the Donald Leonard Papers, box 19 (Jackson Prisons Riot, 1952), at the MHC, Ann Arbor, which includes a blow-by-blow of state police operations during the riot. The press was allowed ready access to the prison during the riot; several reporters talked with inmate leaders in 15 Block, and there were regular briefings and many informal discussions with prison authorities during the four-day stalemate. As a result, press reports were remarkably full, and a review of archival material reveals little in the way of a "secret," or "untold," side of the story. The most serious gap in information pertained to the condition of the hostages being held (a maximum of thirteen at the height of the riot); the warden sought to keep the press from talking with hostages who were released, whether to avoid alarming the families of those officers still in captivity or to prevent word from getting out that the hostages were, in fact, being well treated and protected by the inmates in 15 Block. See, for example, the taped interviews with released hostages, in Department of Corrections, Bureau of Correctional Facilities, SPSM, box 1, file 12, which apparently were never made public.

to do."[2] Of his two key deputies, George Bacon, the deputy warden for custody and a twenty-year veteran of the guard force, was the most experienced, but he had no contingency plan in place and no riot squad available to intervene in the first confused hours of the upheaval. When the night shift came on, he had a double compliment of guards with which to seal off 15 Block, but he was apparently most concerned about the danger of a mass breakout and devoted his attention to cauterizing the revolt and keeping the inmates bottled up inside 15 Block. His opposite number, Vernon Fox, deputy warden for the new department of individual treatment, was a thirty-six-year-old sociology Ph.D., committed to a psychological approach to corrections that relied more upon counseling than custody. He was inclined to negotiate an end to the insurrection but had no personal knowledge of the insurgents in 15 Block, because counselors had been barred from the segregation unit on Bacon's orders.

Earl Ward and "Crazy" Jack Hyatt were certainly well-known to these officials, at least by reputation; two years before, at Marquette, Hyatt had joined with another inmate, Ralph Sterns, in a bold attempt to kidnap Governor G. Mennen Williams as he toured the prison dining hall and to use him as a shield for escape. Ward, whose psychological profile warned that he was an "impulsive opportunist," had not been party to the plan, but he had readily joined in the fray, urging other inmates to rise up and give the escapees cover. The break had been foiled by the governor's bodyguard, who (quite against regulations) had carried his revolver into the institution. Recaptured, Sterns, Hyatt, and Ward were all transferred to Jackson.[3] It was thus hardly surprising that Bacon smelled an escape plot in the melee in 15 Block or that none of the officials sitting around in the warden's office that evening saw much hope of talking these rebels into an early or peaceful submission.

There was, in fact, no plan to escape—no plan for anything. The insurrection was genuinely spontaneous. After several hours a kind of improvised order began to emerge in 15 Block. From the accounts

---

2. Quoted in Martin, *Break Down the Walls*, 88. Frisbie was a very direct, honest man with little political guile. He followed orders and expected others to do the same; his testimony (Attorney General Investigations, 1952, box 6) was refreshingly candid.

3. Sterns, who had also masterminded the attempted escape from Marquette in 1939, in which the warden and parole board were kidnapped, sat out the 1952 riot at Jackson in his cell, refusing to take part in actions that would not, so far as he could see, lead to his own escape.

of both prisoners and hostages it was Earl Ward, a twenty-eight-year-old serving fifteen to thirty years for armed robbery, who emerged as a key figure, the "natural" leader, of the rebellion. The press referred to Ward as a "dangerous psychopath," an "inadequate personality" with an "exaggerated ego."[4] His prison file spoke of "emotional blunting" as a child, and he does seem to have had an exceptionally cruel father; scrappy and quick to fight, he had been repeatedly in trouble with the law as a child, though never for anything more serious than petty vandalism and joyriding. He seems to have gained his reputation as a "misfit" from reports of juvenile authorities that he was a "loner" who "befriended Negroes." But, before he held up a real estate office with a gun in 1949, his most serious crime was to pose as a physician in order to get a job as a hotel doctor. He never killed or seriously hurt anyone—at least not for the record—and his behavior during the riot of 1952 would tend to belie a diagnosis of "dangerous" or "unstable."

With the help of one or two comrades, Ward managed to lock up some of the more dangerous inmates in 15 Block and to curtail the activities of wolfpacks set loose by the takeover. He made Jack Hyatt responsible for the hostages, a clever move that immeasurably increased their security, since no prisoner was about to challenge this highly unstable man of large reputation, whose nickname, "Crazy," was, it seems, richly deserved. Ward established himself in a small corner office on the ground floor, and from this "command post" he carried on conversations with the warden and his deputies by telephone and through a window that opened onto the yard. As he moved to create a semblance of order inside, moreover, he began to formulate inmate demands and give the insurrection some focus. "They had no more idea what the hell they wanted than flying in the air," he said later. "I was six or eight hours with some of the leaders trying to see why the hell they were doing it. They couldn't think of anything."[5] This personal detachment, the assumption of leadership by default, proved characteristic of Ward's conduct throughout the affair, and, while initial negotiations proved very confused, both Frisbie and Commissioner Brooks, arriving from Lansing, began to sense

---

4. See John Bartlow Martin's long biography of Ward, based on prison files and press reports (*Break Down the Walls*, 70–78).

5. Ibid., 83.

that, with Ward in charge inside, there was some hope for a peaceful solution.

Just as Ward was establishing some control in 15 Block, however, Frisbie lost it in the rest of the prison. The warden was also seeking to assert a semblance of order, and, throughout the first night of the insurrection in 15 Block, he debated with Deputy Bacon over what to do about breakfast on Monday morning. Should they treat the events in 15 Block as an isolated incident and feed the general population in mess hall as usual, or should they keep the whole prison on lock-down and feed inmates in their cells. The latter option promised to be a laborious undertaking, likely to take much of the morning and to cause widespread discontent, perhaps additional trouble. In the end Frisbie decided to take what he later called "a calculated risk" in the name of normalcy and marched his charges to breakfast. The north side—twenty-five hundred prisoners—moved smoothly through the chow line, ate, and returned to their cells without incident. As the cell blocks on the south side lined up, however, trouble began. In a mysterious act of provocation that no one was ever able to explain, someone put salt in the coffee. At one of the tables someone yelled, "Arsenic." Plates, trays, and uneaten food flew through the air; six hundred prisoners surged through the kitchen onto the yard; others waiting in line joined them. "They came out of the blocks like kids pouring out of a schoolhouse on a nice day," Frisbie recalled, "whooping, throwing their caps in the air."[6] Outnumbered and unarmed, the guards retreated. The warden had precipitated a general insurrection.

All that day prisoners had the run of the place: they seized knives and cleavers in the kitchen, smashed up the laundry, burned the library and the chapel, and plundered the commissary. Whole quarters of beef were hauled into the yard and roasted on bonfires in a continuous, impromptu barbecue, while enough canned food and processed meat to withstand weeks of siege was carried over to 15 Block and passed in through the windows. Eight more guards were taken hostage and turned over to Ward's custody. Yet, interestingly, though no one bothered afterward to ask why, the insurgents inside 15 Block never took down their barricades and joined the general insurrection. There was no attempt to take over the whole prison, although inmates in the general population were clearly prepared to

---

6. Quoted in ibid., 13.

support the garrison in 15 Block. In the late afternoon units of the state police were deployed to sweep the yard; using tear gas and live ammunition, they drove hundreds of inmates back inside the cell blocks, where they could be locked up again. One prisoner was killed and dozens injured in the melee, but during the night, as rain began to fall, the custodians regained control of the institution. The general riot was over.[7] The main prison lay in shambles, the cell blocks knee-deep in debris and water running from broken toilets, the service facilities wrecked or burned. And the insurgents in 15 Block now had twelve hostages and plenty of food; all hope of starving them out had evaporated, and the likely stakes in human life, should the warden decide to storm the barricades, had been grimly raised.

Donald Leonard, the chief of state police, was not ready on Monday night for an assault on 15 Block; he needed time to prepare, and, meanwhile, he told Frisbie and Fox, "maybe this can be settled by conference."[8] Fox was only too ready to try. All during the general riot on Monday, while guards had withdrawn to the walls and roof-tops awaiting the deployment of the state police, Fox had moved boldly among the prisoners on the yard, speaking to the ones he knew by name and trying to persuade the more "passive, follower-types" to abandon the riot and return to their cells. He wrote later that his intention had been to "establish face-to-face relationships with the men on the fringes" and to show them all that he "wasn't afraid of anything."[9] Undoubtedly he relished the fact that he, a counselor, could go where guards now feared to tread, and he baldly ignored signals from Deputy Bacon, worried about more hostages, to come in off the yard. But Fox was not simply enjoying his rival's discomfiture; he was also apparently developing a singular view of the riot itself. He came to regard it as a test of wills, in which the authorities had to show not so much force as leadership, aimed at channeling inmate thinking and orienting their actions away from riot toward more constructive ends. Like a kind of rehabilitation in action, Fox found in the riot positive possibilities for making change.

Once the state police had swept the rioters from the yard, Fox set about applying his new understanding of "the riot mentality" to the

---

7. Martin, who leaned heavily on sexual and psychological metaphors, likened it to an orgy that had spent itself (ibid., 91).

8. Fox, *Violence behind Bars*, 106.

9. Ibid., 93, 99.

situation in 15 Block. Over the next two days, while the warden and custodial staff busied themselves in the main prison—sorting out inmates, organizing the cleanup of cell blocks, repairing locks, restoring food service, and reestablishing the security of the institution— Fox moved, on his own initiative, to engage Ward directly in conversation. The Deputy for Individual Treatment treated these exchanges as a kind of counseling session, in which he tried to size up Ward and "also to give [him] emotional catharsis by permitting him to verbalize his aggressions."[10] Central to Fox's purpose was a more complex objective: to place himself at the "head" of the inmate insurgents, "to delineate in my own thoughts what the inmates wanted" and "to align inmate thinking with my thinking."[11] In Ward he found an ideal opposite: "Look, Dep," Fox recalled Ward saying on Tuesday morning, "you know prison administration. I know the inmates' gripes. Between the two of us, we ought to be able to work up a good set of demands." Since the insurgents would not talk with Deputy Bacon and Warden Frisbie was inclined to try and "talk them out," Fox was given his lead. During Tuesday and Wednesday, events came to turn on his developing bond with Earl Ward. Often Hyatt or one of the other inmate leaders would join Ward at the window; Frisbie came out once for an exchange with Ward, and Fox was joined from time to time by Seymour Gilman, Brooks's assistant, or a captain of the guards. But Ward and Fox remained the center of attention, playing out an elaborate psychodrama with each other, each inclined to inflate his own importance and both groping for legitimacy within their respective "camps" by finding grounds of accommodation with the other.

Both men were operating at the outer edges of their competence and experience, but it would be a mistake to treat them as equal partners in negotiation. Ward was not going anywhere; he knew that his only choice, basically, was to negotiate or die and that his only real leverage was his threat to go berserk and wreck everything in a double-cross of self-destruction. But, having found himself leading a prison rebellion, he seemed determined to emerge as a hero in the eyes of fellow prisoners and "not to let the boys down." So he drove an extremely hard bargain, playing his weak hand with nerve and

10. Ibid., 91.
11. Ibid., 106–7.

calculated shrewdness. Each new demand, as it took shape, was fully discussed among the prisoners in 15 Block, and Ward often altered or amended the text in response to suggestions from his comrades. Nor did he let words pass for action but insisted at every turn on material evidence that specific steps were being taken to implement each point of the emerging agreement. When negotiations faltered, he turned wild and menacing, hurling insults at the warden over the telephone or threatening to execute the hostages; when progress was made, he released a hostage to show good faith. He kept Fox off balance with hints at a double-cross just as conclusions were being reached. At one point a raving Hyatt telephoned to say that he had overthrown Ward and was about to kill all the hostages; the "coup" proved a hoax, apparently intended to ginger prison negotiators (though perhaps also to entertain Hyatt).

Though his position was never entirely secure and he was certainly not in complete control of the situation inside 15 Block, Ward kept up appearances, balancing the moods and whims of the inmate insurgents against the growing impatience and material strength of the state police to keep negotiations alive and Fox in play. Not only did he maintain the air of someone who knew what he was doing, but he was nervy enough to allow events to take their course. He never forced the pace, and in the end he had Fox making pleas and promises in order to preempt an armed assault, which the deputy feared more than Ward. And at all times Ward insisted on full publicity, calling newsmen out for photographs and interviews, demanding that the negotiations be reported on the prison radio, and following the coverage in the press—at one point calling Frisbie to account for some statements quoted in the Detroit newspapers. Not only did Ward understand the importance of the media in building reputations, but he recognized that the press covered the authorities as well as the rioters and could thus be used as an independent check on what prison officials did and said, keeping them honest in their negotiations with him.

For his part Fox felt that Ward was trying to insure himself a place of respect in prison society—to make himself a "big shot"—and he apparently concluded that this was a small price to pay for a peaceful settlement. He later insisted that throughout the negotiations he was only playing Ward along, succoring his vanity and making him feel important, while hoping that Ward could carry his comrades with him. But, while he tried to win Ward's trust, Fox himself never trusted Ward; not only did everyone tell him that the inmate leader was dangerous and unstable, but Fox's own paternalistic approach to the crisis precluded trust. The deputy conceived himself to be in charge of the relationship with Ward, establishing a personal ascendancy over him and coaxing, even manipulating, him toward a peaceful conclusion against his own baser instincts. He recognized Ward as the inmates' spokesman and sought to bolster his claims of leadership. He accepted inmate grievances about the brutality of guards in 15 Block, not because he was so horrified by the strap chains, "wrist-breakers," and rubber hoses that the inmates produced as evidence but because he felt that, by aligning himself with these grievances, against the custodians, he could win their trust. Indeed, at several points Fox suggested what demands the prisoners might want to make in order, as he always said, "to orient their thinking" and lead them toward things he could deliver.[12]

However clever he was in all this—and later he would boast that "none of the [final] terms were what the inmates really wanted"[13]—Fox was also deeply invested in his own agenda. He too was intent on emerging as a hero, of using the situation for his own ends. In the crisis of custody he saw an opportunity to expand the domain of "individual treatment." He was delighted to record a remark made by Commissioner Brooks, as they drove up to Lansing together to lay the emerging terms before the governor: "Custody has had its way, and now, look what has happened! As soon as this riot is over, you are going to have your chance to run the prison with your Individual Treatment."[14] He came to see himself as an indispensable figure in the crisis ("because I knew more about the inside of the prison and the inmate mind than anyone else at the prison")[15] and to assume that he was the only person the prisoners were prepared to trust ("my word was good enough for them").[16] He regarded the final terms he negotiated with Ward not only as a victory for his department—"Individual Treatment had paid off in a crisis of violence when Custody was

---

12. Ibid., 109.
13. Ibid., 135.
14. Ibid., 117.
15. Ibid., 116.
16. Ibid., 130.

helpless"[17]—but as "a victory for progressive penology." By negotiating with the insurgents, by helping them shape their grievances into specific demands, by advocating to prison authorities the demands they (jointly) formulated, Fox sought to place himself on the inmates' side and, with Ward's help, to become the inmates' spokesman. And he happily recorded the applause and handshakes that greeted him in the dining hall on Thursday afternoon after the peaceful surrender of 15 Block. But Fox was not only bidding for local popularity; he was also grasping at what he believed to be a new model of corrections, one in which the keepers worked with and for the incarcerated in the name of change. This was a progressive vision of penology that required, in his view, the displacement of custody preoccupations. Paradoxically, the riot became a means to that end.

In the end there were eleven demands.[18] Several had to do with conditions in the detention block; several had to do with medical and dental care and with the treatment of mental patients; two demands—giving counselors access to the detention block and placing counselors on the custodial board reviewing disciplinary cases—clearly reflected Fox's personal agenda; and two demands were watered-down versions of deeper inmate grievances: calls for the abolition of the parole board became a demand for "a letter on prison stationery asking the parole board to revise its procedures" and calls for a committee, selected by prisoners, to review rules and regulations became a demand for "an inmate advisory council." A final item was added on Wednesday, pledging "no reprisals against any ringleader or participant in the revolt."[19]

The outlines of this agreement were already sufficiently clear on Tuesday afternoon to present to the governor, who went along in the interest of saving lives, though with a weather eye to his political opponents. But the final terms were not worked out until Wednesday evening, and even then it remained unclear when and how the actual surrender would be effected. With the guard force growing more impatient, the state police commissioner began pressing for a military

---

17. Ibid., 147.

18. The text is in Department of Corrections, Bureau of Correctional Facilities, SPSM, box 1, file 5. It was also discussed by the special "Dodd Committee" report, in Williams Papers, box 83, Corrections Department, 1952, Jackson Prison Riot: Special Reports.

19. These are reviewed in Fox, *Violence behind Bars*, 108–15.

assault on 15 Block. Fox, defending his containment strategy against mounting pressure for rollback, managed, with the backing of Brooks and Frisbie, to postpone action until Thursday, while he worked out a protocol for ending the siege: once the final agreement had been drafted and signed by the governor, the commissioner, and the warden, it would be communicated to the press; once the prisoners in 15 Block saw the terms reported in the morning papers, they would come out, disarm themselves, and file "into the dining room to be served an abundant meal of steak, ice cream, and appropriate trimmings."[20] Mennen Williams agreed to this exchange, and Fox went out for the last act. His account conveys the flavor of the entire drama, as experienced and rendered by the Deputy Warden for Individual Treatment:

> When I took the agreement over to 15-block with the governor's letter, I met considerable resistance. They had decided that the agreement wasn't what they wanted at all. Ward was beginning to have difficulty with the group. He hadn't got enough. I tried to support him by indicating that they had won a great deal—that these were major principles that would go down in the annals of history. They objected because nothing at all had been said about food! Brutality in 15-block wasn't even mentioned! They wanted to abolish the parole board . . . Jack Hyatt began to doubt that it was actually the governor's signature. . . .
>
> I moved closer to the window and prepared my pen for signature. "This is a historic document," I began. "It will go down in the annals of history. The commissioner signed with my pen, the warden signed with my pen, and I signed with my pen. Will you [Ward] sign with my pen?" I handed him the pen in the signing position. He signed the document. Then he would not give the agreement to me. There was further argument. . . . Somewhat reluctantly, they agreed to let these terms stand, weak as they were from their vantage point. I took the agreement and my pen, thanked them, and left.[21]

---

20. A copy of the final terms is in the Department of Corrections, Bureau of Correctional Facilities, SPSM, in box 1, file 5; and reproduced in Fox, *Violence behind Bars*, 133.

21. Fox, *Violence behind Bars*, 133–34. As the tone here indicates, it is never quite clear if Fox is leading the cons along or if he too believes the "historic" importance of the document.

But there was a last-minute hitch. Although the newspapers reported the terms of settlement on Thursday morning, Ward announced that the inmates would not to surrender until Friday. A prisoner, escaping from 15 Block, told authorities that Ward intended to double-cross them. Was this, like the staged "coup," an attempt to tighten the screws and raise the bid? Or had Ward lost control inside? Or was he simply giving his comrades a final twenty-four-hour fling in freedom before yielding to the inevitable? No one knew. But, if Fox had "conned" Ward into signing an agreement that his followers thought inadequate, Ward now drew Fox into an untenable position. Leonard and the state police were ready to go: "I'm not going to sit on this powder-keg for another twenty-four hours!" he yelled. "I don't think we should coddle these people any longer."[22] A revolt of the guards was also brewing: "Sociology, sociology, sociology is all you ever hear around this place."[23] Several threatened to quit if negotiations continued. Fox went home in despair; Ward telephoned him there, and a final deal was struck: the prisoners would surrender that afternoon, and, in exchange, Fox would broadcast a statement on the prison radio acknowledging Ward's success in winning concessions. Elated, Fox hurried back to the prison to report the good news and to draft a speech, the tone and phrasing of which were entirely his own, reflecting both his eagerness to end the ordeal and, no doubt, his own sleepless exhaustion:

> The boys in 15-block have won, they have won every single demand they made. . . . Earl Ward, Jack Hyatt, and Jarboe and all of the others in charge are men of their word. . . . Earl Ward is a natural leader. He and the other boys are to be congratulated on the good faith with which they have bargained. Their word has been good. My word has been good. This may presage a new era of good, sound inter-relationships between inmate and administration in American prisons. They have done a service. Congratulations to you, men of 15-block![24]

"When I heard that speech," Frisbie said later, "I threw my hat on the floor, I was so mad." Many guards thought the deputy warden had

---

22. Ibid., 138.
23. Martin, *Break Down the Walls*, 97.
24. Quoted in Fox, *Violence behind Bars*, 142–43; and Martin, *Break Down the Walls*, 98.

got lost on his own "ego trip" and "gone over." Fox would always insist that the speech was a final condition, a necessary "bit of psychological warfare," to bring the siege to an end. It was his narrative contention that Ward would have surrendered on Friday anyway but that Leonard's ultimatum on Thursday and the increasing restlessness of the custodial force compelled him to pressure Ward for an earlier surrender, and this, in turn, required a further concession to Ward's ego. A telephone operator at the prison, who monitored the conversation between Ward and Fox, later claimed that Ward made no particular conditions for an earlier surrender and that the idea for a speech was Fox's own. The question of who was manipulating whom remains open. In any event, the moment the speech was given, the inmates surrendered, and, as promised, they were all given a meal of steak (industrial grade) and ice cream before being locked up again in their cells.

Explaining the Riot

Recriminations began instantly. Mennen Williams, who had supported Fox in his negotiations, found his congratulatory broadcast "utterly inexcusable" and demanded that Brooks deliver a reprimand.[25] He was barely ahead of a full-throated uproar in the state legislature and the press. Fox was told that "he had no future in penology in the United States after that speech,"[26] and he resigned. Meanwhile, Ward and the other leaders of the insurrection were transferred to holding cells in several county jails, pending disciplinary action. Investigators descended on Jackson prison from several quarters—a Governor's Select Committee (the Dodd Commission), deputies in the attorney general's office, and Austin MacCormick of the Osborne Association, invited by Williams to do another of his independent inquiries—seeking to determine the causes of the riot and possible remedial action and participating in a broader public debate about the prison and its problems, which dominated the press in ensuing weeks.

Riots are the central moments of any prison's history. Like wars, they are the ordeals of fire that illuminate hidden landscapes and

---

25. Williams Papers, box 83, Corrections Department, 1952: Jackson Prison Riot; letter, Williams to Brooks, 25 April 1952.

26. Martin, *Break Down the Walls*, 100.

form the benchmarks or turning points in time, long thereafter remembered by participants and forever prepared against by those fearing recurrence. And like wars, riots require large explanations. Yet
the litanies of causality that circulated among politicians, administrators, and reporters in the weeks after the Jackson riot were both too
vague and too contradictory to be entirely convincing. Everyone
agreed that the prison was too large, too crowded, and too hetero-
geneous; certainly there was rivalry between custodial and treatment
staffs and the respective deputies in charge at the prison, and the
warden had apparently been too remote to reconcile everyday tensions among his staff; the commissioner and his assistants in Lansing
had interfered a lot—perhaps too much—in the day-to-day operations of the prison and the movement of its inmates. Exactly how
these factors produced a riot in 1952 was not clear, and the various
recitations of causality arising from politicians and commentators, as
well as guards and prisoners at Jackson, seemed to bump into one
another: some said that guards were unjust and discipline too strict;
others claimed that discipline had become too lax and criminals were
being coddled. Some said that custody had too much power; others
insisted that counselors and treatment programs were compromising
security. Some pointed to a shift from liberal to more conservative
practices; others insisted that a move from a conservative to a more
liberal regime at the prison was to blame. Some said the prison was in
a state of flux and transition, with confusion at the top and in the
ranks; others averred that the prison was massively unresponsive to
progressive initiatives, thwarting change and creating frustration
among staff and inmates alike.

We need not here inquire into the sources of these competing
poles of analysis to establish a preliminary point: these opinions suggest not so much the causes of the riot as perspectives upon it. No one
really knew what had caused it, or the causes were too many and too
disparate for anyone to be sure. In any case the views expressed
during the preliminary inquiries represented opinions already
formed on other grounds. The riot was an occasion for extending and
elaborating an ongoing debate; it was a field of action in which positions already held by various actors were put into play. In this sense
the riot revealed a set of conditions that existed beforehand and provided an event that everyone could explain from the vantage point or
perspective they would have held in any case. A search by the histo-

rian for definitive causes is thus bound to be elusive. Yet it is possible to set the conflicting opinions about causes in their historical context and to provide a framework of explanation for the riot that places it within, and makes it a part of, the ongoing history of the state and its main prison.

To take such a position on causality poses additional problems, however. If it is impossible to specify "deep" causes or to be sure that contemporaries knew what caused the riot of 1952, we arrive at a custodian's view of the event: it was a chance occurrence triggered by a simple mistake on the part of a rookie guard. From this perspective the only meaningful causes would be "immediate" or "sufficient" ones, discernible at the moment of insurrection. This position also implies a particular view of prisoners themselves: as a bunch of wild animals, barely held in check by the constant vigilance of custodians and liable to explode in revolt at the least lapse of custodial supervision. In this view riot is explicable in terms of the failure of repression. Most of the investigations of the Jackson riot lent themselves to this conclusion by stressing such general factors as crowded conditions, poorly trained guards, lack of effective segregation, and tensions between custody and treatment—all conditions that pointed, in one way or another, to possible cracks in the patina of control that might, under certain momentary, even accidental, circumstances, allow pent-up pressures to vent themselves in riot.

This picture of the prison as a pressure cooker contained only by custodial vigilance was strongly reinforced by popular accounts of the riot that appeared in its aftermath. Relying heavily on psychological categories and therapeutic language, these narratives suggested an atomized society of isolated individuals susceptible to mobbing and vengeance. John Martin spoke of Jackson prison as a "dumping ground" for the psychotic and mentally ill, and his picture of "the men of 15 block" stressed individual case histories and the rhetoric of sickness—"brain damage," "psychopath," "inadequate personality," "mentally defective." Austin MacCormick was quoted as saying that Jackson was "a madhouse": "How can you run an orderly prison with so many of these off-trail types with nothing being done for them, all cluttering up the landscape?"[27] Such images disseminated in the popular press suggested a disorganized mass of misfits, with clutches of

---

27. Quoted in ibid., 49.

crazies and lunatics, ready to rise at the least sign of inattention by authorities. Set into this seething cauldron of danger a rookie guard, and one had all the elements of high drama: the all-American, clean-scrubbed, well-meaning young innocent meets the mentally defective, personally inadequate, violently disposed criminal. That this encounter could happen at any time implied that the specific, or efficient, cause of the riot on 20 April 1952 was purely accidental, a serendipitous happening.

The belief that the cause of the riot was to be found in the lapses of custody effectively silenced the rioters and rendered irrelevant any negotiations that may have been carried on with them or any agreements that had been forced upon the administration by the unnatural circumstances of the riot itself. No one bothered to interview Earl Ward or the other leaders of the insurrection, and no attention was paid to the list of demands that were produced during the course of negotiations. In the official view Ward had no legitimacy after the surrender; the eleven-point agreement he had worked so hard to develop had been elicited by Fox, and Fox was now discredited. Thus the list of demands could have no bearing on the question of causes. Anything they said about brutality, medical treatment, or the parole board was either ginned up for the occasion (i.e., not real) or put into their minds by an ambitious official like Vernon Fox (again, not real). What motivated prisoners was already known and, in any event, beside the point: they would riot if they got the chance. The only reason to interview them afterward was perhaps to identify the specific lapses in custody that enabled them to go on a rampage and then to identify which rampaging inmates might be liable to criminal prosecution.

The attorney general's office, which conducted the most extensive interviews with inmates after the event, was primarily interested in securing indictments.[28] Investigators quizzed selected prisoners on specific acts of assault, kidnapping, or rape that might promise successful prosecution. They focused much attention on the treatment of hostages—who held a knife to whom and what threats were uttered—and they followed any lead that might shed light on the apparently quite extensive homosexual activity that went on in 15 Block

---

28. The interviews under consideration here are collected in Attorney General Investigations, Criminal Law, boxes 5–6: Investigations Regarding Riots at SPSM, 1952.

during the four-day upheaval. Here a revealing sequence of blame amplified the general imagery of dangerous "off-trail" types ready to go on a rampage. Investigators, needing evidence of illegal activity to sustain prosecutions, were on the lookout for criminal acts and inclined to treat any homosexual activity during the riot as nonconsensual sex—hence, legally rape. They hauled in several prisoners from 15 Block who were thought to be especially mean-spirited or aggressive and interrogated them about wolfpacks and gang rapes. In trying to avoid the trap of criminal prosecution, several pointed the finger at practicing homosexuals, who were often segregated from the general population and confined in 15 Block. During the riot several had apparently been "open for business," with long lines outside their cells; guard hostages could refer to them by name: "Roxy Billings," "Madame Phillips," and "Josephine Simes."[29] When these prisoners were called in for interviews, they naturally feared prosecution for whatever activities they had engaged in during the riot and so insisted in every instance that they had been sexually forced by gangs of inmates to do unnatural acts. The inmates whose names came up in questioning (perhaps the only ones homosexuals in prison felt safe naming) and whom investigators then chose to pursue were all black. The chain of finger-pointing, which ran from assaultive prisoners to homosexual prisoners to black prisoners, was altogether too precarious, involving too much fudging and winking, to sustain criminal prosecutions, even though it gives us fleeting sight of the tatty hierarchies maintained even on the margins of prison society. But what the attorney general's office developed was a symbolically reassuring picture of homosexuality in the prison—as the singular behavior of deranged blacks with unnatural appetites let loose among the innocents—which, in turn, acted as a shadow image for all prison rioters. Not only did such people act atavistically and opportunistically, without "normal" motives, but, if society ever relaxed its guard, "they" would rise up and do unspeakable things to "us." They deserved to be kept down and had nothing to complain about when custody bore down upon them.

A nagging problem with this "eruption" theory of the Jackson riot was that it was not an isolated event. During 1952–53 prisons in the United States experienced a wave of violence, ranging from short-

29. See testimony of Paul Jackson, 9 June 1952, ibid., box 5.

term disturbances to full-blown riots.[30] Even at the time, this syn-
chrony of events strained arguments from serendipity and prompted
a more careful, sociological quest for systemic causes. The best of
these studies focused on moments of change in prison life that desta-
bilized the ordinary routine of control.[31] Gresham Sykes's study of the
"big house" penitentiary at Trenton, New Jersey, was the classic of
this genre; it was also the first to center an analysis of routine order
inside a prison around the tacit collaborations and corrupt deals between keepers and kept. Sykes argued that, for all the asymmetries of
power in a prison, custodians depended upon their captives' cooperation for a smooth-running institution. The threat of force and the use
of punishments could not alone secure compliance, since prisoners
were not easily cowed by the available repertory of sanctions and
often drew strength as inmate leaders from their willingness to stand
up to disciplinary threats. Instead, tacitly, and by degrees, custodians
let prisoners "run the joint": they came to know, even like, many
prisoners; they tolerated a good deal of deviant behavior, rule infractions, and noncompliance in the interest of quiet; they came to depend on prisoners for a lot of minor chores and services and rewarded them with small favors in return; thus they bought into the
inmate codes about the "right guy" and the "square shooter," in
which loyalty and consistent favoritism toward selected inmates was
taken as a mark of "fairness," while uniformity of discipline and
equality of treatment was likely to produce a reputation for "harshness." In short, custodians came to hold sway, less through the
power of their guns than through dense layers of personal relations,
connections, and friendships with inmates, often extended over
many years and involving a long, invisible record of reciprocities. The

30. A partial list includes New Jersey (both at the penitentiary at Trenton and the
prison farm at Rahway), Louisiana, Massachusetts, Georgia, Kentucky, Utah, Pennsylvania, Arizona, Washington (at Walla Walla), New Mexico, Minnesota, and the North
Carolina central prison. These and other disturbances are described in Martin, *Break
down the Walls*, 209–14.

31. For example, Richard McCleary's study of the Hawaii penitentiary in the late
1940s, "The Governmental Process and Informal Social Controls," in *The Prison: Studies
in Institutional Organization and Change*, ed. Donald Cressey (New York: Holt, Rinehardt
and Winston, 1961); Frank Hartung and Maurice Floch, "A Social-Psychological Analysis of Prison Riots: An Hypothesis," *Journal of Criminal Law, Criminology, and Police
Science* 47, no. 1 (May–June 1956); and, of course, Gresham Sykes's study of the New
Jersey penitentiary, *The Society of Captives: A Study of a Maximum Security Prison* (Princeton: Princeton University Press, 1958).

inevitable compromises that custodians made with their captives produced, for Sykes, the central paradox of prison: "They can insure their dominance only by allowing it to be corrupted."[32]

These concessions of power were continuous and incremental, and, although specific acts were often innocuous, even invisible, the cumulative image of Sykes's analysis was of a general draining of authority over time. Once conceded, moreover, power was very hard to reclaim. Indeed, over time, pressures of habit and culture accumulated against any effort by guards to reassert their authority or reverse the patterns of corruption. Yet public conventions, political calculation, and the ideology of custody itself had to deny that power was being transferred from officials to inmates. At some point—"it is admittedly difficult to date these matters precisely"—officials found it necessary, Sykes contended, to reverse the flow of concessions, to reassert custodial authority, and to bring inmate power under control. When it came, this "tightening up" inevitably undercut the cohesive forces within inmate society that had developed around the collusions and corruptions of authority; as rules were re-enforced, preferential treatment ended, and the social order "reformed," prisoners necessarily experienced a massive disruption of settled arrangements, a loss of benefits, and a collapse of the immunities that had, heretofore, protected them from custodial interventions and enabled them to organize life behind the walls. The displacement of settled hierarchies not only threatened established inmate leaders, who had a positive interest in institutional peace, but gave expanded scope for "crazies" and insurgents, who could be expected to thrive on the destabilization of prison society. Discontent combined with instability to produce a riotous brew, and the prison in transition moved toward another expression of the central paradox: "The system breeds rebellion by attempting to enforce the system's rules."[33]

Though not its primary purpose, Sykes's study provided a powerful explanation for prison riots. Two aspects of his argument are most striking. First, it was keyed to change: seeking to understand how regime changes upended patterns of control, he located prison riots in transitional moments, when prisoners felt most caught in the unpredictabilities and uncertainties of carceral life and prison admin-

---

32. Sykes, *Society of Captives*, 58.
33. Ibid., 123–24.

istrations were least able to rely on settled modes of containment. Second, Sykes was prepared to impart agency to inmates. While prisoners did not necessarily resist change in his argument, they did not like it; this was especially the case among inmate leaders and "merchants" with a stake in the old order—precisely those upon whom custodians depended for internal stability. Change produced grievance, dissent, and opposition, even as it weakened the internal network of collaboration and consent around which control was built. Riots, in Sykes's view, expressed both administrative confusion and inmate hostility to change. While he did not develop a fully interactive theory of insurrection in prison, the implications and possible nuances of his thesis on riots are extremely suggestive; unfortunately, they have been lost on (or rejected by) recent critics,[34] who seem more inclined to treat riots as natural upheavals that are allowed to happen and have sought to silence prisoners by stressing lax administration and interruptions in the patina of repression rather than inmate agency and the possibility that prisoners found in moments of change reasons to act.

Sykes was concerned with universals, with establishing essential "laws of movement" in the prison, and he drew from his analysis a "cyclical rhythm from order to disorder to order" that, in his view, held for all prisons across time and place. His analysis has been criticized by other sociologists,[35] who have failed to find in later riots the same pendulum aswinging and have sought to advance other uniformities across time and place as better models for explaining upheavals inside. We do not need to enter into these sociological debates, however, to appropriate Sykes's model to our historical inquiry, for whatever its universal saliency, it grew out of the study of a specific riot in a "big house" penitentiary in 1952, and it sought to understand the crisis of custody not simply as a momentary breakdown in the apparatus of repression but as an expression of deeper, systemic changes in the social fabric of the prison and the structure of rewards that organized keeper and kept alike. In following his lead into an investigation of deeper changes at SPSM, we will resist, however, the socio-

---

34. Here, in particular, see the work of Bert Useem and Peter Kimball, *States of Siege: U.S. Prison Riots, 1971–1986* (New York: Oxford University Press, 1991), esp. 218–31.

35. Most notably in John Irwin's *Prisons in Turmoil*, more obliquely in James Jacob's *Stateville*, and most cogently by Useem and Kimball in *States of Siege*.

logical temptation to encase the Jackson riot of 1952 into a history of prison riots as a generic type or to make it representative of prison riots in that era. We seek, instead, to understand the riot as an expression of a distinct and particular history, a product of factors "peculiar to this institution and this state."[36] In this way we will come to view the riot as an aspect and outgrowth of a transformation of carceral practices in Michigan that began not just with the downfall of Harry Jackson in 1945 but with the collapse of Harry Hulbert's dream of an industrial prison, and we will analyze the riot as part, not merely of a transition in disciplinary routines inside the prison but of a broader reconstitution of politics in the state.

The Roots of Riot (I): Sigler's Political Crusade

The moment in the history of Jackson prison that most closely corresponds with the turning point in Sykes's argument was, of course, the overthrow of Harry Jackson in the summer of 1945. The immediate beneficiaries of Harry Jackson's ouster were his superiors and rivals in Lansing. When the scandal broke, Garrett Heyns, the director of the Department of Corrections, moved quickly to take charge of the prison: Ralph Benson, the warden at Marquette and before that a parole supervisor in Detroit, was brought down to replace Jackson, and Gerald Bush, a member of the parole board, was dispatched north to replace Benson. A new group of deputies, several from the parole field, were also installed at SPSM, while Heyns's old ally Joel Moore was put in charge at Ionia. In effect, the entire state prison system came under the control of close associates and friends of Garrett Heyns and Ross Pascoe. Those close to Harry Jackson saw the hand of the parole board in the entire affair; there was talk of a coup d'état.[37]

The immediate effect of the turnover was a greater coordination of operational policy among the three main prisons in the state and a greater degree of disciplinary uniformity throughout the system. At

---

36. These were the words of the Dodd Report, 13, Williams Papers, box 83.

37. See letter from G. I. Francis to Murl Aten, 4 Mary 1947, Records of the Executive Office, 1947–48, box 8, file 7. D. C. Pettit maintained in the spring of 1946 that his ouster was the result of a plot involving Ross Pascoe and David Phillips. See his letter to Thomas J. Wilson, 3 April 1946, sent to the newspapers and widely reproduced on 6 April 1946.

Jackson this took the form of a massive disciplinary crackdown. Benson moved quickly to assert control over the prison and to show outsiders that prison professionals were now in charge. He took as his marching orders Dethmers's recommendation that prison administration should henceforth "be based on the premise that the first duty of the prison is custodial," and he took guidance from a group of guards and lower officials at SPSM, who had been dissidents in the Harry Jackson administration, allies of G. I. Francis, and cooperative with the Dethmers's investigation. This group now sought to act as a "sounding board" for Benson, forwarding a number of recommendations to the new warden aimed at fostering a uniformity of procedures and conditions behind the walls.[38] They stressed the importance of eliminating all special privileges, all differentials in dress and material resources, and all variations in the standards of discipline; they urged the elimination of inmate clerks, which in their view gave prison "big shots" space to operate; and they pressed hard for the regular rotation of officers "to break up favoritism with pet inmates, to break up the differences which exist between the shifts themselves, to acquaint officers with the entire routine, to guarantee uniform administration of regulations, and to enable men to demonstrate their ability." The general aim was to insure that "administration discipline should be uniform and inevitable."

Benson adopted these recommendations wholesale. He moved immediately to transfer many of the inmate "big shots" to Marquette and to stop the use of inmate clerks in the classification department and the offices of deputy wardens.[39] This gave him direct control over cell assignments and internal movements. He then abolished all "late" details, enforcing a strict eight o'clock curfew, and discontinued the "blanket" passes that had given prisoners free movement

38. A memorandum, dated 30 July 1945, on disciplinary matters at Jackson circulated widely in the days after Benson's arrival. It was written by Sidney Moskowitz and based on conversations with several guards, one of whom was Al Fingel, a former parole field officer, who had become a major critic of, and witness against, Warden Jackson and, with Sid Gilman, the parole board investigator who had played a key role in Dethmers's investigation. Copy in Williams Papers, box 83, Corrections Department, 1957; interview with Fingel, April 1979.

39. *Ann Arbor News*, August 6, 1945. The scale of Benson's crackdown is perhaps best captured in his own testimony before the Civil Service Commission Hearing on 9 April 1946 (Attorney General Investigations, box 10; Civil Service Commission, Michigan Corrections Commission vs. Harry Jackson).

in the institution. He severed the outside trusty division from the inside deputy, establishing a separate administration outside the walls and drastically curbing movement in and out of the prison. He reviewed all work assignments, discovering in the process that nearly 60 percent of the men assigned to the farms and trusty divisions were there without the knowledge or approval of the classification committee.[40] Guard stations and floor patrols were reviewed and procedures tightened; the supervision of the gymnasium was intensified. Most strikingly, the new warden instituted a series of prison-wide shakedowns and cell checks to seize contraband goods, weapons, money, and unauthorized personal property. He was determined, he reported, to see that everyone was treated alike, strictly and without favor; and to enforce his hard line he brought in several handpicked subordinates, notably Charles Cahill, a stern disciplinarian who was made inspector of the guards and charged with bringing the custodial force into line with the new cadence, and George Bacon, an imperious man of spit and polish who was appointed deputy warden for custody. In Lansing Heyns followed the recommendations of Dethmers's report and finally filled the long-vacant post of assistant director in charge of the Bureau of Prisons, appointing a military colonel and former head of Michigan prison industries, William Burke, who promised an administration of "common, every day horse sense, with no freak experiments."[41]

Every effort was made to insure continuity and reassure the public; in Heyns's words, "There has been no vacuum at the prison; we all know what is going on."[42] The public relations position of the department was simply that "an unfortunate situation" had been solved by the dismissal of the responsible culprits, and a new professional administration was now moving to insure that the prison functioned smoothly and without lapse of security. The Corrections Commission, which at first had bridled at Dethmers's grandstand presentations and the suspension of the seven officials,[43] also fell into line: all ap-

---

40. This was reported to the Corrections Commission on 11 September 1945. See Department of Corrections, Pardons and Parole, box 1, Minutes of Prison Commission Meetings.

41. *Detroit News*, 5 September 1945, for the appointment; 24 January 1946, for the quotation.

42. *Detroit News*, 27 July 1945.

43. This according to press reports (viz. *Detroit News* 31 July 1945). There is no indication of debate in the minutes of the commission.

peals hearings for those ousted in the scandal were shunted to the Civil Service Commission, while the Corrections Commission turned with ostentatious public resolve to address the future of the prison system. For weeks the press watched anxiously for signs of trouble, on the premise that, as discipline became more severe under the new administration, riotous responses were to be expected.[44] But there was no interruption of custodial control, no recorded disturbance; to outside observers the prison seemed calm and the administration fully in charge: "One can't always tell what is under the surface," Heyns told reporters, "but everybody seems to be doing his job." That fall Heyns delivered the keynote address, as national president, to the American Prison Association, which voted to hold its next annual meeting in Detroit. It was, perhaps, the high point of his career.

There were, of course, no newsmen present behind the walls to register the reaction of guards and inmates to these events. But there is little doubt (and subsequent evidence certainly indicates)[45] that the disciplinary crackdown at Jackson was very unpopular among keepers and kept alike. Cell searches and shakedowns, which had been rare and never systematic in Harry Jackson's day, could not help but to have upset inmate hierarchies and disturbed settled practices in ways that we can no longer detect. The restriction on movement inside, and on the traffic between the prison and the farms, shut down trade and exchange, while the new disciplinary rigors put an end to the gambling, lending, and numbers running that had been staples of the internal economy.[46] "Most privileges have been abolished and inmates are being punished for offenses which were condoned while Jackson was warden," one inmate told the Civil Service Commission, and more prisoners were reported in the bull pen, now located in 15 Block, formerly "aristocrats' row" and home of the "big shots."[47] Years later Donald Clemmer would report that "inmates transferred from Jackson to Marquette almost to a man make the statement that during their residence at Jackson, they were frequently

44. See *Detroit News*, 11 September 1945; *Ann Arbor News*, 4 August and 27 September 1945.

45. See discussion later in this chapter.

46. See report in *Detroit News*, April 9, 1946, on the demise of gambling since Harry Jackson's day.

47. *Detroit News*, 11 September and 9 April 1945. See testimony in Civil Service Commission, Michigan Corrections Commission vs. Harry Jackson, box 10, at the State Archives.

searched, their quarters were searched frequently, and the personnel at Jackson constantly 'bothered' them."[48]

By the same token old-time guards found themselves under new orders that made it difficult to carry on business as before or even to protect favored inmates from disciplinary actions by other custodians who were more in step with the new regime. A number of guards quit in disgust, and several were fired for misconduct. Early in 1946 the Department of Corrections established a special panel, including George Kropp, the personnel director, William Burke, the new assistant director for prisons, and Harold DeWitt, the assistant manager of prison industries, to review the charges against prison employees that had arisen in the recent scandals and to recommend disciplinary action.[49] While its recommendation for reprimands and transfers proved relatively mild and the intent seems to have been to smooth the waters and reassure regular line personnel, the mere existence of a special disciplinary group created nervousness within the custodial force, many of whom regarded it as a "kangaroo court": "Anyone who has made a remark that they felt in any way criticized the present administration is brought before [the panel]."[50] Fear, factional jostling, and bitterness were widespread, and when, in the spring of 1946, the Civil Service Commission overturned the suspension of "Chuck" Watson, the classification director, on the grounds that the charges against him were matters of deportment and outlook, not conduct, the dissident elements inside the prison found an outspoken leader, deeply devoted (as were many of them) to the old regime and the memory of Harry Jackson.

These dissensions and grumblings behind the walls, while they

---

48. Staff Report to the Michigan Joint Legislative Committee on Reorganization of State Government, Michigan Department of Corrections, March 1951, 17. This report was written by Clemmer, who was then director of prisons in the District of Columbia.

49. The body was apparently created in February 1946, as a result of a meeting of the three main wardens, in an effort to air tensions and settle differences between the new managers of the prison and the older employees. By the time it set to work the civil service commission hearings had produced, in public, a good deal of testimony about custodial misbehavior, and the panel found itself reviewing charges that had been made and recommending disciplinary action or transfers. See Minutes of Prison Commission Meetings, box 1, 20 July 1946, for a report from George Kropp; and the *Ann Arbor News*, 16 May 1946.

50. Statement by Earl Ragar, head of education, 17 February 1947, Case Files: Investigation, 1947, Pardons and Parole Board, Leonard Papers, box 19.

do not yield a coherent narrative of change, do suggest that Warden-Benson had begun to police up inmate society in Jackson. He had broken the power of the "big shots" and reclaimed much of the authority that had been conceded to them in Harry Jackson's day. This had undoubtedly produced a general sharpening of distinctions between keeper and kept. The increasingly uniform, or homogenized, treatment of prisoners was accompanied by a multiplication of minor showdowns between custodians and their captives. But, while there was a good deal of pining for the "good old days," on the one hand, and no little uncertainty about what would be erected once the ground was cleared of all vestiges of the Harry Jackson regime, on the other, there is no indication that the disciplinary crackdown per se fostered confusion or a sense of incoherence behind the walls. Everyone knew exactly what Warden Benson was doing, and the carping and complaining that accompanied his purge would surely have been treated as the residual aftershocks of a great institutional upheaval, largely self-contained and themselves of little consequence, had it not been for Kim Sigler's dramatic reappearance at center stage. His election as Michigan's governor in 1946 posed a sudden and quite unexpected threat to the recently triumphant Heyns-Pascoe coalition. On top of the grating transformation in disciplinary routines and social relations within the prison came a new round of unwelcome exposure and highly politicized interference from outside. Carceral practices and political practices—both in transition—combined again during 1946 and 1947 to shape the history of SPSM.

As we have seen, Sigler lost his case against Frank McKay in the spring of 1946. His job as a special prosecutor was then eliminated, just as the hearings of the Civil Service Commission gave his political rival John Dethmers yet another chance to monopolize headlines with a public recitation of his changes against Harry Jackson. Under a cloud and eclipsed by his rival, Sigler responded with a preemptive move: he announced he was running for governor. As an outsider with few affiliations in the Republican Party, his primary campaign relied heavily upon Sigler's well-established image as "the scourge of corruption" and on his extensive connections with news reporters, many of whom were personally attracted to Sigler's flamboyant style and penchant for making news. Behind the scenes he got support from dissident Republicans, most notably the former governor Alex

Groesbeck, now an aging lawyer in Detroit,[51] and Wilbur Brucker, leader of the anti-McKay forces in Detroit. The themes of his campaign combined Sigler's by now vintage flair for linking all his opponents to Frank McKay—Governor Kelly and Attorney General Dethmers were mere tools of McKayism, "part of the Lansing Political Machine which permitted graft and corruption in state government"—with a projection of himself, in Groesbeck fashion, as the can-do man of affairs, in touch with the people and able to promote efficiency and accountability in state government.[52]

Ironically, Sigler's early success was due largely to the demise of Frank McKay. Without his patronage machine the Republican Party had great difficulty maintaining cohesive internal organization or financial solvency. Governor Kelly had attempted to rebuild party cohesion around a cautious program of continuity and experience, relying on a circle of political insiders and professionals in Lansing to manage affairs and counting on a general wartime policy consensus to deflate internal challenges. But this arrangement proved peculiarly vulnerable to Sigler's insurgent style of attack. As an outsider, Sigler was well positioned to further disrupt an already fragmented party apparatus, and he had nothing to lose in doing so. At the same time, his promotion of the "good government line," his image as an activist, hands-on advocate, and his apparent determination to make the government work more efficiently were all themes directly relevant to the most urgent ideological question facing the Republican Party in 1946: how to address postwar voters, especially returning veterans, and postwar domestic problems, especially housing, education, and disability assistance, with an agenda for governmental action that could compete with—or at least go beyond mere attacks on—the New Deal and yet not abandon base-constituency commitments to lower taxes and less government.

Sigler's brand of scandal mongering and exposé had answers that cut several ways: it attacked the corruption of party patronage systems and made good press copy out of the discomfiture of the old

51. See Frank Woodford, *Alex Groesbeck: Portrait of a Public Man* (Detroit: Wayne State University Press, 1962), 306–19.

52. The attacks on Kelly and the "Lansing gang" are in the *Detroit News*, 18 and 22 June 1946. Sigler's relations with Kelly turned intensely sour in the summer of 1946: "It is no reason to elect a man governor because he happened to be the man to prosecute a few crooks," Kelly was quoted in the *Ann Arbor News*, 17 June 1946.

bosses; it created a media presence, an image of boldness and movement that compared favorably with the bland professionalism of Lansing insiders whom Kelly had relied on to heal rifts and bridge organizational gaps in the party; and it bespoke a commitment to activist
efficiency without dwelling on the specifics of content and costs in a
way that appealed both to penny-pinching regulars in the party and
to more progressive elements looking to recapture the White House
in 1948. Sigler won the August primary in part because his rival in
scandal production, John Dethmers, stepped aside to allow Lieutenant Governor Vernon Brown, a more colorless but senior "insider," to
lead the Kelly forces against Sigler's challenge.[53] He then handily
defeated Murray Van Wagoner, a reluctant candidate and indifferent
opponent, in the November elections, thus becoming part of a national Republican surge that fall.[54]

Scandal mongering proved addictive. Having parlayed his reputation into a successful campaign to root out corruption and clean up
government, Sigler was more or less obliged, once he took office, to
expose illicit goings-on and conduct purges of state agencies. Aside
from his personal penchants and predilections in this, Sigler now had
to devise a basis for governing. He had won office by attacking party
regulars; he could hardly count on them to sustain him in office. His
links with county and local organizations remained tenuous, and
many Republican leaders in the state legislature were openly hostile
to him. His key supporters, Groesbeck and Brucker, came from very
disparate quarters of the party and had little influence over it; they
disliked each other and harbored serious reservations about Sigler: "I
never met up with a fellow that ran for public office that was as
ignorant of what his responsibilities were," Groesbeck complained;

---

53. When Sigler won the August primary, he made it clear that he did not want
Dethmers on the ticket again for attorney general; Kelly secured Dethmers's appointment to the state supreme court by way of compensation.

54. Many said Kim Sigler won because Democrats did not vote. Former governor
Murray Van Wagoner was persuaded to run, after much importuning, by party leaders,
all nonentities, whose disagreements among themselves threatened to leave the party
without a candidate in 1946. There was even some talk of nominating Kim Sigler as a
Democrat and mounting a sort of unity, or coalition, movement. Though the press
made much of Democratic disunity, several Republican regulars observed after the
election that the problem of the Democratic Party was mainly low voter turnout: a
quarter of a million voters, most of them Democrats in Wayne County, stayed home.
They did not vote Republican (see comments by Hale Knight, *Detroit News*, 10 November 1946; and reports in the *News*, 7 November 1946).

"he will two-time anybody . . . to obtain a little notoriety or advantage."[55]

With no organizational base in, or access to, party machinery, Sigler was forced, like Groesbeck in the 1920s, to rely upon his command of the state apparatus to galvanize popular support and neutralize opposition. Groesbeck, of course, had been able to use patronage—state jobs and contracts—to shore up his leadership and consolidate his gains. Sigler could not. But he seems to have absorbed enough of Groesbeck's advice to see that he might fabricate a political base and statewide following independent of his party through governmental initiatives and extensive press coverage of an energetic governor-in-action. In any case the vigorous pursuit of malfeasance and wrongdoing, combined with reform initiatives aimed at increasing administrative consolidation and executive accountability, became the ideological mainstays of the Sigler administration. He conducted a sort of continuous ideological mobilization from above, restlessly pursuing any issue or cause that might serve to cultivate his cherished self-images as the "buster of corruption" and the "champion of efficiency."

To sustain the effort Sigler kept dishing up emergencies. He repeatedly called the legislature into special session, and, while these were supposed to be for exceptional legislation, Sigler piled on work and extended these sittings, until special sessions became regular ones, and the legislature found itself in session more than not during his two years in office. In 1947 he laid out a number of schemes for governmental reorganization—to reduce the traffic in political influence, to make the highway commissioner an appointive office, to abolish the Liquor Control Commission in favor of a single "liquor Czar," to renovate the state police, and to overhaul the state prison system—and, when the legislature hesitated, he launched a stream of public criticism and exhortation, denouncing delay and "obstructionism" in the name of an impatient people. His rhetoric was often bold and assertive, urging the need to modernize state government and give the governor the tools for efficient management. And his style, always flamboyant and highly provocative, provided maximum press coverage in an environment of urgency—the governor in the thick of things, doing the people's business.

---

55. Woodford, *Groesbeck*, 312, 318.

There was also a kind of naive rectitude in Sigler's approach, a straight-arrow's inflexibility. He seems to have believed that government could somehow be made to operate like a civics textbook, with the governor presiding over the executive branch, neatly divided into departments responsible directly to him and standing by to do his bidding, while the legislature, over in its sphere, deliberated and voted on laws proposed to it. As the governor, he proved reluctant to cross the boundaries, to work the invisible lines of influence or lobbying, to barter for votes, or to shape a legislative floor strategy. His aloofness was, perhaps, an act of self-preservation—a determination to remain wrapped in a clean cloak of righteousness, forever unsullied by the machinations of insider politics. But it also expressed his continuing effort to cast himself as the outsider, the people's advocate spreading havoc and panic in the venial back rooms of the state capital. Since the state legislature and most of the permanent bureaucracy in Lansing were dominated by Republicans, Sigler was thus perpetually at loggerheads with his own party and administrative subordinates.

This approach to governing soon irritated and exhausted the legislature. Most of its leadership were stalwarts of the "in crowd," upon whose denunciation Sigler had built his career; most of its members, well rooted in their constituencies and local party machinery, did not need Sigler's kind of activism to maintain their political viability: "The less time we spend here, the better off the people of Michigan will be."[56] Sigler, trying to move the reluctant, cast his reform agenda in partisan terms. All he wanted to do, he insisted, was to fix what the Democrats had done. In this perspective the Murphy reforms of 1937–38, in attempting to break up the power of patronage masters by inserting civil service rules and bipartisan supervision into state administration, had actually made government less efficient. Part-time commissions of worthy citizens, operating between the governor and administrative departments, might shortcircuit patronage networks, but they also tended to diffuse authority and make decisive action impossible. Moreover, the consolidation of a civil service system was beginning, in this view, to infringe upon the policy-making prerogatives of the executive office. When high-level administrators

---

56. A legislator quoted in the *Detroit News*, 4 April 1948.

were protected by civil service and their access to the top was diverted through intermediate, bipartisan commissions, there was no way a chief executive could shake up his administration or insure that his orders were carried out.[57] Sigler's remedy for all this was what he called "streamlining"—specifically, the elimination of the various commissions and boards in favor of single high-profile administrators, brought in from the outside without civil service protection to serve at the governor's pleasure.

For those in government, however, Sigler's remedy was clearer and more clearly dangerous than the problems it addressed. Many legislators saw in the creation of topflight administrative positions in the governor's gift a throwback to the days of the "little Mussolini" and a dangerous concentration of executive power. The only reason to support streamlining was to save money and reduce taxes. But here Sigler's promises were always ambiguous; his principal political appeal was to those in the Republican Party (and perhaps also Democrats disenchanted with FDR) who wanted to see government take an active role in postwar society, addressing its needs and solving its problems in competition with the promises of the New Deal. But this activist rhetoric alarmed a legislature dominated by outstate Republicans from small towns, whose values and outlooks were more modest and who believed that, with the wartime emergency passing and the state facing a deficit, it was time to scale back initiatives and cut costs. Their caution was echoed by the state bureaucracy. For the new insider establishment of permanent officials now taking shape in Lansing behind civil service protection and greater professionalism in government, Sigler's penchant for "supermanagers"—outsiders with a mission to crack down, shake up, and overhaul—seemed purely disruptive, promising a kind of permanent revolution that raised the specter of endless purges and continuing instability in administrative routines. It is hardly surprising, then, that state administrators co-

---

57. Sigler laid out this case in his Inaugural Address, 1 January 1947. Kim Sigler Papers, box 1, Speeches, MHC, Ann Arbor. The archival papers left by the Sigler administration, both in Lansing and in the MHC, are skimpy and disappointing. See also *Ann Arbor News*, 15 May 1948; and the general discussion of the issues in Albert Applegate, "The Search for Responsible State Government in Michigan" (Honors thesis, Woodrow Wilson School of Public and International Affairs, Princeton University, 1949).

alesced with legislative leaders to block most of Sigler's high-flying reforms, balling them up in legislative committees and stalling them in lengthy floor fights.[58]

It is in this context that we can begin to appreciate why Sigler's only success in the renovation of government came in the state's prison system. The Department of Corrections had been created by a Democratic reform in 1937; its director reported to one of those bipartisan commissions Sigler so heartily disliked. The department was also heavily populated by "Democratic holdovers" who had passed under civil service protection and were now making careers in state service as advocates of professionalism in corrections. Moreover, these elements had only recently consolidated their control within the system, eighteen months before Sigler's inauguration, and they had done so by ousting Harry Jackson, a pillar of the Republican old guard and well connected among conservative lawmakers. The efforts of the newcomers to stabilize lines of authority and build alliances in the legislature were still going on in 1947, attended by considerable confusion and contention within the prison system. Here was an opening for Sigler, one that brought his nose for scandal and his need for a crusade into harness with the antipathy of some Republican lawmakers for Garrett Heyns and their partisan instincts for an assault on a supposedly "Democratic" stronghold in state administration. Not only was the department vulnerable to a corrective intervention because its permanent bureaucracy lacked defensive alliances with key legislators, but this very vulnerability tended to bridge some of the crosscurrents and tensions between Sigler and fellow Republicans that otherwise divided them and frustrated the governor's reform agenda.

During 1947 Sigler seized this opportunity. Restlessly, if not aimlessly groping for a usable rhetoric and ideological platform for governing and trying to forge an administrative program that would sustain his image as the scourge of corruption and champion of good government, Sigler reached down into Jackson prison and appropriated the continuing struggle over Harry Jackson's legacy to his own ends. He used Jackson prison to make a scandal and then "salvaged" it with decisive reform. Once again the state prison became an exten-

---

58. A fuller account of his legislative battles over the veterans bonus, labor legislation, the sales tax, etc., can be found in the Undergraduate Report, *The Transformation of Michigan Politics in the 1940s*, SFRC Monograph no. 10, Residential College, UM, 1985.

sion of, and a constituent element in, state politics—this time caught up in the partisan imperatives and experimental logic of postwar Republicanism and the efforts of a political newcomer to solve the question of his own future by providing an ideological and programmatic answer to the New Deal that would mobilize support. Yet, though submerged in politics, Jackson prison was never a passive object of Sigler's conjuring. Prisoners and custodians alike, especially friends of Harry Jackson, found an unlikely ally in Kim Sigler; they used his interest in scandal production, even as he used them to produce a scandal, in order to sustain the internal struggle over administrative authority and carceral practices, the continuation of which, in turn, provided Sigler with openings to find scandal. The common target of these dual but disparate purposes was the Heyns-Pascoe coalition so recently triumphant in the struggle with Harry Jackson.

Producing Scandal in the Reformed Prison

Harry Jackson was certain that Ross Pascoe had engineered his downfall. But the warden was not alone in his dislike of the parole board and its chairman. A number of leading jurists in the state, including, most prominently, W. McKay Skillman of Detroit Recorder's Court and Guy Miller of the Wayne County Circuit Court, had serious reservations about the system of parole established under the 1937 reform act. For them it was a question of jurisdiction: Did the sentencing judge retain jurisdiction over convicted felons after they were sent to prison, or did control over the inmate pass to the Department of Corrections and the parole board at the moment of incarceration? Skillman insisted on a continuing supervision until final discharge; Pascoe firmly resisted such "meddling," claiming that the trial judge's purview ceased with the sentence and that the final disposition of any felon in prison lay entirely in the hands of the parole board.

The specific point of contention was the minimum sentence. Skillman and others argued that a sentence with a minimum and maximum term was intoned by the judge for the good of the felon, not the guidance of the parole board; most prisoners, he argued, should be released on the expiration of their minimum sentence, less good time earned, unless *institutional* behavior warranted some extension of incarceration—and, then, only upon consultation with the sentencing judge. Many wardens, and none more vehemently than Harry Jackson, agreed. If institutional authorities granted good time and imposed disciplinary punishments, they were in a position to promise (or threaten) reductions (or extensions) of sentence—provided, of course, that the parole board could be counted on to grant release at the expiration of the minimum term on a more or less routine and predictable basis. The parole board, for its part, took a far more independent view of this question, preferring to treat the minimum sentence as "the moment" when the board reviewed a prisoner's record and determined how much time he would have to do. Pascoe firmly defended his autonomy in these matters: the board would issue no guidelines, make no promises, hold out no predictable pattern of behavior. The fundamental point for Pascoe was that parole was a privilege, to be received with joy and surprise, like good luck or gifts, not a right to be expected or counted on, let alone demanded.[59]

Judges, of course, had political influence, and Skillman's position found resonance among state legislators, especially conservative Republicans, who regarded the 1937 reform act as a piece of Democratic legislation and the Department of Corrections it created a "hotbed" of liberalism. None were more prominent in their criticism, especially of the parole board and of Pascoe and Heyns personally, than Elwood Bonine and Elmer Porter, both powerful Republican senators and senior members of Senate committees dealing with prisons. In April 1945, as the scandal broke over SPSM, the Senate set up a special committee of its own to look into prison affairs and assess the workings of the 1937 reforms; Bonine and Porter, together with one liberal Democrat with connections to the labor movement, Stanley Nowak, were its only members. The committee moved slowly, operating for only a few months each spring when the legislature was in regular session and seemingly unsure of what to study. During the spring of 1946 Bonine and Porter sat in on every session of the civil service hearings, listening carefully to Dethmers's charges and Harry Jackson's defense. By May the two senators seem to have found their

---

59. These issues were clearly spelled out in a document prepared for the *Detroit News* by Pascoe and Gerald Bush on 30 January 1945 and later included in Noel Fox's *Survey of the Michigan Corrections System* prepared in June 1949 for Governor G. Mennen Williams. A copy may be found in Fox's report and in the Williams Papers, box 14. See also a perceptive account of these issues in the *Detroit News*, 5 August 1945.

stride, announcing to the press that their confidential hearings would now center on Jackson prison and inmate complaints about parole.[60] Their final report was ready a year later, in April 1947.[61]

It was thus during the early months of 1947 (which were also the first months of the Sigler regime) that Bonine and Porter spent a good deal of time in and around Jackson, interviewing inmates and guards. The word was soon out that they were not friends of the department or the current administration at the prison and were receptive to criticism of the parole board. Charles Watson, restored to his job as classifications director by the Civil Service Commission, worked closely with the committee, feeding it cooperative prisoners and collecting affidavits and sworn statements on his own. With little prompting the stories poured in—stories of the parole board, of hearings in which board members retried criminal cases and held inmates up to ridicule, of promises for special consideration made by parole board members to anyone who agreed to testify against Harry Jackson, of shakedowns of parolees by parole agents in Detroit; stories of harassment and intimidation, of Warden Benson and his immediate superior, Assistant Director Burke, threatening prisoners who testified before the Senate committee and conducting reprisals against inmates and guards who remained loyal to Harry Jackson; and stories of graft and corruption—Heyns having free suits made, Bush having repairs done on his home by inmate workers, Burke receiving free furniture for his home in Owosso, and other officials getting goods made, cars repaired, and labor performed by inmates "off the book." And from a more murky distance came stories of massive fraud in Prison Industries during the war—illegal sales of cloth and other goods, traffic with black marketeers in New York, and other schemes to defraud the government. Bonine and Porter listened to it all with sympathy, uninterested in the details but apparently convinced from what they heard that there was much more to be uncovered:

> I can't talk to you as I would like under present circumstances [the inmate clerk in the garment factory told the senators]. You are in no position to offer me any security. I have seen what has happened to others who became involved in past investiga-

---

60. *Detroit News*, 9 May 1946.
61. See press reports, *Detroit News* and *Free Press*, 15 and 17 April 1947.

tions. . . . You will learn nothing of any value from inmates here who are in a position to help. They are all concerned over their own welfare [sic].[62]

As leads and stories piled up, pointing beyond the committee's mandate or involving possible criminal activity, Bonine and Porter asked the state police to join in, and the threads of inquiry began to branch out again through all aspects of Jackson prison.[63]

Prison officials watched with alarm this rising tide of tales told out of court. Publicly, Heyns insisted that they had nothing to hide: "We are as eager as anyone to find out if anything is wrong, and are quite willing to cooperate."[64] The department sought to give every appearance of cooperation; when reports of wartime graft in Prison Industries surfaced, the department announced that it had itself uncovered an "unusual practice" in the disposal of surplus and obsolete material and "ordered it stopped." Heyns insisted that it was "an error of judgment more than anything else" but that the official concerned, Fred Munnell of Prison Industries, had been told "that it will no longer be done that way."[65] But behind the scenes officials were rather more anxious to contain the damage. Convinced that a "fifth column" was at work in the prison, Heyns and Benson took measures to curb its activities—Charles Watson was transferred to the Trusty Division outside the walls in April and then fired, again, in May for insubordination; inmates considered too devoted to the old regime were transferred to Marquette, although officials vigorously denied any intention to interfere with the investigation.[66] The director met

62. Testimony of George George, 23 March 1947, Donald Leonard Papers, box 19.

63. Most of the information we have on these hearings comes via the material turned over by the Senate committee or collected by state police investigators and passed on to Lansing for review by Donald Leonard, the new state police commissioner (Donald Leonard Papers, box 19).

64. *Detroit News*, 15 April 1947.

65. *Detroit News* and *Ann Arbor News*, 13 March 1947.

66. *Detroit News*, 16 April 1947. Watson was transferred by his immediate superior, Sidney Moscowitz, a former parole examiner, who was appointed to the new post of assistant deputy in charge of inmate welfare in February 1947, a position that included supervision of inmate classification. After repeated clashes (see statement by William Patterson, 23 March 1947, the Leonard Papers, box 19) Moscowitz transferred Watson outside in late March and then brought action to fire him in late April. The department upheld his dismissal in early May (*Detroit News*, 2 May, 1947); the Civil Service Commission then reinstated Watson in June; he was fired again in August, ostensibly because of low scores on the civil service exam, which was administered to

with the new governor several times in the spring of 1947 to urge upon him "the necessity of bringing current investigations to a speedy conclusion," and the Corrections Commission joined in with a strong letter of support.[67] In a report submitted to Sigler in late April, Heyns rejected the notion that there was a " 'Jackson situation' in the sense that there is in that institution administrative mismanagement, widespread unrest among inmates or discontent among employees."[68] Such allegations, he insisted, were the work of "disgruntled former employees," "malcontent prisoners," and "biased outside interests" who were being allowed to concoct an aura of scandal where none existed.

But Sigler, never one to allow facts to distract him from appearances, could not let this opportunity pass. He had said little in his gubernatorial campaign about the state prisons, except to link them in a general way to McKayism and the corruption that he said ran rampant in state administration. The archives shed no light on his intentions, although, given his dislike of bipartisan commissions and his critique of the Murphy reforms, it is likely that he had an eye on the Department of Corrections as a possible target for his streamlining projects. He does not seem to have shared Bonine and Porter's dislike of Heyns nor to have had any strong opinions about the parole board or the question of its jurisdiction. But the possibilities of combining his agenda with the senators' was clearly present. And it may be surmised that, as the odor of scandal began to rise again from Jackson prison, Sigler was drawn powerfully to the possibility of showing that Dethmers had not done a complete job. In any event, two days after he met with Heyns to hear pleas for an early end to investigations, Sigler ordered his attorney general, Eugene Black, to take charge of the inquiry and press it home.[69] For several days the press was full of stories of a vigilant governor "awaiting a report," "reviewing allegations," "studying options." What he had before him was a memorandum from the state police, really an unedited compendium of everything that had come up in the testimony of inmates and guards at

---

him when he was reinstated (*Detroit News*, 6 June and 21 August 1947). No departmental records of actions against Watson appear to have survived.

67. See Minutes of Prison Commission, 13 April 1947, Department of Corrections, Pardons and Paroles, box 1.

68. *Grand Rapids Press*, 19 April 1947.

69. *Detroit News* and *Grand Rapids Press*, 15 April 1947.

Jackson, coupled with a short response from Heyns defending the prison against the allegations and charges contained in this collection.[70] What was at issue had less to do with prosecutable illegalities than with political confidence: Was the new regime at the prison going to receive the endorsement and support of the governor, or was it to be laid open to renewed attack from critics in several quarters? For Sigler the choices were purely political.

While he was contemplating his options, the Senate committee issued its report. As expected, Bonine and Porter recommended broad changes in the 1937 Corrections Act, including the elimination of the four-member commission and its replacement by a full-time appointive commission of three, an expansion of the parole board to four members, with its director and chair appointed by the governor, and a sharp reduction of departmental supervision over the individual wardens, who were to be removed from civil service protection but also given broad autonomy in the running of their institutions. The lone Democrat on the committee, Stanley Nowak, issued a blistering minority report, denouncing his two colleagues for listening to a few vocal critics in the pursuit of "rumors and suspicions" and for recommending the creation of "seven politically controlled positions," in place of the part-time bipartisan commission and professional management of the department provided under the 1937 reform.[71] At the same time, the report got little applause in the Sigler camp, where the replacement of a four-man commission with a troika and the recommendations for weakening centralized control over prison wardens did not look like bold acts of streamlining. No one thought much would come of the report so late in the legislative session. Indeed the weakness and obviously partisan character of the Bonine-Porter study, coupled with the clutter of unsubstantiated and legally rickety charges collected by the state police, may have given prison officials some hope that they had finally weathered the crosscurrents of investigation and innuendo.

But they reckoned without the governor and his political needs of the moment. Declaring that enough suggestion of "impropriety" and "malfeasance" had arisen in the course of the Senate hearings and

---

70. The state police report is in the Leonard Papers, box 19, dated 12 April 1947.

71. Press criticism of the report was widespread; see, particularly, the jaundiced reaction of Guy Jenkins, the widely syndicated capital correspondent (*Ann Arbor News*, 3 May 1947); Nowack was interviewed by the *Grand Rapids Herald*, 4 May 1947.

police investigations to warrant concern, Sigler suddenly announced the launching of yet another probe—this time "an investigation to end all investigations." He insisted that his only intention was to lay suspicions to rest by airing them all fully, and, to insure an aura of impartiality, he reached outside state agencies for "new faces" to conduct the probe, appointing Thomas McAllister of Bad Axe, who had managed Sigler's gubernatorial campaign in the "thumb" area of the state, and Edmund Blaske of Battle Creek, a personal friend, to be his special investigators.[72] Brought hurriedly to Lansing to receive instructions, these two soon established themselves at the state police post at Jackson, across the road from the prison, and during the summer months proceeded to interview nearly two hundred and fifty inmates without ever setting foot inside the prison.[73]

Predictably, Blaske and McAllister were at sea, only vaguely aware of the recent history of the prison and unsure what to believe of what was told to them. They wandered off on tangents, down old trails already well explored before, through the thickets of the Hooper murder again, and around in circles over parole proceedings. They became hopelessly balled up in contradictions, as one inmate told them not to believe the words of another and one group of guards told stories on others. And they found no way out, since they were determined to preserve their status as impartial outsiders and refused, on principle, to visit the prison or fraternize with Warden Benson and his staff. A considerable bias, already implied in their appointment, accumulated around this stance. It was deepened by their procedure, which was to interview one prisoner and ask him who else they should talk to, building lists of witnesses upon such chains of association and thus laying themselves open for covert lobbying.

As novices with inquisitorial powers, however, Blaske and McAllister posed a serious threat to prison professionals. Battle lines between Jackson's administrators and Sigler's investigators were soon drawn. Benson and his staff held back, wary of the investigators and uncertain of what charges were being leveled against them and what they might have to answer for when they were called across the street. This gave the floor to prisoners, and hundreds signed up for a

---

72. *Grand Rapids Herald*, 18, 20, and 22 May 1947; *Ann Arbor News*, 22 May 1947.
73. The transcripts of these interviews are in Attorney General Investigations, Criminal Division: Investigations of SPSM, 1921–47, box 3, continuing into box 4.

chance to talk about their affairs. The hearings became a forum to speak bitterness, and, as Blaske and McAllister listened to the lamentations and complaints of aggrieved inmates, they formed the opinion that the prison was being massively mismanaged and that Benson was being uncooperative and hostile in an effort to cover up wrongdoing.

The pushing and pulling across Cooper Street soon got into the newspapers. The department in Lansing, not knowing what was being talked about in the state police barracks and unable to control where prisoners might lead the investigators, issued general alarms. Heyns worried about institutional morale, and Pascoe warned prisoners that they were subject to criminal libel if they made false statements.[74] The attorney general shot back that the probe was turning up "wrong-doing from top to bottom inside the prison" and that "indictments may be expected."[75] Warden Benson responded publicly that he was "almost reaching the limit" watching these "prize saps" being made into the "dupes" of prison malcontents; Blaske and McAllister were unwittingly contributing to insolence and indiscipline among prisoners, who, knowing that they could carry grievances across the street, resisted orders and, in effect, dared custodians to crack down. In view of Benson's concern about disciplinary problems, the Corrections Commission again urged Sigler to bring the investigation to an early end.[76] But Blaske and McAllister replied with charges of their own—that prison officials were destroying evidence, interfering with their call for witnesses, and threatening those who did testify with reprisals or transfers. "We have plenty of ore and there is some gold in it," they told reporters, but progress was being hampered by official stonewalling and by jokes told around the institution, with official encouragement, about "backwoods lawyers" and "Hoosier hotshots."[77]

Sigler's response was imperial: he summoned Heyns and Benson to his presence, rebuked them for talking to newsmen, and placed a gag order on all prison employees, investigators, and ("the governor mentioned specifically") Ross Pascoe. He had complete confidence in

74. *Detroit News*, 28 June 1947.

75. Ibid., 30 June 1947.

76. Minutes of Corrections Commission, 1 July 1947, Department of Corrections, Pardons and Paroles, box 1.

77. *Grand Rapids Herald*, 28 and 29 June 1947; *Detroit News*, 28 and 30 June 1947.

his two investigators, he told Heyns, and "if in the future there is anything amiss . . . you are to come and tell me."[78] Sigler then dispatched his attorney general to Jackson to supervise the continuing inquiry; his task was to help Blaske and McAllister "make decisions as to the particular line of inquiry" and to report directly to the governor on the condition of morale and discipline at the prison. Before leaving Lansing, Black assured Sigler that "prison morale has not been adversely affected"; indeed, "it was a known condition of unrest in the prison which was one of the originating causes of the investigation. The investigators are obtaining evidence of both maladministration and wrong-doing. We want all the facts."[79] Sigler needed little encouragement. He had received wide notice and editorial praise for his forthright intervention and for his insistence that a professional silence be maintained by state officials while serious allegations were being sifted.[80] The governor appeared to be in charge, getting the job done. In press reports SPSM was described as engulfed in "innuendo," "clouds of suspicion," and "rumors of misconduct"; while nothing was clear, the mere existence of such charges seemed sufficient reason to continue the probe. In effect, the investigation was feeding itself.

For the next six weeks Blaske and McAllister concentrated their inquiry on the question of wartime graft in Prison Industries, primarily because it offered fair promise of criminal prosecutions. The essence of the matter (though there were many tangents) was that Fred Munnell, head of Prison Industries at Jackson during the war and an employee of the system since 1919, had sold remnants of cloth, mostly celanese and rayon used in coat linings, that had been purchased by the prison's garment factory to meet army contracts for uniforms, to a certain Alfred Goldstein, the federal inspector for military contracts in Michigan prisons; Goldstein had then disposed of this material through his brother, Solly, in New York, on the open market at considerable personal profit. When the charge first surfaced in the spring of 1947, Heyns had not considered it a serious breach, since the material in question had consisted of bolt ends and remnants, some of them damaged, and Prison Industries had been paid

---

78. *Detroit News*, 2 July 1947; also *Ann Arbor News*, 2 July; *Grand Rapids Press*, 2 July; and *Grand Rapids Herald*, 4 July 1947.

79. *Detroit News*, 10 July 1947.

80. *Grand Rapids Herald* editorial, "Good Work, Governor," 5 July 1947.

forty thousand dollars by Goldstein for the goods. Munnell insisted he was merely trying to dispose of unusable surplus, and Heyns noted that all money realized had gone to the state treasury. But the transactions were technically illegal under the Munshaw Act, which forbade sale of prison property to private individuals or the transport of prison goods across state lines. This was, admittedly, thin gruel for scandal, but the subsequent disappearance of the Goldstein brothers and their apparent use of false addresses in New York added a dash of criminal zest to the story, and, as Blaske and McAllister focused on Munnell and his superior at that time, William Burke,[81] a process of titration brought other charges to light: perhaps Munnell had suits (even a zoot suit!) made for his personal use by prison industries or had juggled the accounts to cover items of prison property sold off to other private connections; perhaps Burke had converted steel kitchen cabinets to his personal use and made off with some venetian blinds, a trellis, and a picnic table that belonged to the state; and perhaps, when Jesse Shanks, a rather seedy individual who later took gifts from Goldstein, was hired by Burke to run the garment factory, he and Munnell were already in a conspiracy to defraud the state.[82]

Although Blaske and McAllister regularly gave Sigler oral reports of their findings, none of this got into the press, thanks to the governor's "gag order." By the end of September, however, with the investigation showing no discernible results and the press starved for stories, complaints began to arise about its mounting costs; both Blaske and McAllister were receiving a per diem of fifty dollars plus expenses, and the total charge for the "prison sift" was now running over eleven thousand dollars.[83] This was five times what Dethmers's probe had cost, and it revived memories of Sigler's own overblown expense account when he had been special prosecutor in 1944–45. With the legislature summoned to begin a special session in November, the governor needed something other than bills to show for his efforts. It was time for a media blitz.

81. Burke had been head of Prison Industries from 1939 to 1942 then went on active duty until 1946, when he returned to Michigan and was appointed assistant director for prisons by Garrett Heyns.

82. These and other charges, stories, and speculations are contained in a Report of Investigation to Donald Leonard, n.d., in box 19, Case Files: Miscellania (4); and in the preliminary report of Blaske and McAllister, 4 October 1947, in Attorney General Investigations, box 4.

83. *Grand Rapids Press* and *Ann Arbor News*, 24 September 1947.

On 30 September Sigler broke his own command for silence and announced that an unnamed underling at the furniture factory in Ionia had confessed to burning records that indicated "that products made for the state actually were delivered to private individuals." In the governor's retelling of the story of this "rather important official," members of the Corrections Commission had received furniture for "private" use, and these deliveries had been recorded as "state repairs" to disguise the fraud. When questioned, commissioners were perplexed; perhaps, said one member, the governor was referring to a two-drawer file cabinet given to each commissioner to hold official papers—but no one was sure, and all were insulted by the governor's uncharacteristically ham-handed public attack. Pressed by reporters, Sigler "rechecked the confession and decided that the commissioners had been wrongly accused." In retreat he stressed the complexities of the investigation and the instances in which "guilty parties" tried to alter, hide, or destroy records in an effort to conceal wrongdoing. "There is a lot more connected with this that I don't want to disclose now."[84]

With the press thus baited, Sigler struck again two days later. At a news conference he announced proceedings against William Burke and Fred Munnell for "misfeasance, malfeasance, and gross neglect of administration" and signed an executive order commanding the two to show cause why they should not be fired.[85] The Corrections Commission protested; several officials at Jackson expressed dismay; and Arthur Wood, writing for the Michigan Corrections Association, a private citizens' group, spoke for them all when he called the charges "an exaggeration" and told Sigler that "the reiteration of such charges, some of them rather vague, together with the long process of

---

84. This is drawn from *Grand Rapids Press, Detroit News,* and *Grand Rapids Herald,* 30 September 1947.

85. The story was broken by Guy Jenkins, whose contacts in the capital were extensive (see *Grand Rapids Press,* 2 October 1947; *Ann Arbor News,* 3 October 1947); it became official on 9 October, when formal charges were laid, based on Blaske and McAllister's preliminary report of 4 October. There was some dispute about the procedure, which was invented for the occasion: Sigler ordered the two by executive decree to appear at a public hearing of charges on 27 October, but it was not clear if this would be binding on the Civil Service Commission or the Corrections Commissions or if either or both of these bodies would also hear appeals. The Corrections Commission also protested, in a letter of 12 October, that some of the charges against Burke occurred in an earlier time, when prisons were operating under "a political party system, when such things were common practice."

investigation, keeps the public and the management at Jackson in a state of jitters, obscuring the unquestionable fact that the general conduct of our prison affairs in recent years has been sound and progressive."[86] But Sigler was no longer listening. With the same erratic, even heedless, intensity, the same flair for surprise and newsworthy possibilities that had characterized his pursuit of Frank McKay, he now chased Burke and Munnell. Chairing a public "executive review" that he concocted ad hoc for the occasion, Sigler led the interrogation, hectoring witnesses, taunting the hapless "defendants," and pointing Blaske, who served as state prosecutor, to the main points. Munnell was first in the dock; he had already "confessed" his mistakes and sought now to explain his actions. But the governor would hear none of it. Leaving his seat as presiding officer to become the inquisitor, Sigler badgered and questioned Munnell, ridiculing his answers, warning him not to lie, indicating where he had changed his testimony, pressing him for details he could no longer remember, and throwing out rhetorical questions—"Is this an example of your slipshod methods of running prison industries?"— to instruct his audience.[87] On the third day, after seventeen hours of hostile grilling, Munnell began to mount his defense; led carefully by his attorney, he laid out the logic of his wartime deals, showed where the money had gone, produced data on prison industry profits, and, in all, effected a remarkable resurrection: the shady lightweight, easily tricked by wily con artists and (probably) in cahoots with them, whom Sigler had left cringing on the stand, was transformed into a shrewd and experienced man of prison business, who, while he may have been guilty of some errors of judgment, was otherwise a loyal servant of the state and certainly no crook.

This was not where Sigler wanted to go. From the presiding chair he spotted Berry Beaman of the Corrections Commission in the audience, interrupted the defense to summon him forward, and proceeded to "blast" the commission for failing to supervise Prison Industries effectively or to discipline Munnell when irregularities were

---

86. Executive Office Records, box 8, file 7: Corrections Commission, contains copies of letters sent to Sigler from several quarters. Woods's is dated 11 October 1947. See also Department of Corrections, Pardons and Parole, box 1, Minutes of Prison Commission, 10 October 1947, at which the letter to Sigler, dated 12 October, was discussed and agreed upon.

87. Full accounts appeared in the press on 27, 28, and 29 October 1947.

first uncovered. Beaman defended his colleagues: they had taken timely and appropriate action the previous spring; they had not fired Munnell because, in their judgment, the case did not warrant the dismissal of a civil servant; they had not pursued the inquiry because Sigler had horned in with his own team of investigators. Sigler responded with a speech:

> One of the troubles with our present government in Michigan today is the fact that many boards and commissions and various departments of government say, when trouble arises, "There is nothing we can do about these matters because of civil service." [The Corrections Commission complains that] prisons have been the subject of repeated and almost continuous investigation. That is true, and it will continue to be true as long as men conduct affairs like Mr. Munnell conducted them.
>
> I want the prisons run so that every citizen will have complete confidence and respect in the administration—and you are not going to have that kind of respect so long as you have a man like Mr. Burke at the head of it. I want this business of investigations stopped, but I want it to be stopped by you and your department. Is that clear?

"That is clear, your honor," conceded Beaman.[88] His point made, Sigler adjourned the hearings. The next day he suspended them entirely, fired Munnell, and commanded the Corrections Commission to dismiss William Burke.[89] The commission refused. Declaring that "the Corrections Department needs very little housecleaning except the multitude of investigators who have been passing in and out of our institutions for the past four years," the five commissioners collectively resigned: "We don't have to stand for public humiliation."[90] "Quitters," taunted the governor in retort.[91]

But Sigler had turned the tables. With the scandal in war industries that he had cultivated all summer about to fizzle out, he had deftly shifted the focus of attention from the patently skimpy facts of

---

88. *Detroit News*, 30 October 1947.

89. *Ann Arbor News, Detroit News*, and *Grand Rapids Press*, 30 October 1947.

90. Minutes of the Commission, 30 October 1947; public statements to the press, *Grand Rapids Herald* and *Detroit News*, 31 October 1947.

91. *Grand Rapids Press* and *Ann Arbor News*, 31 October 1947.

the case against Munnell and Burke to a debate over the effectiveness of the commission system itself. The resignation of the entire commission added a grist of conviction to his mill. He now controlled the pace of events. He could blame the prison commission for failing to face up to its responsibilities "despite the fact that all the evidence had been turned over to it," thus preserving the impression that there was more to the scandal than had come out in the public hearing while making it seem that it was the commission itself—its "lame defense of Burke and Munnell," its inability "to devote the required time to the job"—that had made such a long investigation necessary in the first place. "Conscientious as they may be, they simply cannot give their entire time to direct the department for which they are responsible."[92] The solution was implicit: with a stronger, more centralized executive authority, there would be no need for further investigations, indeed nothing to investigate.

A week later Sigler opened the special session of the legislature with a ringing call for decisive action—"I've only got a few short months to do things. I'm starting now"[93]—and laid out a plan to overhaul prison administration, replacing the four-man, bipartisan commission with a single, appointed commissioner of corrections. His bill passed in a single day. The crisis the governor had manufactured, coupled with the aura of scandal that he had cultivated all summer, now combined with Bonine and Porter's long-standing dislike of Heyns, whose job was conveniently abolished by the new arrangement, to produce quick results. Sigler then invited Austin MacCormick to come for consultations and, at the latter's suggestion, named Joseph Sanford, warden at the federal penitentiary in Atlanta, as his new "supermanager." "It's a honey of a set-up," he told newsmen at the end of the year.[94] It was also politically rewarding: the press applauded Sigler's decisive leadership and found little to criticize in his revamped system; early in the new year a meeting of party leaders and financial contributors agreed that Sigler should get the funding he needed to carry his reform campaign right through to the fall elections.[95] The search for scandal had served its purpose, and Munnell and Burke slipped between the cracks and disappeared.

92. *Ann Arbor News*, 31 October 1947.
93. *Detroit News*, 9 November 1947.
94. *Ann Arbor News*, 27 December 1947.
95. *Detroit News*, 26 February 1948.

Inside the Reformed Prison

The 1947 Corrections Act was a monument of sorts to Kim Sigler's character and political needs of the moment. He never made clear how the new, more centralized structure prevented scandal or, indeed, how the old system designed in 1937 had promoted it. And the archival record sheds no light at all on Sigler's motives or calculations. The narrative sequence constructed here, leading from his political needs to his interest in scandal to the prison and its administrative renovation, rests entirely upon a reading of his actions in the public record, not upon any inside information. The claim, put simply, is that good government themes were the flip side of scandal, and dependent upon it, and that both were essential to Sigler's ability to govern without a political base or secure access to party machinery. Thus stated, the prison was irrelevant, and, indeed, it is not apparent from the public record that Sigler spent much time briefing himself on the prison and its problems. His reform measures were of a generic sort, derived from his general interest in streamlining, but they indicated no particular insight into the administration of prisons. When asked, experts and progressives in penology, such as Austin MacCormick, found both the 1937 and 1947 acts imminently acceptable, arguing that it was less a question of choosing one over the other, or changing from one to the other, than of settling on something and allowing the system to stabilize around it. The Democratic platform in 1948 promised to restore the 1937 commission system, but after they won office, they concluded, on expert advice, that any change was worse than none and left things as they were.[96] Sigler's monument stood until after the riot because no one had the energy to tear it down.

---

96. The legislative history of this is not clear, but a special advisory committee chaired by Earnest Brooks, an author of the 1937 law, and Arthur Wood urged the new governor to leave things as they were (Report of the Governor's Advisory Committee, n.d., Williams Papers, box 14), and by the spring of 1949 all thoughts of going back to the 1937 system had been abandoned (see *Detroit News*, 30 April 1949). Another attempt, in 1951, also failed; this time the Department of Administration came down strongly against change (memo from the Department of Administrations, 2 April 1951, Williams Papers, box 58, Corrections Department file). After the riot the system was changed again, with a Corrections Commission reinstalled as the overall supervisor of the department and its director.

If the reform had no compelling substance, neither did the scandal that produced it. Sigler himself always had less interest in what happened than in what use he could make of what was uncovered; this was his strength as a prosecutor of corruption and a producer of scandal. But the investigators who spent time at Jackson during 1947, including Bonine and Porter as well as Blaske and McAllister—not to mention the state police who assisted them all—talked to real people and heard real stories. In between chasing lost bolts of rayon from World War II and trying to prove that Warden Benson, or Burke and others in Lansing, were impeding the investigation by threatening or transferring would-be witnesses (subjects that took up a lion's share of the transcripts they generated), these investigators heard stories about harsh discipline and controversies among guards, bad food and poor medical facilities, homosexuality and gambling, missing goods and tampered records, and, above all, stories about the parole board and its lack of consideration for inmates, its unfair procedures, and its capricious, unpredictable ways. This litany might be heard in any prison at anytime and is not indicative of anything particular about Jackson. None of the investigators ever found a way to put the undigested jumble of stories together or to reconcile their contents in a continuous narrative about the management or operation of the prison. It is significant that, in the end, the only indictable offenses uncovered—indeed, the only activities that could constitute (marginally) plausible grounds for dismissal—had taken place five years earlier, during Harry Jackson's tenure, when corrupt practices could be tied to a sustained description of social order and patterns of administration behind the walls.

Given the context, however, the stories told to investigators in 1947 tell us something about Jackson prison after Harry Jackson's downfall. What is most obvious, of course, is that Harry Jackson's cronies and dependents in the prison used the investigation, and Sigler's need to continue it, to keep up a sustained guerilla campaign against Heyns and Pascoe, to discredit the new order at SPSM, and even to effect a rehabilitation of the former warden. Heyns certainly thought this was the crux of the matter. Harry Jackson had many friends in the Republican Party, especially among conservative legislators, such as Bonine and Porter, who shared his dislike of Heyns and Pascoe, and the former warden was in touch with his friends in Lansing during these months.[97] There is no doubt that Chuck Watson, one of Harry Jackson's most devoted and openly sentimental followers, was deeply involved in the production of witnesses for Bonine and Porter. It is also apparent that the flurry of stories about prison industries during the war was stimulated, at least in part, by the fact that then industry head, William Burke, was a close personal friend and protégé of Heyns, who had only recently been appointed the new assistant director for the Bureau of Prisons; Prison Industries had been know as "Heyns's territory" during the war, part of the department's domain, not the warden's, and, insofar as Harry Jackson's loyalists were leading the investigators, the pursuit of Fred Munnell in 1947 reflected an insider's understanding that wrongdoing in Prison Industries could be laid at Heyns's doorstep. Finally, while it may register some real grievance, the fact that the preponderance of evidence against the parole board in the Blaske-McAllister transcripts had to do with attempts by various members to bribe or entice prisoners to testify against Harry Jackson—offering favors to those who cooperated, threatening those who refused—is surely suggestive of a chain of selectivities in who came forward, what they thought the interrogators wanted to hear, and what the investigators chose to pursue. It tells us something about how the Blaske-McAllister probe was viewed inside the prison that many inmates took pains to boast, in 1947, about how they had resisted pressure to testify against Harry Jackson in 1945.

In this context we may read the testimony of prisoners and guards in a double light: as interested attempts to defeat the new order and bring back the old and as implicit expressions of internal reactions to the changes that followed Harry Jackson's ouster.[98] Espe-

---

97. *Grand Rapids Press*, 18 March 1948; *Detroit News*, 30 March 1948. Jackson also had a brief meeting with Sigler and left behind a memorandum, dated 20 March 1948, rehearsing the injustice done to him—"how, through political intrigue, conspiracy, coercion, intimidation, and bribery I was ultimately removed from office by false changes proffered by the political machine of the Corrections Department"—and asking for reinstatement.

98. Here the testimony collected by the Senate committee and by state police in the spring of 1947 is more revealing, hence helpful, than that collected by Blaske and McAllister during the summer, when the inquiries began to narrow onto prosecutable actions; the latter two focused the bulk of their time on Prison Industries and the Munnell-Burke case, or, more tangentially, on who got whom to testify against Harry Jackson. They seemed rather impatient with talk of life inside or with guards' career

cially among the rank and file of the custodial force, there seems to have been widespread discontent. Older guards spoke of being pushed around by the newcomers. Those who had been, or continued to be, loyal to Harry Jackson felt they were being shunted aside and passed over for promotion; there was considerable resentment of "outsiders" who had come in with Benson. Laurence Muck, a veteran hallmaster, summed up the feelings of many older guards:

> The prison can't go on the way it's going. All the oldtimers are being "horsed around." The new officials are taking advantage of the old experienced men because they are near retirement. They have to take it or get fired. They don't want to lose out now with retirement so near. Young and inexperienced men are taking their places and don't know the score.[99]

The tension and bickering among custodians was visible to prisoners and affected them. One wrote to Governor Sigler directly, to say that the prison

> is being operated under the worst conditions I've seen in many years, and I have been here a great number of them. It don't seem possible that the officials could be as they are in this day and age, that old proverb of "Dog eat Dog" still holds true within these walls, from Heyns on down to the cell-house screw, they're all sparring for the chance to stab each other in the back.[100]

Paradoxically, such sentiments probably only stiffened Sigler's resolve to pursue an investigation that, in turn, only intensified the tensions and suspicions among custodians and between guards and prisoners.

Many veteran guards felt Benson's disciplinary crackdown was a mistake. The imposition of uniform procedures, the intensification of rule enforcement, and the elimination of special privileges struck many old-timers as a provocation to inmates that also, by stripping custodians of inducements and favors, placed them in personal dan-

worries. Although I have drawn on the Blaske-McAllister transcripts (Attorney General Investigations, boxes 3–4), I have found the material in the Donald Leonard Papers (box 19) more helpful in reconstructing conditions inside Jackson in 1946–47.

99. Statement taken 26 March 1947, ibid.

100. Copy of letter, H. Meyers to Kim Sigler, 3 February 1947, Leonard Papers, box 19.

ger. For some, such as Captain Stetekluh, the new rigidities made his job harder. He approved of uniform discipline when handling prisoners en masse, on the yard, or at dinner: "There you must handle them all the same." But uniform discipline should not be inflexible discipline, he continued:

> You have got to take into consideration the individuals. If you can recognize a man's work, if he does you a good job, why not compensate him some way . . . by granting them a little extra privilege, such as a detail that would allow them a little bit more liberty out of their cells; that is, the occasional man that you pick out for doing special work. You have them working for us.[101]

This was the voice of the old order, hedging his bets perhaps ("that is, the occasional man") but sticking to his guns. More venal veterans, such as Laurence Muck, who had had his fingers in many tills during Harry Jackson's tenure, no doubt had more pointed things to say in private about Benson's bleaker and less remunerative prison, but most guards would probably have echoed Stetekluh's assessment that "the present administration has tightened up considerably on inmates" but that this policy had only generated resentment and "hasn't improved the morale of inmates."

Prisoners certainly agreed. Many expressed frustration with the crackdown, the intensified discipline, the cell checks, the harassment—"there is too much supervision"[102]—and lamented the loss of easy contact and reciprocity: "It used to be we could stop and talk with any of the officers and members of the parole board when we would meet them in the corridors. But not any more."[103] When inmates complained to Blaske and McAllister about "low morale," "lack of consideration," and "terrible conditions," they were responding at least in part to a more uniformitarian world in which prisoners had fewer freedoms and diminished opportunities and prison society was conditioned by greater scarcities and less privileges. The discord among guards came down upon prisoners in the form of greater pressure and less trust. Old-timers, who had to be careful not to offend the new regime, could not be as flexible or forgiving with

---

101. Attorney General's File, Special Investigations, SPSM, box 4, vol. 23.

102. Testimony from George George, 23 March 1947, Leonard Papers, box 19.

103. Statement of William Patterson, 23 March 1947, ibid.

inmates as before. New guards came with instructions to bear down, and veteran guards were no longer able to protect their favorites or reward cooperation. As opportunities for profitable collaboration diminished and the new disciplinary emphasis increased the number of hostile encounters between keepers and kept, tensions rose. "You know the way they are running this place is a shame. They are creating so much discord that anything can happen. No inmate has any respect for the officers here anymore."[104]

As the rules changed, prisoners saw the hierarchies of status and connection that had once organized prison life dismantled. The dense web of exchange that had bound keeper and kept together in forms of tacit, at times illicit, collusion, came unraveled, leaving in its place greater caution, a mood of betrayal, and a feeling of helplessness among inmates and old-timers alike. The sense of distance, of interrupted intercourse, of lost intimacy, congealed into a kind of nostalgia for the old order.

Cast in this way, we begin to mimic the language of the witnesses, recalling "lost worlds" and waxing by degrees more wistful and nostalgic as the remembered stability of the old is set against the confusion and uncertainty of the new regime. This conforms rather too readily to familiar conventions of narrative history, and we must be careful of the interpretive gloss we give to the evidence. Yet what prisoners said is suggestive. While the jumble of testimony collected by Bonine and Porter, Blaske and McAllister, does not permit us to construct a stable picture of life inside Jackson prison in 1946–47, we can glean intimations of how the new rules unsettled the social fabric of the prison and created new anxieties.

The endless complaints about harsh discipline, for example, may be read as a register of grievance against the new regime's crackdown, but they also suggest that custodians were handling a growing number of infractions through official channels. Perhaps this is only a measure of stricter enforcements, but it may also indicate that officials were intervening in situations that they had heretofore let prisoners handle, that the internal solidarities and organization that had enabled inmates to resolve conflicts and disputes among themselves was not functioning well. These are hints that the capacity of inmates to govern themselves—to "run the joint"—was weakening, that the

104. Ibid.

old terms of standoff and collaboration no longer held. Similarly, the fact that so many inmates were willing to carry grievances across the street to investigators may be taken as a measure of discontent, but it may also be a sign that internal solidarities were breaking down; the inhibitions (and sanctions) against talking, informing, "ratting" to officials, and the reticence required by corrupt collusions were less apparent by 1947. The unending confusion of evidence collected by the investigators suggests that just about anybody and everybody was willing to talk; there is no sign of inmate leaders, no references to key figures or hierarchies that investigators might follow in developing their information. And, while it is now impossible to give anything like clear shape to the impression, the amount of direct contradiction, denial and cross-denial, that Blaske and McAllister "uncovered" from and among their witnesses suggests that they had fallen into a thicket of small, antagonistic factions. This too would be consistent with a leveling of inmate hierarchies and a weakening of "self-governing" capacities. As custodians reclaimed powers once conceded to the "cons," the authority of old inmate leaders narrowed to their immediate circle of friends; the links that once made prison society function as a reluctant community were cut or foreshortened, and the internal spaces, once organized as the coherent satrapies of "big shots," came under the control of small, rival factions.

If these speculations are consistent with now invisible developments, we may conclude with the sociologists of the 1950s that the disciplinary crackdown and the leveling of inmate hierarchies produced a more atomized, less cohesive society inside. The effort to increase official "protection" for individual prisoners by eliminating the grip of the "big shots" and intensifying custodial supervision tended to increase official interventions in prisoner affairs. This deepened the reliance of prisoners upon authority, even as it broke up lateral connections among inmates and multiplied the factions competing inside. The result, among prisoners, seems to have been a sense of greater insecurity and less safety. For us it exposes a curious inversion. Harry Jackson's prison, which seemed to outsiders to have been heedlessly corrupt, conceding control to convicts and neglecting the most elementary principles of carceral control, was, for its inmates, a relatively orderly and predictable universe that had channeled their energies and regulated their expectations. Ralph Benson's prison, by contrast, while promoting a uniform discipline and procedural regime that was fully comprehensible on the outside because it was in accord with free world expectations of what a prison should be, fostered among prisoners a sense of uncertainty, unsettledness, even danger, that had not existed before. The chorus of complaints, of finger-pointing and head shaking, that arose in 1947 registered, but did not itself explain, the growing disease behind the walls. Yet we need to understand this new specimen of disorder if we are to understand what prisoners were saying when they rioted.

A New Kind of Disorder

We may begin by rehearsing Garrett Heyns's view of the changes in train. In his keynote address as president of the American Prison Association in November 1945, he took as his theme "the time of transition is with us."[105] For Heyns this meant, rhetorically, that the war was over and, in turning again to peacetime corrections, it was time to take stock: "We are not certain," he said, musing over the biblical metaphor, "that we want these plowshares shaped exactly as they were before." Cautious and diffident as ever, Heyns sketched a progressive agenda for change in the fields of probation, juvenile justice, and prison operations. He worried about disciplinary practices and personnel problems, but the burden of his remarks on prisons underscored the importance of education, vocational training, clinical services, and, above all, classification. For Heyns effective classification—the segregation of inmates according to types of crime and prospects for reclamation, the separation of "defective delinquents," "the sex deviate and the psychopath," from ordinary offenders, and the distribution of inmates across a range of custody classifications, from maximum to minimum—was the necessary prerequisite for an effective program of rehabilitation and hence the very essence of "individualized treatment." In recommending these changes to his listeners, Heyns quoted from the Prison Association's declaration of principles and held out a transcendental vision of the more perfect prison, not just the "best . . . in the country," but the "most effective system . . . humanly possible."

Heyns's notion of a transition was thus securely nestled between

---

105. "Swords into Ploughshares" (presidential address), *Proceedings of the American Prison Association*, New York, 15 and 16 November 1945, 3–18.

old and new, darkness and light, with progress cast as a struggle against reactionary forces. Many of "our co-workers" dislike "modern penology," he warned: "We find among our officials many who resent any breakdown of the old routine. Such men can sabotage any progressive program." An idealized future set against the hard struggles of the present transition but already better than the dark days of yore—these were by now conventional images in national correctional circles, and, in using them, Heyns was locating himself among the "advanced thinkers" of his profession. He was also rendering an implicit commentary on developments in Michigan prisons: reflecting on the terms of his recent struggle with Harry Jackson; reading the continuing opposition to change at SPSM as a "fifth column" of malcontents who clung to old practices and sabotaged the efforts of progressive managers; and seeing prisoners who complained as benighted and feckless and unaware of what was good for them. It also helps us understand Heyns's dismay at Kim Sigler's intervention, for the governor was, if nothing else, a paragon of reform and champion of the anticorruption crusade—an ally of progress, among whose minions Heyns counted himself and thus the last person from whom Heyns, his attention focused on retrogressive forces in the prison, would expect an attack. Sigler disrupted Heyns's scenario of change.

Other speakers who addressed the association in this period also spoke of change, but their words hint at a problem of larger and more complex dimensions. Joseph Sanford, Heyns's predecessor as president of the association in 1944 (and his successor as head of Michigan corrections in 1947) also framed his keynote address in terms of preparations for peace and developed the theme of a "new epoch in prison administration and penology."[106] But his tone was far grimmer and more discouraging. Refusing to present a prescription for change because, he said, "the future . . . is so completely unstable," Sanford devoted his remarks to critiquing "our principal failings." Chief among these were "an all pervading pessimism, a stagnant cynicism," and a lack of vision: "We are short on constructive objectives." Lamenting the lack of positive models, he chided his listeners on the intellectual emptiness of the profession: "Hardly a book has been

---

106. "Prison Administration Must Prepare for Peace" (presidential address), *Proceedings of the American Prison Association*, New York, 12 and 13 October 1944, 107–20.

written, hardly a voice has been raised in our time that would tend to provide us with a sound and effective program of reform. The simple truth is that we suffer from a dearth of leaders and a drouth of ideas." There was no coherent account of what prisons were trying to do or what standards might be applied to measure success. The challenge to professionals in the new epoch was to reassemble in new circumstances the core intentions and practical claims of penology.

This was not a new lament in national prison circles. Throughout the 1940s leading figures in the profession called for new thinking, reassessment, and reform, and these recurrent pleas were closely tied to discussions of the future of prison practices, the acceptable boundaries of discipline, the need for improved classification, and the changing criteria of rehabilitation. The pivotal issue, always at the center of these discussions and key to the crisis of direction, was the question of prison labor. The collapse of prison production in the Depression had been rendered permanent by restrictive legislation in the mid-1930s, and by the time the Supreme Court ruled, in 1937, that "the sale of convict-made goods in competition with the product of free labor [is] an evil," prison administrators had come to realize that idleness was no temporary problem, nor one that existing programs was likely to solve. It was "a desperate situation,"[107] which "could hardly be worse."[108] The "busy workshops of the past . . . have been swept bare"; "the fight to drive prison products from the open market . . . is practically over."[109] "You are now with your backs to the wall, and unless some way can be found to get prison industries upon the state use system, you may lose the most powerful instrumentality you ever have had to maintain discipline and promote the rehabilitation of your charges."[110]

It was not only that prison managers felt an effective tool of discipline had been knocked from their hands or that a dangerous idleness was rising on all sides; the crisis of the industrial model of corrections threatened the penal project with incoherence. "I am overwhelmed," Richard McGee told the convention in 1938, "at the

---

107. "Prison Labor—Past and Future," *Proceedings of American Prison Association*, St. Paul, Minn., 2–7 October 1938, 327.

108. "Prison Labor—the Existing Situation," *Proceedings of the American Prison Association*, Philadelphia, 10–15 October 1937, 229.

109. From discussion of prison labor, *Proceedings* (1937), 229, 232.

110. *Proceedings* (1938), 329.

evident futility of much of what we do, and I am baffled by a thousand obstacles. The machine of which we are a part has become more powerful than its operators."[111] The doors clanked, the prisoners shuffled to and fro, the guards rotated their shifts, but the point of it all was lost. Not only was there little meaningful work, but prison industries, starved for investment and shunted off into limited "state-use" markets, offered little in the way of skills or training that could lead to substantive work in the free world. One of the basic assumptions of penology, still persuasive only twenty years before—that there was a continuous flow in casual work from prison industries to the labor market in the free world—had been permanently undercut. This made it difficult for prison managers to deliver a coherent account of what they were doing: of who criminals were (the lazy and indolent had become, in the Depression, the chronically unemployed), what made them misbehave (a rebellious or surly nature had become, in the Depression, a desperate need), what was done to them in prison (discipline and hard work had become, at best, intermittent work at tasks irrelevant to a depressed job market), and what criteria were applied to release (a steady job had become a pious hope of adjustment).

On the surface it would seem that the expansion of war production would have offered prisons a timely solution. Not only did the level of demand—over fifty million dollars in industrial and agricultural goods in the first year[112]—increase employment in prisons, but federal contracts offered a new flexibility in the legal application of state-use provisions.[113] More impressive to prison officials, however, was the notable rise in productivity among prison workers: "The morale of the inmates in our penal and correctional institutions is higher than ever before in their history." This, more than additional jobs, was believed to insure peace and good order. And the model

111. "Realism in Prison Administration," *Proceedings* (1938), 53. McGee went on to be president of the association in 1943.

112. Aggregate date for state and federal prisons was offered in a session on "Problems of Prison Industry in War and Peace," in *Proceedings of the American Prison Association*, New York, 20–22 November 1943, 67–68.

113. The state Administrative Board ruled in 1942 that sales to the federal government were illegal under the law, if solicited by Prison Industries, but entirely legal if the United States government needed war supplies and came asking. The Munshaw-Frey Act was subsequently amended to reflect this interpretation. See Corrections Commission minutes, 10 November 1942.

presented in wartime of a carceral community full of well-adjusted prisoners, who not only worked hard but were happy and coopera- tive in doing what they were told, lingered long after the war. Yet prison managers were also aware that war production masked, rather than solved, deeper dilemmas. The surge in demand for war goods interrupted efforts to develop stable state-use markets within the states; it strained existing facilities while delaying investment in new plant and equipment; it distorted prison industry programs, as a shortage of raw materials forced cutbacks and layoffs in some plants (binder twine, stamping and metal work) while overworking others (textiles, canning, and shoe making). And few had illusions about the future; as Fred Munnell commented in a discussion at the association meeting of 1943, "One does not have to be a prophet . . . to accept the fact that once this present emergency is over, the urge or the necessity to produce in prison industries will no longer exist."[114] When the "temporary period of flush production" is finished, "what then?" Some, impressed by the communal solidarity of inmate workers, reached for optimism:

> Even greater is the promise which lies ahead, if we hold the gains and make them a springboard from which we can invade the future with new and better aims and more constructive methods. This means . . . bold and constructive planning for the post-war world in the penological realm.[115]

But this merely restated the problem Sanford sketched the following year, papering with rhetoric the holes in sustained thought. More typical was William Burke's worried call at the 1946 meeting for voca- tional training, more farms, industrial pools, sharing arrangements— anything to keep up the momentum and the high morale of the war effort.[116] The moment war contracts were suspended, the deeper problems—how to keep industries alive, how to keep prisoners busy,

---

114. "Tomorrow's Industrial and Agricultural Program" (discussion in *Proceedings* [1944], 123 ff; Munnell's comments are on 127–28).

115. "Practical Problems of Administration Projected by the War: Part II," *Proceedings* (1943), 68.

116. "A Travesty of Justice," *Proceedings of the American Prison Association*, Detroit, 4–8 October 1946, 185–88.

how to keep the ideology of corrections intact—reasserted themselves in the "new epoch."

Lamentations are rarely raised in total darkness, of course, and corrections officials had at least rhetorical solutions ready at hand throughout the 1940s. Indeed, a recitation of difficulties was often a prelude to sketches of progressive possibilities. "The solution comes in a new penology . . . the past is behind us."[117] Few thought they could undo the restrictive legislation on prison industries or restore the industrial model to its full glory. Coming to terms with the new, now permanent, limits meant, among other things, recognizing that in the future "there is likely to be less manufacturing in the institutions."[118] While an old-fashioned response might be to raise the alarm of idleness, the path of the "new penology" was toward a multiplication of other activities and programs to occupy inmates. Charles Osborne laid out the progressive agenda as early as 1937,[119] when he warned his listeners not to allow "prison industries to become an end in themselves" but, rather, to integrate them more closely "with the remainder of the prison program":

> By all means, let us stand firm on the principle that prisoners must work, but let us not lose sight of the fact that work is one element in a program of rehabilitation and it should be coordinated with the other elements and not allowed to dominate them.

Austin MacCormick took up these themes the following year in a lyrical evocation of the "dynamic penology":

> The head and the staff of the dynamic institution are doing their best to fill the waking hours of their prisoners' day with activities that interest them, stimulate them, and fit them to participate effectively and satisfyingly in a free social existence after they are released.[120]

---

117. Harold E. Donnell's remarks, *Proceedings* (1937), 236.

118. This from a discussion, "The Problems We Face: Education, Vocational Training, and Adequate Employment of Prisoners," *Proceedings* (1945), 68–73.

119. "Prison Labor as Seen by the Osborne Association," *Proceedings* (1937), 240–42.

120. "Paregoric Penology," *Proceedings* (1938), 42.

This displacement of the point of incarceration, from producing docile and disciplined workers to promoting a satisfying social existence, was replicated in discussions of industrial training during the war. Training, rather than production, had become the central rationale for prison industries by 1945, and its principal intent was not to discipline the body to industrial work but, instead, to prepare the inmate, in an "integrated total program" that combined education, training, religious instruction, and counseling, for a successful life as a free citizen.

> The real job of the prisons [is] not to produce binder twine or automobile tags but to develop men better able to get along in the community. Our problem is a human one.[121]

Industries were thus repositioned within the prison, to become one element in a larger, more complexly articulated agenda of rehabilitation.

> Into the plan and the program for the individual prisoner [declared MacCormick] comes the techniques of the administrators, the classification service, the medical service, the industrial men, the educators, the librarians, and the chaplains.[122]

And such an institution, he added, would pay for itself many times over, not in the profits of its industries but "in men and women reclaimed to useful and lawabiding lives." Prison industries, Fred Munnell told the Detroit convention in 1946, had "attained a place in present-day penology that a decade or two ago . . . would have seemed to be unattainable," because now "the worker [has] become a trainee."[123]

This new configuration of the penal project did not entirely break the link between prison work and social discipline that had governed the industrial model. It was still assumed that hard work in prison

---

121. William Ellis, *Proceedings* (1943), 72; see also the discussion "Problems We Face," *Proceedings* (1945), 68 ff., in which "training" becomes the leitmotif of the entire discussion.

122. *Proceedings* (1938), 44.

123. "Prison Industries Are Basic to a Well-Organized and Administered Program of Correctional Treatment," *Proceedings* (1946), 189–95.

promoted self-discipline and good order; it was still assumed, or hoped, that skills learned in prison would be salable in the job market outside; a good work record was still important in a parole hearing; and parole was still, more or less, contingent on having a job on the outside.[124] But at every link in this equation there were now added caveats and additions. With the shrinking of prison industries, not everyone could work, certainly not in industrial jobs; thus a more refined classification process was necessary, to sort out those deemed "reclaimable" (mainly younger and first offenders) and to forge up for the lucky few the "right" combination of work, training, education, and counseling that would foster the promised rehabilitation. At the same time, it could no longer be assumed that industrial work in the prison had much relevance to the free labor market; "there is," admitted the warden of San Quentin, "no place where a jute mill graduate can find work in a community identical to that he performed in a mill,"[125] but with an integrated program, geared to the specific needs of each individual, it was possible to hope that work in the mill might, in addition to work habits, promote "training in care of equipment, observance of plant safety rules, cooperation with co-workers, etc"— skills for getting along in the free world. And, while a good work record might still impress the parole board, it had to be conceded that the more threadbare and transparent work opportunities available in prison required some embellishment of the record; prison industries had now to contribute to the counseling process by producing constant reports on workers aptitudes, skills, and habits, which could be used not only by the parole board in determining readiness for release but also by parole officers in the field trying to find job placements for those released. And, finally, "it is not enough to release a man and place him in a job. He needs constant help through a carefully prepared program of follow-up work."[126] More comprehensive parole procedures would not only intensify supervision after release but extend the rehabilitation process deep into the free world.

All the myths of reinclusion still prevailed; imprisonment was still supposed to change criminals, correct their wayward impulses,

---

124. See the discussion on "The Function of an Industrial Program in a Penal Institution," in the *Proceedings of the American Prison Association*, Long Beach, Calif., 12–16 September 1947, 145–52.

125. Ibid., 150.

126. "Problems We Face," *Proceedings* (1945), 70.

and restore them, whole and rehabilitated, to the community. Only this was no longer achieved through hard labor. Work in prison was now permanently decentered. The shrinking sphere of prison industry—not only the constriction of product lines and markets but also the increasingly trivialized nature of available jobs and their increasing irrelevance to the world of industrial work outside—displaced labor within carceral practice, repositioning it to the sidelines as an ancillary or contributory activity, no longer central to the rationale of incarceration. In its place classification was given pride of place as the new coordinating science, around which the satellite arts of education, vocational training, group counseling, individual therapy, and, also, industrial work were assembled into a "total program," a whole rhetorical fabric, a continuous account of what prisons were doing. A new "mix" had emerged by the late 1940s, one that clung to the industrial model but amended, modified, and supplemented it to close the gaps opened by limited work and widespread idleness and to reaffirm the redemptive ideals of incarceration in altered circumstances.

This mix proved infinitely adjustable. What was made necessary in the first instance by the Depression and restrictive legislation became by the 1950s the preferred option. A triumphant Fordism had no place for prison labor or prison-made goods. As labor unions became more organized and watchful, as the labor market became more segmented, specialized, and tightly controlled, embracing high-tech production and requiring fewer, more highly skilled workers, the notion that there was a link between what a prisoner learned inside and employment opportunities on the outside became increasingly frayed and unconvincing. And the notion of therapeutic rehabilitation—not disciplined work at a job but, rather, successful adjustment to the community—became increasingly prominent in the rationales of incarceration. Therapy could take account of the "whole man"; the social background of need, the elements of "disfunction" and "instability" that made unemployment chronic; the "antisocial" character that turned an admittedly frustrating search for work into a crime of opportunity; the mental difficulties that got in the way of finding an "appropriate" placement or developing an "adjusted" understanding of real prospects—all these contextual problems could be addressed through counseling and remedial programs. And what began as a supplement to repair and preserve the industrial model became, by the 1950s, its substitute, a new model prison promising the same things, only through different means.

We must, of course, be cautious in transposing this national discourse to a local plane. There were huge gaps between rhetoric and practice, and the annual gatherings of professionals promoted a kind of "group talk" among an in-crowd that had more to do with mutual reassurance than decisive action. Yet to see the transition of the 1940s in the broader context of a crisis in the industrial model prison is to cast a very different light on events in Michigan at mid-decade. The problems at Jackson prison would appear to have little to do with corruption or the overthrow of Harry Jackson's regime. Indeed, Harry Jackson's system might be seen as one possible way to cope with the collapse of industrial production in the "big house." It was the first solution essayed in Michigan, only because patronage practices had become so well entrenched in the state prisons during the 1920s and because the completion of Hulbert's massive industrial prison in the midst of depression and the face of restrictive legislation made for a particularly acute crisis of correctional ideology in Michigan. But this did not make Harry Jackson's solution the only one imaginable; his political and bureaucratic opponents quickly embraced the alternative language of the new penology heard in national circles and applied it not only against Harry Jackson's methods but to the crisis of the industrial prison that the old warden was, also, trying to master. Harry Jackson's defeat in 1945 had more to do with the political indefensibility of his increasingly corrupt patronage practices than with any strong evidence that the new penology would be better at managing SPSM in a postindustrial era. By the same token, in dismantling Harry Jackson's system, his successors merely laid bare the continuing crisis of the industrial prison and made plain the incoherence of the hard labor rationales that had underwritten Harry Hulbert's ambitious project.

Benson's disciplinary crackdown and the inmates' response to it was not the crux of the matter either. To be sure, the new regime moved quickly to slice through the informal traces of collaboration and reciprocity around which Harry Jackson had built his regime, but a disciplinary crackdown was not itself a regime of control. Heyns, Pascoe, and Benson all espoused the tenets of the new penology, and they clearly assumed that, in destroying the old regime, now rendered obsolete and old-fashioned by scandal, they were clearing the ground for new and improved carceral practices. Benson reaffirmed the importance of the Classification Committee and tried to clarify its procedures; he created a new post, a Deputy Warden for Inmate Welfare (soon renamed the Deputy Warden for Individual Treatment), in an effort to give salience to the new priorities. But most of his efforts in 1945–46 were directed at rooting out the old regime, and it remained unclear how the rhetoric of a new corrections would cohere in practice or how it would become articulated with the existing everyday operations of the prison.

Moreover, the crackdown coincided with the suspension of war contracts and a rapid collapse of prison industries. The reimposition of limits upon work options inside was further reinforced by the bizarre pursuit of Fred Munnell, whose offense was in the violation of certain legal restrictions on the sale and movement of prison-made goods in the economy and whose removal in 1947 symbolically proclaimed an end to all wartime looseness of enforcement or tolerance for shortcuts in the marketing of prison-made goods. And Benson only made the job crisis worse when he abolished hobby craft production (on the grounds that the jobs involved offered inmates too many illicit opportunities).[127] Thus, in dismantling Harry Jackson's system, prison managers were not only depriving themselves of numerous tried-and-true levers for the control of SPSM, they were also reengaging some of the same dilemmas of industrial penology that Harry Jackson had sought to solve through informal and illicit means. And, beyond the rhetoric they had rehearsed, the epigoni had trouble making the new regime as clear or as tangible as the old had been.

Not only did prison managers have difficulty offering a continuous account of what they were trying to do, but prisoners had trouble reading the "new line" for clues about how to win release. It is in this context that we may understand the bitter criticisms of the parole board in 1947. It was not just that Ross Pascoe was mean and unapproachable or the parole board too stingy in letting inmates out— though these aspects were undoubtedly important; what inmates

---

127. The process itself is instructive: first, Benson put a limit of $1,200 per man on profits from hobbycraft sales and banned the highly popular trade in canaries. Then he moved to impose a flat wage on all inmates engaged in hobby crafts, based on prison pay scales, but, when this was challenged by labor organizations, who argued that a flat wage made the prison, not the individual prisoner, the producer, the warden simply discontinued hobby crafts altogether.

most hated were the mixed and uncertain messages they got from the board or that circulated as story and rumor through the prison. Though work was no longer the centerpiece of rehabilitation and all prisoners were told they must earn parole by participating in a "fully integrated program," the alternative paths were neither spelled out nor sufficiently developed, and almost every inmate could tell a story of how the board had discounted efforts to meet its expectations or had proven suspicious of those who had, in Pascoe's words, "taken the easiest course, avoiding work through pretending a yearning for 'education.'"[128] The only certain guideline, hardly reassuring, was Pascoe's general view that "a man who has for many years lived outside the law may rarely be restored to good citizenship by a brief term of incarceration, but may be by a longer and more intensive correctional procedure." The smug self-assurance of this remark could hardly disguise, for prisoners, its profound vagueness; it was the uncertainty that proved excruciating.

In this respect the widespread bitterness and sense of grievance that investigators found in 1947 registered the confusion that attended the displacement of work as the path to release and a growing impatience with the absence of a clear substitute narration of conditions. Tearing down Harry Jackson's regime merely brought these problems to the surface. Inmate complaints captured the need, which everyone felt and which even Harry Jackson had tried to articulate, for a new and continuous account of the prison process and of the location of parole in it, so that prisoners had some idea of what was expected of them and how they might hasten their release. This was not so much a nostalgia for the old regime as an impatience with the new—a call not to go back but to get on with it. And it was not sensational scandal or the downfall of Harry Jackson that conditioned this reading of transition but, rather, the continuing failure of Harry Hulbert's industrial prison and the strains in the synapses of the carceral project that were exposed when Harry Jackson's remedial regime was dismantled. In the midst of exposé and political upheaval, prison officials experienced considerable difficulty in developing an alternative model of penality, and their efforts to juggle the balls of uniform discipline, less work, better classification, more education,

---

128. "Parole Indictment and Responses, 1945," in Noel Fox, *Survey of Michigan Corrections,* 20 June 1949, Williams Papers, box 14.

and uncertain parole were only complicated by the wild card intrusions of Kim Sigler, looking for something scandalous.

The new mix of correctional rationales and the uncertainty that accompanied the new regime were neatly captured in the mural-like picture the department chose to put on the cover of its quarterly bulletin in 1946 and 1947. At the center of the picture, against a backdrop of cell blocks and tiers, stands a well-dressed inmate with books under his arm; we have to look up to him, as he gazes off to the right of the picture into the distance, perhaps at some future yet to be realized. To the left, below the main figure and slightly off center, is another large portrait, this one of a prisoner-worker looking down at his task; we know he is working because his shirt is off, but it is impossible to tell quite what he is doing with his hands. Around him are grouped some symbolic props—a draftsman's compass, some test tubes, a few unrecognizable plants, an engine—that evoke the powers of science, careful planning, and study and suggest not so much the tools of prison labor as the instruments of correction. On the right, opposite the prisoner-student, stand two guards in profile under a giant fist gripping a bar. Below the guards, and marching in close order between them and the prisoner-student, is a line of faceless inmates, their backs to the viewer, headed "down" into the cell blocks. The main elements of the new penology are all present—education, work, and custody; uplift, self-discipline, and control. Classification is present by implication: presumably it sorted out and set to the forefront those prisoners considered reclaimable through learning and labor and is sending the rest, the recalcitrant and irredeemable, shuffling off into oblivion. Missing from this representation of prison life is the main currency of prison—time and the main regulator of that currency—the parole board. The picture thus offers clues, but no coherent account, of the one thing that mattered to inmates: how to win release. The picture is an assemblage of elements that foregrounds individual prisoners without connecting them to a "readable" process—a collage of counterpoints that conveys multiple meanings but a confused message.

The Roots of Riot (II): Settling Uncertainty Inside and Out

Charitably, one might argue that Kim Sigler was dealing with similar confusions in 1947. Having led an assault on Frank McKay and swept his would-be heirs in the moderate Republican center aside, he found that he had only exposed a deeper problem: how to govern through a party whose internal cohesion and political monopoly had been destroyed in the Depression and the subsequent collapse of patronage politics. Sigler found his solution in the politics of exposé and in a continuous mobilization of good-government crusades, carried on through the media over the head of, and at times against, his own party, not to mention officials of his own government. When, in 1947, he ginned up a scandal in the prison and used it to ram his reorganization plan through the legislature and win the blessings of the press for decisive action and good management, his principle victims were officials in the Department of Corrections who had participated in the overthrow of Harry Jackson and believed themselves to be the governor's allies in the campaigns against corruption and political patronage. The beneficiaries of reform became its first victims. Sigler, feasting on the discontent, factionalism, and uncertainty of a system in transition and turning everything upside down in his hunt for something to expose, nullified the efforts of prison officials to address the continuing crisis of the industrial prison or to articulate the terms of a new carceral order.

"Good clean administration" remained his watchwords as he summoned the legislature to session in March 1948.[129] In a series of radio addresses he laid out a sweeping agenda of governmental overhaul. Ideally, he said, the state should have a new, thoroughly modern constitution, but in the interim he proposed a series of constitutional amendments to extend the term of the governor, make the offices of attorney general and secretary of state appointive, and remove salary ceilings for state employees, so that the most high-powered outside managers could be brought in to run the state.[130] In his opening speech to the legislature he coupled these proposals with a plan to create a new Department of Administration that would consolidate budgeting, purchasing, and accounting as well as management of state supplies and equipment under a single agency that, as a "tool of the governor," would insure his control and promote accountability and efficiency. "The key to good government," he opined, "is good organization."[131] Briskly dismissing concern about

---

129. *Ann Arbor News*, 1 January 1948; *Detroit News*, 8 February 1948.

130. Radio Address, WKAR, 2 March 1948, in a collection of speeches, Sigler Papers, box 2, State Archives.

131. *Grand Rapids Press*, 16 March 1948.

cost with the claim that monies saved through streamlining would make new taxes unnecessary, Sigler hitched his political fortunes to the program of consolidation and renovation, betting that the combination of aggressive executive leadership and an ideology of good government would carry him through the elections in the fall.

But the political problems of the previous year quickly revived. Legislators continued to have mixed reactions. A few were openly contemptuous of the governor—"just plain insipid rantings"—and urged him to drop "this foolish reform business."[132] The bold program soon got bogged down; lawmakers dragged their heels, prolonging committee hearings, extending their weekend recesses, and dissipating Sigler's urgent momentum in interminable procedural debates.[133] Sigler responded with yet more calls to action; he showered the legislature with a bewildering array of proposals—to provide pensions for state judges, to make use of federal airport funds, to allow banks to close on Saturday, to inaugurate daylight savings time, and to permit state institutions to use margarine—that had little to do with streamlining government and a lot to do with his need to appear the bold and far-sighted governor striding ahead of the legislature in service to the people. The odd spectacle of a legislature held in session against its will by a governor determined to force action by heaping on more work ended in a shouting match, with Sigler denouncing the legislature for obstructionism and the lawmakers voting to adjourn without further action.[134] Only an elaborate, last-minute compromise (in which the legislature adjourned but agreed to reconvene for one day in May and pass a thin version of Sigler's package) saved the governor from the worst legislative reversal in living memory.

Sigler's overhaul of the state prison administration was nearly lost in this general imbroglio. His new high commissioner for corrections, Joseph Sanford, arrived in the new year under orders from Sigler "to inquire into the fitness of employees and report to me."[135] The governor made it clear that he was not finished with the Department of Corrections: "Certain individuals will be given an opportunity to resign," he told newsmen in that now familiar blend of officiousness and imprecision. "If they do not, there will be public

---

132. Ibid., 15 April 1948.
133. See *Detroit News*, 15 April 1948.
134. *Ann Arbor News*, 29 April 1948; *Detroit News*, 30 April 1948.
135. *Ann Arbor News*, 3 March 1948.

hearings. I don't care to tell you who they are right now, and I am not prepared to say how many."[136] It was clear that all of Harry Jackson's successors—Heyns, Pascoe, Joel Moore (at Ionia), Gerald Bush (at Marquette), Ralph Benson (at SPSM), and Seymour Gilman (in the parole office)—were candidates for removal.[137] Behind the scenes Sanford apparently told lawmakers that he had no further use for the services of his predecessor;[138] whether this was a clumsy attempt to nudge Heyns to resign or a bid to win favor with Senator Porter, Heyns's old enemy and chair of the Senate committee that would have to confirm Sanford's appointment is not clear. But it is clear that the "insiders" quickly rallied in the legislature to block Sanford's confirmation; a group of senators from western Michigan also coalesced to protect Heyns, holding Sanford's confirmation hostage until they had substantive assurances from Sigler.[139] The governor quickly discovered that he could neither fire Heyns nor keep him without alienating key legislators, and, needing all the allies he could muster in a fractious legislature, he began cutting deals. He allowed Heyns to retreat to a seat on the parole board and guaranteed his job, albeit at reduced salary, and, after an initial defeat, the Senate confirmed Sanford's nomination by a narrow margin at its one-day special convocation in May, with the friends of both Sigler and Heyns joining in support.[140]

Immediately heads began to roll. Sanford declared war on "the

---

136. As Sigler told the Advisory Council on Corrections, he wanted to given Sanford full latitude in settling his staff (Minutes of Advisory Council, n.d. [March 1948]; Administrative Records, State Boards and Commissions, 1948, Records of the Executive Office, 1947–48, box 39, file 3).

137. *Detroit News*, 13 March 1948; *Grand Rapids Press*, 11 March 1948.

138. *Detroit News*, 17 March 1948.

139. James Milliken (Traverse City), Perry Greene (Grand Rapids), and William Vandenberg (Holland) were leaders of this effort (*Grand Rapids Press*, 18 March 1948). The coalition against Sanford consisted of liberals who followed the American Civil Liberties Union (ACLU) in criticizing Sanford's record at Atlanta, prison reformers who had not approved of Sigler's overhaul the previous fall, and friends of Pascoe and Heyns.

140. Much of this went on "off the record" and involved tradeoffs on other legislative matters before the special session. The *Detroit Free Press*, 28 March 1948, said the bewildering maneuvers were like "watching a ping-pong game and a yo-yo contest at the same time" (see also *Detroit News*, 19, 27, and 30 March 1948; *Detroit Free Press*, 29 March 1948; *Ann Arbor News*, 21 May 1948; *Detroit News*, 22 May 1948). Bonine joined with Milliken and Vandenberg in supporting the nomination; both Porter and Greene abstained.

subversive group" in the department that had opposed his nomination. The first to go was Gerald Bush, warden at Marquette since
1945; although there were formal charges—"reported breaches of regulations"—the reasons for dismissal were plain: Bush "admitted
lobbying against my confirmation," said Sanford; "I felt—and still
feel—the Department will not benefit by [Sanford's] tenure," replied
Bush.[141] Joel Moore was reported next on Sanford's list; the two had
apparently feuded since the 1930s, when they were both in federal
corrections, and the warden had made no secret of his distaste for the
new commissioner.[142] But Moore, who was almost seventy years old
and unwell, was legally compelled to retire in 1949, and, though
Sanford apparently tried to force an early retirement, on grounds that
Ionia "is a mess," he let the matter rest when the old man adamantly
refused to be budged. Instead, in August he fired Warden Benson at
SPSM, on grounds of "inattention to duty," "lack of cooperation," and
"excessive use of intoxicating liquor."[143] The press assumed that
Heyns and Pascoe were the ultimate targets of the purge; Sanford was
quoted as saying "either they go or I go."[144] Yet both were politically
connected, and Heyns was protected by Sigler's promises to senators.
Instead of dismissal, they were forced to watch helplessly from the
sidelines, unable to protect their friends in the department as the

---

141. *Detroit News*, 8 June 1948; *Grand Rapids Herald*, 5 June 1948; *Ann Arbor News*, 5
June 1948. Sanford claimed that, on the day before the Senate vote in May, Bush made
two dozen phone calls to friends in Lansing urging rejection.

142. *Grand Rapids Press*, 5 and 9 June 1948; *Detroit News*, 8 June 1948; *Ann Arbor
News*, 9 June 1948. Victor Anderson of Sigler's office told Pliny Marsh, who had entered
a strong defense of Joel Moore, that Moore was among the "very foolish people in the
Department who have resented [Sanford's] coming to Michigan" (letter, 24 August
1948, Records of Executive Office, 1947–48, box 39, file 2).

143. *Grand Rapids Press*, 11 August 1948; *Detroit News*, 14 August 1948. There is no
independent evidence of Benson's drinking, but it seems likely that the charge originated from an incident the previous year, when Blaske and MacAllister, annoyed by
delays in the appearance of inmate witnesses, suddenly summoned Benson to the state
police post on his day off. He had apparently been over at the Jackson County fair that
afternoon, having a few drinks "with the boys"; one of the investigators smelled liquor
on his breath, and there followed a hostile exchange between the warden and Sigler's
probers about whether Benson had entered the prison under the influence. Although
Benson vehemently denied mixing liquor with work, the investigators remained dis-
trustful of the warden, and their report apparently lodged the notion in Sigler circles
that Benson was a drunkard. See Attorney General Investigations, 1947, box 4: Interview with Benson, 28 August 1947.

144. *Detroit News* 12 August 1948.

purge rumbled on down through the ranks, knocking off lesser figures and threatening others.

This was almost entirely a "turf" fight, with very little substance. The professional and philosophical differences between the camps were slight. Sanford's views on correction were in step with his time, and his standing in the profession was high; he had carved out a respectable career in federal corrections, as warden of the Chillicothe (Ohio) industrial facility and, more recently, as warden at Atlanta, and he came highly recommended by Austin MacCormick, whom Sigler consulted on the appointment. In his interviews with the press Sanford spoke of bringing stability and accountability to the system, instituting modern classification and training facilities, and moving the corrections system toward a therapeutic future. But he was an outsider, with a reputation for toughness and a mandate from the governor to shake things up. Insiders who had not enjoyed Sigler's confidence did not offer Sanford theirs.[145] The incumbent wardens apparently feared that his talk of a "chain of command system" meant a centralized administration on the federal model and greater interference by the department in the day-to-day operations of their prisons; they all resisted the master in Lansing and ended up echoing, apparently without hearing it, Harry Jackson's complaints of four years before.[146]

While Sanford felt a purge was necessary in order to get control of the department, it soon became apparent that his needs were not serving Sigler's. On the face of it, to be sure, dismissals looked like decisive action or a salutary housecleaning, and all summer the governor's office staunchly supported Sanford's purge. But there was a growing recognition in the press that the governor's campaign to streamline administration, in the one department in which it was being fully implemented, was becoming purely disruptive. "It's beginning to look as if the chief job is to go around and fire somebody,"

---

145. *Ann Arbor News*, 21 May 1948; *Grand Rapids Herald*, 26 September 1948. George Kropp, in an interview, said flatly, "He was plain dumb." The ACLU believed Sanford was a racist, apparently based on reports about his tenure as warden at the Atlanta penitentiary, and their charge was soon echoed in liberal circles of the legislature and became fixed in Democratic Party rhetoric by the fall of 1948; in his campaign for governor G. Mennen Williams warned that Sanford would establish a Georgia-style chain gang in Michigan and promised to fire him (*Grand Rapids Press*, 19 January 1948; *Grand Rapids Herald*, 26 October 1948).

146. *Ann Arbor News*, 3 March and 21 May 1948.

grumbled one senator; others worried that the old practices of job rotation under patronage were being reconstituted in the techniques of modern government: "A situation is developing where any new Governor will be forced to get rid of Sanford and his supporters. Sanford will personify the Sigler Administration. Any new Governor will have to make a change in self-defense."[147] In effect, Sigler's highly personal, media-sensitive brand of politics, far from broadening his appeal or his political reach, had begun to personalize, and thus make petty, everything he did. It had been easy enough, four years earlier, to detect personal pettiness in the feud between Harry Jackson and Garrett Heyns, but there had also been real issues of policy at stake and enough substance in the scandal of 1945 to justify an overhaul of the department. Sigler's own pursuit of Frank McKay had also been very personal, but the many stories about the "boss" had been true, or at least credible, enough to give lift to Sigler's revelations and to make his crusade appear to be about something much larger and darker than simple facts suggested. Sigler's scandal in 1947 was threadbare by comparison. While it won him the power to overhaul the Corrections Department (and the political credit for decisive action), it lacked richness or staying power and failed to hold the attention of the media, upon whom Sigler depended for political significance. In applying his streamlining remedies, moreover, Sigler relied as always on appearances—a strong outside administrator, acting for the governor in shaking up a seemingly "corrupt" administration—rather than substance; in time it became apparent that there was no reason for doing it other than the doing of it.

By the autumn of 1948 Sigler had played out the available possibilities of a politics of scandal. His crusade for good government sputtered to an end just as the campaign season began. While it is possible that Sanford's summer purges, in their early stages, helped Sigler win renomination by amplifying his call for clean, decisive administration, his primary victory was largely due to a lack of unified opposition—itself a measure of the disarray of his party—and to a determination among state Republican leaders not to allow disunity or dissension to spoil a campaign they all believed would, finally, bring a national victory over the hated New Deal. There was very little enthusiasm evidenced for Sigler himself at the party convention

147. *Detroit News*, 14 August 1948.

in September, and what support he had seems, if anything, to have ebbed during the fall. On election day many Republicans withheld their vote for governor; Dewey carried Michigan, and every Republican seeking state office was elected, except Sigler and his attorney general. It was a vote of no confidence directed at him personally.[148]

None of Kim Sigler's problems in his final year as governor had anything to do with the Democratic opposition. With only two state senators and five representatives, the party had hardly been a presence in the legislature. As a political organization, it was directionless and in disarray, divided between pre–New Dealers, pro–New Dealers, and anti–New Dealers. Despite FDR's commanding presence in national politics, the state Democratic Party was not a viable contender for office in Michigan after 1940, and without officeholders it lacked the leaders and the patronage to discipline or hold the loyalty of a rank and file. Van Wagoner's last campaign in 1946 was little more than a gesture. In late 1947, however, a convergence of developments began to revive party fortunes. A group of young New Deal activists, many of them with experience in wartime Washington, began organizing Democratic Clubs around the state in an effort to draw out "closet" liberals—those who voted for Roosevelt in national elections but stayed home or voted Republican in Michigan ballots—and to develop the basis for a progressive state campaign platform.[149] These developments coincided with, and indeed made possible, a movement among labor leaders in the state toward closer ties with the Democratic Party organization. Walter Reuther of the United Automobile Workers, in particular, having used the growing tide of domestic anticommunism to defeat left-wing factions and capture the presidency of the UAW, was forced to accept the affidavits on party affiliation demanded in the Taft-Hartley Act of 1947 and to reject the

148. On the twists and turns of this election, see SFRC, *Transformation of Michigan Politics in the 1940s*, 73–75, 90–97. The Democrats won the governorship by 160,000 votes and picked up several seats in the legislature, mostly from Wayne County. But in statewide elections Republicans prevailed, reelecting a U.S. senator (Homer Ferguson), the secretary of state (Fred Alger), and the state treasurer (Hale Brake).

149. A full discussion of these clubs and the famous meeting in Hicks Griffiths's basement in November 1947 that got the movement started is to be found in *Transformation of Michigan Politics*, 77–90. I have also drawn on Ruth Wassem, "The Michigan Democratic Party in 1948: The Emergence of the Liberal-Labor Coalition," MHC, Ann Arbor; Aaron Horowitz, "The Michigan Election of 1948" (Senior thesis, Residential College, UM, spring 1984); and interviews with G. Mennen Williams (30 April 1985) and Neil Staebler (23 April 1985).

third party movement for Henry Wallace, widely supported by the labor left, in 1948. These moves brought labor toward the political center, just as liberal activists in the Michigan party began shifting the Democratic center to the left.

The possibilities of a connection between liberal party activists and moderate labor leaders was seized by G. Mennen Williams, a young, likable war veteran with New Deal credentials and established political connections around the state. Though closely associated with the reform movement, he was not selected by the Democratic Clubs, whose focus was on long-term party building, but once he declared his candidacy he drew strong support from the network of liberal activists that the clubs were developing. Similarly, while not a candidate of labor, his cold war liberalism, his firm rejection of the Wallace breakaway, and his New Deal platform placed him in close alignment with the positions of the Reuther leadership group, who welcomed his entry. The UAW Political Action Department worked hard to get out the labor vote in Wayne County: "Never before in the history of the Democratic party in Michigan have we been given a program as progressive and liberal as the one submitted."[150] It would be too much to claim that Williams's victory in November 1948 was a product of this labor-liberal coalition (it owed more to Sigler's political exhaustion). But it is fair to say that his campaign made such a coalition possible, and his narrow election victory in 1948 made the alliance a permanent feature of the state's political landscape.

In key respects Williams's triumph did not appear different from earlier Democratic victories; he won in a presidential election year, when a national candidate led the ticket and got elected. This had been the pattern throughout the Roosevelt years, except in 1944, and in each case the party lost again two years later. If Williams was not to be another one-shot governor—if, indeed, he was to be the first Democratic governor reelected since 1912—he had to demonstrate his qualities as a leader and consolidate the elements of the new coalition that was lining up behind him. Yet, as a lone Democrat in a sea of Republican officeholders and legislators, he had little hope of getting

---

150. The discussion of the UAW is drawn from Martin Halpern, *The UAW and the Politics of the Cold War* (Albany, N.Y.: SUNY Press, 1988); and from *Transformation of Michigan Politics*, 81–90. The quotation is from a memo by Gus Scholle of the Michigan CIO-PAC to union locals, in the UAW–Political Action Department, Roy Reuther Papers, box 3, folder 14, Walter Reuther Library of Labor and Urban History.

much done; his "Fair Deal for Michigan" became hopelessly stalled in the legislature. Unable to deliver on his promises, he fell back upon ideological appeals. Like Sigler before him, Williams came to rely on his access to the media and the formal occasions his office afforded for policy speeches to articulate his own agenda and define an ideology of change that could appeal over the heads of politicians in Lansing directly to the people.

There was, however, a crucial difference: Democrats were genuine political outsiders. In battling the legislature, Williams was not attacking his own party; rather, he was positioned to use progressive initiatives—and their almost inevitable defeat at the hands of a Republican legislature—to attract new voters to the Democratic fold and solidify the allegiance of constituencies that had voted for him in 1948. And, because his aim was to mobilize and include new voter blocs, he was able to enhance the Democratic appeal and draw new strength simply by defining more clearly the ideological differences between the two parties; every showdown with the Republican legislature helped him do this. Williams was thus able to make advantage of his weakness. Indeed, in contrast to Sigler's blend of scandal and reform, it was now possible for the governor to pose as a champion of good government without attacking the agencies and departments of government or its civil servants, and this meant that, potentially, the stabilization of administrative routine and the pursuit of reform could, for once, go hand in hand.

All good Republicans, of course, opposed the New Deal. But after five straight national defeats and now, with a Democratic governor about to "bring the New Deal home," there was some understandable confusion among Republican leaders over how to respond: Should they trim to the liberal winds or stand by their principles? "There seems to be quite a feeling in the legislature," Hale Brake, the new state treasurer, told Wilbur Brucker, "that now we must become more liberal and some of the more jittery members are going off 'half cocked' with so-called liberal ideas."[151] This struck Brucker as lunacy: "I wish some of the Republicans who are sounding off about our party changing its policies in order to curry favor with pressure groups would tell us how they could possibly out-deal the new deal. . . . Do

151. Letter, Brake to Brucker, 24 November 1948, Brucker Papers, box 5; see also *Grand Rapids Press*, 24 November 1948, reporting an inconclusive meeting of Republican lawmakers concerning what strategy to adopt in the face of Williams's victory.

they want us to promise 'me to'?"[152] But there was, in fact, no easy choice between compromise, which was an extension of the constructive engagement of Fitzgerald and Kelly but was easily branded "me-too-ism" in the frustrated and angry climate of 1948, and rejectionism, which could be called a devotion to principle but could easily paint the party into a self-defeating corner and cut it off from tiers of potential voters. The dilemmas were fully apparent at the party convention in February 1949, where delegates listened to Brucker rail against creeping socialism and the deadly embrace of liberalism and then passed resolutions in favor of fair employment practices, increased old-age assistance, aid to dependent children, better education, improved unemployment benefits—all without tax increases.[153]

In the next several months, however, the new party chairman, Owen Cleary, steered the party decisively to the right. Responding to what he called "the voice of the rank-and-file,"[154] Cleary sought to establish a emphatic ideological line

> against present trends of the Democratic party towards socialism with its ultimate threat of communism. You may be sure [Cleary told party fund-raisers] that we shall not hesitate to support free competitive enterprise and to attack increased taxation and government spending. . . . You may rest assured that we shall fight with every ounce of energy we possess all proposed radical legislation on a State or National level. We are determined that "me-too-ism" shall have no part in the Republican party.[155]

Tactically, Republican speakers sought, at every opportunity, to yoke the Democratic Party to the labor movement and to insist that Mennen Williams was a "cryptosocialist" who had allowed his party to be "kidnapped by labor elements tending toward socialism."[156] Guy

---

152. Letter, Brucker to Murl Aten, 3 December 1948, ibid.

153. *Detroit News*, 13, 17, 19, and 20 February 1949; *Ann Arbor News*, 18 and 19 February 1949.

154. Owen Cleary Papers, box 1, MHC, Ann Arbor, is full of letters from rank-and-file party activists, pleading with him to "draw a line," "stand for something," and "stop playing 'me-too.'"

155. Letter, Owen Cleary and Arthur Summerfield to Party Finance Offices, 19 March 1949, Owen Cleary Papers, box 1.

156. The *New York Times* ran a special two-part series on the political situation of Republicans in Michigan (21–22 June 1949).

Jenkins of the Booth newspaper chain and William Muller of the *Detroit News*, who covered Lansing and state politics and provided copy for many smaller newspapers around the state, adopted as fact that labor leaders, in particular Gus Scholle of the Congress of Industrial Organizations (CIO) Political Action Committee in Michigan, controlled Williams and intended to give "Michigan residents a liberal helping of British socialism."[157] The image of the governor calling up Scholle before every initiative transformed Republican rejectionism into a brave stand by the people's representatives against alien values, in defense of the American way. But it also deepened the impasse between the governor and the legislature and thus amplified Mennen Williams's ability to define a clear ideological alternative to the Republican majority.

As both parties unfurled ideological banners during 1949–50, they also reached down into the grassroots constituencies, seeking to mobilize the electorate into permanently organized rival camps. Neil Staebler, the Democrats' organizational wizard, built a statewide network of county committees, with subcommittees to deal with special issues and finance committees linked to statewide fund-raising efforts.[158] Meetings and rallies were held throughout the year to educate and mobilize voters; as elections approached, a coordinated program, "You and Your Government," was organized across the state to enable voters to meet Democratic candidates and officeholders and discuss issues of local concern. Cleary answered with Republican county committees, which canvassed voter opinions through meetings and questionnaires and sought to build from this sample of opinion a "representative platform." He traveled the state reviving grassroots organizations and, with Arthur Summerfield, the state finance chairman, built a network of contributors, keyed to automobile dealers associations, who gave money to the party, not to individual candidates. Staebler, in turn, drew pledges of money and cadres of canvassers from organized labor. Indeed, by the 1950 elections both parties had laid the bases of permanent organizations that, drawing upon distinct elements of the automobile industry in the state, were entirely independent of their candidates and officeholders. Campaigning became a continuous and full-time activity, with party orga-

157. *Detroit News*, 13 March 1949; *Ann Arbor News*, 26 March 1949.
158. Staebler's papers, which track these tireless organizational efforts, are in the MHC, Ann Arbor.

nizers planning two and three elections ahead; advertising contracts were signed, campaign budgets laid out, and the main outlines of rival platforms drafted before anyone was nominated.[159] Both parties had entered a kind of permanent campaign, in which clearly defined and relatively stable ideological differences were deployed in an effort to incorporate categories of voters and interests into a partisan fray organized by two parties whose chief function was to coordinate alignments of difference with each other.

The state prison system did not lie along the ideological divide between Democrats and Republicans after 1948; in partisan debates over housing, disability, education, and labor laws, the prison was neither a participant nor a target of political combat. No one could call the Department of Corrections a hotbed of socialism. Moreover, thanks to the Sigler reform, Mennen Williams was able to appoint his own man as commissioner of corrections in place of Joseph Sanford. Thus a Democratic administration, facing an unbroken phalanx of hostile Republicans everywhere in state government, was able to chart a course unopposed in the one administrative department that had been successfully "streamlined" by the other party. This gave a strong boost to progressive change in the prison, assuring the proponents of the new penology expanded resources and strong executive support. Because the Department of Corrections was, in effect, a small Democratic preserve, the Williams administration also had every reason to shield it from political interference; this provided a cocoon of neutrality in which the modalities of "modern" administration—of professionalism, bureaucratic rationality, and institutional subordination—could be consolidated. There was little plausible partisan gain to be had from stirring the prison pot again. For the first time since the 1920s the cause of progressive reform in the prisons was bound securely to the movement for a stable, routinized administration. The elements of a new articulation of the carceral project were in place. The fact that this produced a riot is what requires explanation.

The new commissioner, Earnest Brooks, who replaced Sanford in 1949, was a staunch ally of the governor. A wealthy man, for whom politics was both a public duty and personally fun, Brooks was not a prison professional like Sanford nor well versed in prison affairs,

159. See *Detroit News*, 13 November 1949.

although as a state senator, he had a (rather light, it seems) hand in drafting the 1937 legislation that established the Department of Corrections. His intention was to serve as a caretaker, until the 1947 act was repealed, but when these plans unraveled,[160] Brooks stayed on, growing more attached to the job he had intended to fill only temporarily. Mild and easygoing, with strong liberal convictions, he saw his chief role as a peacemaker, stabilizing a troubled department. He visited the prisons regularly, listening to complaints and suggestions from prisoners and custodians alike. He missed no opportunity to stress the importance of education and vocational training in the prisons; he did much to promote classification procedures; he strongly backed efforts to develop a minimum-security camp program.[161] And he tried to bring a quinquennium of investigations to a close by having Noel Fox, lately the unsuccessful Democratic candidate for secretary of state, compile a comprehensive survey of Michigan corrections, in which all the recommendations and proposals for change were assembled, discussed, and assessed. This gave Brooks programmatic guidance. In personnel decisions he seemed determined to lower the profile of the department, contain its intramural bickering, and promote continuity. Garrett Heyns, his career in Lansing checked, was returned to Ionia where he had started, replacing the retiring Joel Moore as warden. There was a confused and unsuccessful attempt in 1950 to transfer Ross Pascoe from the parole board and make him warden at Marquette.[162] And at Jackson prison Brooks stuck with Julian Frisbie, who had arrived in Michigan on election day as Sanford's warden designate, mainly because he wanted to avoid yet another administrative turnover; Ralph Benson was returned to duty as Frisbie's deputy.

Brooks spent a great deal of time on the yard at Jackson prison.

---

160. See n. 96.

161. An outline of these efforts, "Corrections-Conservation Camps" may be found in Noel Fox, *Survey,* 72–76. The first camp, at Cassidy Lake, was converted from a prisoner-of-war camp, the inmates being used to maintain the Waterloo recreational area. Its success prompted creation of others. They were used for minor and first-time offenders and for pre-parole programs.

162. The correspondence surrounding this proposed move is in Williams Papers, box 38, Corrections Department, General, 1950. It was also widely discussed in the press; see *Detroit News,* 12 April 1950. The plan was stopped largely because Emery Jacques, the warden at Marquette, vehemently objected to a transfer that he regarded as a demotion and found support in the legislature and civil service commission. But Pascoe was also cool to the idea, and, typically, Brooks did not press it.

He believed the commissioner should be primarily concerned with inmate welfare, but he seems also to have been fascinated with the powers of the paternalistic touch. "I'd go there," he told Martin after the riot, "sit down in the yard on a bench, let the guys hover around me, take out my notebook, write down complaints. I got a kick out of it."[163] And then he would take action, on personal cases (changing a work assignment, moving an inmate to another cell block, seeing to someone's medical appointment, tracking down a lost letter) and on general complaints (lengthening yard time, relaxing mail censorship, expanding visiting privileges, altering the way inmate money was accounted, adding law books to the library). Among inmates he was known as a soft touch, a sucker for the hard luck story. No one doubted his good intentions, but many guards felt he was silly and naive—"a two-year-old toddling along with TNT in each hand."[164] Some felt the commissioner's interventions undermined the warden, although Frisbie seems not to have noticed. Unlike Brooks, Frisbie, a rather remote figure committed to paperwork and the delegation of authority, was rarely seen on the yard and, some said, lacked the "subjective feel" for the prison that a warden was supposed to have. But in both individual cases and institutional matters he obeyed orders from his superior and, whatever his personal views, aligned himself closely with the liberal line enunciated by Brooks's office.

After the riot, of course, there would be much controversy about the commissioner's hands-on style of management. Several guards told investigators that, by being soft on the inmates, Brooks had undermined custodial authority. But others felt that his friendly, accessible style had not only ameliorated conditions in the prison but actually made the guards' job easier, in that his highly personal response to individual needs and complaints made it easier for custody to stand by the new uniform standards, which allowed no favoritism. There was also, later, much disagreement about whether the many, often ad hoc changes he initiated made any difference. The claims that he had done much to improve inmate morale were vitiated when prisoners rioted in 1952. And it remains unclear whether discipline was actually more or less relaxed under Frisbie and Brooks. There were promising reports in 1951 that Brooks's humane ways had be-

---

163. What follows is drawn mainly from Martin, *Break Down the Walls* (38–40), based on interviews he did in 1953.

164. Ibid., 40.

gun to ease the department's reputation for harsh discipline,[165] but Clemmer's survey later that year singled out the toughness of disciplinary practices at Jackson as a problem needing review; both the length of time prisoners were confined to punishment cells and the condition of "solitary" were, he said, "more severe than in many other northern prisons."[166] It is possible, even likely, that discipline remained stiff throughout the late 1940s and early 1950s but that exceptions to rules became more common and more easily obtained. Indeed, if Brooks was prone to give "breaks," and if guards resented this outside interference, it seems quite likely that, in reaction, custody bore down more heavily on inmates. We may also assume that Brooks, in his visits to the yard, never encountered the inmates confined to the isolation cells in 15 Block, where the dour sternness of the disciplinary crackdown continued uninterrupted by the commissioner's goodwill.

It was in the areas of treatment and counseling, however, that Brooks believed his progressive instincts in penology could do the most for inmate morale. In March 1949 he instituted an ambitious program for classification and counseling at Jackson.[167] In order "to provide a maximum of individualized and personalized attention" to inmates, ten trained counselors were hired at the prison. Every inmate sent to Jackson was to be assigned a counselor, who would do an "intake" interview, write "a concise, meaningful report which treats primarily with the problems of the prisoner," recommend a program of activities and placements to the Classification Committee (on which counseling supervisors sat), and follow the inmate through his term, responding to his needs, writing progress reports, representing him in disciplinary hearings, and preparing his file for parole appearances. Brooks made a public commitment that "every institutional inmate will be seen and his personal problems discussed at least twice a year by his own particular counselor."[168] In a kind of institutionalized version of his visits to the yard, he intended the counselor to combine the roles of therapist and friend, giving each

165. *Lansing State Journal*, 2 January 1951.

166. Staff Report to the Michigan Joint Legislative Committee on Reorganization of State Government, no. 15, March 1951, 17–18, 55.

167. The directives establishing the program are included in Noel Fox's *Survey*, 33–41.

168. *Detroit News*, 23 March 1949.

prisoner guidance in individual "sessions" but also helping out with
his mail, personal problems, medical needs, family worries, legal and
financial affairs, and collisions with custody. As the "founding document" opined:

> The counselor is actually considered the working tool through
> whom the institution will attempt to so change and modify the
> attitude of prisoners that they shall more readily make proper
> adjustment to institutional life and be better prepared to assume
> the responsibilities and privileges of citizenship when they are
> released.

And the file that the counselor compiled and kept was supposed to
play a key role in the all-important parole hearing.

To manage this new program at Jackson, Brooks picked Vernon
Fox, a young social worker with advanced degrees, who had enjoyed
considerable success at the Cassidy Lake Technical School as chief
psychologist and classifications director.[169] Appointed deputy warden for individual treatment, Fox took charge of all activities at the
prison not directly related to custody: classification, academic and
vocational schools, the library, the gymnasium, the print shop (which
put out the prison newspaper), the mailroom, a new arts and crafts
program, and, above all, the counseling program. This ungainly
amalgam did not have much institutional clout, and compared to the
nearly five hundred officers and staff involved in custody, Fox's staff
was a puny twenty-five or thirty. But the new deputy came to Jackson
with substantial leverage, because everyone knew that he had the
personal backing of the commissioner.[170] We do not know Frisbie's
opinion of individualized treatment, though his letters to Brooks
echoed the official line while evidencing a fetching lack of clarity
about what counselors actually did:

> The counselor program, which will for the first time bring into
> the prison case work in the accepted and fullest sense, will enable

169. Vernon Fox gives his own background in *Violence behind Bars*, 77–79. He
claims that he never intended to make a career in corrections but, returning from the
war, had been persuaded that he could "make a difference" with the young offenders
at Cassidy Lake.

170. Interviews with Robert Northrup and Al Fingel, April 1979.

each prisoner to have a close personal relationship with one man in the prison who will seek, through the usual techniques of case work, to modify the attitudes and behavior of the men who comprise his case load. No man is born with bad habits or anti-social habits; he learns them.[171]

Fox felt that, after initial hesitations, he got full support and cooperation from the warden.

But counseling got a rough reception from custody. A cold war between individual treatment and collective security quickly developed, firing off crises and turf fights on all sides. The bitterness and recrimination between guards and counselors was later included in everyone's litany of causes for the riot. Fox and his opposite number, George Bacon, the deputy in charge of custody, never got along; the warden was incapable of resolving their disputes, largely it seems because, while he tended to agree with Bacon, who favored tough discipline and no-nonsense handling of prisoners, he usually sided with Fox, who reflected the views of his superiors in Lansing. The biggest fight was for control of the "labor pool." Fox contended that, if prisoners were to be involved in individual treatment programs that included work, education, and vocational training, it was essential for the counseling staff, which determined classifications, to have control over job assignments. Bacon objected on grounds that guards needed control of assignments as an instrument of control. Frisbie passed this to Brooks, who decided in Fox's favor; the power to threaten a transfer or a less desirable job slipped from custody's hands. There was also a great battle for the control of inmate files. At first two separate files were kept on each prisoner, one by counselors, reflecting the treatment program and progress being made in it, the other by custody, including the disciplinary jacket and representing institutional behavior. Eventually, however, counselors won physical control of the files and gained (so guards believed) the ability to kill a "ticket" or "prep" a file before crucial parole hearings. Only in one area did Bacon prevail: he stoutly refused to allow counselors into 15 Block, the disciplinary unit, and Frisbie backed him.

As the authority of the counseling staff grew, and the division of

---

171. Letter, Frisbie to Brooks, 22 March 1949. Executive Office, Commissioner of Corrections, 1949, box 8.

powers between custody and treatment became more apparent to prisoners, guards felt outflanked.[172] To the old line officers, who had once controlled all incentives and regulated the everyday flow of rewards and favors, the growth of treatment came directly at their expense and entailed a painful loss of status. Placing treatment on a par with custody was not only an affront to veteran guards, many of whom saw themselves as friends and informal counselors to inmates anyway,[173] but also a sign that brains, degrees, and fashionable ideas counted for more than steady work and long experience. Fox arrived at the prison with a title, office, and salary equal to Bacon, twice his senior. Counselors came in five days a week, working eight hours a day, enjoying coffee breaks and cheerful offices, while custody personnel had to work seven-day rotations, around the clock, on their feet and in uniform. Counselors were generally younger, but invariably better paid.

The retreat of custody, and the gradual shrinkage of its resources and authority, was the direct corollary of the expansion of a new postindustrial penology. Hard work and a clean record were no longer considered secure measures of rehabilitation (or, for prisoners, a clear pathway to parole). Instead, the "right" mix of work, education, and counseling was to be applied, and gauging the extent of rehabilitation (and the terms of parole) was left in the hands of professionals. "The assumption of the treatment prison," observed Donald Cressey in his 1965 discussion of tensions between custody and counseling,[174]

> is likely to be that of a "stream of action" in which clients or patients, like raw materials, pass through the prison and have various rehabilitation operations performed on them, each according to his needs. The security and housekeeping activities are, at most, a "framework" in which these operations take place.

Discipline—both the conformity of inmates in prison and the correction of their "problems" in preparation for release—was secured less

---

172. "Do you believe that guards have as good control over the inmates as they previously have had? No" (interview with Harry Goodall, a sixteen-year veteran, 27 May 1952, Attorney General Investigations: 1952 riot, box 5).

173. George Bacon was loud in making this claim, see Williams Papers, box 106.

174. Donald Cressey, "Prison Organizations," in *Handbook of Organizations*, ed. J. March (New York: Rand McNally, 1965), 14.

through the body, in the form of hard labor and punitive coercion, than through the mind: prisoners were "won over" by their counselors, acting as friends and advocates, and they were "worn down" by the authoritative operations of scientific expertise, promulgating diagnoses and programs that sent them groping through unfamiliar mazes in search of release. And this was accomplished in a context of indeterminacy that kept prisoners guessing. Indeed, to make the promise of release utterly conditional, hence entirely dependent upon those applying treatment, was considered essential in establishing the ascendency of corrective counseling over deviant dispositions. According to Dr. David Phillips, the first psychiatrist hired at Jackson, every sentence should be for one year to life imprisonment: "Then it would be up to a group of trained experts to decide when release would be granted."[175] Elaborating, the doctor explained, "I am certain that some murderers given life terms might be eligible for release at the end of one year, while some larcenists given one year terms should be incarcerated for life." The superior knowledge of the expert confronted the lowly inmate and kept him guessing. As Pascoe put it, "There is little, if anything, that the individual could advance in his own behalf that is not already known to the board."[176]

But, however cogent in theory, the impact of the new penology upon SPSM was, in practice, diffuse and uneven. The sheer size of the prison tended to swallow up therapeutic initiatives. There was space for only 325 prisoners in the school program, which was staffed almost entirely by inmate teachers, and the vocational programs (which included metalworking, sign painting, drafting, and typewriter repair) could barely handle 100 prisoners.[177] And while the plan to have extensive dossiers on social background and personal problems compiled by sympathetic counselors sounded good, such intimacy was virtually impossible in a prison where each counselor had a case load of 500 to 700 inmates and where, even optimistically, "if we could get a 'good morning, Joe' on an individual basis to every man in the prison three times a year, it would in itself be an advance for the treatment program."[178]

---

175. *Jackson Citizen Patriot*, 27 May 1937.

176. Attorney General Investigations, box 1, "Parole Inquiry," n.d., containing the substance of Pascoe's long interview with the press on 30 January 1945.

177. The programs were reviewed by Clemmer, *Prison Community*, 17–19; and Noel Fox, *Survey*, 50–53.

178. Fox, *Violence behind Bars*, 68.

Moreover, with few jobs remaining in prison industries at SPSM, compiling a good work record of the traditional kind was difficult and, with the parole board now intoning the virtues of education and counseling, probably not persuasive. Prisoners, intent on getting out, had to deal with and get along with the counselors, yet all too often this landed them in the cross fire between individual treatment and custody. A prisoner who asked a guard for a favor might be told to see his counselor; a counselor trying to be responsive might then run into custodial opposition or interference.[179] A prisoner who relied too heavily on a counselor positively invited a "hassle" from guards, but, as counselors gained control of inmate files, a prisoner who sided with the guards or avoided counseling might find a note of reprimand entered in his record. And always, the uncertainties that flowed from the competing domains of custody and treatment were compounded by the remoteness and punitive capriciousness of the parole board, which paid little attention to the elaborate social background profiles or the diagnoses and progress reports that counselors produced, preferring to "retry" the original crime and to gauge from its own tried-and-true rules of thumb whether repentance had been done or genuine reform effected. Thus the new penology, far from transforming carceral practices at Jackson, generated a series of competing, often contradictory, accounts of what the prison was doing and under what conditions imates might win release.

Incoherence in the official line implied to prisoners not only a lack of accountability but a perverse refusal to acknowledge that there was even a need to be accountable. In part this was a calculated element of the therapeutic model; deliberately kept guessing, prisoners throughout this period expressed deep hatred for the parole board—"stonehearted, pagan, miseducated misfits."[180] But at Jackson the deep uncertainties of parole—the imprecise guidelines, unpredictable decisions, and indeterminate sentences—only aggravated inmate impatience with the scattered, beleaguered, and hopelessly inadequate programs of individual treatment. In this respect the insertion of the therapeutic model of penology into Jackson prison did

179. See Testimony of George Brown (14 May 1952), Attorney General Investigations, box 5: "If the convicts got any beef, we just give them a pass, and let them go see the counselor" (testimony of Henry Curry, 19 May 1952, ibid., box 6).

180. Comment by Frank Martin (n.d.), Department of Corrections, Bureau of Correctional Facilities, box 1, file 2.

nothing to make life more predictable for prisoners or to render the account of what was being done to them more coherent. If anything, the coming of scientific penology and individual treatment after 1948 only compounded the effects of the disciplinary crackdown of 1946–47.

Yet something very profound was being altered. At the center of the new penology was the expert or professional, equipped with diagnostic tests, case histories, scores, standards, norms, and results. While the older structures of custody and control were by no means effaced by the intrusion of a few college-trained counselors behind the walls, the new order profoundly affected fundamental social relations in the prison. For the very process of elevating expertise and legitimizing the ascendancy of professionals required that the objects of corrections be altered into something clinically different—into dysfunctional, incompetent, disturbed misfits. This necessitated a new distance, even a rupture, between keeper and kept that cut against the continuum of society and outlook between guards and inmates that, under earlier conditions, had made informal collusion, face-to-face accommodation, and "secret" recognitions possible. Indeed, for all the attitudes of helpfulness and support that were embodied in the notion of treatment, its dominant message to inmates was one of sorting, separation, and individualization—promising an atomized world in which each prisoner, labeled and classified, his particular case distinguished from that of all other inmates, was attached as an individualized dependent to a counselor who combined, ambiguously, the roles of helper and authority, friend and disciplinarian.

In this we confront one of the paradoxes of reform: on the outside New Deal politics was built upon new mobilizations and the inclusion of new groups and voices, but, as it entered the prison, reform promoted disconnection and disenfranchisement. The ascendancy of the treatment specialist in penology not only repositioned the subordinate objects of power; it disenabled the prisoners and, by making them incompetent, disenfranchised them. The premise of the therapeutic prison—that prisoners were "sick," "disturbed," "sociopathic," "defective"—meant in practice that they were pushed away, isolated, labeled as "problems," and then invited or compelled to attach themselves, individually, to the new processes of corrective treatment, in order to get out. But, since at Jackson the "way out" was not clear and the counselors who were supposed to provide guidance along the way were without influence on parole decisions, the result was that the pushing, isolating, and labeling was experienced as something purely punitive—"they try to make you fell like you're nobody"[181]—and, far from raising inmate morale, it tended to reinforce Jackson's reputation for harshness. Custodians bore the brunt (and the dangers) of inmate anger directed at ineffectual counselors and irresponsible parole, yet they were themselves crowded by the claims of treatment and felt they lacked the tools or the official encouragement they needed to fall back on older techniques of co-optation and concession that, in the past, had elicited the cooperation or soothed the nerves of their charges. Embattled and resentful in this uncertain environment, guards tended to react with rigidity and harshness—"a little too heavy on the penal"[182]—adding their own element of tension to a festering situation that no one seemed able to control.

Reading the Riot and Its Aftermath

We might narrate these brooding tensions into the causes of riot in 1952. We could look into the conflict—or the lack of integration—between custody, treatment, and parole and probably see the breaks in the patina of control that, under certain circumstances, became the openings for insurrection. And, if we did, we would soon find ourselves rehearsing the debates of the post-riot investigations: Was discipline too harsh, or too lax; was treatment too powerful, or too weak; was Brooks too meddlesome or Frisbie too ineffectual; was the clash between custody and treatment inevitable or the product of weak leadership; was it a liberal turn in penology or the deeply conservative core of the prison that best explains why there was a riot? We could push these questions further and treat the riot not as some momentary breakdown in the apparatus of repression but as an expression of a transitional moment in the history of the prison. Here we would reconnect with the powerful traces of Sykes's analysis. As authorities moved to reclaim powers conceded to inmate collaborators and "big shots," they disturbed deeply entrenched hierarchies and patterns of reciprocity, weakening the capacity of prisoners to orga-

---

181. Ibid.
182. Harvey Robb, a fifteen-year veteran, Attorney General Investigations, box 5, 14 May 1952.

nize themselves, destabilizing the bases of custodial control, breeding resentment, and fostering nostalgia for the good old days. As such, the riot of 1952 arose from a transitional break in which an older order was being dismantled but new structures and rules had yet to congeal in its place.

Such readings of the riot, while not entirely wrong, tend to isolate events inside the prison, as if the riot had only local causes, and thus to miss the contextual and conjunctural dimensions of an explanation. Clearly, the transformation of Republican politics in the mid-1940s made the reformation of the internal regime at Jackson prison possible, even necessary, yet the continuing elaboration of a politics of scandal in 1946–47 disrupted, even prevented, the consolidation of a reformed alternative inside. The election of a Democratic governor in 1948, and the subsequent relocation of the prison in the evolving terrain of party combat in the state, did not automatically bring a solution. Indeed, the elaboration of treatment programs as a further extension of reform tended to deepen the confusion and amplify the incoherence of the carceral regime at Jackson; not only were prisoners denied avenues of corrupt collaboration by the disciplinary crackdown, but they were then recast as the topographical "other" in treatment, misfits who could not be included in the production of carceral order. Neither the disciplinary determination of Benson nor the good intentions of Brooks were enough to secure a reform regime. This was because the articulation of a new order required more than just changes at the political center or at the top of prison administration—or even at the level of the warden and quotidian operations; it required also that lines of connection and assent be established with the objects of correction.

This can be clearly seen in two aspects of the riot of 1952. In the first place what is missing from a hydraulic model of riot, which sees it erupting inevitably, if serendipitously, from lapses in repression, is what was missing from the prison itself during the four days of rioting—namely, some way of looking down into the social relations of the prison. When the guards pulled back to the walls and rooftops and Vernon Fox moved about the yard seeking to influence inmates, individually, to return to their cells, their actions, together, exposed the absence of interior networks and linkages among prisoners and between prisoners and the authorities. This may reflect, at least in part, the particular conditions of insurrection, but these missing linkages are especially dramatic if one imagines D. C. Pettit, rather than Vernon Fox, trying to pull strings and curb disturbance. What was not available to prison managers in 1952 was a network of allies and retainers among the prisoners who had a stake in preserving order and who could enable the keepers to reach down into the yard or the cell blocks and enforce order. There were no prison leaders available during the riot who could command assent and steer the conduct of other inmates. Fox sought to make himself a spokesman for inmates, and Earl Ward emerged as his collaborator in this effort. But both were temporary figures, thrown up by the crisis of control and quickly brushed aside when the emergency had passed. The fact that so much came to hang on such a tenuous and personalized connection between two men who had not known each other before 20 April 1952 suggests not just a crisis of custody—a momentary breakdown in the apparatus of repression or the organization of consent—but a much deeper dissolution of the social fabric of the prison, a full-blown crisis in the social relations that organized life inside.

Thus cast, we might be tempted to follow Sykes toward an analysis of the riot as a conservative or nostalgic gesture by prisoners seeking, in a transitional moment, to resist change or recapture lost worlds. Yet this would be to follow authorities in neglecting what prisoners were demanding. For in the list of demands that the prisoners formulated and debated there is no hint of nostalgia for the old regime and no sign of notable resistance to change. Indeed, if we take these demands as the legitimate voice of the inmates in revolt, we can detect, or at least infer, clear intentionality. They attacked disciplinary harshness and the cruel means of punishment employed in the segregation unit, called for better medical and dental care and for more humane treatment in the mental ward, demanded an expanded purview for treatment staff, allowing counselors into the disciplinary block and on the segregation committee, and urged the creation of an inmate council, initially to review all rules and regulations and to veto those that were disliked but eventually boiled down to an elective body for discussing rules with the treatment staff. Above all, they insisted that the parole board be abolished in favor of a flat-term sentence or automatic release at the expiration of the minimum, an unshakable demand that Fox managed with difficulty to water down to a request for a clarification of procedures and criteria. While one might see registered here ongoing inmate resentment toward transitional confusions in prison administration, and especially in the parole process, the aim of these demands was, overwhelmingly, toward achieving greater clarity and an end to uncertainty. Reviewing the rules, eliminating indeterminacy in sentences, reducing the discretionary power of the parole board and of custodians, clarifying procedures for segregation and disciplinary action, all amount to establishing, not destroying, a new, not an old, order. And it is significant that these demands were formulated by inmates who had been marked as misfits, sociopaths, and defective delinquents in the new therapeutic regime—that is, by those who were the farthest from inclusion in treatment programs and yet the most in need of therapy. Moreover, the link established between Fox and Ward in the course of the riot, which became the only corridor through which deals could be crafted and agreements negotiated for a restoration of order, was a strangely private liaison that took the form of a therapeutic session—precisely in the sense that the counselor sought to lead and manipulate Ward to win his trust, and the inmate sought to play along with Fox's agenda in the hopes of getting a break.

The riot at Jackson thus bore all the marks of the new penology and of prisoners' engagement with the new rules. In this light we recapture the agency of prisoners. Denied the capacity and the space to organize the prison themselves—to run the joint—by the disciplinary crackdown of 1945–47 and then transformed by the treatment regime of 1949–51 into mental and behavioral "problems" who needed help and expert guidance, prisoners had been turned into objects of therapy, infantilized and denied agency. Treated like children, unable to organize or govern themselves, they had been forced to depend on external frames of order. But when the prison failed to provide these frames—indeed continued to deliver incoherent and self-contradictory messages—prisoners moved, in the context of a riot, to create their own order, to seek a clarification of rules and procedures, and to demand (and insist that their counselors advocate for) more channels for rehabilitation and treatment and a real chance to win release through the new modalities of the therapeutic prison. Through insurrection prisoners involved themselves in the continuing debate among prison managers over how to integrate the carceral elements that the new penology had rearranged. Not only did the content of their demands seek to clarify and extend the new order in a way that was coherent and comprehensible to its objects, but the act of negotiating these demands became, in Ward's skillful manipulation of Fox, a model of how prisoners would seek to extend and bend the new treatment modalities to make space for themselves. In this sense the riot was at once the first fruit of reform, a call by prisoners for its extension and an experiment in how to appropriate the therapeutic encounter to the reproduction of inmate *Eigensinn*.

Significantly in this context, a coherent narrative of corrections did not congeal at Jackson until after the prisoners had spoken. It was the riot that nudged the "big house" along the final steps in its transformation. Not that prison officials paid much attention to inmate demands, but during the riot a form of communication was conducted that, in its aftermath, informed the policies of the keepers as they reconstructed order. Those seeking control implicitly registered the limits and requirements of compliance articulated in action by those being controlled. In practices a de facto deal echoed the formal agreement between Ward and Fox, though it was never acknowledged.

There were few recriminations and no search for scandal after the riot. The governor, who had every reason to reinforce and protect the Department of Corrections, appointed a commission of investigation to make recommendations and a new warden to carry them out. William Bannon, a professional with credentials and a reputation for toughness, hands-on administration, and "yard smarts," was given carte blanche to restore normal routine at the prison and ample resources to enlarge the guard force, improve security procedures, and renovate the physical facility. But, in bolstering custody, Bannon also placed heavy emphasis upon cooperation between guards and counselors and on the administrative integration of therapy and custody. With the backing of his superiors, he made guards part of treatment outreach (e.g., in referring prisoners to therapy or group counseling) and turned counselors into security operatives (e.g., placing them in cell blocks and on shift duty). The prevailing idiom of Bannon's prison was that of delivering services, tailored to the individual needs of prisoners and premised upon the inmate's recognition of "a personal problem."[183] While the number of industrial jobs at Jackson continued

---

183. From the minutes of a meeting of prison counselors and parole board members, 13 April 1954, Department of Corrections, SPSM, Selected Subjects, box 5, file 1. "We quickly learned," wrote Malcolm Braly years later, "that we were expected to view this journey through prison as a quest, and the object of our quest was to discover our

to shrink (as several production facilities, including binder twine and the cannery, were shut down) and the proportion of prisoners employed in institutional maintenance chores rose, all jobs in the service-oriented prison came under the rubric of "social education" and were treated more as adjuncts to expanded academic programs than as instruments of discipline.[184] By the 1960s, when the state created a separate school district at the prison with elementary and high school degrees, nearly twice as many prisoners were involved in academic study as in industrial work. In the same period social and psychological services for mental patients, for individual treatment, and for group counseling were steadily expanded, providing prisoners with therapeutic channels to "exchange ideas," "relieve pent-up emotions," and even "find themselves" as individuals ("I never knew myself like I do now")—all the while compiling a dossier for parole.[185]

The consolidation of treatment and the rationalization of its administration, which gave prison officials a more coherent form of address to prisoners, was closely linked to an overhaul of the parole process. When Ross Pascoe died in 1954, parole was rapidly integrated into the programming for individualized treatment. Procedures were clarified, meetings were held to align parole criteria with counseling activities, and the treatment and educational staff at Jackson were delegated to create a "continuous process," leading from initial classification at Reception and Guidance through institutional programming to a date with the board, parole camp, and release: "Preparation for parole release should begin immediately upon the inmate's admittance."[186] To address inmate complaints and to create incentives for rehabilitation, prison administrators sought to establish predictability in parole by making release contingent upon serious participation in treatment programs.

---

problem" (*False Starts: A Memoir of San Quentin and Other Prisons* [Boston: Little, Brown, 1976], 156).

184. See memo by Darwin Clay on the Educational Program at SPSM, 24 June 1954, in Attorney General Investigation, box 5.

185. Quotes from a news report in the *Jackson Citizen Patriot*, 12 April 1959, touting the successes of group counseling.

186. See minutes of meeting between counselors and the parole board, 13 April 1954; and Darwin Clay's memo on educational programs at Jackson, 24 June 1954, Attorney General Investigations, box 5.

By 1958 the National Council on Crime and Delinquency gave the state high marks for its liberality in parole and for its efforts to grant parole at the earliest opportunity.[187] While an appearance before the parole board lost none of its contingent terror for prisoners, the linkages between what an inmate did in prison and what the parole board looked for in considering release became considerably clearer. In time prisoners figured out how to work this system, "conning" their counselors, bending treatment programs to other, more immediate agendas, and feigning redemption for the benefit of the board—recreating in the therapeutic context the little lies of compliance that gave the appearances of reform and made discipline seem complete. But the games prisoners played were bound to rules and remained responsive to the new map of expectations in a treatment regime; whatever openings were found for appropriating and adapting official programs to unintended ends, the new modalities could be seen to work toward the one end that really mattered: "If I hadn't taken the counseling, I'm convinced I wouldn't have received parole."[188]

The reign of treatment fostered a proliferation of statuses within the prison system. Hierarchies among prisoners, based on differential access to resources and privileges, were permanently leveled in a system-wide insistence upon uniform standards in the handling of inmates. Instead, differentials among prisoners were established laterally, in a proliferation of classifications and categories that sorted one inmate type from another and distributed them among an assortment of facilities, security gradations, and individualized programs. The operation of this system depended upon the development of standardized tests, classification procedures, and uniform markers of baseline and progress, and it entailed continuous coordination among, and an ever deeper integration of the main prison into, a statewide network of institutions, with inmates and staff moving from place to place and transfers or assignments being shaped by the operational needs and constraints of the whole system. At Jackson the first and most dramatic effect of this integration was the rapid shrinkage of its population; a sustained effort to redistribute prisoners within the system—moving them out of the main prison into a new youth division for young and first-time offenders, an expanded camp

187. National Council on Crime and Delinquency, "The Costs of Michigan's Corrections Program, a Review of Trends" (mimeograph, December 1958, 22–23).
188. *Jackson Citizen Patriot*, 12 April 1959.

program for minimum-security classifications, a trusty division for long-term and low-risk inmates, and a special parole camp for inmates about to be released[189]—insured that the population at Jackson was smaller in 1960 than thirty years earlier[190] and, by 1967, it was at an all-time low of 3,155, half the count at the time of the riot and 2,500 below its standard capacity. This reduction, which made counseling and treatment programs easier to run and probably more effective, was entirely dependent upon the positioning of the main prison within a statewide organization of correctional activities.

As the prison system multiplied the gradations and options for corrections and absorbed its main prison into a more rationalized network of classifications and distributions, the day-to-day operation of the prison was subjected to ever closer supervision from departmental authorities. Gus Harrison, who became director of corrections in 1953 and remained on the job for two decades, proved an adept bureaucratic centralizer: punctilious about the chain of command, prolific in his production of directives, he demanded regular reports from all wardens and administrators, took charge of budget planning (producing regular surpluses on current account), subordinated the parole board to departmental guidelines, reviewed all personnel changes and inmate transfers, and, in his determination to stamp out cliques and centralize management, insisted that all internal correspondence on policy matters go through his office, thus effectively eliminating cross-talk and static within the agency.[191] Altogether, Harrison's administration brought to fruition the patterns of professionalization that had been in the making since the Murphy reforms of 1937. During the 1950s a new generation of prison professionals emerged who were making their careers in the department, moving frequently from one institution to another, with regular promotions,

189. A good deal of the rapid growth in inmate population at Jackson during the 1940s reflected internal transfers from Ionia and Marquette to the new (and capacious) facility at Jackson. The relative measures of increase and decrease among Michigan's main prisons between 1930 (100) and 1955 were estimated by the department to be 162 (Jackson), 97 (Marquette), and 68 (Ionia). See memos on population trends and projections in Department of Corrections, Executive Division, Correspondence of the Director, 1940–1976, box 8, file 3.

190. The average for 1930 was 4,950; the average for 1960 was 4,777.

191 Department of Corrections, Directors File, 1952–58, box 4, contains Harrison's initial orders and directives; his reign as director is reviewed in SFRC, *A History of Jackson Prison*, chap. 6, much of which was based on interviews with Robert Northrup and Albert Fingel in April 1979.

pay raises, and union representation. Increasingly, prison managers were school-based professionals, their academic credentials displayed on their office walls, and they collaborated closely with other civil servants in the department, many of whom they got to know along the migratory circuits of their careers. They met regularly, formulated shared objectives, and protected one another from outside criticism. Their efforts to promote departmental coordination, to bring parole and counseling into sync with custody, to expand treatment and educational programs, to routinize procedures and make standards clear were expressions not only of the bureaucratic milieu that nurtured them but of their determination to deploy a coherent account of the correctional project in the wake of the riot.

In this they had the full backing of the governor, who had as much interest in routinizing procedures and tightening accountability within the system as he had in insuring discipline at the main prison. As a lone Democrat perched precariously atop a state government dominated by Republicans, Williams was determined to cauterize the prison system from political interference and make it a showpiece of progressive administration. This accorded perfectly with departmental efforts to restore credibility to prison management and to wrap everyday routine in a bureaucratic rationale that fostered confidence and fended off criticism. The development of a "company line" in corrections promoted a depoliticization of prison management and nurtured a kind of professionalizing calm in the system that valorized the reign of the experts. This helped consolidate a narrative of corrections, built around treatment and therapeutic rehabilitation, that provided a coherent account of what was done in prison, to criminals, with what effect. It was a narrative that incorporated the goals of a reform Democratic administration, the outlook of an increasingly professionalized prison administration, the priorities of a security conscious but progressive warden at Jackson, and (at least implicitly) the demands articulated by prisoners in the riot of 1952. It could thus guide administration, cater to the morale and esprit of prison employees, and lay out clear and redeemable expectations for inmates. On the one hand, it spoke to a popular faith in governmental institutions and trained experts and to a view of crime and delinquency as residual social problems; it presented criminals as mental defectives with dispositional disorders and corrections as a professionally designed system for managing the remaining or recurring anomalies of behavior in an otherwise orderly and self-disciplined society. On the other hand, it provided the rationale for an internal prison regime that combined tough, uniform standards of custody with counseling and educational programs, and it marked out, for inmates, a path of reformation leading to release that was, at last, echoed in the criteria for parole.

Thus emerged a coherent account of carceral practices that linked the imperatives of custody, the promises of reformation, and the expectations of prisoners to broader themes of political discourse and to prevailing assumptions about what prisons were for and what they were expected to do. While this account was not without interruptions and contradictions—and lasted no more than twenty years before it too unraveled in the general crisis of the 1970s—its consolidation in the 1950s provides an appropriate point to end this narrative and reflect upon its trajectory.

Chapter 5

Dressage to Dungeons: Marking Trajectories of Change in Modern Penology

No doubt, there were prisoners incarcerated at Jackson in the 1920s who were still there in the 1950s and who watched the procession of wardens, the opening of the new facility, the scandals, the riot, and all the other turnovers and upheavals described in this study without seeing any profound alteration in the routines of everyday life. Years slipped by and disappeared in a cadence of unremitting sameness. Yet the regime that congealed at Jackson in the wake of the 1952 riot was vastly different from Harry Hulbert's prison in the 1920s. Its internal routines, though invariable from day to day, were orchestrated differently; its rational was articulated in new iterations and with different emphases; and its location in the field of political power in Michigan was profoundly altered.

We could make a genealogy of difference by assembling the symbolic essences of two moments in the history of the prison, in the 1920s and the 1950s, and catalogue changes as a movement from one to the other. Thus we might mark a shift from mechanical to flexible punishment. The prison of the 1920s was the apex of a hierarchical structure of punishment, in which legal judgment decided between fine, probation, and prison (for specific terms), and each prison disposed of those remanded to its charge. The prison of the 1950s was embedded in what David Garland, in another connection,[1] has called an "extended grid of non-equivalent and diverse dispositions," in which diagnosis was made on a case-by-case basis and individual prescriptions formulated in consultation with experts. Thus we move

---

1. David Garland, *Punishment and Welfare: A History of Penal Strategies* (London: Gower, 1985), 24. Garland's analysis of British penology in the early twentieth century was especially suggestive in the contrasts I am attempting to make here.

from a mass address to an individual focus. The industrial prison of the 1920s regarded all prisoners as more or less the same, recalcitrant but bendable fodder for the industrial productivity machine; the therapeutic prison of the 1950s made individualization a central principle and sought to replace the regimentation of mass discipline with a specific address to individuals who might be studied, won over, and reformed.

In this move from *Verteltungsstrafe* (a mechanical and exact legal retribution) to *Zweckstrafe* (a multiplicity of sanctions deployed for instrumental or utilitarian ends), we move from a classical to a modern view of the criminal. The prison of the 1920s treated the criminal remanded to its charge as a wayward but not essentially different species of being. Again to use David Garland's helpful formulation, criminals "differed from non-criminals only in the contingent and non-essential fact of their law-breaking,"[2] and they could thus be dealt with according to a scheme of "metaphysical equality." By the 1950s the prison had deployed a battery of classifications and categories that spoke of the particularities of individuals, diagnosed their specific needs, and developed programming to meet them. Thus we move from the formal equality of legal subjects to the uneven particularities of therapeutic subjects; the criminal ceased to be like any other save in the commission of crime and became essentially different—a sick, psychotic, or maladapted personality whose crime was merely the summation of a life that was "other" than normal. The response of corrections moved from a discipline of subordination and docility, with all the echoes of nineteenth-century carceral dressage, to a discipline of specialized adjustment, with all the clinical ramifications of personal exploration and self-discovery, self-discipline and inner change. Such a shift implied, finally, a fundamental alteration in the position of the state with respect to the convicted felon: from the stern adjudicator, dispensing penalties for delinquent acts, the state became the helping hand, offering aid and threatening interventions in the best interest of the delinquent. As we have seen, this shift was the paradoxical analogue of a movement in political practices from patronage-based coalition building among political insiders to an image-based media politics of mass mobilization.

Two kinds of prison, in the same place, with directional move-

---

2. Ibid., 14.

ment from/to but much that is carried over from one to the other—such a formulation invites a debate on the "progress of reform" and draws us into a standard paradigm of explanation in the historiography. Progressive forces, expressing social movements or plain good intentions, mount campaigns to change the prison (for the better) but are inevitably frustrated by the combined forces of habit, convenience, and reaction (which explains why so much remains the same) and, retreating, leave behind only faint traces of reform (which accounts for the halting march of progress in penology). Whatever its yields, this explanatory framework misses the continuously (re)negotiated nature of the prison at all points along the way. In this book I have tried to avoid the sterility of discussing prison history in terms of change versus no-change but also the ahistorical determinism of Foucault's genealogies, by focusing on the construction of coherent narratives of carceral practice. Putting the discursive articulation of practices at the center of the analysis has given me ground for a narrative history that retains agency (coherent narratives have speakers), contingency (coherence is always partial, passing, and conjunctural), and necessity (narrations that impart meaning to practices are not merely an effect of action but also something practitioners need and actively seek)—without assuming a predetermined direction or privileged insight into intentionality. The formulation of coherent narrative accounts, and the need to keep making these narratives cohere, proved pivotal in three ways that are important to the argument: in what linked the political sphere with prison operations; in what drove change and shaped the available spaces for reform; and in what continually reopened the possibility of inmate self-activity, the space in which prisoners could act and thus assert their presence in the story. We must now pan the possibilities of this approach for its analytic returns.

Prison and Politics

In exploring the interpenetration of the prison and state politics, I was concerned with the prison as an extension of political practices and especially with how the prison was rendered accountable to politics, whether through patronage obligations, probes and investigations, or formal bureaucratic oversight. But I was also interested in the prison as an institutional presence and player in these political processes, a contributing participant in the constitution of the political sphere and in its transformations. From this perspective the prison was not only an instrument of power or extension of political practices in another setting; nor was it a purely technical or neutral agency of the state. Rather, the prison was a constituted site of power—in Foucault's terms, a position built of the accumulated and ordered effects of power practiced among unequals—which combined with other positions of power in the state to form the alliances and circuitries that, in turn, came to express and amplify the discursive formulations and hegemonic practices of the power combinations to which it belonged.

In this sense Jackson prison was part of the construction of a public discourse about order—about who deviants were, what behavior was intolerable, and what forms of punishment or reclamation were possible or acceptable; it was, at the same time, an expression and carrier of these forms of discourse, hegemonic ideologies, and terms of political competition that constituted order in the public sphere. Indeed, to the extent that prison managers were able, with the means available, to construct a coherent account of what they were doing, the state prison contributed to the credibility of the regimes of order predicated upon these hegemonic ideologies; it could make politicians appear competent. There were thus deep and abiding connections between the processes of bringing things to order in the public sphere and bringing things to order behind the walls.

In these transactions, practices forged in one place found expression in the other. Patronage masters became prison managers, while correctional experts engaged in political combat. The terms of political compromise framed the terms of prison administration, even as the evolving aims of corrections found combination with political agendas of reform. The disciplinary practices and regimes of control that were possible inside the walls were conditioned by what was politically permissible outside and were subjected to periodic, often disruptive intrusions from the political sphere; yet what was ordered inside the prison became a part of the process of constituting public order, underwriting the electoral prospects of incumbents and contributing the experts of knowledge and experience who helped frame political discourse and public policy about crime and social order. The people sent to prison were, in part, the objects of that discourse as well as the targets of the policing that flowed from prevailing views of who criminals were and what they deserved. But in prison they were turned into an ever-replenished store of usable delinquents, offered back to society as the visible problem that highlighted certain kinds of crimes and criminals, not others, and established the moral high ground against the deviant other.

These linkages between the prison and the political process depended upon the continuing capacity of prison managers to naturalize problems of crime and social order within the language and terms of existing institutions. This was a proactive and everyday process of adapting available means to new challenges or defining novel problems in terms of the means already at hand. Prison managers were often engaged in a precarious balancing act, claiming, on the one hand, that the crisis they faced was unprecedented and alarming while offering, on the other, public assurance that matters were under control in professional hands. Their success over much of this century was sustained by the central truism of modern penology, that "crime and deviance are social problems for which there can be a technical institutional solution,"[3] and by a normative social science that studied crime for its social roots and found in the institutional processes of the penitentiary the possibilities of discipline and correction. This institutionally centered paradigm enabled prison managers to formulate coherent, if frequently revised, accounts of the carceral project that, again and again, made the prison its own best solution to failure. It was this faith in the efficacy of penal institutions that allowed Harry Hulbert to cram an old prison full of modern machinery and call it redemptive; it was this continuing faith, even after the prison lost its industrial rationale, that not only masked Harry Jackson's perilous experiments but also made credible the sequence of exposé and reform that revitalized the redemptive ends of imprisonment under the guise of treatment.

The production of connectedness was an ideological project, not of masking some "other" reality (although a certain amount of deceit or fudging was always present) but of constituting public discourse and public policy. Again and again, prison managers at Jackson put up rhetorical accounts of themselves; when these "matched" prevailing conceits of political practice and public opinion, it produced a contingent "fit," neither fully functional nor wholly self-sustaining.

---

3. Garland, *Punishment and Modern Society,* 7, from whose general discussion in chap. 1 I draw inspiration in what follows.

Harry Hulbert's efforts to elaborate a vision of industrial corrections conformed to popular images of the criminal as lazy layabout in need of corrective work, which itself did double duty for a host of shadowy figures—foreigners, drunkards, spendthrifts, bootleggers, and drifters—who constituted the imagined world of undisciplined labor. The rhetoric of hard work harmonized nicely with Alex Groesbeck's carefully cultivated public image of himself as the state's premier public servant. And the way the governor mobilized a party political base dovetailed with the way the warden organized his authority over employees and inmates at the prison. To be sure, the reliance of political practice and prison administration upon a continuum of patronage transactions and informal perks tended to blur distinctions and, in one variant of development, to elide the worlds of keeper and kept, criminalizing authority even as it disciplined criminals. At the same time, however, the ideology of hard labor helped reaffirm distinctions between the world of politicians, their retainers, subordinates, and dependents, and the world of criminals, who were different in this respect, that they refused gainful employment and the disciplines of work. The language of work effected a rhetorical separation of the two spheres yet bound the project of law enforcement to its objects, making possible a coherent account of what penal correction was trying to do and producing in the process the typical delinquent of that age.

The collapse of the industrial logic of the prison in the 1930s made it increasingly difficult for Harry Jackson to frame an account of his practices that did not strain either the truth of his regime or public credulity about what corrections was supposedly doing. By embracing a reform agenda, his critics tried to preserve the credibility of the carceral project while jettisoning Harry Jackson's practices, a circle they squared by repositioning their rhetoric on the high ground of expertise and treatment and recasting the now old regime as corrupt. In this effort new model prison administrators found echoes in Sigler's campaigns against corruption and his call, as governor, for streamlined administration. But the articulation of a coherent account on this new ground was stymied by Sigler's quite opportunistic use of the prison as the target of his political crusades. The governor's claims of incorruptibility and executive élan were established through a continuing disruption of reform agendas at the prison. The static between Jackson and Lansing, and the continuing lack of fit between the regime at the prison and politically viable agendas in the state, produced tensions and resentments among inmates seeking, in the new but incomplete rules of the game, openings to make life tolerable and release more likely. While these complaints were registered in the governor's recurrent investigations, they could not be coherently addressed by prison managers—nor the internal regime stabilized—until a viable modus vivendi was worked out between the carceral and political spheres.

It was not until after the Democrats resumed office in 1949, and really not until after the riot in 1952, that the elements of a fit between politics and prison practices were shaken out once again. A liberal ideological articulation of social betterment and Fair Deal progressivism found clear echoes in the rhetoric of rehabilitation through individualized treatment. The interests of a minority Democratic regime in shielding the prison from interference by a Republican legislature conformed precisely with the instincts of prison professionals, especially after Gus Harrison's arrival, for bureaucratic consolidation and self-cauterization. In the 1950s Governor Williams's interest in avoiding the political damage of another prison riot coincided exactly with Warden Bannan's determination to master the prison and make the internal order coherent. And throughout this period the elaboration of new ideological rules of political combat, which placed a premium on incorruptibility and media images of professional efficiency, comported well with the reign of penal experts bent on disentangling prison administration from its criminal charges and establishing ties with individual inmates on a professional, that is nonpersonal, basis.

The face-to-face political order and prison regime of the 1920s, based on small differences and reciprocal obligations, gave way to a regime built on synaptic distances. The more crime was naturalized as a deeper asocial deviance that had to be labeled and corrected, the more criminals were made to appear as essentially "other," different, set apart, and encountered from a distance. In the spaces of incomprehension created by distance, politicians sallied forth to deal with the unknown, relying on experts to provide relevant knowledge from tests, assessments, and specialized studies that would tell them, and the public, what needed to be done. Political practice shaped an encounter with crime that fit with the prison's growing reliance on professional standards and treatment techniques. Expert management, informed by scientific knowledge, confronted deviants with an intimidating expertise that told them the problem was theirs, the state was there to help, and treatment was the only pathway to release. Again, the prevailing rhetoric bound the normalizing forces of political discourse to the object of penal correction, making possible a coherent account of prison practices and producing in the maladjusted, sick, or psychotic deviant the characteristic delinquent of the age.

Chronicles of Change

Reform was the language of narrative coherence in an era when prisons were supposed to rehabilitate criminals. It was therefore a potent word in the penology of the "big house" and on the lips of many, quite unlikely characters in the years under study here: Harry Hulbert considered himself a progressive in his advocacy of industrial rehabilitation; Harry Jackson was widely regarded as a modern prison manager who inaugurated classification programs, psychological testing, and guard training at the prison before he fell victim to scandal; his fiercest critic, Ross Pascoe, was very much in the vanguard of the new therapeutic penology yet, in his management of parole practices, proved a major barrier to the consolidation of a coherent treatment regime; Joel Moore and Joseph Sanford both came to Michigan with sizable reputations for innovation and advanced thinking in federal corrections only to become fierce personal enemies in the state system; two directors of the department in this period, Sanford and Garrett Heyns, served as presidents of the National Prison Association, affirming Michigan's reputation in national circles as one of the most advanced and effective prison systems in the country, even as they divided it into rival camps. Reform language was clearly part of prison politics throughout the period under study, not as some alien intrusion but as a tool of routine administration and a weapon in factional power struggles.

This cannot be explained solely by reference to the good intentions of prison managers, for their intentions were never pure, and their focus, in speaking of reform, was usually elsewhere. Nor was the prevalence of reform talk in Michigan corrections a product of outside efforts to open the gates of prison to the winds of change. There was, briefly in the late 1930s, an effective reform lobby in the state, grounded in elements of the Murphy administration, but its salience is best explained in terms of the growing crisis of the carceral order occasioned by the collapse of industrial work, not as an independent variable intruding upon the prison system. Indeed, if anything, reform agendas are best treated as a political language emanating from within the prison system, whose rhetorical power lay not in some vision of a better carceral world nor in the charismatic sway of good intentions but in the capacity of reform talk to address current, quite quotidian problems. And the power of such talk turned upon its utility in forging and sustaining conceptual links between what was done to criminals by the processes of punishment and what were the prevailing notions outside of who criminals were, what they deserved, and how they or the problem they posed could best be contained. The narrative coherence of corrections in the 1920s (built around the industrial prison and the criminal as layabout) and in the 1950s (built around the therapeutic prison and the criminal as psychotic misfit) was sufficiently compelling to rule out competing formulations and to allow prison managers to appear as knowledgeable progressives in effective charge of the carceral project. In the 1930s and 1940s, by contrast, as the narrative coherence of the industrial penitentiary came apart, innovative formulations found a hearing, and reform rhetoric was quickly appropriated by various factions in the prison system as they groped competitively for ways to restoring coherence to the carceral project.

Yet, if reform agendas offered a language of narrative coherence, talk alone settled nothing. To be credible, the rhetoric of reform had to be linked to available means. Hulbert's promotion of an industrial model penitentiary went hand in hand with his campaign to build a prison in the new idiom. The nub of most factional infighting during the period between 1938 and 1945 was the struggle for effective control over the means of punishment—parole, prison industries, placements and privileges in everyday operations—without which reform formulas had little credibility. The riot of 1952 was, in effect, a challenge to prison authorities to get their practices aligned with their promises.

The riot also demonstrated that a rhetorical connection of means and ends in a strategy of corrections was, by itself, not enough. It also had to "work," a word with multiple tests. Strategic formulations had to encompass the tactics of routine custodial control in the prison as well as methods for the correction and rehabilitation of criminals. It had to speak to multiple audiences at once: to inmates (fair punishment plus viable steps toward redemption and release), to prison employees (everyday marching orders plus a sense of purpose and a boost to morale), to politicians (the promise of firmness in dealing with criminals coupled with the assurance of a constructive purpose), and to the public (a guarantee that prisons made them safe yet also carried a solution to the problem of criminal deviance).

Thus, finally, what rendered a strategic formulation credible was not simply the persuasiveness of the official account nor its powers to rationalize the interests of multiple audiences but also its "fit" with specific political configurations and particular social and political contexts—not others. Tensions and tears in the narrative were continually produced by changes beyond the control of prison managers, and, while language was always fungible and stretchy, it is significant that, in patching and reformulating the account of corrections throughout this period, the rhetoric of reformation was repeatedly deployed in forging links between concrete means of punishment and desirable social ends.

Focusing on the production of coherent accounts allows us to see ideology not as a mask or cover for something else but as an integral, creative process of producing connectedness. Reform talk was a way of forging meaningful links between prison and society, and the history of reform emerges not as an autonomous subject of study but as an important element in the ongoing hard labor of giving meaning and location to the carceral project within specific contexts at particular historical moments. From this perspective we may turn back to the sociologists' preoccupation with the location of prisons in society and see less a problem to be analyzed than a discursive formation; and we may also begin to find a way of studying these relationships without reducing the prison to social and material determinants that lie elsewhere.

Central to most studies of prison is the problem of the relationship between modes of punishment and the rest of society. For Durkheim, in the earliest sociology of punishment, the moral judgment and retribution embodied in acts of punishment reflected back upon society and informed it of the values and norms it held in common. In the twentieth century, however, most sociologies of prison have moved with the more technical approaches of corrections to focus on how transgressors of norms might be corrected and made over.[4] Punishment has been something done to others. It proceeds from a set of "givens," social norms embodied in law, and is applied to deviants beyond the view of ordinary society but with a view to their eventual re-inclusion. The prison takes a surplus on the penalty in order to create a separate zone of correction in which the disciplining of the criminal, not the punishment of the crime, is the central concern. From this perspective a sociology of what works has been centrally concerned with what might interrupt or block the effectiveness of these disciplinary applications. In such discussions Durkheim's interest in the effects of punishment upon society have mattered only obliquely, finding voice in the study of the "deterrent effect" of punishment, a field long hampered by vagueness and imprecision.[5] The interaction between prison and society has become the study of the prison as an instrument of society, reflecting, expressing, or carrying dominant values and thus capturing "all the major societal changes."[6]

Yet the process by which these transformations were brought into the prison, or the nexus of interaction between prison managers and political centers that mediated these "registrations," have not often been the object of sociological study. Rather, what has defined the prison in any given period has been its distance from society. For Clemmer inmate society formed a closed, cohesive world that resisted the ministries of rehabilitational programs and formed a cluster of practices outside, beyond, and over against the imperatives of normative society as represented in the custodial regime of the prison. With Sykes the administration of prison was grafted onto Clemmer's inmate society to form a separate, albeit functionally coherent, society operating outside, and thus tending to distort, social norms. James Jacobs then studied the incorporation of this prison society into the bureaucratic and administrative apparatus of the state, claiming to follow "the movement of the prison's place in society from the periph-

---

4. On this evolution, see Ian Taylor, Paul Walton, and Jock Young, *The New Criminology: For a Social Theory of Deviance* (London: Routledge, 1973), esp. chaps. 3–4; and Garland, *Punishment and Modern Society*, chaps. 2–3.

5. See Franklin Zimring and Gordon J. Hawkins, *Deterrence: The Legal Threat in Crime Control* (Chicago: University of Chicago Press, 1973), for an intelligent assessment of research problems.

6. Jacobs, *Stateville*, 2.

ery toward the center."[7] What in the older sociology was a study of prison as a microcosm of society outside itself, separate but functionally cohesive, became, in later installments, the study of prison as an indicator of social organization, registering the deepening professionalization, bureaucratization, and legal equality of "mass society."

A closer focus on the processes by which larger social changes intersect with prison operations suggests a rather different picture. First, there is little in the history of the Jackson "big house" to suggest that the prison was ever very far from the political center of the state. While the ties that bound it in the 1920s were neither bureaucratic or rationalized, they were dense and continuous. Moreover, practices in the prison not only reflected prevailing patronage relations in state politics but also helped to constitute and reproduce these relations. The struggles in the system during the 1940s were all about realigning the prison to changing administrative structures at the state level and reflected the quest for, as well as the crisis of, articulations between prison operations and broader social and political contexts. The media attention lavished on the prison in this transition was not only unprecedented then but unparalleled since. Yet the crisis of the 1940s registered, if anything, the perceived dangers of *not* maintaining close links between prison and society and the imperatives of sustaining a coherent connection, in order to rationalize what was done in prison.

It is hardly incidental, then, that the most fruitful sociological studies of prison were done between the mid-1930s and the late 1950s, in precisely the period when the carceral narrative was most disrupted, the strings of coherence most frayed, and the receptivity of prison managers to new ideas and reform experiment most open. A sociology that was concerned with what works, in a period when the definition of *works* was the reformation of prisoners, not only partook of a reform discourse but, through its production of knowledge, contributed intellectual material to prison managers who were grouping for the articulations that would convincingly bind their practice to society in ways meaningful to the general public, politicians, guards, and prisoners as well as to themselves. The problems addressed most effectively in the sociological literature of this period—the formation of inmate subcultures, the resistant cohesiveness of inmate society, the patterns of resistance to rehabilitation, the necessary invitations

---

7. Ibid., 6.

to collusion, the consequent corruptions of authority—were all problems made salient by the task of maintaining a coherent account of the carceral project. In making plain what was done, with what effect, upon whom, the great sociologies of prison clarified what might be done and pointed to other, potentially more viable regimes. They were thus part of a dominant discourse about prisons in the rehabilitational era, and their concern with the relationship between prison and society arose from *within* the loop, its problematization being part of the very process of inventing connectedness and thus not something to be studied unreflexively, as if it were found, outside itself.

The Marxist tradition comes somewhat closer to an interactive and historically specific analysis of change by focusing not on what works but on what is revealed by the workings of the system of punishment. The effort to understand penal policy and carceral regimes in terms of the conditions for the reproduction of capitalism is a move toward understanding punishment, not primarily as a mechanism of crime control but as a tool in the class project of reproducing unequal social relations. It is, of course, not easy to bind the particularities of punishment to broad movements in the political economy of class domination without becoming reductionist, but Rushe and Kirchheimer's early exploration of the relationship between penal systems and labor markets and their principle of "less eligibility" clearly have relevance to the story told here. Jackson prison in the 1920s was plainly designed to conform to the rapidly expanding labor market in low-skilled industrial jobs. The factory model penitentiary put prisoners to work and secured internal order through labor disciplines at the same time that it established a plausible account of how this regime might foster the reformation of felons and their productive reintegration into a society of mass production. The Depression closed down this industrial avenue of carceral development and severed the connection between the prison regime and the conditions of the free world labor market. Without an anchor in industrial work, the prison's account of itself buckled and unraveled.

By the late 1940s, however, the adaptations of treatment successfully repaired the coherence of punishment in a fully industrialized world. At the highpoint of Fordism in American industry, when capital moved toward new investments in technology and the first round of automation, Jackson prison underwent perhaps the first essay in restructuring and deindustrialization. In a general sense the deployment of new forms of non-employment-based discipline, anchored in medical models and the therapeutic production of adjustment, was a move to accommodate the new conditions of the labor market, in which fewer, more highly skilled workers reduced the demand for casual and unskilled labor. By the 1950s prisoners were being invited, through counseling, to accommodate themselves to a permanent position at the margins of a low-wage job market, without much hope of upward mobility but under a continuing imperative to go straight and live clean. In this context a new rationale for punishment was cobbled together from the inappropriate means left over from the industrial moment; rather than training the body for hard work and relying on the job market to absorb and discipline the parolee after release, the prison now tried to discipline the mind through counseling, remedial training, and the vagaries of the indeterminate sentence and then to insure continued conformity after release, not through the external disciplines of job, community, and family but through an expanded institutional capacity to supervise those on parole.

Yet there remains a powerful reductionism in *Punishment and Social Structure* that turns the prison into a derivation of something else and blocks the study of carceral practices themselves. Without doubt, long-term secular changes in the political economy, the labor market, and the requirements of capital get mimicked, even replicated, by changes in the carceral regime. But prisons are ultimately irreducible institutions with internal dynamics and histories that cannot be made into dependent variables of other social processes—any more than they can be turned, as prison sociology would have it, into expressions of social change or normative imperatives generated elsewhere. Jonathan Simon's formulation of the relationship of prison and labor market is thus helpful: "modern punishment . . . relied for its coherence on its fit with the disciplinary forms of social life being generated by the industrial labor market."[8] This way of putting the matter assumes no causal priority; the notion of a "fit," which is presumably made from several directions, implies both processes of negotiation and a "life" outside such negotiation. That a fit produces

8. Jonathan Simon, *Poor Discipline: Parole and the Social Control of the Underclass, 1890–1990* (Chicago: University of Chicago Press, 1993).

"coherence" brings us back to the rhetorical, even ideological nature of the link between prison regimes and social processes. Unlike the sociologies that are themselves part of the ideological production of connectedness or the studies in a Marxist tradition that treat ideological formulations as a kind of effervescence masking deeper forces, we find here a way of addressing directly the problem of producing coherent narratives of meaning. Like strategic military doctrine, these accounts serve to coordinate tactics and provide the minions of the system with everyday guidance and a sense of purpose while linking particular operations to larger objectives. Their production invites us to study how positions of power are assembled from the effects of unequal social relations and how articulations are achieved among these positions in a field of power relations.

Here we draw on Foucault's insights into power and its creative possibilities, and into the analogical articulations he made among social institutions, including prisons, under the guiding rubric of disciplinary practices. Foucault was, of course, inclined to see prisons (and much else besides) as variable expressions of the same general disciplinary impulse that swarmed all over society, diffusely but unidirectionally, on many fronts but from no definite source. Though he was fascinated with official discourses on punishment and with the interpretive possibilities contained in the instruments of punishment themselves, he preferred to avoid detailed study of historical processes in which human beings with values, emotions, and mixed motives turned abstract movements into everyday routines. His habit of eliding complex histories into ideal-type essences to be assembled oppositionally, in invitations to explore genealogies, blocks historical narration in ways that are both suggestive and misleading. Certainly there was little of Foucault's disciplines at work in Jackson prison in the 1920s; indeed, most of the key elements of his carceral regime— isolation, silence, the precise monitoring of movement, and the compartmentalization of the body in daily routines—had been abandoned in favor of an industrial society in which days were divided into work and time off, months into workdays and weekends or holidays, and inmate life was organized around the relative sociability of the shop floor and road gang. In principle, of course, the prison was "like" a factory, but in practice industrial discipline inside the prison was a crude, if workable, quotidian stand-in for the sort of mental command that Foucault postulated in the disciplinary panopticon. Later on, with the deployment of therapeutic techniques, one might say that Jackson prison began to take on some of the omnipresent surveillance of Foucault's imagining. Parole policies certainly claimed an "excess beyond the sentence" and tried to turn that to the remaking of inmates, and the pretensions of an all-seeing counselor to know what was best for each inmate partook, in some measure, of the individualizing disciplines Foucault described. But the history of treatment at Jackson—its thinness, its interruptions, and its early demise—suggest that what was done in detail was less important than how it was talked about; this returns our attention to the centrality of narrative accounts. The gaps between rhetoric and reality only underscore the fact that, in grasping for essences in the construction of genealogies, Foucault was not especially interested in how prisons were actually run, day to day, or in how change came about.

In focusing on the formulation of coherent accounts, my intention has been to confer agency upon both prison managers and prisoners and thus to reposition the question of the connection between prison and society. Instead of proceeding from a policy framework, in which one studies what works (on the assumption that in punishment something is done to someone for instrumental ends), or from a causal framework, in which one studies the workings of punishment to discern deeper driving forces (on the assumption that causal determination is necessarily to be found somewhere else), I have taken a less directional path by studying practices and their effects. Relying on historical particularity rather than theoretical exegesis, I have tried to show how, in practices, linkages were established interactively among different levels and disparate agendas and how ends were coordinated with means through negotiation among volitional actors with different skills and diverse motives. The production of social order became a study of how, in practices, disparate elements were brought together, incompletely and unstably, under the same umbrella of meaning by historical figures who, while operating within specific contexts not of their choosing, appropriated, adapted, and exploited possibilities in contingent and open-ended ways.

Bringing Prisoners Back In

Throughout the era of the "big house" the language of rehabilitation provided the broad ideological framework within which accounts of the carceral project were formulated and reformulated. The underlying principle was always to make criminals over—whether into diligent workers or well-adjusted individuals—through a carceral process designed to address whatever it was decided had made them criminals in the first place. Thus the implied destination of those banished from society for a term of imprisonment was always release and re-inclusion. The proofs of rehabilitation that were required for parole—a good work record, serious involvement in therapy, indications of adjustment to prison that promised a successful reentry into society—were all marks of normalization, signs that once criminally deviant souls could be returned to the folds of society and made to lead unexceptional lives of elementary conformity. What changed over the years was not the intent but the tactics employed to achieve this end. Changes in the method reflected political and control dynamics within the prison system as well as amended ideas about who criminals were, what made them misbehave, and what public policies were required to contain or change them.

This persistent mythology of inclusion in twentieth-century corrections was analyzed, at least indirectly, by Rushe and Kirchheimer in their effort to understand the relationship between punishment modes and the conditions of the labor market. In this view the constant, disruptive motion of capitalist development, destructive in its restless creativity, was continuously disturbing, disorganizing, even destroying "yesterday's" forms of stabilization, undermining the social prohibitions and constraints that kept people within the law. The criminal justice system generally, and its modes of punishment in particular, thus stood at a juncture in social policy between affirmations of capitalist development, on the one hand, and efforts to cope with its wreckage, on the other. Here the notion of punishment as a means of reforming and reintegrating criminals into society became the promise (and pretense) of a system claiming to be able to close the gap between economic progress and social disruption, not only by containing the losers but also by bringing "them" along. Liberals might emphasize the redemptive nature of this effort, while conservatives might prefer to see in it a reaffirmation of norms and an enforcement of conformity, but, for all, the criminal becomes simultaneously the "other" (a product of damage, disorder, or difference) and yet potentially "like us" (wanting the same things, thus reformable, but needing useful strategies for conformity, skills for survival, and a firm but helping hand for the inevitable moments of backsliding). As always, this apparent humaneness in the administration of justice is, following Rusche and Kirchheimer, linked to a guarantee of bourgeois class assumptions about the benign and beneficial nature of progress.

The importance of this doctrine of reclamation, however, was not that there were gaps between rhetoric and reality but that prison managers, in bridging or fudging these, always needed the cooperation of inmates—at both ends of the equation: rehabilitation only carried conviction if prisoners got with the program and made at least an appearance of change; the smooth operation of the institution, in which the everyday rubs, frustrations, and brutalities of an imperfect reality generated tensions, confrontation, and recurrent control problems, required at least the tacit collaboration of prisoners. To succeed, the "big house" had to offer its charges incentives for compliance. These were proffered in different terms at different times: through the informal opportunities of an illicit economy in the 1920s, through an outright concession of power in the 1940s, and through the games of group counseling and the promise of early parole in the 1950s. But precisely because the prevailing goal of rehabilitation necessitated the presentation of practical models of acceptable behavior and pathways back from, that is out of, incarceration when these models were properly mimicked, the ground for negotiation and accommodation between keepers and kept was always tacitly open. The pretense of reformation, not its fact, had to be sustained, and this continually renewed the small lies of compliance that were always to be found at the heart of the disciplinary order.

Because of this necessity, moreover, spaces of inmate self-activity were continually refreshed in the "big house" prison. Whatever the differences of content, every carceral regime in this period carried certain presumptions about how prisoners were supposed to behave, what they were supposed to do, and to what they were expected to aspire—both for their own good and in the pursuit of rehabilitational goals. Prisoners took the injunctions and invitations of their masters and bent them to other ends, which might include making some money, protecting their property or themselves, subordinating others, winning a favor or getting a break, improving the quality of their lives, or getting out for a few hours or even on parole. We saw how, in the industrial prison of the 1920s, the factory floor became both the site of industrial discipline (rehabilitation) and a space of more limited surveillance in which inmate business was transacted (self-activity). In the 1940s, when concerns for routine custodial control became paramount in a prison that was without jobs and short of staff, inmates' self-activity exacted a price for cooperation, effectively taking over the lower echelons of prison administration. In the scandals and disciplinary crackdown of the late 1940s, these spheres of autonomous self-activity were rapidly and radically reduced, but, even in the constricted straits of the disciplinary crackdown, we saw indications of inmate cliques exploiting the continuing investigations (and the naïveté of investigators) to outmaneuver one another and undercut the new administration. The riot of 1952 briefly broke open channels of inmate self-organization and self-articulation that revealed signs of an enduring, if smothered, narrative among prisoners about the practices, as well as purposes, of incarceration. And in the treatment prison of the 1950s inmates quickly learned to inflect the programs of therapy and self-improvement to new and unintended ends, finding ways to take over academic classes, to turn group counseling and writing courses into vehicles of self-expression, to use religious freedoms to organize politically, and to build on liberalized mail and visiting privileges the legal and political contacts that made possible a challenge to prison management from the outside.[9]

We speak here of recurrent patterns of resistance—but only in part. The din, crowding, scarcities, indignities, and dangers of prison life, combined with the uncertainty and powerlessness of prisoners to create, at all times, festering resentments—accumulations of bile that prisoners spit back, in moments of desperation or bravado, at one another, at their keepers, and on themselves. The cumulative *effect* of this seething hostility and defiance was, perhaps, a form of resistance to the prison and its minions. But in the "big house" penitentiary these oppositional positions were constantly leavened by countervailing invitations for inmate cooperation and incentives for compliance. And it was at the points where defiance and compliance intersected that the requirements of the keepers could be inflected to the needs and practices of the kept, and it was here that prisoners were able to carve out spaces of limited autonomy within the custodial regime

---

9. For an excellent general discussion of this process, studying California, see Eric Cummins, *The Rise and Fall of California's Radical Prison Movement* (Palo Alto: Stanford University Press, 1994).

where they could be and act with minimal interference from authorities. These zones of nonacquiescent compliance or noncompliant consent (*Eigensinn*, in Alf Lüdtke's term) were marked by constant, always mutual surveillance—guards watching, checking, anticipating; prisoners observing, testing, inventing—and by constant, albeit tacit negotiation: how much prisoners could get away with; how much authorities were able or prepared to see or put up with. These were necessarily contingent and unstable spaces, always shifting and subject at any moment to a sudden, violent foreclosure. Nevertheless, they were kept open, and continually reopened, because authorities needed inmate cooperation to run the prison and effect rehabilitation, and prisoners could do very little without a wink or a nod from their keepers.

Historical Perspectives on the Present

These reflections throw light on the present condition—light that both historicizes the prison we have studied and illuminates the nature of difference shaping contemporary corrections. As a coherent account of carceral practices, the model of individual treatment held ends and means together for a little over a decade, before it too began to unravel. The paternalism (and implicitly white models) of individualized treatment did not respond well to the vast demographic changes of the 1960s, in which prison populations became, quite rapidly, both younger and blacker, nor did it offer mechanisms for coping with the radical politicization of prisoners in the late 1960s. This turmoil and resistance among inmates was amplified by a sharpening progressive critique of treatment modalities[10] and by growing technical doubts about the rehabilitative effects of therapy.[11] By the early 1970s the treatment model of corrections was in full-blown crisis, and prison professionals were thrown on the defensive, trying to maintain the established narration of policy while adapting to rapidly changing conditions. It was in this crisis of articulation that the

---

10. The most famous of these was the American Friends Service Committee, *Struggle for Justice: A Report on Crime and Punishment in America* (New York: Hill and Wang, 1971).

11. The most notable statement of failure was in Robert Martison's famous study, "What Works?—Questions and Answers about Prison Reform," *Public Interest* 35 (Spring 1974).

most trenchant critiques of imprisonment,[12] as well as the most hopeful reevaluations of the treatment model[13] and the most bizarre experiments in behavior modification,[14] were developed, and it was in this context that a number of alternative formulas—for community corrections, deinstitutionalization, and inmate democracy[15]—were essayed.

In this transitional passage Michigan's contribution to experimentation was the so-called responsibility model developed by Perry Johnson, as warden of Jackson prison (1970–72) and as Gus Harrison's successor in Lansing (1972–84).[16] Responding to the new pressures from inside and outside the institution, Johnson sought to shift the central form of address between keeper and kept from one of dependency and treatment to one of coexistence and relative autonomy. His injunction to his staff was to back off, "give them air and then hold them accountable." In an effort to reduce the rubs and hassles of everyday life, prisoners were no longer required to attend counseling or to participate in rehabilitational and treatment programs, and they were allowed as many material goods (telephones, TVs, tape decks, street clothes, and personal possessions) and as much freedom of movement and association (including religious and political meetings) as possible—all on the assumption that, if treated fairly ("man to man"), prisoners would take responsibility for themselves and cooperate in organizing the everyday peace and order of the prison. A

---

12. For example, Jessica Mitford, *Kind and Usual Punishment: The Prison Business* (New York: Knopf, 1973).

13. Robert Sommer, *The End of Imprisonment* (Oxford: Oxford University Press, 1976).

14. A seminal statement was by J. V. McConnell, "Criminals Can Be Brainwashed—Now," *Psychology Today,* April 1970. See also P. Sanford, "A Model, Clockwork-Orange Prison," *New York Times Magazine,* 17 September 1972; Philip Hilts, *Behavior Mod* (New York: Harper's Magazine Press, 1974), chap. 6; and Robert Geiser, *Behavior Mod and the Managed Society* (Boston: Beacon, 1976), chap. 3.

15. See Charles Stastny and Gabrielle Tyrnauer, *Who Rules the Joint? The Changing Political Culture of Maximum-Security Prisons in America* (Lexington: D. C. Heath, 1982), for the experiments in inmate councils (the "citizenship model") at the Washington State Penitentiary at Walla Walla; and Ronald Berkman, *Opening the Gates: The Rise of the Prisoners' Movement* (Lexington: D. C. Heath, 1979), for a study of the problems of representation and "pluralism" in prisons in California and New Jersey. Andrew Scull, *Decarceration: Community Treatment and the Deviant—A Radical View* (New York: Prentice-Hall, 1977), is a programmatic statement; see also the essays in Y. Bakal, ed., *Closing Correctional Institutions* (Lexington: D. C. Heath, 1973).

16. See John DiIulio, *Governing Prisons: A Comparative Study of Correctional Management* (New York: Free Press, 1987), chaps. 3–4; and the SFRC report, *A History of Jackson Prison,* chap. 7.

perfectly liberal response to the crisis of control inside, and especially sensitive to the growing racial tensions between keepers and kept, the responsibility model was an attempt both to cope with the disarray of the treatment model and to formulate a plausible alternative that would combine custodial preoccupations with inmate expectations in an articulation that resonated in a liberal political context.

Yet it was this context that proved most unstable in the early 1970s. The space opened for innovation by the crisis of treatment was soon closed down by economic recession and fiscal crisis and by the rising conservative mobilization around issues of law and order that combined a critique of welfare and social service spending with demands for tougher, no-nonsense measures against criminals. This shift in the terms of public debate over crime and its control cut the ground from under alternative formulas of correction, in that it turned the critique of treatment, as a means to reformational ends, into a crisis of rehabilitation itself—that is, into a critique of correction as such.[17] A mounting skepticism about both the institutional means and the reformational ends of punishment shook the foundations of the "big house" penitentiary. Beginning with the Federal Bureau of Prisons in 1975, one prison system after another jettisoned rehabilitational programs and abandoned the rhetoric of correction that had underwritten the carceral narrative and the sociologies of prison for a half-century. The central question at the core of prison scholarship—what blocks or impedes reformation—simply lost its point, and prison managers were fatally compromised in their efforts to make public concerns about crime and social order fungible with available institutional programs and capacities. Perry Johnson's responsibility model represented an attempt to rationalize what was being done in prison to insure peace and avoid harm with a rapidly shifting public discourse on crime and its control; it fell increasingly out of step with a public and political climate that was rapidly losing faith in institutional solutions and was developing expectations of the prison so diminished that a managerial scheme designed to avoid trouble merely invited it. Always embattled, the experiment was quickly terminated after inmate disturbances in 1981 seemed to confirm the hard-line view that prisoners were not to be trusted.

---

17. See Francis A. Allen, *The Decline of the Rehabilitative Ideal* (New Haven: Yale University Press, 1981).

Seen in historical perspective, it is clear that the Perry Johnson regime of the 1970s was, like the Harry Jackson regime of the 1940s, a makeshift strategy, devised in the face of rapid changes to cope with the growing incoherence of the carceral project. It is telling that, in both instances, when prison managers lost a coherent form of address to prisoners—for example, the clear models of behavior, the pathways to parole, the invitations to collaboration, and the lies of compliance that had characterized both the industrial and treatment eras—they moved, in both cases, to insure control and maintain quiet in their institution by expanding efforts to win inmate compliance: Harry Jackson bought their collaboration with massive concessions of power; Perry Johnson assumed their cooperation with a general concession of privileges. In neither case did the tactics of custodial control "fit" well with prevailing or emerging views outside: Harry Jackson came under mounting criticisms from reform currents oriented toward treatment and greater professionalism; Perry Johnson faced a gathering storm of conservative penology, committed to an eradication of coddling privileges and to a refusal of collaboration with prisoners in the management of the prison. Both strategies thus failed to provide a coherent narrative of the carceral project; both faced internal dissensions from elements of the custodial staff; both were unstable in their address to prisoners; and both found their denouement in a riot.

Looking back from this perspective on the history we have recounted, it is apparent that the form of penal discipline studied here, the centralized, mass-managed, Fordist institution of the "big house," was in an almost continuous state of crisis. Each carceral regime at Jackson, however impressive its layout and rhetoric, proved ad hoc and improvised, unstable and short-lived—Harry Hulbert's no less than Harry Jackson's, the therapeutic model no less than the responsibility model. The difference was that some regimes were able to cobble together a convincing account of themselves that at least temporarily held penal practices and public expectations together, while others were unable to effect such a fit. But what made the "big house" continuously viable through the whole period was a combined faith in rehabilitation and institutional solutions; when rehabilitation faltered, the institutional means continued seeking ways to rationalize itself in terms of reclamation and re-inclusion; when the institution lost its bearings, the ideology of rehabilitation underwrote efforts to reform practices and refocus institutional policy. Always a blend of elements, the reform agenda was tenable only so long as the prison was seen, politically, as the most effective means of addressing social problems, while the prison remained a viable institutional solution only so long as it was invested with a rehabilitational ideal that gave a politically convincing promise of social effectiveness. It is not as if rehabilitational ends could not exist without the prison, for they have continued to thrive in community-based and noncarceral forms of corrections long after prisons have abandoned them; it is not as though prisons could not function without rehabilitational goals, for clearly they do so today. But the specific combination of ends and means, and the possibilities this offered for a coherent account of the carceral project, were specific to a particular era and mode of punishment. And it may well be that the deep complicity of prisons in the production of political discourse, and of politics in the production of prison regimes, was also peculiar to this period and thus historically specific. This would suggest, in turn, that the continuities we observed—in rehabilitational goals, institutional architecture, and patterns of inmate collaboration as well as self-activity—were not the hardened boulders of habit resisting the tides of reform nor recurrent features, somehow timeless and essential to the prison, but, rather, specific characteristics of the dialectic reproduction of the "big house" penitentiary in a particular era, now past.

The grand metaphor of the panopticon, in which a continuous presumption of surveillance, imagined more than real, schooled its objects in self-control, appealed to Foucault because it was quietly efficient and light in its touch. There was no need for the scourge and whip in punishment. Yet there was a hidden assumption in the metaphor, which Foucault largely disregarded but which all penitentiaries discovered in practice. The smooth operation and silent effect of the panopticon could only work if the person under surveillance cared (or could be made to care) very much about being observed. Why else would authorities pretend to watch when they were not? Why else would a prisoner care what was seen? The prison made its famous claim to a surplus on the penalty, turning punishment into correction, on the assumption that the offender being punished would want to be reconciled and reunited with the society that punished—or, more precisely, that the process of surveillance, of expert knowledge and its applications in corrective discipline, would *create* a delinquent soul eager to be free and anxious to do whatever was required to secure release. The panoptic science, and Foucault's use of the panoptic metaphor, thus rested on the twin pillars of exclusion (punishment) and the promise of re-inclusion (correction). In the actual operation of the prison it was quickly discovered that the disciplinary core of the carceral, so deftly described by Foucault, depended upon a tier of implied sanctions, additional punishments, and further deprivations, the existence of which were only revealed when someone said, in effect, "I don't care what you see." But at the same time the promise of re-inclusion and the possibility of its refusal created the conditions for those invitations to compliance that the "big house" repeatedly proffered its charges.

The highway to redemption was not only paved with good intentions. It was also littered with billboards and road signs marking the route to release and advertising the corrected life. Routine prison operations were full of what Garland has called "signifying practices," which "hold out specific conceptions of subjectivity and . . . authorize forms of individual identity."[18] Discipline displayed to its objects the kinds of "personhoods" that were available and laid out models of behavior for how to become (or seem to become) one of these "available" people. From the point of view of prisoners, these were often ironic iterations, designed to entangle them in various games and deceits that would secure the approval of the parole board and provide the public with models of carceral success. But these were also broadcast messages that helped to shape public expectations of what can or should be done to criminals in the name of protecting society. Imprisonment was, as Durkheim recognized, a kind of "moral communication" that told prisoners about authority, normality, morality, and personal obligation and, by constituting the delinquent and the modes of his correction, organized and clarified public perceptions of itself—speaking to society at large about what was tolerable and what was not, about how boundaries could be marked and where zones of danger lay.[19] It was not so much a question of whether industrial discipline or therapeutic techniques could be shown to work but, rather, that they provided a plausible account

18. Garland, *Punishment and Modern Society,* 250.

19. See ibid., chap. 11; also Howard Becker on labeling theory, *Outsiders: Studies in the Sociology of Deviance* (London: Free Press of Glencoe, 1963); and the discussion in Cohen et al., *New Criminology,* chap. 5.

of what ought to work, given the games prisoners played, the promises authorities made, and the expectations the public held. This was
precisely what enabled the modern mode of punishment to address
several audiences at once: convicted felons were linked to the lawabiding public by a rhetoric of carceral transformation that was articulated by professionals in the field (often talking among themselves) but
found its confirmation in the (apparent) transformation of prisoners
and in the resulting public belief that these institutional effects were, in
fact, keeping society safe. This could not be done without the tacit
collaboration of inmates. The little lies of compliance that were necessary to keep the narrative of corrections intact produced the invitations
to inmate cooperation that created, in turn, the space of *Eigensinn*
behind the walls. In effect, a prison that was part of the production of
political life and the constitution of moral knowledge was itself constituted by its inmates, who were empowered in historically specific,
albeit limited, ways by the redemptive promises of the prison.

In the turmoil of the 1970s and the hard-line reaction of the 1980s,
the promise of re-inclusion and the programs of rehabilitation that
had sustained it were shut down, and the language of dumping,
warehousing, three strikes, and throw-away-the-key came to dominate correctional discourse. Without a ritual of redemption to give a
persuasive account of the linkages between punishment and re-inclusion, criminal justice moved toward exercises in pure exclusion. This
may be taken as the coercive moment in the shift to a postmodern,
post-Fordist, and postliberal society, in which uneven growth and
minimal upward mobility foreshortened opportunity and limited access; an individual's record, or lack of it, became a kind of permanent
computerized quarantine channeling those without good credentials
away from jobs, and whole sectors of employment, into perpetually
marginal, excluded statuses. As community constraints and the social
disciplines of the labor market have eroded—and, with these, the
very norms to which corrections aspired—the narrative certainties
that linked carceral disciplines with free society and made a regime of
punishment cohere have become increasingly threadbare. Postmodern penology thus lost its individualized address and became
concerned with marking and containing whole categories of people;
"the task is managerial not transformative."[20]

---

20. Malcolm Feeley's description of "the new penology" as discussed in Nils
Christie, *Crime Control as Industry* (New York: Routledge, 1993), 164–65.

Here a deep alteration has taken place in the disciplinary project imagined by Foucault. For at the margins the workings of the panopticon have been reversed. Increasingly, surveillance has become preoccupied not with forming the thresholds of conformity and the ritual subordinations entailed in the taxonomic project of orderly compliance and re-inclusion but with identifying those who do not belong and are to be permanently excluded.[21] Here the illusions of compliance that the prison once sustained are no longer necessary, because, in a regime of postliberalism, inclusion is no longer a goal and willing compliance no longer expected of those with no prospects of access. Public assurances that discipline is intact now depend upon the technical competence of security forces in keeping "them" away.

Without a strategy of re-inclusion, moreover, prisons become battlements in the social war against the excluded. There are now no models of the corrected life and fewer linkages, however tacit or implied, between keeper and kept upon which to build common ground or negotiate the terms of a social contract. The internal regime is no longer anchored in strategies, however tatty and contradictory, for re-inclusion; offering no substantial or programmatic way back, the prison has fewer receptors calibrated to read what inmates say or do as purposive or meaningful. Prisoners, denied the spaces of self-reliance from which to surveil authority and act on that knowledge, are in no position to contest—or to give consent to—the carceral order. Without the context of mutual collusion to frame events and give meaning to what is observed, there are fewer signs and messages being exchanged in prison. There are no promises to betray, no terms to negotiate, no need for authorities to channel a self-activity that is denied. The logic of this trend in corrections is toward ever closer supervision at ever greater arm's length—monitors, intercoms, automatic doors, manacles, leg irons, and minimal human contact, all characteristics of the "maxi-maxi" units that have sprung up around the country.[22] Here, as Foucault predicted, "the isolation of the convicts guarantees that it is possible to exercise over them, with maximum intensity, a power that will not be overthrown by any other

---

21. See Mike Davis's discussion of panoptic shopping centers, in *Cities of Quartz: Excavating the Future in Los Angeles* (London: Verso, 1990), chap. 4.

22. Cummin, *Rise and Fall*, 270–74; and Bill Dunne, "The U.S. Prison at Marion, Illinois: An Instrument of Oppression," in *Cages of Steel: The Politics of Imprisonment in the United States*, ed. Ward Churchill and J. J. Wanderwall (Washington, D.C.: Maisonneuve Press, 1992).

influence; solitude is the primary condition of total submission."[23]
Paradoxically, key features of the most modern American prisons
hark back to the incarceration of perfect isolation and silence that the
Quakers sought to attain in the first penitentiary at Eastern State in
Pennsylvania, but without any of the redemptive intent of this earlier
essay in punishment. Professional management nowadays seeks absolute control, which can only exist in isolation—static spaces frozen
in time.

A power that seeks to erase all autonomy in the subordinate rules
out all relational connection with its object. Without a program of re-
inclusion, there is no strategy of corrections to combine with inmate
strategies of compliance to produce a logic of incarceration. There is,
as a result, little connection between the corrections profession and
academic research; the profession, says one longtime observer,
"seems to have lost its moral defense—its sense of purpose. Corrections appears to have become an institution without an ideal—a set of
practices without purpose of direction."[24] This general aimlessness
may, in fact, mark the outer limits of carceral discipline itself. For the
failure to renew the promises of re-inclusion and the creation of permanent, nonnegotiable categories of exclusion suggest that the production of usable delinquencies (the representative criminal figures
that "sum up symbolically all others"), which Foucault regarded as
central to the carceral project as a whole, has now moved outside the
prison—or, more precisely, the prison can no longer be found where
Foucault tried to locate it, "at the point where the codified power to
punish turns into the disciplinary power to observe . . . at the point
where the redefinition of the juridical subject [the offender] by the
penalty becomes a useful training of the criminal [the inmate]."[25]
Perhaps this is because surveillance is now more complete, more
generalized, diffuse, and total and thus no longer needs an anchor in
the prison. The panoptic project has moved onto the streets and into
the squad car, the rap sheet replacing the prison record in the production of usable delinquents.[26] But this is possible precisely because the

---

23. Foucault, *Discipline and Punish*, 237.

24. Peter Scharf, "Empty Bars: Violence and the Crisis of Meaning in the Prison,"
in *Prison Violence in America*, ed. Michael Brasell, Steven Dillingham, and Ried Mont-
gomery (Cincinnati: Anderson Publishing Co., 1985).

25. Foucault, *Discipline and Punish*, 224.

26. On this, see Diana Gordon, *The Justice Juggernaut: Fighting Street Crime, Controlling Citizens* (New Brunswick, N.J.: Rutgers University Press, 1991).

"representative" delinquent in our time is the black male, who is constituted as criminally dangerous prior to imprisonment and is put in prison as a confirmatory act, part of a continuing and generalized process of exclusion. The carceral archipelago in this interpretation has slipped its anchor and now floats free of core practices in the prison. For its part the prison, now relocated at the dead end of the line, cauterizes itself in the interest of more perfect control, its custodial instincts droning on without coherent narration of purpose or meaningful links to the outside world, mindlessly producing carceral cocoons for the excluded, simply because no alternative procedure has yet been dreamed up, except in the movies.

Index

DATE DUE			